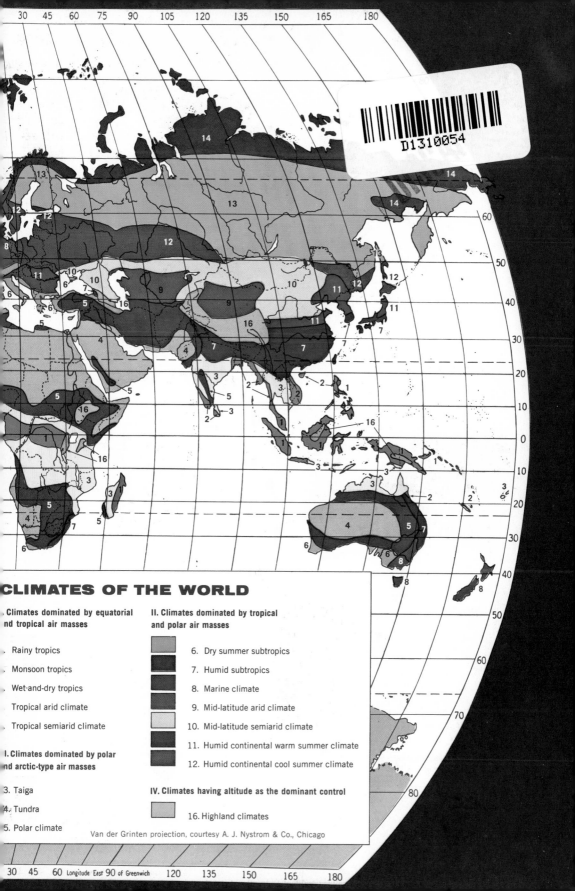

CLIMATES OF THE WORLD

I. Climates dominated by equatorial and tropical air masses

1. Rainy tropics
2. Monsoon tropics
3. Wet-and-dry tropics
4. Tropical arid climate
5. Tropical semiarid climate

III. Climates dominated by polar and arctic-type air masses

13. Taiga
14. Tundra
15. Polar climate

II. Climates dominated by tropical and polar air masses

6. Dry summer subtropics
7. Humid subtropics
8. Marine climate
9. Mid-latitude arid climate
10. Mid-latitude semiarid climate
11. Humid continental warm summer climate
12. Humid continental cool summer climate

IV. Climates having altitude as the dominant control

16. Highland climates

Van der Grinten projection, courtesy A. J. Nystrom & Co., Chicago

GENERAL
CLIMATOLOGY

second edition

GENERAL CLIMATOLOGY

HOWARD J. CRITCHFIELD
Professor of Geography
Western Washington State College

Prentice-Hall, Inc. Englewood Cliffs, New Jersey

Current printing (last digit):

10   9   8   7   6   5   4

Library of Congress Catalog Card No.: 66–13327

Printed in the United States of America. (35024-C)

PRENTICE-HALL INTERNATIONAL, INC., *London*
PRENTICE-HALL OF AUSTRALIA, PTY. LTD., *Sydney*
PRENTICE-HALL OF CANADA, LTD., *Toronto*
PRENTICE-HALL OF INDIA (PRIVATE) LTD., *New Delhi*
PRENTICE-HALL OF JAPAN, INC., *Tokyo*

PREFACE

Although climate is but one of the many factors that impinge upon our lives, it merits our fuller understanding if we are to make intelligent responses to a complex environment. This book aims to introduce the fundamentals of general climatology in a manner that will serve students in the natural and social sciences as well as those who intend to pursue meteorology and climatology as distinct fields of study. I hope that the examples of applied climatology in the later chapters will not only stimulate an interest in climatology but also develop an appreciation of basic scientific investigation and the interdependence of fields of knowledge.

This second edition retains the organization of the first. Numerous emendations recognize recent developments in the sciences that deal with the atmosphere. Others aim for greater clarity and an improved sequence in presentation. The division of the broad field of climatology into three parts provides for flexibility in both emphasis and organization of a college course to fit various instructional patterns. Part One is an introduction to the elements of weather and climate and the related atmospheric processes that involve transfer of heat, moisture, and momentum. It includes brief discussions of the techniques used to gather the building blocks from which we have constructed our understanding of weather changes and regional differences in climate. Part Two deals with the classification of climatic types and their geographic distribution, employing the fundamental pattern of world climates as a framework for explanatory description. Part Three relates the elements of weather and climate to the biotic environment and human activities, concluding with a chapter on climatic change. It has been arranged to facilitate the treatment of separate sections in conjunction with topics in Parts One and Two if desired.

Throughout the book an attempt has been made to incorporate recent discoveries and revised theories, but rapid developments in several phases of meteorology, climatology, and related sciences require reference to current journals for reports on research. The reading lists at the ends of chapters have been selected to encourage thought and investigation beyond the scope of an introductory work. The interested and capable reader will wish to pursue many topics in greater detail than is possible here.

I am greatly indebted to my teachers, who laid the foundation that made this book possible, and to my students, who made helpful suggestions during the evolution of both the first and second editions. Comments from teachers who have used the first edition in their classes were valuable guides to revision. I am especially grateful to Douglas B. Carter for a detailed critical reading which has been the basis for many corrections and changes in emphasis from the first edition. Any errors, inconsistencies, or omissions remain my responsibility, however.

HOWARD J. CRITCHFIELD

Bellingham, Washington

CONTENTS

part one

THE
PHYSICAL ELEMENTS
OF
WEATHER
AND
CLIMATE

introduction 1

The many specialized fields of study that concern the planet we call Earth may be grouped into three broad categories embracing the *lithosphere,* or solid portion of the earth; the *hydrosphere,* or water portion; and the gaseous *atmosphere.* Although the envelope of gases is the most significant in the study of weather and climate, heat and moisture are continuously exchanged between land and water surfaces and the atmosphere, making all three integral parts of the whole.

The processes of exchange of heat and moisture between the earth and the atmosphere over a long period of time result in conditions which we call *climate.* Climate is more than a statistical average; it is the aggregate of atmospheric conditions involving heat, moisture, and air movement. Extremes must always be considered in any climatic description in addition to means, trends, and probabilities. Climate is an important element of the physical environment of mankind, for, although man usually thinks of himself as a creature of the land, he actually lives at the bottom of a deep "ocean" of air that surrounds the earth. *Weather* is the day-to-day state of the atmosphere and pertains to short-term changes in conditions of heat, moisture, and air movement. Weather results fundamentally from processes that attempt to equalize differences in the distribution of net radiant energy received from the sun.

Climatology is the science that seeks to describe and explain the nature of climate, how it differs from place to place, and how it is related to man's activities. It is closely allied to *meteorology,* which deals with day-to-day atmospheric conditions and their causes. Meteorology is often defined as the physics of the atmosphere; it uses the methods of the physicist to interpret and explain atmospheric processes. Climatology broadens the findings of meteorology in space and in time to cover the whole earth and periods of time as long as observations and indirect evidence will permit. Because climatology involves collection and interpretation of observed data it necessitates statistical techniques; however, it is more than statistical meteorology. It makes abundant use of the tools of the geographer, including maps, and through its concern with climate as an element of man's physical environment has a close relationship with geography.

In this study of climatology we shall be concerned with three fundamental subdivisions: physical, regional, and applied. The basic question to be answered in physical climatology is: What causes the variations in heat exchange, moisture exchange, and air movement from time to time and from place to place? That is, why do we have different climates? As a first step toward the solution, we seek, through observation, facts relating to these variations. Several observable elements aid in the description of atmospheric conditions: radiation, duration of sunshine, temperature, humidity, evaporation, cloudiness and fog, precipitation, visibility, barometric pressure, and winds. The occurrence of these elements in a particular combination is the result of a number of processes involving the transfers of heat, moisture, and momentum which occur within the atmosphere and between the atmosphere and the earth's surface. Processes of weather and climate are influenced, in turn, by differences in latitude, altitude, land and water surfaces, mountain barriers, local topography, and such gross atmospheric features as prevailing winds, air masses, and semipermanent pressure centers. The roles of these factors and processes will be discussed in Part One.

Regional climatology has as its goal the orderly arrangement and description of world climates. It encompasses the identification of significant climatic characteristics and the classification of climatic types. The third division, applied climatology, explores the relationship of climatology to other sciences and considers it as a means for improving our well-being.

HISTORY OF METEOROLOGY AND CLIMATOLOGY

Climatology is at once an old and a new science. It is as old as man's curiosity about his environment. It is as new as the invention of the airplane, radio, and radar. Primitive man was greatly affected by the phenomena of weather and climate but was largely unable to explain them logically. Superstition and pagan religion served to interpret atmospheric mysteries such as rain, wind, or lightning. In the early civilizations gods were often assigned to the more important climatic elements. Thus to the Greeks Boreas guided the north wind; Ra was the Egyptian god of the sun; Jupiter Pluvius was the Roman god of rain; and Thor was the god of thunder in Norse mythology. Indians in the arid southwest United States still hold ceremonial dances to implore the gods to produce rain.

Advances in knowledge of weather and climate parallel the general development of science from ancient times. The Greek philosophers showed great interest in meteorology and climatology. In fact these two words are of Greek origin. Meteorology was literally a "discourse on things above" and included meteors and optical phenomena. Climatology comes from the Greek words *klima,* which referred to the supposed slope of the earth, approximating our conception of latitude, and *logos,* a discourse or study. The division of the world into five climatic zones (torrid, north and south temperate, north and south frigid) is attributed to Parmenides, who lived in the fifth century B.C. Among other Greek contributions to these sciences are Hippocrates' work on medical climatology, *Airs, Waters and Places,* written about 400 B.C. and Aristotle's *Meteorologica,* dated about 350 B.C. Over the centuries weather sayings were developed relating storms and other atmospheric conditions to phases of the moon, the orbital position of the earth, or the constellations. Some of the weather lore of the ancients was based upon intelligent observation of recurring weather types and was quite logical.

The period of weather lore and superstitions in the development of meteorology and climatology lasted until the beginning of the seventeenth century, when the invention of instruments and recording of observations furnished a basis for more accurate climatic description and for a scientific analysis of weather phenomena. Two instruments in particular marked the turning point in understanding of the atmosphere and its processes of change. In 1593 Galileo constructed a thermometer, and in 1643 his pupil, Toricelli, discovered the principle of the mercurial barometer. Many refinements on these instruments followed, as well as the invention of increasingly complex devices for measuring and recording weather elements. As soon as instrumental observations could be made and recorded, it became possible to compare weather data for different times and places. One of the first climatological maps was that published by the British astronomer Edmund Halley in 1686 to accompany his *Historical Account of the Trade Winds and Monsoons.*

It was some time before the importance of weather records was fully appreciated. By 1800 dependable weather observations were being made at only twelve places in Europe and five in the United States. The first systematic records of instrumental observations in the United States were begun in 1738 in Charleston, South Carolina, by John Lining. Early weather records at New Haven, Connecticut, date back to 1780. Baltimore and Philadelphia have records beginning in 1817 and 1825 respectively. Many of the early records in the interior of the country were taken at army posts, beginning in the 1830's. On the Pacific Coast, Sacramento and San Francisco have records from 1849 and San Diego from 1850.

The modern period of instrumental observation did not begin until the middle of the nineteenth century, when a great increase in the number of reporting stations occurred. However, there are still large areas over the oceans and continental interiors which are not under adequate surface observation. The greatest impetus to the use of meteorological data came after the development of the telegraph in the 1830's. Rapid communication of observations facilitated plotting of weather charts. In Holland, Buys-Ballot, a professor at Utrecht University, began the compilation of daily weather maps in 1852. Admiral Fitzroy, who formulated some of the first rules relating pressure and storms, made an accurate forecast of a storm in England from a weather chart in 1861. In the United States the Smithsonian Institution began collecting weather data and plotting them on maps in 1865. Cleveland Abbe made map forecasts in 1869–70.

In the nineteenth century the discovery of several principles related to gases and atmosphere circulation served as a basis for theoretical meteorology. About 1850 Heinrich Wilhelm Dove of Germany developed the idea that storms occur when polar and equatorial air come together. Study of world charts of winds and ocean currents prepared by Matthew Maury in the United States made it possible to reduce the sailing time from England to Australia from four to three months. During the American Civil War, Sir Francis Galton of England postulated the existence of anticyclones as well as cyclones in the mid-latitude circulation. In 1857 Buys-Ballot published his famous rule relating winds to pressure distribution: If you stand with your back to the wind in the Northern Hemisphere the low pressure will be on your left.

Most of the early rules of forecasting could be applied only locally, for they were based on familiarity with surrounding conditions and average weather patterns rather than on an analysis of general atmospheric movements. Until World War I, progress in weather science was largely in improvements in quantity and quality of observations and records, which in themselves were important bases for theoretical studies in meteorology and climatology. The dawn of present-day meteorology actually came when man could probe the upper atmosphere. Both the airplane and the radio played a large part in this development. Near the end of World War I, Vilhelm Bjerknes and his son Jacob formulated the polar front theory and initiated studies of air masses and fronts in Norway. In the United States, this was followed by extensive examination of the upper air under the leadership of Carl-Gustav Rossby. Aviation not only made upper-air observations possible—it made them imperative. For the purpose of meteorological observation, however, the airplane was to be replaced by balloons, rockets, satellites, and electronic devices, which extended knowledge of the upper air to ever greater heights. As a result, theories of atmospheric circulation are constantly being revised. Studies in long-range forecasting and climatic change as well as daily weather changes are making increasing use of information on the chemical, physical, and electrical properties of the atmosphere at high levels. Weather forecasting, which was primarily concerned with surface observations a half century ago, is today based on a three-dimensional atmosphere.

The present phase of research in weather and climate has broadened to include, on the one hand, investigations of atmospheric conditions at ever greater heights and, on the other hand, detailed examination of extremely thin layers of air immediately adjacent to the surface of land, water, or vegetation. That the sciences of meteorology and climatology are coming of age is evidenced by the growing practical application of their discoveries and techniques to the activities of man. Knowledge of weather and climate is being applied in the solution of such seemingly diverse problems as the best design for homes, the proper planting times for peas to insure a succession of maturity over a period of weeks, the best clothing for members of the armed forces at stations in all parts of the world, and most favorable conditions for launching space vehicles.

Worldwide exchange of meteorological and climatological information is today coordinated through the World Meteorological Organization (WMO), a specialized agency of the United Nations with headquarters in Geneva, Switzerland. The WMO took on its present form in 1951, having developed from the International Meteorological Organization, which had been established in 1878. In the United States the Weather Bureau is the primary organization for collection, analysis, and dissemination of information on weather and climate. In carrying out its objectives the Weather Bureau cooperates with a number of private and government agencies both in North America and abroad. The early history of the Weather Bureau dates back to the establishment of a Weather Service in the Army Signal Corps in 1870, although the Government Land Office began observations as early as 1817. The Signal Corps Weather Service was transferred to the Department of Agriculture in 1891 and became the United States Weather Bureau. In 1940 the Bureau was transferred again to the Department of Commerce. A Department of Commerce reorganization in 1965 consolidated the Weather Bureau and the Coast and Geodetic Survey in a new agency known as the Environmental Science Services Administration. These organizational changes have reflected the expanding demand for weather services as techniques of observation, forecasting, and application of weather information have developed during the past century.

NATURE OF THE ATMOSPHERE

The atmosphere is a deep blanket of gases which entirely envelops the earth. It is as much a part of the earth as the land or the water but it differs from them in several respects. Air is colorless, odorless, tasteless and cannot be felt except when it moves as wind. It is mobile, elastic, compressible, expansible, and can transmit compression waves. It is transparent to many forms of radiation. Although air is not nearly as dense as either land or water, it does have weight and exerts pressure, but, because it is compressible, its density decreases rapidly with altitude. The total mass of the atmosphere has been calculated at about 56×10^{14} tons. About half of this mass lies below 18,000 feet, and more than 99 per cent lies within 20 miles of the earth's surface.

Fortunately, air offers resistance to objects which move through it so that the friction which results when meteors pass into the outer atmosphere creates enough heat to destroy most of them before they can reach the earth's surface.

Without the atmosphere life could not exist and there would be no clouds, winds, or storms—no weather. Besides being an essential for life and a medium for weather processes, the air acts as a great canopy that protects the earth from the full force of the sun by day and prevents the loss of too much heat at night. If there were no atmosphere the temperatures of the earth would soar to over 200° Fahrenheit in the daytime and drop to approximately −300° at night.

ORIGIN OF THE ATMOSPHERE

The more plausible explanations of the creation of the atmosphere are based in part upon study of the atmospheres of other planets of the solar system. The elements which comprise the earth's atmosphere appear to be scarce elsewhere in the universe. Matter in the outer reaches of the atmosphere consists largely of the two lightest elements, hydrogen and helium, but these are rare in the air near the earth's surface. Presumably this condition developed through eons of geologic time along with slow changes that produced the present lithosphere and hydrosphere. In the early stages of formation of the planet from "cosmic gases" a weak gravitational field may have allowed light gases like hydrogen and helium to stray off into space. Even the gases of the present atmosphere probably are not direct residue of the earliest form of the planet. Rather they are a secondary atmosphere which evolved from volcanic eruptions, hot springs, chemical breakdown of solid matter, and, later, contributions from vegetation. Evidence points to a stabilization of the atmosphere in something like its present form by the Cambrian period, about 500 million years ago.

Yet an interaction of land, water, air, and plant and animal life constantly uses and renews the atmosphere. For example, the weathering of rocks, burning of fuel, decay of plants, and breathing of animals all use oxygen and release carbon dioxide. Nitrogen follows a complex cycle through bacterial activity in the soil, animal tissue, organic processes in decay, and back into the air. Plants, animals, bacteria, and chemical interaction in soil and water all help to maintain an intricate balance among land, water, life, and the air.

COMPOSITION OF THE ATMOSPHERE

The air is a mixture of several gases, each of which acts independently of the others. The Greeks classed air as a single element, and that idea was held until the late eighteenth century when chemists began to isolate and identify separate gases. Simple experiments in chemistry and physics can be performed to demonstrate that air is neither a single gaseous element nor a compound of gases. Because of the continuous churning and diffusion of these gases in the lower atmosphere they are found in the same proportions at different times and places, so that the Greek concept of air is neither surprising nor entirely illogical.

Four gases—nitrogen, oxygen, argon, and carbon dioxide—account for more than 99 per cent of dry air. Nitrogen alone constitutes nearly four-fifths of the air by volume and oxygen one-fifth. The principal remaining stable gases are neon, helium, methane, krypton, hydrogen, nitrous oxide, and xenon. Various other less stable gases, including ozone and radon, also occur in air.

TABLE 1-1

Principal Gases Comprising Air

	By Volume	By Weight
Nitrogen (N_2)	78.088%	75.527%
Oxygen (O_2)	20.949	23.143
Argon (A)	0.93	1.282
Carbon dioxide (CO_2)	0.03	0.0456
	99.997	99.9976

Of these gases oxygen is the most important for life. It combines readily with many other chemical elements and is necessary for combustion. Carbon dioxide is a product of combustion and is exhaled by animals and used by plants. It absorbs a part of long-wave radiation from the earth. Nitrogen does not combine readily with other elements, but it is a constituent of many organic compounds. One of its main effects in the atmosphere is to dilute oxygen and thus regulate combustion and other kinds of oxidation. Ozone is a powerful oxidizing agent but it occurs in such minute quantities and at such great altitudes that its function in this respect is extremely limited. Of greater significance is its capacity to absorb a part of the sun's ultraviolet radiation and thereby limit the quantity which reaches the earth's surface to the amount essential for life.

Up to this point we have considered the gases of dry air; however, of far more importance than any of them in weather and climate is water vapor. Water vapor has characteristics which set it apart from the other gases of the air. The proportion of water vapor in the air varies from minute amounts to a maximum of about 4 per cent under extremely humid conditions. This variability is one of the main concerns of the meteorologist. In Chapter 3 it will be discussed in detail along with another unique feature of water vapor, namely, its ability to change from a gas to a liquid or solid while a part of the atmosphere. The three forms of water in the atmosphere have restrictive effects upon solar radiation; they are able to absorb, reflect, and scatter certain wave lengths of the solar spectrum.

Up to altitudes of 50 or 60 miles (80–100 km.) the composition of the atmosphere remains fairly constant. The proportion of ozone increases; carbon dioxide, water vapor, and dust decrease. Besides the water droplets and ice crystals which occur as fog, haze, or clouds in the atmosphere, there are large quantities of suspended dust particles. The amount of dust varies greatly over the earth, but even over the oceans, hundreds of particles per cubic centimeter of air have been counted. Most of these particles are invisible to the naked eye and some are submicroscopic in size. Dust absorbs a part of the incoming solar radiation and also is an agent of reflection and scattering. It is one of the factors in the intensity and duration of dawn and twilight. The blue color of the sky and the red of sunsets are due to selective scattering of the visible solar spectrum by gas molecules and dust. Condensation of water vapor begins on nuclei of fine dust particles. One might suppose that the atmospheric dust would eventually be washed down to earth by rains, but it is constantly being replenished. The sources are many and varied: dry soil particles, smoke, salts from ocean spray, bacteria, seeds and spores, volcanic ash, and meteoric dust. The number of dust particles is great in industrial centers and relatively greater in dry regions than in humid areas. The concentration of dust generally decreases with altitude although the smallest particles reach heights of several miles and meteoric dust is introduced at the outer limits of the atmosphere.

VERTICAL DIVISIONS OF THE ATMOSPHERE

The vertical extent of the atmosphere is difficult to ascertain, for there is no sharp boundary between the air and extraterrestrial space. Atmospheric phenomena associated with the earth's magnetic and gravitational fields extend outward for several thousand miles to a vague zone of nebulous gases and radiation particles that become rarer and rarer until at last the terrestrial characteristics of the atmosphere cease.

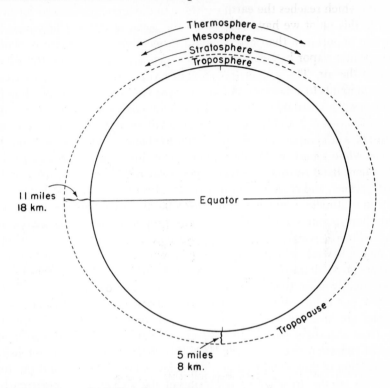

Fig. 1-1   Major vertical divisions or "shells" of the atmosphere.

On the basis of vertical temperature differences the atmosphere may be divided into four major layers, or "shells"—the *troposphere,* the *stratosphere,* the *mesosphere,* and the *thermosphere.* The troposphere is the lower portion of the atmosphere, extending up to about 5 miles at the poles and 11 miles at the equator. It is the realm of clouds, storms, and convection currents and is therefore of primary concern to meteorologists and climatologists. Thermal convection, being better developed in the tropics, is responsible for the greater vertical extent of the troposphere near the equator. It also explains the somewhat greater height of the troposphere in summer than in winter at a given latitude. The outstanding characteristic of the troposphere is the fairly uniform decrease in temperature with increase in altitude until minimums of −70° or −80°F are reached. The zone marking the end of this temperature decrease is called the *tropopause*. Above the tropopause lies the stratosphere, which exhibits little vertical change in temperatures that approximate those of the Arctic winter at the surface. The stratosphere is thicker over the poles and sometimes does not exist over the equator. Near its outer limit, the *stratopause*,

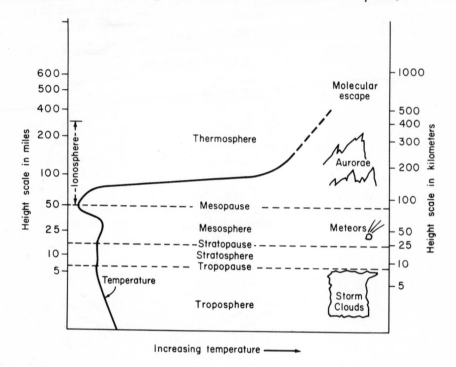

Fig. 1-2 Vertical divisions of the atmosphere and related phenomena.

are the greatest concentrations of ozone, and rare nacreous clouds occasionally appear. Beyond the stratopause, which has a mean altitude of about 15 miles in the middle latitudes, is the mesosphere. Temperatures in the mesosphere increase and then decrease to a minimum near the *mesopause*, at 45 to 50 miles. Most meteors burn and disintegrate in this layer. In the thermosphere the temperature again rises to values approaching 2000°F at an undefined upper limit. Such temperatures are not strictly comparable with those observed by ordinary thermometers at the earth's surface, however. They result from collisions among molecules being too infrequent to maintain thermodynamic equilibrium. Orbiting satellites have invaded the thermosphere and space probes have penetrated it.

Coinciding with the lower portion of the thermosphere is the *ionosphere*, an atmospheric layer at 50 to 250 miles delimited on the basis of ionized particles and their effects on the propagation of radio waves. Little was known of the ionosphere until it was found that radio waves are reflected by ionized layers at great heights. The aurora borealis and its Southern Hemisphere counterpart, aurora australis, apparently result from excitation of the ionosphere by high-energy radiation particles from the sun. Their maximum occurrence is near the magnetic poles, toward which the particles are deflected by the earth's magnetic field. Aurorae have been observed to increase with an increase in sunspot activity. There is no proven relationship between auroral displays and weather in the troposphere. Another phenomenon of the ionosphere, *air glow*, originates with self-luminescent gases. It exhibits no significant correlation with sunspot or magnetic activity.

In the chapters that follow we shall be concerned almost entirely with the lower part of the troposphere, for it is the sphere of weather, but the unity of the atmosphere must be kept in mind. Variations of density in upper atmospheric layers may logically be expected to produce changes in lower layers. Much of what is not now fully understood about our weather and climate may be explained ultimately with reference to the upper atmosphere, the nature of which is being investigated in ever greater detail by researchers in the field of aeronomy, the science of the upper atmosphere.

ADDITIONAL READINGS

Blench, Brian J. R., "Luke Howard and His Contribution to Meteorology," *Weather*, 18, 3 (1963), 83–92.

Court, Arnold, "Climatology: Complex, Dynamic, and Synoptic," *Ann. Assoc. Am. Geogrs.*, 47, 2 (1957), 125–36.

Hare, F. Kenneth, "The Stratosphere," *Geog. Rev.*, 52, 4 (1962), 525–47.

Jastrow, Robert, "Artificial Satellites and the Earth's Atmosphere," *Scient. Am.*, 201, 2 (1959), 37–43.

Landsberg, H. E., "Origin of the Atmosphere," *Scient. Am.*, 189, 2 (1953), 82–86.

Leighly, John, "Climatology Since the Year 1800," *Trans. Am. Geophys. Un.*, 30, 5 (1949), 658–72.

Reichelderfer, Francis W., "The World Meteorological Organization," *Weatherwise*, 17, 5 (1964), 213–23; 234.

Shaw, Sir Napier, *Manual of Meteorology*, Vol. 1, Meteorology in History. Cambridge, England: Cambridge University Press, 1926.

Whitnah, Donald R., *A History of the United States Weather Bureau*. Urbana, Ill.: University of Illinois Press, 1961.

heat 2
and temperature

The primary source of heat for the earth and its atmosphere is the sun. The amount of heat which the earth receives from the stars and other celestial bodies is negligible. Radiant energy from the sun that strikes the earth is called *insolation*—a contraction of "incoming solar radiation." Insolation consists of rays of radiant energy made up of various wave lengths. The longer waves, called infrared rays, are largely absorbed in the atmosphere. At the other end of the solar spectrum are the shorter ultraviolet rays, which are capable of producing certain photochemical effects. Between these bands of invisible radiation is the visible portion of the spectrum that we know as sunlight and that is the most effective in heating the earth. When the rays of the solar spectrum reach the earth they are partially absorbed and converted from short-wave to long-wave radiant energy, that is, heat. Energy gained in this way provides the "fuel" for the processes of weather and climate, and it is transferred both vertically and horizontally, creating a variety of temperature conditions. Eventually it is lost by radiation from the atmosphere to outer space.

THE HEAT BUDGET

Only a small part of insolation is absorbed directly by the air through which it passes. The processes of radiation, convection, and conduction bring about heating and cooling of the air by transferring heat between the earth and the air and between **14** different levels in the air. In addition, heat is exchanged between various surfaces and the atmosphere by the processes of evaporation and condensation.

Radiation is the process of transmission of energy by electromagnetic waves and is the means by which energy emitted by the sun reaches the earth. Of the total solar radiation which reaches the outer limits of the atmosphere about 32 per cent is reflected by clouds or scattered back to space by suspended particles and is never used to heat the air; 2 per cent is reflected to space from the earth's surface. This total reflectivity is known as the earth's *albedo*. The albedo of different surfaces varies greatly; clouds have an albedo about ten times that of land. The average value for the entire earth, including the atmosphere, is about 34 per cent, although it is greater in polar regions than at the equator. About 19 per cent of solar radiation is absorbed by gases (principally water vapor) and suspended particles, 24 per cent is absorbed directly by the earth, and 23 per cent is absorbed by the earth after diffuse scattering by clouds and atmosphere. Thus approximately two-thirds of the total insolation is effective in heating the earth and its atmosphere. (See Figure 2-1.)

By virtue of its absorption and conversion of insolation into heat, the earth itself becomes a radiating body. Although the components of the atmosphere collectively are able to absorb only a small portion of the incoming short-wave radiation, they can capture a large part of the outgoing long-wave radiation. Water vapor and carbon dioxide are especially

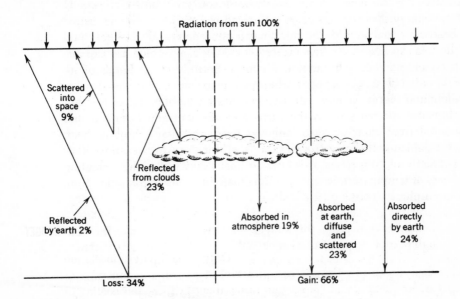

Fig. 2-1 Heating of the earth and its atmosphere by insolation.

effective in absorbing long-wave energy. This ability of the atmosphere to admit most of the insolation and retard the re-radiation from the earth is known as the *greenhouse effect* because of the analogy to the function of a glass covering on a greenhouse. Besides the long-wave (heat) radiation from the earth's surface there is also radiation from cloud layers and from the atmosphere out into space. The total amount of energy coming into the earth over a considerable period of time is equalled by total outward losses. If this were not so, the earth would soon become either very hot or very cold. Actually there is a deficit of heat at high latitudes and a surplus in low latitudes owing to radiation gains and losses. Horizontal transport by winds and by water in ocean currents prevents the progressive accumulation of heat in equatorial regions.

Conduction is the heat transfer process which occurs when two bodies of unequal temperature are in contact. Heat passes to the colder body as long as the temperature difference exists. Thus, when the land is absorbing radiation and is warmed above the temperature of the air, conduction transfers a part of the heat to the lower layer of air. If the land is cooler than the adjacent air the heat transfer is reversed and the air is cooled. The latter phenomenon is common at night and in winter in the middle and high latitudes.

Air itself is a poor conductor of heat. If conduction alone provided transfer of heat upward from the earth's surface, the air would be very hot along the ground on a summer day and quite cool a few feet up. Within the air heat conduction is insignificant compared with *convection*, which accomplishes transfer of heat through movement of the air itself. Air heated by contact with the warm earth surface expands and becomes less dense. The lighter air thus created is replaced by cooler, heavier air from above and a convectional circulation is established with horizontal as well as vertical components. The same principle is involved in the circulation of warm air in a room. Liquids, being mobile like gases, also develop convectional systems. The oceans exhibit convection on a grand scale in their pattern of currents. Although much of the convective activity is due to heating at the earth's surface, it is important to remember that the principle of convection will operate also through cooling at higher levels. An example of this occurs when cold air temporarily pushes in above warmer air, producing a sudden overturning of air as the denser, cooler air above replaces the lighter, warmer air below. Winter thunderstorms sometimes result from this kind of convection.

Although part of the net radiation gained by the earth's surface is transferred upward by long-wave radiation and as sensible heat by the processes of conduction and convection, much of it reaches the atmosphere as latent heat in water evaporated from land and water surfaces, and especially from oceans. Moist air masses may move great distances before condensation of their water vapor releases huge quantities of latent heat. Thus we see that the processes of heat and moisture exchange are closely interconnected.

Taken together, the processes of heat transfer maintain a complex exchange of heat between the earth's surfaces and the atmosphere, but ultimately the total amount of energy coming into the earth is equalled by total outward losses to space. In this way the over-all heat budget of the earth is balanced.

VARIABILITY OF INSOLATION

The amount of insolation received on any date at a place on the earth is governed by:

1. the *solar constant*, which depends on:
   (*a*) energy output of the sun
   (*b*) distance from the earth to the sun
2. transparency of the atmosphere
3. duration of the daily sunlight period
4. angle at which the sun's noon rays strike the earth.

The first of these influences upon insolation is of least importance. Measurements and calculations of the amount of heat coming into the outer limits of the atmosphere have resulted in an average figure of about 2 gram calories per square centimeter per minute. If the solar constant seems small, consider that it may also be represented as more than 4½ million horsepower per square mile.

Although referred to as the *solar constant*, it actually varies slightly. The variation has not been found to have a great effect upon daily weather, but it may be related to certain climatic fluctuations. Variations in specific components of the solar spectrum, especially ultraviolet radiation, are probably of greater significance in affecting atmospheric conditions.

The distance between the earth and the sun varies between 94.5 million miles at *aphelion* (July 1) and 91.5 million miles at *perihelion* (January 1). Neither of these is a great variation from the average distance of 93 million miles, and although the amount of radiation reaching the outer atmosphere is about 7 per cent greater at perihelion than at aphelion, other factors influencing insolation and temperature largely override the difference.

Transparency of the atmosphere has a more important bearing upon the amount of insolation which reaches the earth's surface. The effect of dust, clouds, water vapor, and certain gases in reflection, scattering, and absorption was discussed previously. It follows that areas having heavy cloudiness or polluted air will receive less direct insolation. Transparency is also a function of latitude, for at middle and high latitudes the sun's rays must pass through a thicker layer of reflecting-scattering atmosphere than at tropical latitudes. (See Figure 2-3.) This effect varies with the seasons, being greatest in winter when the sun's rays are lowest on the horizon.

The duration of daylight also varies with latitude and the seasons, and

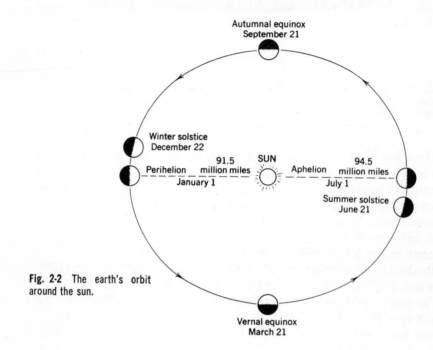

Fig. 2-2 The earth's orbit around the sun.

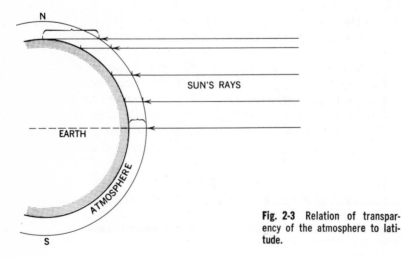

Fig. 2-3 Relation of transparency of the atmosphere to latitude.

the longer the period of sunlight the greater will be the total possible insolation. At the equator day and night are always equal. In the polar regions the daylight period reaches a maximum of twenty-four hours in summer and a minimum of zero hours in winter. At the respective summer solstice, under clear skies, a polar area may receive more radiation per 24-hour day than other latitudes, though the net radiation used for heating is reduced by the albedo of ice and snow surfaces.

TABLE 2-1

Longest Possible Duration of Insolation

Latitude	0°	17°	41°	49°	63°	66½°	67°21′	90°
Daylight	12 hr.	13 hr.	15 hr.	16 hr.	20 hr.	24 hr.	1 mo.	6 mo.

The effect of the varying angle at which the sun's rays strike the earth can be seen in the daily march of the sun across the sky. At solar noon the intensity of insolation is greatest, but in the morning and evening hours, when the sun is at a low angle, the amount of insolation is small. The same principle has a broader application with respect to latitude and the seasons. In winter and at high latitudes even the noon sun's angle is low; in summer and at low latitudes it is more nearly vertical. The oblique rays of the low-angle sun are spread over a greater surface than are vertical rays and, as a consequence, produce less heating per unit area.

The angle at which solar radiation strikes the earth's surface also depends upon the surface configuration of the land. In the Northern Hemisphere southern slopes receive more direct rays, whereas northern slopes

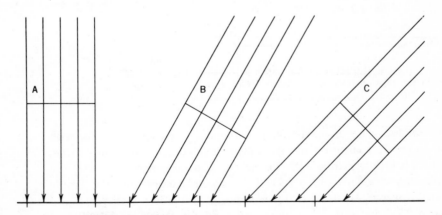

Fig. 2-4 Relation of sun angle to effectiveness of insolation. A—sun directly overhead, highly effective; B and C—smaller angles of incidence, less effective insolation.

may be entirely in the shade. The possible hours of sunshine in a deep valley may be greatly reduced by surrounding hills. Certain valleys in Switzerland, for example, receive direct sunlight in winter for only two or three hours around noon.

WORLD DISTRIBUTION OF INSOLATION

From the foregoing it is evident that the world distribution of insolation is closely related to latitude. Total annual insolation is greatest at the equator and decreases regularly toward the poles. At the equator the annual receipt of insolation is about four times that received at either of the poles. As the rays of the sun shift seasonally from one hemisphere to

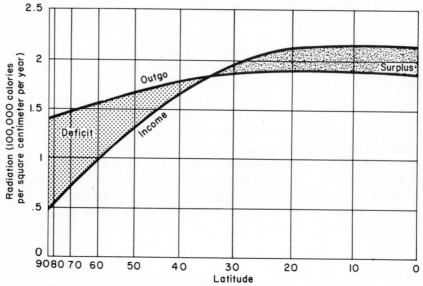

Based on data from Henry G. Houghton, "On the Annual Heat Balance of the Northern Hemisphere," *Journal of Meteorology*, 11, 1 (1954), 1–9.

Fig. 2-5 Latitudinal distribution of the earth's heat budget. From about 38° N. and S. to the poles there is a net annual loss of heat by outgoing radiation. Between 38° N. and S. income exceeds outgo.

the other, the zone of maximum possible daily insolation moves with them. In tropical latitudes the amount of insolation is constantly large, and there is little variation with the seasons. But in its annual journey the sun passes over all places between the Tropic of Cancer and the Tropic of Capricorn twice, causing two maximums of insolation. In the latitudes between 23½° and 66½°, maximum and minimum periods of insolation occur at the summer and winter solstices respectively. Beyond the Arctic

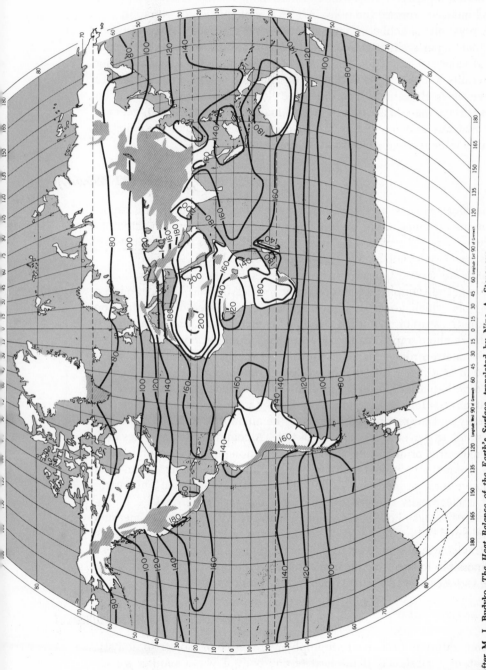

After M. I. Budyko, *The Heat Balance of the Earth's Surface*, translated by Nina A. Stepanova. U.S. Weather Bureau, 1958. Van der Grinten projection, courtesy A. J. Nystrom & Co., Chicago.

Fig. 2-6 Total annual insolation at the earth's surface. Values are in kilogram-calories per square centimeter per year.

and Antarctic Circles the maximum coincides with the summer solstices, but there is a period during which insolation is lacking. The length of the period increases toward the poles, where it is of six months' duration.

Observations of actual insolation at the earth's surface show a distribution that departs slightly from a simple latitudinal pattern. Maximum annual values of insolation occur at about 20° latitude, where the drier air permits a greater proportion of the radiant energy to penetrate to surface levels. Regions with considerable cloudiness receive less insolation at the surface than do areas with predominantly clear weather. In general, high plateaus and mountains are favored by more effective insolation because of the relatively clearer air at high altitudes.

MEASUREMENT OF SUNSHINE AND INSOLATION

The effects of sunshine as distinct from heat and temperature are important in maintenance of life, and they play a large part in human activities. Everyone is familiar with the claims of many chambers of commerce that theirs is a climate with a great number of sunshine hours.

There are several types of instruments which measure the duration of sunshine. The Campbell-Stokes recorder focuses the sun's rays through a glass globe which, acting as a burning glass, chars a record of sunshine on a graduated strip of cardboard. Modified cameras have also been devised which use photographic paper to record the sun's light rays. Another class of sunshine recorder depends upon the fact that a black surface absorbs radiation at a faster rate than a white or translucent one. The resulting heat differential is transferred mechanically or electrically to a recorder.

Instruments for the determination of insolation, called *pyrheliometers,* generally make direct measurements of the amount of radiation absorbed on a small area over a short period of time. A common type operates on a thermoelectric principle. Incidence of radiation upon black and white rings of equal area produces differential heating which generates an electromotive force proportional to the intensity of the radiation. The instrument is electrically coupled to indicating and recording devices. Photoelectric cells and photospectroscopic apparatus are also used to measure sunlight and to investigate special components of the solar spectrum such as ultraviolet radiation. By means of net radiation meters, or *radiometers,* it is possible to measure the radiant transfer of heat upward from the earth's surface as well as that which is directed downward.

AIR TEMPERATURE AND ITS MEASUREMENT

Temperature is a relative term implying a degree of molecular activity, or heat, of a substance. If the heat of one body flows to another we say

Fig. 2-7 The Eppley pyrheliometer. A thermocouple connects black and white rings of equal area in the activating element. It generates an electromotive force proportional to the intensity of solar radiation.

that the former has the higher temperature. To measure the temperature of a body an arbitrary scale of reference is employed. The two most common scales used in the measurement of air temperature are the Fahrenheit and Centigrade, or Celsius, scales. The Fahrenheit scale fixes the boiling point of water at 212° and the melting point of ice at 32°. The Centigrade scale's boiling point of water is 100° and its melting point of ice is 0°. It is the scale now most widely used in reporting temperature data and in meteorological analyses. The two scales indicate the same temperature at −40°. Fahrenheit temperatures may be converted to their Centigrade equivalents by the following formula:

$$C = 5/9(F - 32)$$

Similarly:

$$F = 32 + 9/5C$$

Still another scale, the Kelvin, or Absolute, is based upon *absolute zero,* the point at which a gas theoretically would cease to exert any pressure.

The value of each degree on the Absolute scale equals that of a Centigrade degree but Absolute zero is −273° Centigrade. Centigrade temperatures may thus be converted to Absolute simply by adding 273.

The most common type of thermometer consists of a sealed glass tube
with a uniform bore and a bulb at one end filled with either mercury or
alcohol. Changes in temperature produce expansion or contraction of
the contents of the tube, which is graduated to facilitate reading of the
indicated temperature values. The accuracy of temperature measurements depends on the care with which the thermometer is constructed
and calibrated as well as on its exposure to the air. For official measurements of surface air temperature the thermometer is mounted in a louvered instrument shelter which has its base four feet above the ground.

Another type of thermometer indicates temperature differences as they
affect the shape of a bimetallic element. Two strips of different metals are
welded together to form a bimetallic bar. An increase in temperature
causes the bar to expand, but the two metals expand at different rates,
causing the unit to bend. The curvature is translated into temperature
values on a calibrated dial. A simpler version of the principle of expansion employs a metallic coil which produces varying tension on an indicating mechanism in response to temperature changes.

Thermocouples and *thermistors* indicate temperature electrically. Their
accuracy and rapidity of response make them suitable for microclimatic
observations in air, soil, plant tissues, clothing, and other specialized
exposures. The thermocouple consists of a pair of junctions of two unlike
metals. When one junction is kept at a constant temperature and the other
is exposed to a different temperature, the electromotive force generated
in the circuit can be measured by a potentiometer calibrated in degrees.
The thermistor, a semiconducting ceramic element, offers less resistance to
the flow of current as its temperature increases. Temperature can thus be
indicated as a function of current.

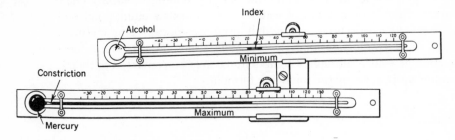

Fig. 2-8 The maximum and minimum thermometers.

For climatic records it is useful to know the highest and lowest temperatures that occur during a certain time. Registering thermometers have
been developed for obtaining the maximum and minimum temperatures.
The simplest *maximum thermometer* is a mercury thermometer with a
constriction in the bore near the bulb. (See Figure 2-8.) The constriction
allows the expanding mercury to pass as the temperature rises, but when
cooling occurs the column of mercury breaks at the constriction leaving
a part in the bore to register the highest temperature attained. The maximum thermometer is mounted horizontally and is reset by whirling so that
centrifugal force pulls the detached thread of mercury down past the
constriction. The fever thermometer used by physicians is a specially
calibrated maximum thermometer.

The *minimum thermometer* has a larger bore and its fluid is colorless
alcohol. A tiny, dark index in the shape of a long dumbbell is placed in
the bore below the top of the alcohol column. The minimum thermometer
is mounted horizontally and as the alcohol contracts with the decreasing
temperature the meniscus (concave surface) of the alcohol pulls the index
down. When the meniscus moves up the bore, however, it leaves the index
behind to register the lowest temperature. Resetting of the minimum
thermometer is accomplished by inverting the stem until the index slides
down to the meniscus.

Fig. 2-9 Double-recording thermograph. The Bourdon tube on the right activates a pen arm
to record air temperature. The element in the foreground translates temperature changes to
the second pen arm via a capillary tube from another location in air, water, or soil.

Courtesy Belfort Instrument Company.

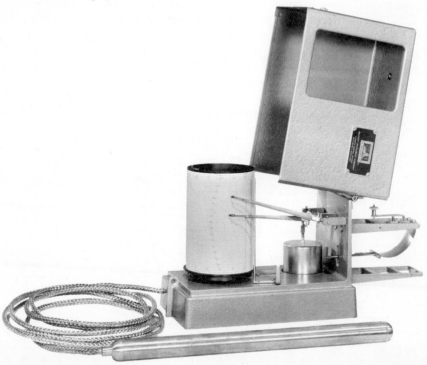

Where a permanent, continuous record of temperature is desired a *thermograph* is used. The thermograph consists of an element responsive to temperature changes, a system of levers to translate these changes to a pen arm, and a cylindrical clock drum around which a calibrated chart is mounted. Most thermographs have eight-day clocks and a chart which provides for a continuous ink trace of temperature for seven days. A common temperature element employed is the *Bourdon tube,* a flat, curved tube of phosphor bronze filled with alcohol. The tube changes its curvature in response to temperature changes. Bimetallic elements are also used in thermographs. The readings obtained from a thermograph are not as accurate as those from a mercury thermometer, but frequent checking of the thermograph trace against an accurate thermometer makes a corrected thermograph chart valuable for climatological work.

For most purposes thermometers are read to the nearest one-tenth degree. Temperature differences smaller than one-tenth degree cannot be indicated accurately without special instruments, and the results would be of no added value for most ordinary climatic records.

TEMPERATURE RECORDS

For climatological purposes, several kinds of temperature values are desired. Comparatively few stations in the world take hourly temperature readings although an hourly record or a continuous record is highly desirable. From a thermograph trace or from hourly records the daily march of temperature may be determined. Probably the most-used basic tem-

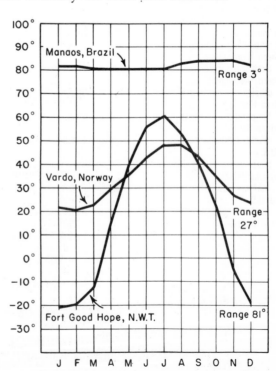

Fig. 2-10 Variations of mean monthly temperatures at selected stations.

perature value is the *daily mean,* from which monthly and annual values may be computed. The daily mean temperature is found by adding the 24-hour maximum to the 24-hour minimum and dividing by two. (Hourly temperatures during the 24-hour day would provide a better basis for the mean, but at many stations they are not recorded.) The difference between the highest and lowest temperatures of the day is known as the *diurnal* (daily) *range.* Ordinarily the observations of the maximum and minimum thermometers are the bases for the daily mean temperature and the diurnal range. The *mean monthly* temperature is found by adding the daily means and dividing by the number of days in the month. Mean monthly values for the year indicate the *annual march* of temperature through the seasons. The term *annual range* is applied to the difference between the mean temperatures of the warmest and coldest months. For most stations in the Northern Hemisphere the warmest month is July and the coldest January. When corresponding temperature values for a number of years are averaged, a generalized value useful in climatic description is obtained. However, such averages tend to obscure the year-to-year variability and climatic changes or cycles.

TABLE 2-2

Records of Extreme Temperatures*
(in °F)

Record	Temperature	Location	Date
Highest official air temperature	136°	Azizia, Libya	Sept. 13, 1922
Highest temperature in the U.S.	134°	Greenland Ranch, Death Valley, Calif.	July 10, 1913
Highest annual average temperature	88°	Lugh, Somalia	13-year average
Lowest official temperature in Northern Hemisphere	− 90°	Verkhoyansk, Siberia	Feb. 5 and 7, 1892
Lowest unofficial temperature in Northern Hemisphere	−108°	Oimekon, Siberia	Winter, 1938
Lowest official temperature in Western Hemisphere	− 87°	On Greenland ice cap at 9,820 feet	Dec. 6, 1949
Lowest temperature on North American Continent	− 81°	Snag, Yukon	Feb. 3, 1947
Lowest official temperature in the U.S.	− 76°	Tanana, Alaska	Jan., 1886
Lowest temperature in the 48 contiguous states	− 70°	Rogers Pass, Mont.	Jan. 20, 1954
Lowest unofficial temperature in the U.S.	− 78°	Fort Yukon, Alaska	Jan. 14, 1934
Lowest official record by U.S. Weather Bureau	−109.8°	Amundsen-Scott Station (90° S.)	July 14, 1963
Lowest world temperature	−126.9°	Vostok Soviet Station, (78° 27′S.; 106° 52′E.) at 11,440 feet	Aug. 24, 1960

* United States Weather Bureau.

Especially in the middle and high latitudes the length of the *frost-free season* is commonly a part of the temperature record. Frost-free season is defined as the number of days during which temperatures are continuously above 32°F. The mean frost-free season is the difference in days between the mean date of the last frost in spring and the mean date of the first frost in autumn. It is regarded as an important consideration in agriculture, but there is actually no simple, direct relationship between plant growth and freedom from frost.

HORIZONTAL TEMPERATURE DISTRIBUTION

The differences in temperature from place to place are quite as important as the differences from time to time. An ever-expanding network of temperature recording stations makes it possible to describe areal differences with increasing accuracy. On maps, the horizontal distribution of temperature is commonly shown by means of *isotherms,* lines connecting points with equal temperature values. (See Figures 2-11 and 2-12.) On weather maps of small areas the actual observed temperatures are used as a basis for drawing isotherms, but on continental or world maps mean temperatures are frequently reduced to sea level equivalents by adding about 3.3F° for each 1000 feet of elevation. This adjustment essentially eliminates the effect of altitude on temperature and thus facilitates the mapping of horizontal temperature differences. Vertical distribution of temperature will be discussed in the succeeding section.

The general pattern of world distribution of temperature is determined by a number of factors. It has already been noted that the effectiveness of insolation in heating the earth's surface is largely determined by latitude. The general decrease in temperatures from the equator toward the poles is one of the most fundamental and best known facts of climatology. If the effect of latitude were the only controlling factor affecting the receipt of net radiation we would expect a world temperature map to have isotherms lying parallel to each other in the same fashion as parallels of latitude. Of course, such is not the actual case.

The irregular distribution of land and water on the earth's surface tends to break up the orderly latitudinal arrangement. Land areas warm and cool more rapidly than do bodies of water, with the result that annual temperature ranges are greater over land. There are three primary reasons for the contrasts in land and water temperatures. (*1*) Water is mobile and experiences both vertical and horizontal movements which distribute heat energy absorbed at the surface throughout its mass, whereas insolation is absorbed by land only at the surface and is transmitted downward slowly by conduction. (*2*) Water is translucent and is penetrated by radiant energy to a much greater depth than is opaque land. Thus a given quan-

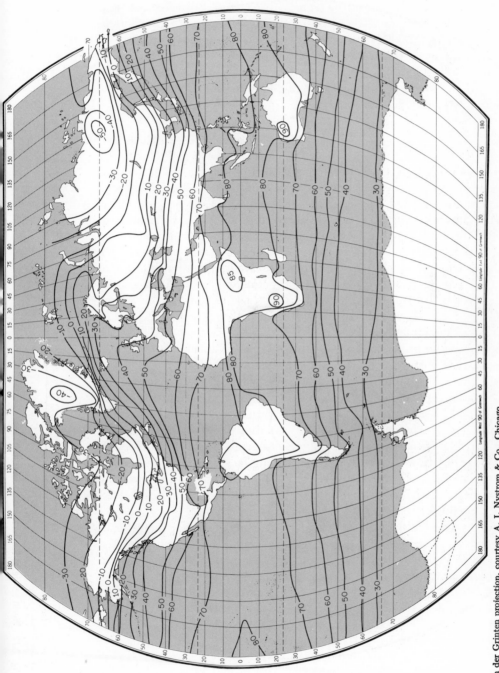

Van der Grinten projection, courtesy A. J. Nystrom & Co., Chicago.

Fig. 2-11 World sea level temperatures in January in °F.

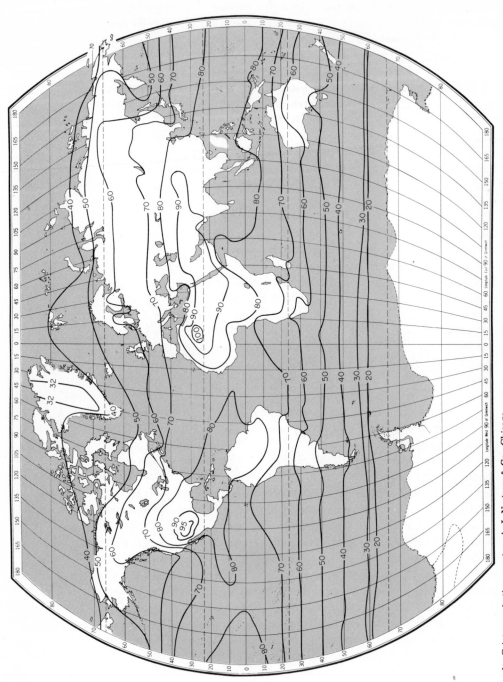

Van der Grinten projection, courtesy A. J. Nystrom & Co., Chicago.

Fig. 2-12 World sea level temperatures in July in °F.

tity of insolation must be distributed through a greater mass of water than of land, even though their surface areas are the same. (3) The *specific heat* of water is higher than that of land. That is, a given mass of water requires more heat energy to raise its temperature 1° than does an equal mass of dry land. Consequently, the same amount of insolation will produce a higher temperature on a land surface than on a water surface. Conversely, in cooling, water will have to lose a greater amount of heat than will land to produce the same drop in temperature.

The general effect of the contrast in heating of land and water areas is to produce cooler winters and warmer summers in the center of continents than along coasts and over oceans. Coastal or marine climates tend to be moderate, experiencing no great extremes in either daily or annual temperature changes.

Through the horizontal transport of ocean water in the form of currents and drifts heat is carried from one part of the earth to another. Thus, an ocean current travelling toward a pole will warm air which passes over it, producing air temperatures higher than would normally be expected for the latitude. A current moving toward the equator will produce cooler air temperatures. An outstanding example of the effect of an ocean current upon temperature is that of the North Atlantic Drift off northwest Europe. The January isotherms for 30° and 40° intercept the United States' east coast in the vicinity of latitude 40°N., but the North Atlantic Drift carries warm water into the northeast Atlantic so that these two isotherms strike the coasts of Great Britain and the Scandinavian Peninsula at a much higher latitude. Examples of the effect of a cold ocean current can be seen in the temperature distribution along the west coasts of South America and Africa. The Peru (South America) and Benguela (Africa) Currents flow northward along the west coasts, where upwelling causes temperatures to be lower than in corresponding latitudes on east sides of the continents.

The horizontal distribution of sea surface temperatures results from the effects of latitude and the seasons as well as of ocean currents. Extremes range from below 30°F in high latitudes to about 90°F in certain tropical gulfs. Annual variations in temperature of the sea surface are greatest along the east coasts in the middle latitudes of the Northern Hemisphere, the extremes occurring in February and August. There is thus a lag of about two months in heating and cooling of the ocean surfaces behind the periods of high and low sun. (See Figures 2-13 and 2-14.)

It is obvious that neither oceans nor ocean currents can have their maximum effect upon temperature unless the prevailing winds blow from the water to the land. Prevailing wind direction and the movements of air masses have a direct influence upon the average temperatures of an area. This is well illustrated by the winter flow of air across the United States.

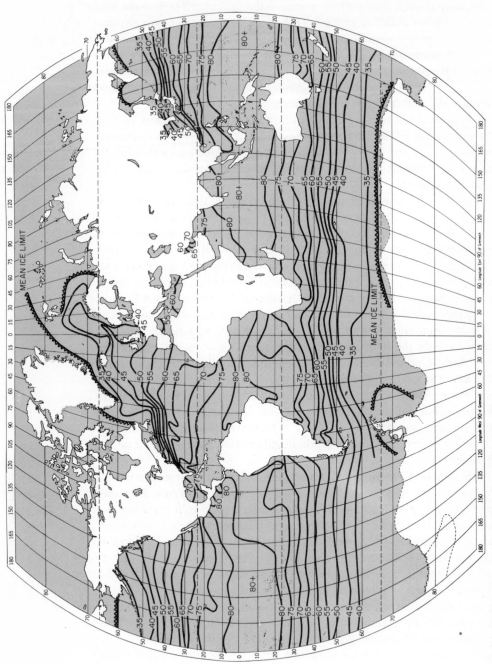

Van der Grinten projection, courtesy A. J. Nystrom & Co., Chicago.

Fig. 2-13 Mean February sea surface temperatures in °F.

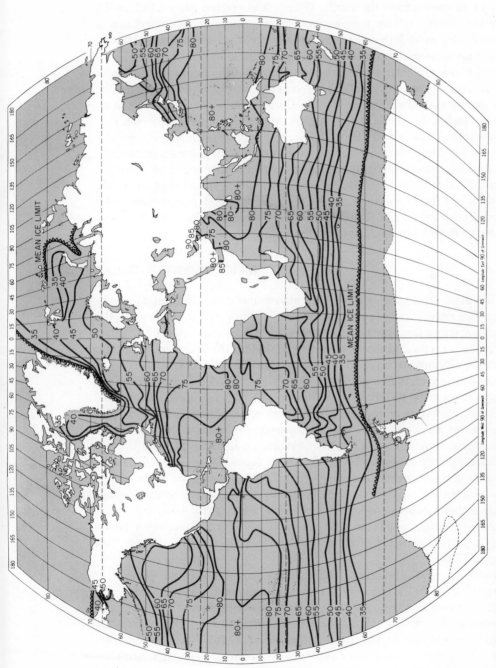

Van der Grinten projection, courtesy A. J. Nystrom & Co., Chicago.

Fig. 2-14 Mean August sea surface temperatures in °F.

The west coast experiences the relatively warm temperatures characteristic of air blown from the Pacific Ocean. The eastern part of the nation
receives cooler air from the continent in the general west-to-east movement of storms and air masses and the immediate effect of the Atlantic
Ocean upon east coast temperatures is somewhat restricted.

Still another influence on horizontal temperature distribution is mountain barriers. The barrier effect of mountain ranges tends to restrict the
movement of cold air masses. In the United States the Rocky Mountain
barrier assists the prevailing westerlies in diverting most of the cold outbursts from Canada to the east. Similarly, the Himalayas in Asia and the
Alps in Europe protect the regions to the south from polar air masses.

On a local scale, topographic relief exerts an influence upon temperatures. In the Northern Hemisphere north-facing slopes will generally
receive less insolation than south-facing slopes, and temperatures will
normally be lower. Local drainage of cold air into valleys at night will
also tend to affect temperature distribution.

VERTICAL DISTRIBUTION OF TEMPERATURE

The permanent snow caps on high mountains, even in the tropics, indicate the decrease of temperature with altitude. Observations of the
temperature in the upper air by means of instruments attached to kites,
balloons, airplanes, and rockets have shown that there is a fairly regular
decrease in temperature with an increase in altitude. This condition extends upward to the tropopause. The average rate of temperature decrease upward in the troposphere is about 3.3 F° for each 1000 feet of
altitude. This vertical gradient of temperature is commonly referred to as
the *normal lapse rate*. The normal lapse rate represents the average of
many observations of upper air temperature at different times and places
and should not be confused with the *actual lapse rate,* which is indicated
by a single observation over a given location. Indeed the actual lapse
rate of temperature does not necessarily show a decrease of temperature
with altitude at lower levels. Where observations show no change with
altitude, the lapse rate is termed *isothermal.* Such a condition never occurs
over a very great range of elevation nor for a long period of time. (See
Figure 2-15.)

Certain special conditions in the lower troposphere may produce a
reversal of the normal lapse rate so that the temperature actually increases
with an increase in altitude. This is known as a *temperature inversion,* and
the lapse rate is said to be inverted. Temperature inversions near the
earth's surface may be produced in five ways. (*1*) Radiation of heat from
the earth's surface on a clear night, or from surfaces in high latitudes,
results in increasingly cooler surface temperatures and consequently a

cooling of the lower layers of air. Inversions due to radiation are best developed over snow surfaces. They are not likely to occur over water, which is slow to cool, unless the water is already cooler than the overlying air. (2) Because of its greater density, cold air from hilltops and slopes tends to collect in valley bottoms, creating an inverted lapse rate up the slopes as well as in the free air over the valley floor. Air drainage inversions are frequently associated with spring frosts in middle latitudes, and for this reason fruit growers prefer gentle slopes to valley bottoms for orchard sites. (3) When two air masses with different temperature characteristics come together, the colder air, being more dense, tends to push underneath the warmer air and replace it. The boundary zones along which two air masses meet are called *fronts*, and the inverted lapse rate

Fig. 2-15 Components of a vertical lapse rate of temperature.

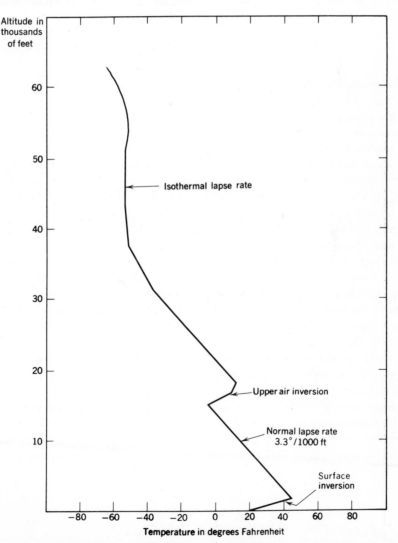

which results is a *frontal inversion*. Frontal inversions are not confined to the lower layers of the troposphere as are the types mentioned previously, but may occur at upper levels wherever cold air underruns warm air or warm air advances above cold air. (4) Advection of warm air over a cold surface will create an inversion in the lower layers of the air mass as the warm air is cooled by conduction. This process is common when warm air passes over a cold water surface but may also occur over cold land or snowfields. (5) Another type of inversion, the *subsidence inversion*, occurs in an air mass when a large body of air subsides and spreads out above a lower layer. In the process the air is dynamically heated more in the upper portion than at its base. Inversions of this type may occur at considerable altitudes.

ADDITIONAL READINGS

Budyko, M. I., *The Heat Balance of the Earth's Surface*, translated by Nina A. Stepanova. Washington: U.S. Department of Commerce, Weather Bureau, 1958.

Court, Arnold, "Duration of Very Hot Temperatures," *Bull. Am. Met. Soc.*, 33, 4 (1952), 140–49.

Drummond, A. J., "Radiation and the Thermal Balance," in *Climatology*, Arid Zone Research X. Paris: UNESCO, 1958, 56–74.

Houghton, Henry G., "On the Annual Heat Balance of the Northern Hemisphere," *Journ. of Met.*, 11 (1954), 1–9.

Ludlum, David M., "Extremes of Heat in the United States," *Weatherwise*, 16, 3 (1963), 108–129.

————, "Extremes of Cold in the United States," *Weatherwise*, 16, 6 (1963), 275–91.

Sutton, Sir Graham, "Scales of Temperature," *Weather*, 18, 5 (1963), 130–34.

atmospheric moisture

Moisture in the atmosphere plays such a significant role in weather and climate that it is commonly treated separately from the other constituents of air. In one or more of its forms atmospheric moisture is a factor in humidity, cloudiness, precipitation, and visibility. Water vapor and clouds affect the transmission of radiation both to and from the earth's surface. Through the process of evaporation water vapor becomes an important medium for conveying latent heat into the air, thus giving it a function in the heat exchange as well as in the moisture exchange between the earth and the atmosphere. Atmospheric water is gained by evaporation but lost by precipitation after complex intervening processes of horizontal and vertical transport and changes in physical state. Only a minute fraction of the earth's water is stored as clouds and vapor in the atmosphere at any one time. The net amount at the end of any given period for a particular region is an algebraic summation of: the amount stored from a previous period, the gain by evaporation, the gain or loss by horizontal transport, and the loss by precipitation. This relationship expresses the *water balance of the atmosphere.*

HUMIDITY

Terminology related to humidity is concerned with the gaseous form of H_2O, that is, water vapor. Several expressions of the amount of water vapor in the air are used. *Specific humidity* is the ratio of the mass of

37

water vapor actually in the air to a unit mass of air. Thus a kilogram (1000 grams) of air of which 12 grams are water vapor has a specific humidity of 12 grams per kilogram. A closely related term is *mixing ratio,* which is the mass of water vapor per unit mass of dry air. The mixing ratio is, in a sense, a recipe for an admixture of water vapor and dry air. A value of 12 grams per kilogram would entail a total of 1012 grams for the mixture. For most conditions, the specific humidity and the mixing ratio differ insignificantly. Another humidity expression based upon separate consideration of air and water vapor is *vapor pressure.* This is the partial pressure exerted by water vapor in the air, and it is independent of the other gases. It is expressed in the same units used for barometric pressure, that is, millibars or inches of mercury.

When air contains all the water vapor it can hold at a given temperature and barometric pressure, it is said to be *saturated,* and its actual vapor pressure will equal its *saturation vapor pressure.* The air will then be at its *dew point* temperature.

A term which represents the actual amount of water vapor in air but which is seldom used in meteorology is *absolute humidity.* It is defined as the mass of water vapor contained in a unit volume of air and is expressed as grams per cubic meter or grains per cubic foot. It has wide application in the field of air conditioning.

Probably the best known and most used reference to water vapor is *relative humidity,* which is the ratio of the amount of water vapor actually in the air to the amount the air could hold at a given temperature and pressure, that is, the ratio of the actual to the saturated vapor pressure. Thus, if a kilogram of air at constant pressure could hold 12 grams of water vapor at a certain temperature but contains only 9 grams at that temperature, it has a relative humidity of 75 per cent. When the temperature of air is increased, the capacity to hold moisture increases. If no further moisture is added, the result will be a decrease in relative humidity. Conversely, when air temperature is decreased, its capacity for

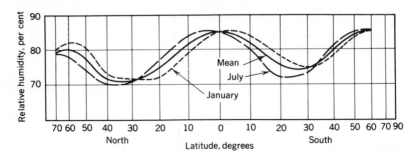

After Haurwitz and Austin, *Climatology* (McGraw-Hill, 1944).

Fig. 3-1 Approximate mean latitudinal distribution of relative humidity.

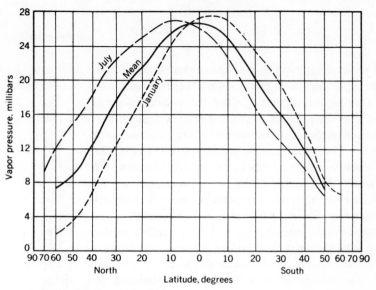

After Haurwitz and Austin, *Climatology* (McGraw-Hill, 1944).

Fig. 3-2   Mean latitudinal distribution of vapor pressure.

moisture decreases and its relative humidity increases. The average diurnal maximum relative humidity occurs in the early morning hours and the minimum in the early afternoon. Relative humidities tend to be greater over land in winter, except where there are strong summer incursions of moist air, for example, in regions affected by the monsoon. Over the oceans, relative humidity reaches a slight maximum in summer. On mid-latitude mountains there is also a tendency to summer maximums because of strong convective flow of moist air. The approximate mean latitudinal distribution of relative humidity is shown in Figure 3-1. Although the actual pattern is punctuated by other climatic controls, maximums generally prevail at the equator and minimums in the belts of subtropic highs. Poleward toward the westerlies, there is, again, an increase because of decreasing temperatures. This zonal distribution of relative humidity contrasts somewhat with the average pattern of vapor pressure or specific humidity. (See Figure 3-2.) Even the desert air of the subtropical high belt holds considerable water vapor though its *relative humidity* is low. In the polar regions, low temperatures produce low specific humidities.

HUMIDITY MEASUREMENTS

Direct measurement of the actual amount of water vapor in the air is not feasible for ordinary observations. Instead the various humidity values are determined indirectly from the *psychrometer*. This instrument is simply two thermometers mounted on the same backing. One is mounted a little lower than the other and has its bulb covered with a piece of   **39** muslin or wicking which can be wetted for the observation. It is known as the *wet-bulb thermometer* and the other is the *dry-bulb.* When the psychrometer is swung freely in the air or is aerated by a fan, the loss of heat required to evaporate water from the wet-bulb will cause it to show a lower temperature reading. The difference between the readings is called the *wet-bulb depression.* When the dry-bulb temperature, the wet-bulb depression, and the atmospheric pressure are known any of the standard expressions of humidity can be determined from a series of psychrometric tables, which have been computed by the use of formulas based on mathematical relationships. If there is no depression of the wet-bulb, the air is saturated and the relative humidity is 100 per cent.

Relative humidity is one of the humidity values for which there is an instrument that makes a direct measurement. The *hair hygrometer* operates on the principle that human hair lengthens as relative humidity increases and contracts with decreasing relative humidity. The tension of several strands of hair is linked to an indicator. Unfortunately there is such considerable lag in the response, especially at low temperatures, that the hair hygrometer is a much less accurate instrument than the psychrometer. For meteorological purposes, its principle is employed primarily in the *hygrograph,* a recording hygrometer which has a clock drum and pen arrangement just as in the thermograph. The activating elements of the thermograph and the hydrograph are often combined in the same case with pens tracing their respective records on the same chart. This combination is called the *hygrothermograph.*

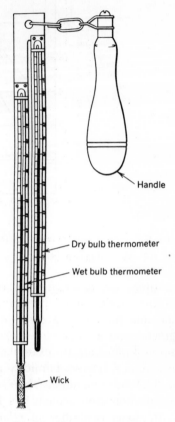

Handle

Dry bulb thermometer

Wet bulb thermometer

Wick

Fig. 3-3 Sling psychrometer.

A device known as the *infrared hygrometer* employs a beam of light projected through the air to a photoelectric detector. Two separate wave lengths of light are used; one is absorbed by water vapor and the other passes through undiminished. The ratio of the infrared light transmitted by the different wave lengths is a direct indication of the amount of water vapor in the light path.

Hygrometers in the home are ordinarily of the hair type. Some "hygrometers" are actually stationary psychrometers, with the wet-bulb covered by a wick which carries a constant flow of water from a small dish or tube. Such instruments may give fairly accurate humidity measurements indoors if the air is calm and proper humidity tables are used, but

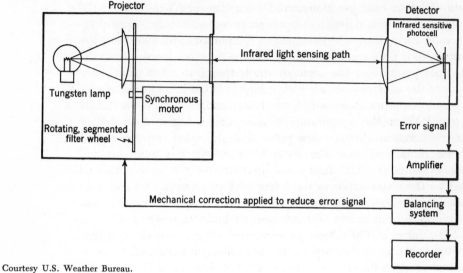

Courtesy U.S. Weather Bureau.

Fig. 3-4   Essentials of the infrared hygrometer.

outdoors the variation of air movement about the wet-bulb produces corresponding variations in the reliability of derived humidity values. A novel humidity "instrument" is the weather house. When the old woman comes out it is supposed to rain; when the young girl appears fair weather is due. One or two strands of catgut, their tendency to twist varying with relative humidity, activate this device.

A type of humidity gauge useful where electrical transmission of the variation is desirable depends upon the fact that the passage of electrical current across a chemically coated strip of plastic is proportional to the amount of moisture absorbed at its surface. This type of humidity element is in common use in radiosondes for upper air observations of moisture conditions. Still other humidity devices employ artificially cooled surfaces to determine the dew point temperature directly.

PHYSICAL CHANGES OF STATE OF WATER

The chemical compound H_2O occurs naturally in the atmosphere in all three phyical states—gas, liquid, and solid—and it may change from one state to any other, always with heat involved.

Evaporation, the change of state from liquid to vapor, results when molecules escape from any water surface, whether it be the surface of water bodies, droplets in clouds or fog, or thin films on solids such as soil particles. The process requires energy and is the means by which vast amounts of latent heat are transferred from the earth's surface to the atmosphere. Its rate is dependent upon three major factors: vapor pressure, temperature, and air movement. Evaporation increases as the saturation vapor pressure at the water surface becomes greater than the actual vapor pressure of the adjacent air. It therefore takes place more rapidly into dry air than into air with a high relative humidity. The rate of evaporation also increases with rising water temperature, other factors being equal. When the temperature of the water is higher than that of the air, evaporation always takes place. Finally, wind movement and turbulence replace air near the water surface with less moist air and increase evaporation. The heat used in carrying out evaporation is retained by the water vapor as the *latent heat of vaporization* and does not raise the temperature of the vapor. The latent heat of vaporization ranges in value from nearly 600 calories per gram of water at O°C to about 540 calories at 100°C because as temperature increases the difference between the kinetic energy of the escaping molecules and the average kinetic energy of all the water molecules decreases. The process of evaporation therefore becomes less selective and requires less heat as a growing proportion of the liquid molecules gain the necessary energy to escape from the water surface.

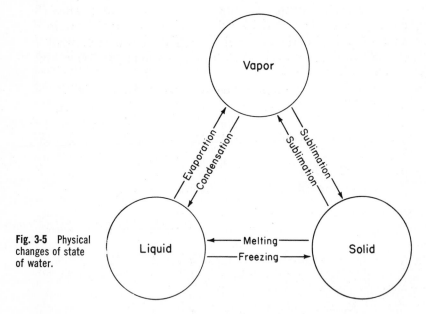

Fig. 3-5 Physical changes of state of water.

A special case of evaporation is *transpiration,* which entails a loss of water from leaf and stem tissues of growing vegetation. The combined losses of moisture by evaporation and transpiration from a given area are termed *evapotranspiration.*

Measurement of the amount of moisture which air will take up by evaporation is commonly accomplished by recording the water lost from an exposed pan or tank, making due allowance for water added by precipitation. More complex measurements to determine the actual amount of water evaporated from soil surfaces and transpired from vegetation prove difficult in practice. Indirect approaches are based on the water balance equation:

$$ET = P - (R + S)$$

where ET is the loss by evapotranspiration, P the gain by precipitation, R the loss by runoff, and S is the water stored in the soil. Thus, if precipitation, runoff, and soil storage can be measured evapotranspiration can be calculated as a difference.

Since evapotranspiration involves an exchange of energy as well as of moisture from the surface to the air, attempts have been made to calculate its value in terms of heat, radiation, temperature, and air movement factors.

Change of state from water vapor to liquid water is *condensation*. When moist air comes in contact with cool surfaces, it may be cooled to the point where its capacity to hold water vapor is exceeded by the actual amount in the air. A part of the vapor then condenses into a liquid form on the cool surface, producing *dew*. When this happens the latent heat of vaporization, in this process called the *latent heat of condensation*, is released. Liberation of the latent heat of condensation always tends to slow down the cooling process. It provides one of the main sources of heat energy for atmospheric processes. The temperature at which air becomes saturated upon cooling and at which condensation normally begins is the *condensation temperature* or *dew point*. However, the dew point temperature is not a definite boundary at which all condensation takes place. Condensation also results from cooling in the free air, but it requires the presence of very small *condensation nuclei*. The most active nuclei are hygroscopic particles, which have an affinity for water, and upon which condensation may take place even at temperatures above the dew point, that is, when the relative humidity is less than 100 per cent. If sufficient water droplets are formed in this way to become visible, *haze* will result, becoming fog or possibly clouds as the number and density of droplets increase. Among the hygroscopic materials in the atmosphere are salts liberated from bursting bubbles in the foam of ocean spray and numerous chemical compounds in industrial smokes. Insoluble dust particles are less effective nuclei, although they may have greater significance in the formation of ice crystals at high levels. A theory proposed by E. G. Bowen suggests that particles introduced into the upper atmosphere by meteor showers are an important source of ice nuclei.[*]

[*] The theory and subsequent developments are discussed in N. H. Fletcher, "Freezing Nuclei, Meteors, and Rainfall," *Science*, 134, 3476 (1961), 361–67.

As cooling and condensation proceed various degrees of *supersaturation* are required to maintain the growth of droplets. The saturation vapor pressure must be considerably exceeded in the air surrounding the smaller droplets and those with nonhygroscopic nuclei. Larger droplets and those having soluble nuclei gain increments of condensation more readily. Laboratory experiments have shown that in carefully washed and filtered air supersaturation as great as 700 per cent is required before the beginning of condensation. Since there is normally an abundance of condensation nuclei in the lower atmosphere, visible condensation products can be expected to form whenever the relative humidity reaches 100 per cent.

Superficially, the process of *melting* and *freezing* appear to be remarkably uncomplicated. Ice melts at a temperature of 0°C (32°F) when warmed, but liquid water does not always freeze at that temperature, contrary to popular belief. Foreign material dissolved in the water, suspended in it, or covering it, and the amount of water involved in the process all may lower the freezing point. In free air, small water droplets are known to exist at temperatures far below the "normal" freezing point. This is especially true at upper levels. The supercooled condition can apparently be discontinued by lowering the temperature below a critical point of about −40°C (also −40°F) or by introducing artificial ice nuclei. In the rainmaking experiments of recent years dry ice has been used to produce low temperatures. Silver iodide crystals introduced into a supercooled cloud result in formation of ice particles when temperatures are below −4°C, being most effective at about −15°C. The smaller the droplets of water the lower the temperature at which they will freeze spontaneously. The processes both of freezing and melting involve the *latent heat of fusion* (80 calories per gram), which is absorbed when ice melts and released when water freezes.

At temperatures below freezing, water may bypass the liquid form in its change of state. When dry air with a temperature well below freezing comes in contact with ice, molecules of the ice (H_2O) pass directly into the vapor state by means of the process of *sublimation*. Sublimation frequently removes snow from the ground in dry winter weather, and it explains why frozen laundry will dry in spite of low air temperatures. The reverse process is also known as sublimation and is a special case of condensation in which both the heat of vaporization and the heat of fusion are released. Sublimation nuclei must be present in free air to produce ice fog or ice clouds. If sublimation occurs on a cold surface the visible product is *frost*. Sublimation nuclei probably play an important part in dispersing clouds of supercooled water droplets. A leading theory is that they initiate the formation of small ice crystals from the vapor in the air adjacent to the supercooled droplets. A part of the supercooled water then evaporates into the drier air and the resulting vapor in turn sublimates on the ice crystals. Thus the supercooled droplets do not freeze directly on the crystals, as might be supposed.

PROCESSES OF COOLING TO PRODUCE CONDENSATION AND SUBLIMATION

Some type of cooling process normally is required to sustain condensation or sublimation. The cooling processes are as follows.

1. Adiabatic processes
   A. A decrease in barometric pressure at the surface, in which case fog might form.
   B. Rising air, which in turn results from
      (a) convection
      (b) convergence of wind currents or air masses (as along fronts)
      (c) orographic lifting
2. Nonadiabatic processes
   A. Loss of heat by radiation. Direct radiation from moist air may produce fog or clouds.
   B. Contact with a cold surface (conduction). Dew, frost, or fog are the normal products. The process may be associated with the movement of air across a cold surface (advection).
   C. Mixing with colder air. If the mixture has a temperature below its dew point clouds or fog will form, assuming sufficient effective nuclei are present.

Of all the types of cooling which air may experience, those due to lifting are by far the most important in condensation in free air. When air rises for any reason there is less pressure upon it at the new level and it expands and cools. Upon subsiding it undergoes an increase in pressure and is warmed. These temperature changes, occurring without any heat being added to or subtracted from the air, are termed *adiabatic*. They result from changes in pressure which in turn alter the kinetic energy of the air. *Nonadiabatic* processes involve the gain or loss of heat by the air from or to an outside source. The rate at which unsaturated air cools as it rises is $10C°$ per 1000 meters or $5.5F°$ per 1000 feet. If rising and cooling continue until condensation begins, however, the latent heat of condensation will be released into the air to reduce the rate of cooling. The new rate of cooling is called the *wet*, or *pseudoadiabatic, rate;* it is the true, or *dry adiabatic, rate* modified by the latent heat of condensation. Its value varies with pressure (and therefore with heights reached by ascending air), averaging about $6C°$ per 1000 meters or $3.2F°$ per 1000 feet.

Adiabatic cooling due to lifting is accomplished by any of the three ways outlined above or by any combination of them. Convection has been discussed previously as a method of heat transfer. As a process leading to adiabatic cooling it is common whenever the earth's surface is warmer than the air above. Convergence occurs when winds of different directions or speeds meet one another. In tropical areas convergence frequently involves air currents with similar temperature characteristics. In middle latitudes there is likely to be a considerable difference between the temperatures of converging winds, and the warmer air will ride over the cooler. This special case of convergence is known as *frontal lifting. Orographic lifting* may be defined as ascension of air caused or intensified by any topographic obstruction on the earth's surface. Ranges of mountains and hills are most effective in orographic lifting, forcing winds which blow against them to adopt vertical components. However, even a slight rise in land elevation, as on a coastal plain, can induce some lifting. Assume that the wind blows in from the sea across a flat coastal plain. The frictional drag of the land is greater than that of the sea, and the lower layers of air will consequently be slowed. The air coming from seaward will be forced to rise over this barrier of congested air in order to proceed inland. Because of the tendency of air to pile up against the barrier, the effect of any surface which induces orographic lifting extends for some distance to windward.

CLOUDS: THEIR FORMATION AND CLASSIFICATION

Clouds are condensation (or sublimation) forms that usually result from lifting processes. Those associated with strong rising air currents have vertical development and a puffy appearance, whereas those resulting from gentler lifting or other methods of cooling tend to spread out into layers. Although their method of formation is largely responsible for their appearance, clouds are classified primarily on the basis of their height, shape, color, and transmission or reflection of light. The World Meteorological Organization has established a detailed cloud classification with categories for genera, species, and varieties and with provisions for naming clouds that have undergone changes in form. Table 3-1 indicates the use of Latin names and the major elements of the classification.

For our purposes it will be sufficient to divide all clouds of the troposphere into four families: high, middle, low, and clouds with vertical development. High clouds are the *cirrus* types, always formed of ice crystals, whose average elevation ranges from 20,000 ft. above the earth's surface to the tropopause. Cirrus is nearly transparent, white, and fibrous and does not yield precipitation. *Cirrocumulus* clouds are a cirriform layer or patch of small white flakes or tiny globules arranged in distinct groups or lines. They may have the appearance of ripples similar to sand on a beach. Cirrocumulus is not a common cloud. *Cirrostratus* is a thin white veil of cirrus. It is nearly transparent so that the sun, moon, and brighter

TABLE 3-1

Classification of Clouds*

Genera	Species	Varieties
CIRRUS	fibratus uncinus spissatus castellanus floccus	intortus radiatus vertebratus duplicatus
CIRROCUMULUS	stratiformis lenticularis castellanus floccus	undulatus lacunosus
CIRROSTRATUS	fibratus nebulosus	duplicatus undulatus
ALTOCUMULUS	stratiformis lenticularis castellanus floccus	translucidus perlucidus opacus duplicatus undulatus radiatus lacunosus
ALTOSTRATUS	—	translucidus opacus duplicatus undulatus radiatus
NIMBOSTRATUS	—	—
STRATOCUMULUS	stratiformis lenticularis castellanus	translucidus perlucidus opacus duplicatus undulatus radiatus lacunosus
STRATUS	nebulosus fractus	opacus translucidus undulatus
CUMULUS	humilis mediocris congestus fractus	radiatus
CUMULONIMBUS	calvus capillatus	—

* From *International Cloud Atlas*. Geneva: World Meteorological Organization (1956), p. 7.

stars show through distinctly. Cirrus clouds frequently can be detected by the *halos* which they create around the sun or moon and can thus be distinguished from haze or light fog. Halos result from the refraction of light by ice crystals suspended in the air.

The middle clouds ordinarily occur at heights ranging from 6500 to 20,000 ft. above ground level. The two principal types are *altocumulus* and *altostratus*. Altocumulus contains layers or patches of globular masses of water-droplet cloud usually arranged in fairly regular patterns of lines, groups, or waves. Vertical air currents in the layers occupied by alto-cumulus may cause the clouds to build upward. Isolated altocumulus may be formed where a current of air rises over a mountain or a convection column, provided the rise is sufficient to cool the air below its dew point. The banner clouds above peaks (or above local "chimneys" of convection) are of this type. Because of their lens shape they are named *altocumulus lenticularis*. Altostratus is a fibrous veil, gray or blue-gray in color, and thicker than cirrostratus although it may merge gradually into the latter. It does not exhibit halo phenomena, but another optical effect, the *corona*, sometimes appears as a circle of light around the sun or moon in both altostratus and altocumulus. A halo is produced by refraction in ice crystals, but the corona results from the diffraction of light by water droplets. The corona is smaller than the halo and its diameter is inversely proportional to the size of the cloud droplets. The red of the faint color band is on the outside, that is, away from the sun or moon; in the halo the red is on the inside. It is common for altostratus to change into alto-cumulus and vice versa. Precipitation may fall from altostratus, or al-tocumulus but it does not necessarily reach the ground. Sometimes this *virga* is visible hanging from the bottom of the cloud in dark, sinuous streaks. When the cloud layer lowers to become somewhat thicker and darker and falling rain or snow obscures its base it is called *nimbostratus*.

The base level of low clouds varies from very near the ground to about 6500 ft. The basic type of this family is the *stratus*, a low, uniform layer resembling fog but not resting on the ground. Stratus is frequently formed by the lifting of a fog bank or by the dissipation of its lower layer. If broken up into fragments by the wind it is called *fractostratus*. Heat loss by radiation from the top of a stratus layer can cause condensation in the cooled layer above the cloud so that it builds upward. This should not be confused with vertical development due to rising air. When associated with the nimbostratus, stratus sometimes builds downward as well. Rain falling from the upper cloud layer may evaporate on falling through dry air and then recondense in lower saturated layers to form stratus. Precipitation from stratus, if it occurs, is usually light.

Stratocumulus clouds form a low, gray layer composed of globular masses or rolls which are usually arranged in groups, lines, or waves. If the aggregates of thick stratocumulus fuse together completely so that

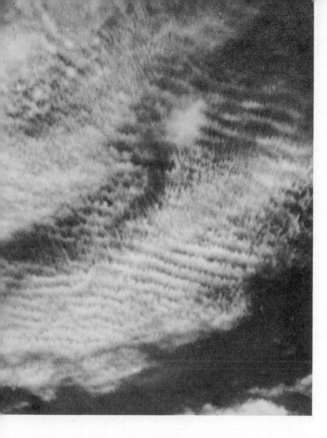

Courtesy U.S. Weather Bureau and E. E. Barnard.

Fig. 3-6 Banded cirrocumulus ("Cirrocumulus stratiformis undulatus").

Fig. 3-7 Cirrostratus with fractocumulus below.

Official U.S. Navy Photo.

Photo by author.

Fig. 3-8 Altocumulus ("Altocumulus stratiformis").

the structure is no longer evident, the clouds are classified as stratus. Note that altocumulus clouds have the same general characteristics. Altocumulus viewed from a mountain or an airplane may be difficult to distinguish from stratocumulus for this reason.

Clouds with vertical development fall into two principal categories: *cumulus* and *cumulonimbus*. Cumulus clouds are dense, dome-shaped, and have flat bases. They may grow to become cumulonimbus, the extent of vertical development depending upon the force of vertical currents below the clouds as well as upon the amount of latent heat of condensation liberated in the clouds as they form. Cumulus with little vertical development and a slightly flattened appearance are commonly associated with fair weather.

Sometimes large groups of cumulus develop a nearly complete covering of the sky and become stratocumulus. Conversely, stratocumulus occasionally break apart into separate clouds and become cumulus.

Cumulonimbus clouds exhibit great vertical development, towering at times to 60,000 ft. or more, where they spread out to leeward and form an anvil of cirrus. These are the thunderhead clouds that produce heavy showers of rain, snow, or hail, often accompanied by lightning and thunder. To an observer directly beneath, a cumulonimbus cloud may cover

50

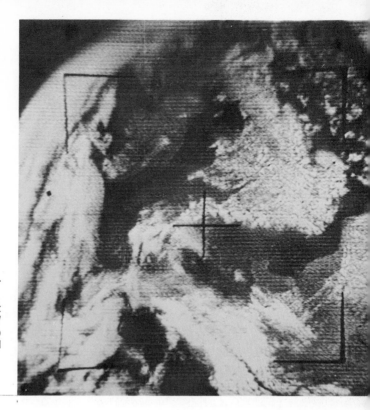

Fig. 3-9 Afternoon cumulus over Great Britain as photographed by TIROS IV on April 13, 1962. The cloud cover to the south and west was associated with a weather front.

Fig. 3-10 Fair weather cumulus ("Cumulus humilis").

Fig. 3-11   Stratus clouds in a valley with altocumulus above.

Fig. 3-12   Stratocumulus ("Stratocumulus cumulogenitus").

Official U.S. Navy Photo.

Fig. 3-13 Rapidly moving cumulus waves developing into stratocumulus.

Photo by author.

Fig. 3-14 Cumulonimbus in early stage of development ("Cumulonimbus calvus").

the whole sky and have the appearance of nimbostratus. In this case its true nature is revealed by the much heavier precipitation that falls from the cumulonimbus or by the preceding evolution of the cloud cover. Turbulence along the front of an advancing cumulonimbus sometimes creates a roll of dark fractocumulus or fractostratus.

CLOUD OBSERVATIONS

Because of their obvious relation to air masses, moisture content, and to vertical and horizontal movements of air, cloud observations are among the most valuable types of information used in weather forecasting and in flight planning. *Cloud types* are determined by visual observations, the accuracy of which depends upon experience and knowledge of the processes of cloud formation. The *sky cover* is obtained visually by viewing the clouds against the dome of the sky as a background and estimating in tenths the sky area covered. Four terms are in common use to express sky coverage:

Clear, no clouds or less than $\frac{1}{10}$ of sky obscured by clouds.
Scattered, $\frac{1}{10}$ to $\frac{5}{10}$, inclusive, covered.
Broken, more than $\frac{5}{10}$ but no more than $\frac{9}{10}$ covered.
Overcast, more than $\frac{9}{10}$ of sky covered.

For meteorological records, the coverage of separate layers of clouds at different heights is determined and recorded. For example, an overcast of cirrostratus may be observed with $\frac{2}{10}$ of low clouds on the horizon. Of course it is not always possible to see upper cloud decks, especially if they lie above a low overcast. Aircraft and radiosonde observations greatly assist the ground observer in such cases.

Fig. 3-15 Weather map symbols used to indicate sky cover.
Courtesy U.S. Weather Bureau.

Symbol	Code Number	Sky Coverage	Symbol	Code Number	Sky Coverage
 ◯	0	No Clouds	 ⊖	5	Six – tenths
 ◐	1	Less than One – tenth or One – tenth	 ◕	6	Seven and Eight – tenths
 ◔	2	Two and Three – tenths	 ⦶	7	Nine – tenths or Overcast with Openings
 ◑	3	Four – tenths	●	8	Completely Overcast
 ◖	4	Five – tenths	 ⊗	9	Sky Obscured

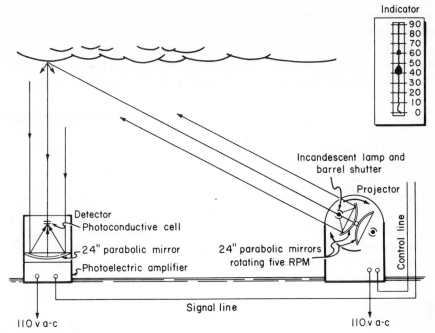

Courtesy U.S. Weather Bureau.

Fig. 3-16 The rotating-beam ceilometer.

Cloud height is the distance between the ground and the base of the cloud. The distance from the ground to the lowest cloud layer which creates a broken, overcast, or obscured sky cover is termed the *ceiling*. Cloud heights may be estimated visually, but for accurate determinations, one of several methods of measurement is employed. In the daytime, gas-filled *ceiling balloons* with a known rate of ascent are timed until they enter the cloud layer to determine height. Under a dark cloud layer or at night, the *ceiling light* is used to project a vertical beam of light onto the base of the cloud. The observer stands at a measured distance from the light projector and measures the angle of elevation of the light spot with a *clinometer*. Height of cloud is then determined by reference to trigonometric tables. The *ceilometer* operates on the same principle as the ceiling light but has a photoelectric element which reacts selectively to the light spot to indicate height. The accuracy of both the ceiling light and the ceilometer decreases with higher clouds and is lessened by a thin cloud cover since the spot of light becomes less definite.

Cloud direction can be observed visually with reference to a fixed object, although for more accurate records the *nephoscope* is used. The principle of most nephoscopes involves a straight rod which is lined up with the direction of movement of clouds. For determination of *speed of cloud movement* it is necessary to know the height of the cloud. Movement with respect to graduations on the rod of the nephoscope is timed and by employing the mathematical principle of similar triangles cloud speed can be calculated. Some nephoscopes are fitted with mirrors so that clouds are observed indirectly.

FOG FORMATION AND FOG TYPES

Fog results when atmospheric water vapor condenses or sublimates to the extent that the new forms, water droplets or ice crystals, become visible and have their base in contact with the ground. Saturation of the air and sufficient nuclei are ordinarily prerequisite to formation of fog, but, as has been previously explained, hygroscopic nuclei may "force" the process at relative humidities below 100 per cent. Very light fogs formed in this way are sometimes referred to as *damp haze.* Heavier fogs restrict visibility and constitute a hazard. The collection of fog particles on vegetation and other obstacles may produce *fog drip,* which contributes to the receipt of moisture at the ground surface.

Observations of fog for meteorological records take into account the composition of the fog (water droplets or ice crystals) and its effect upon visibility. *Visibility* in a given direction is the greatest distance at which common objects like buildings or trees are visible to the unaided eye. *Prevailing visibility* is the greatest visibility value that prevails over at least one-half of the horizon. For determination of visibility at airport runways a device known as the *transmissometer* measures the transmission of light over a fixed path (Figure 3–17). Visibility can be affected by dust, smoke, and other suspended particles in addition to or apart from fog.

Fig. 3-17 Schematic diagram of the transmissometer system used for determining airport runway visibility.

Courtesy U.S. Weather Bureau.

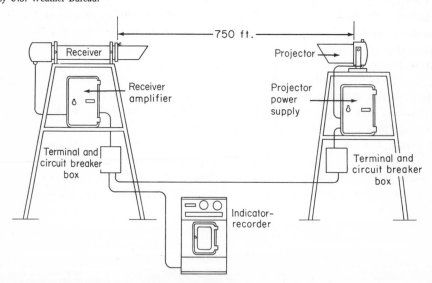

The principal processes that cause saturation are cooling of the air and evaporation of water into it. Accordingly, fogs are classified into two main categories:

1. Fogs resulting from evaporation
   (a) steam fog
   (b) frontal fog
2. Fogs resulting from cooling
   (a) radiation fog
   (b) advection fog
   (c) upslope fog
   (d) mixing fog
   (e) barometric fog

Steam fog forms when intense evaporation takes place into relatively cold air. As water vapor is added to the cool air saturation occurs and condensation produces fog. Steam fog is most commonly observed over bodies of water in middle and high latitudes. On the oceans it is also known as "sea smoke," and in the arctic builds to heights of 4000 or 5000 ft. Steam fog sometimes forms on a small scale over warm, wet land immediately after a rain. In the tropics after a thundershower the air is temporarily cooled so that evaporation from soil and vegetation produces saturation and subsequent condensation.

Along the boundary between two air masses, evaporation from warm rain falling through the drier air below may be followed by saturation and condensation in cooler layers to form *frontal fog*. If the condensation layer is above ground level it is termed stratus cloud. (See discussion of stratus as a low cloud.) Turbulence in the lower air reduces the extent and persistence of such a fog.

Ground fog, or *radiation fog*, is produced when fairly calm moist air is in contact with ground that has been cooled by nighttime radiation. If the air is completely calm only dew or frost is likely to form. Slight turbulence increases the depth of fog, but, if it is violent enough, it will distribute the excess moisture into upper, warmer layers and prevent fog formation, or dissipate that already in existence. Valleys are particularly susceptible to radiation fogs as well as to frosts because of frequent temperature inversions. At sea this type of fog does not form because of the negligible daily variation of the water temperature. In winter, largely in polar regions, radiation fogs may be composed of ice crystals. They are called *ice fogs* or sometimes *diamond dust* because the ice crystals glitter in the light.

Advection fog is formed when moist air is transported over a cold surface. It is especially common at sea where warm moist air masses move over the colder water of high latitudes or across cold ocean currents. In the summer, along arid west coasts, the cold water is provided by upwell-

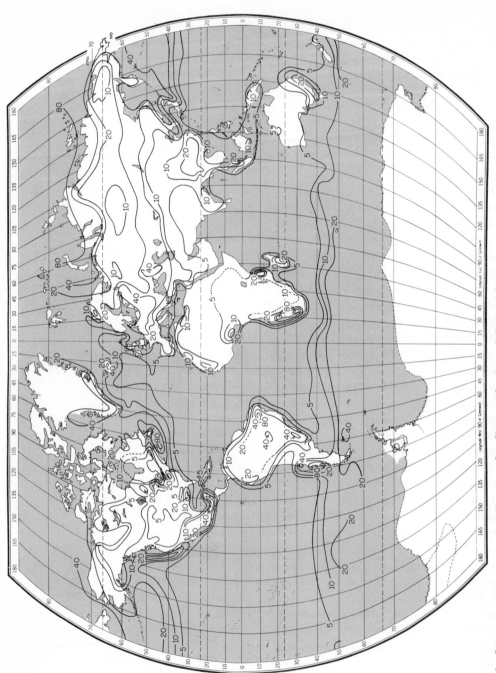

Van der Grinten projection courtesy A. J. Nystrom & Co., Chicago. After Berry, Bollay, and Beers, *Handbook of Meteorology.*

Fig. 3-18 World distribution of mean annual number of days with fog.

ing offshore; fogs of this type are frequent and persistent. Winds blowing onshore tend to carry along both temperature and humidity characteristics, extending the fog inland. In winter in mid-latitudes, the introduction of moist air of tropical or subtropical origin over cold land or snow surfaces likewise can result in advection fog.

The gradual orographic ascension of moist air up a sloping plain or hilly region can cool the air adiabatically to form *upslope fog*, provided the air is already near saturation. If the ascent is too rapid or there is convective turbulence in the air, condensation will likely take place above ground level to form clouds. Upslope fog is fairly common on the high plains east of the Rocky Mountains. In southeastern Wyoming it is locally known as "Cheyenne fog."

When warm moist air comes into contact with cool moist air the mixture in the boundary zone may have a temperature low enough to produce saturation and condensation. If this takes place at the earth's surface a *mixing fog* is the result. The most common occurrence is at fronts between air masses of maritime origin. Convection or convergence will cause it to dissipate or lift, and it is usually difficult to separate mixing as a cause from the other processes which generate fog at a front. When one "sees his breath" on a cold day, it is a special case of mixing fog, though it can hardly be regarded as a major fog type.

Barometric fog is extremely rare, although the cooling process associated with it possibly intensifies other types of fog. If the general pressure distribution over an area undergoes such a change that a layer of moist air at the ground level experiences a lowering of barometric pressure, the resultant adiabatic cooling could lead to condensation. These conditions are most probable in a valley or basin filled with stagnant air which is not immediately replaced as less dense air moves overhead.

The above outline of fog types should be regarded more as a classification of fog causes than as distinct kinds of fog. While most fogs have one principal cause, their depth and density are usually influenced by one or more additional processes which lead to saturation. Figure 3–18 shows the world distribution of the mean annual number of days with fog.

PRECIPITATION: CAUSES, FORMS, AND TYPES

Precipitation is defined as water in liquid or solid forms falling to the earth. It is always preceded by condensation or sublimation or a combination of the two, and is primarily associated with rising air. Although they may contribute significantly to the transfer of moisture from the atmosphere to the earth's surface, fog, dew, and frost are condensation forms and are not considered to be precipitation. The common precipitation forms are *rain, drizzle, snow, sleet,* and *hail.* Of these drizzle and light snow are the only ones likely to fall from clouds having little or no vertical development.

It is obvious that not all condensation, even in rising air, is followed immediately by precipitation. A complete explanation of the mechanics by which some clouds produce rain or snow and others do not is still lacking. The "rainmaking" experiments carried out by various public and private agencies have considerably extended knowledge along these lines. A cloud is physically an *aerosol*, that is, a suspension of minute water droplets or ice crystals in air. In order to fall from the cloud, these water forms must grow to sizes which can no longer be buoyed up by the air. Coalescence may be achieved through collision resulting from turbulence or electrical discharge between droplets or, as is thought more likely, through the tendency of small droplets to migrate to larger, warmer to cooler, or liquid droplets to crystals. Until comparatively recently, the ice crystal theory of heavy precipitation was widely held, and it may be the explanation for many rainstorms in middle and high latitudes. In the upper levels of vertically developed clouds, there are often supercooled water droplets which do not play an active direct role in precipitation. If ice crystals appear in the supercooled cloud, water vapor crystallizes onto them and the water droplets evaporate into the resulting drier air. Ultimately all liquid water disappears and the crystals grow large enough to begin falling. If they fall through cold air, they may reach the ground as snow; if through warmer air, they melt to fall as rain. Unfortunately, this theory does not explain tropical precipitation which occurs from clouds having temperatures above freezing throughout. Nor can it explain the drizzle which falls from relatively thin stratus layers. Probably one or a combination of the other processes of coalescence is the basis of these types of precipitation.

Precipitation is classified in two ways: according to the form taken by the falling water or on the basis of the processes which lead to its formation. Rain is the most common precipitation form. It falls from clouds formed in rising air when the temperature, at least at lower levels, is above 32°F. As pointed out above, raindrops may begin as snow crystals which melt as they descend into warmer air. If the crystals grow and reach the ground level, they produce snow. Unusually large snowflakes are composed of several hexagonal crystals adhering to one another. Rain which freezes as it falls from a warm mass of air through a cold layer near the surface is termed *sleet*. Under wintertime conditions, rain may fall through cold air and freeze upon striking cold surfaces to form *glaze* or an *ice storm*. Freezing rain is a great hazard to vegetation, transport facilities, and overhead wires. In the Pacific Northwest, it is referred to as "the silver thaw" because it ordinarily presages a warmer air mass which moves in behind a warm front.

Drizzle is defined as numerous, uniformly minute droplets of water which seem to float, following the slightest movement of the air. (Technically, drizzle droplets have a diameter of less than 0.02 inch.) It falls continuously from low stratus-type clouds, never from convective clouds, and it is often associated with fog and poor visibility. These characteristics distinguish it from light rain, which falls from clouds (generally nimbostratus) that have progressively lowered. Drizzle is in some places called "Scotch mist," or simply mist.

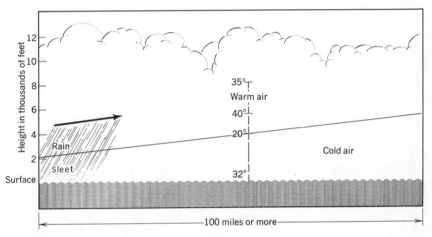

Fig. 3-19 Formation of sleet in the cold air under a warm front.

Strong, rising, convective currents, as in a cumulonimbus cloud, carry the raindrops formed by intense condensation and coalescence of water droplets to higher levels where they freeze to become *hail*. These frozen drops fall again after reaching a level of decreasing convection and take on a coating of ice as they pass through supercooled droplets. Repeated ascending and descending results in alternating layers of clear and crystalline ice and in a concentric structure in the hailstones. Another theory of hail formation holds that a frozen nucleus falls and alternately encounters supercooled water droplets and snow crystals which adhere to the hailstone and account for the concentric layers. The size of the stone depends on the amount of ice and snow it collects in one continuous descent. Hailstones having weights of more than two pounds have been recorded, although these were probably two or more separate hailstones frozen together. Hail rarely occurs in the tropics or at high latitudes.

Under less violent conditions of convection, *small hail* or *snow pellets* may fall. Small hail consists of spherical or conical grains of ice which represent the primary state of hail formation. Usually the grains have a nucleus of snow surrounded by a coating of clear ice, and they have a mushy consistency. Snow pellets are small balls of compacted snow crystals about the size of peas. They are white in appearance and do not have the ice coat. Small hail and snow pellets are both more commonly associated with convective activity in winter and spring, while true hail occurs with the violent thundershower of summer.

Another ice form which may, in one sense, be regarded as precipitation is *rime*. Rime forms on cold surfaces which are exposed to moving fog or clouds of supercooled water droplets. It has a crystalline form and builds to the windward in featherlike shapes. A special case of rime is the rime icing of aircraft which fly through supercooled clouds. It is most prevalent in temperatures below 15°F.

Having previously dealt with the methods of cooling which lead to condensation and sublimation, we can now outline the principal types of precipitation which result.

(1) *Convectional precipitation,* resulting from convective overturning of moist air. Heavy, showery precipitation is most likely to occur. Rain or snow showers, hail, and snow pellets are the forms associated with convective precipitation.

(2) *Orographic precipitation,* formed where air rises and cools because of a topographic barrier. It is doubtful that much of the world's precipitation is formed by orographic lifting alone; on the other hand, it is an important factor in intensifying rainfall on windward slopes and it therefore affects areal distribution. The greatest annual totals of rainfall in the world occur where mountain barriers lie across the paths of moisture-bearing winds. A famous example is Cherrapunji on the southern margin of the Khasi Hills in Assam, India. This station averages 450 inches of rainfall annually. In 1873 the total was only 283 inches; in 1861, when the annual total was a fantastic 905 inches, 366 inches fell in the month of July alone. Mt. Waialeale on the island of Kauai in the Hawaiian group has a windward-slope station that has an annual average of over 475 inches. These and other record rainfalls in mountainous areas should not be ascribed entirely to a simple orographic effect. Besides forcing moist air aloft, orographic barriers hinder the passage of low pressure areas and fronts, promote convection due to differential heating along the slopes, and directly chill moist winds which come in contact with cold summits and snowfields. Even this combination of effects cannot induce precipitation unless wind and moisture conditions are favorable.

(3) *Frontal precipitation,* produced when air currents converge and rise. In tropical regions where opposing air currents have comparable temperatures, the lifting is more or less vertical and is usually accompanied by convection. In middle latitudes, frontal convergence is characterized by the more gradual sloping ascent of warm air over cooler. However,

convectional activity frequently occurs along fronts where the temperatures of the air masses concerned are quite different. Mixing of air along the front also probably contributes to condensation and therefore to the frontal precipitation.

Most precipitation results ultimately from a combination of cooling processes which produce condensation or sublimation. An additional process is necessary to cause raindrops or ice crystals to grow large enough to fall from the clouds.

OBSERVATIONS OF PRECIPITATION

A great deal of important information about precipitation is obtained by visual observation of its form, type, and duration. It is obviously impractical to measure all the precipitation which falls over large areas. Instead precipitation is sampled at a number of places. In the United States there are between 12,000 and 13,000 sampling stations. At a given place, precipitation is measured by the simplest of meterological instruments, the *rain gauge*. The standard rain gauge is a metal cylinder eight inches in diameter and has a capacity of 23 inches. It is usually fitted with a covering funnel which directs the water into a measuring tube and which also reduces loss by evaporation. The measuring tube is so designed that it amplifies the amount of water at the ratio of ten to one. Thus ten inches of water in the tube represent one inch of rain. A thin graduated stick is used to determine the depth to the nearest five thousands of an inch, and amounts are recorded to the nearest hundredth inch. Amounts less than 0.005 inch are recorded as a trace, or simply "T." In most climatological work values to the nearest tenth inch are used. When snow, hail, or other ice forms are expected, the receiver funnel and measuring tube are removed from the gauge and only the eight-inch overflow can is used. In measuring snow and ice, a known quantity of warm water is added to the gauge. After melting is complete, the water is measured in the measuring tube and allowance is made for the warm water. Rain and snow tend to be blown in eddies about the gauge, making collection of a true sample questionable, especially in high winds. Slatted wind shields have been designed for mounting around the gauge to reduce this effect.

Improvements on the standard rain gauge are the *tipping-bucket gauge* and the *weighing-type gauge*. In the former a small divided metal bucket is mounted so that it will automatically tip and empty every 0.01 inch of rainfall collected. The tipping action activates electrical contacts which in turn activate a recording pen arm. The weighing-type gauge weighs precipitation as it falls and by means of a pen arm attached to the spring scale makes a continuous record on a clock chart.

Average snow depth on the ground is determined by averaging three

Courtesy Belfort Instrument Company.

Fig. 3-20 Weighing-type precipitation gauge. When assembled for use a bucket on the weighing platform collects rain and snow that falls through the 8-inch opening at the top. The pen arm makes a continuous record of the rate and amount of precipitation.

or more representative measured depths. In mountain areas where snow depths become great, graduated rods are sometimes installed in representative spots so that depth can be read directly at the snow surface.

DISTRIBUTION OF PRECIPITATION REGIONALLY

In much the same way that isotherms are used to show areal distribution of temperature, values of precipitation may be plotted on a map using lines called *isohyets*. Figure 3–21 is an *isohyetal map* of the world with lines drawn through places with the same annual average rainfall. Note that precipitation over land only is indicated. Knowledge of rainfall over the oceans is extremely limited and for obvious reasons difficult to obtain. For land records, data for several years (at least 35) are desirable to provide representative mean values.

Although several climatic factors combine in a complex fashion to influence the world pattern, some generalizations are evident from the world map of precipitation. The amounts are greatest in equatorial latitudes, decreasing toward the poles with a great deal of irregularity. Where the general circulation of the atmosphere is characterized by ascent of air, for example, in the intertropical convergence zone, there are large annual rainfall totals. On the other hand, where subsidence is the rule, for exam-

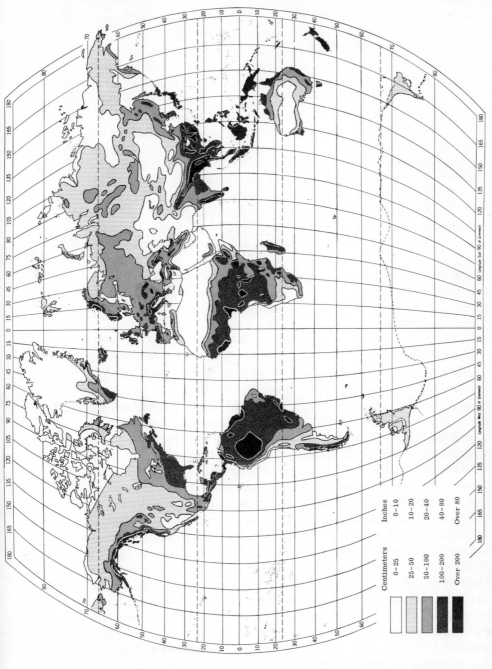

Van der Grinten projection, courtesy A. J. Nystrom & Co., Chicago.

Fig. 3-21 World distribution of mean annual precipitation.

Centimeters	Inches
0–25	0–10
25–50	10–20
50–100	20–40
100–200	40–80
Over 200	Over 80

ple, in the subtropic highs, there is much less rainfall. In high latitudes the colder air has limited capacity for moisture, there are few incursions of moist tropical air, and precipitation is much less. There is also much less thermal convection in the polar regions than in the tropics.

The distribution of land and water imposes an important influence upon rainfall in middle and high latitudes. Regions located in the interior of continents, far from the oceanic sources of moisture, have less precipitation than coasts. The combination of nearby oceanic moisture sources with favorable prevailing winds produces greater rainfall on the windward than on leeward coasts, but ocean currents or drifts may introduce a further modification. Warm ocean currents offshore increase the moisture content of winds which blow across them. This principle operates along the Atlantic slope of the United States, where the warm Gulf Stream flows offshore. Cold currents, on the other hand, decrease precipitation over the adjacent land by cooling the lower layers of air that passes over them, thus inhibiting ascent and lowering moisture holding capacity. The result may be fog or low stratus clouds; vertical lifting and precipitation are unlikely.

Mountain barriers, by forcing ascent of moisture-bearing winds, tend to concentrate precipitation on their windward slopes and produce a "rain shadow" to the leeward. Aside from the tropics, the wettest regions are the mountain sides against which prevailing winds blow from the oceans. Even in the tropics, record annual rainfalls occur where orographic lifting is a significant factor. Among the numerous instances of mountains causing unequal distribution of precipitation are the mountainous trade-wind islands, the Atlas Mountains of North Africa, the Southern Andes along the Chilean-Argentine border, the Southern Alps of New Zealand, and the coastal ranges of western North America. At Henderson Lake on Vancouver Island the annual average precipitation over a fourteen-year period was 262.0 inches, with 323.7 inches in 1931. Paradise Ranger Station in Mt. Rainier National Park, Washington, recorded 1000.3 inches of snow in the 1955–56 winter season.

The fact that orographic lifting causes precipitation to increase with altitude gives rise to certain modifications of its horizontal distribution. This increase is seen on the leeward as well as the windward slopes of mountains but appears to have an upper limit, at least in the tropics, where precipitation begins to decrease again above elevations of about 10,000 feet. At the high elevations, much of the moisture has already been condensed and precipitated from the air, and conditions are analogous to those in polar areas. Moreover, upper-air subsidence, as in the trade-wind inversion, is inimical to precipitation at high altitudes.

It should be remembered that, because the precipitation of a given area usually results from several interrelated factors, its regional distribution is likewise determined by complex causes. "Normal precipitation" is largely an hypothetical concept with respect both to horizontal distribution and the time factor.

SEASONAL VARIATION OF RAINFALL

Quite as important as the actual rainfall totals accumulated in a particular year are the characteristics of *seasonal distribution* from month to month throughout the year, the *dependability* of rainfall from year to year, and the *frequency* of rainfall. The conditions which cause precipitation in a region do not exist in the same combination throughout the year. The latitudinal migration of the general pattern of wind and pressure belts was discussed in the section on general circulation. Precipitation areas associated with the belts of convergence tend to move northward in the Northern Hemisphere in summer and southward in winter. In equatorial regions, which are constantly under the influence of equatorial convergence, rainfall is fairly heavy throughout the year, but a few degrees north or south are areas that are alternately dominated by the equatorial convergence and the subtropic high and have wet summers and dry winters. Certain west coasts in the middle latitudes have dry summers and wet winters as they experience the effects first of the subtropic high, and then of the westerlies with their cyclonic storms. The monsoon circulation brings even more striking seasonal contrasts, producing wet summers as winds blow onshore and dry winters when the circulation is reversed. Seasonal variation in rainfall because of the monsoon is especially well developed in India and southeast Asia. The effect of mountain barriers on seasonal variation can only be to increase the amount when the

Fig. 3-22 Precipitation graphs for Washington and Allahabad.

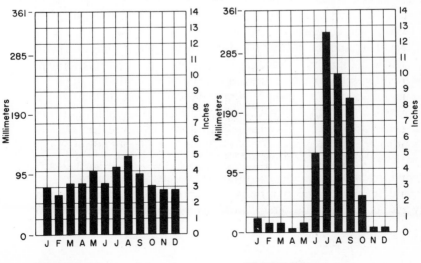

Washington, D.C.
Annual average   40.8in.

Allahabad, India
Annual average   41.8in.

other factors are favorable. Because of its vital importance in human activities, especially agriculture, the annual *regime of precipitation* (monthly distribution through the year) is often more significant than the annual average. Reference to the precipitation graphs for Allahabad, India, and Washington, D.C., in Figure 3-22, clearly illustrates the difference in regimes although these stations have approximately the same annual averages.

Dependability of rainfall refers to the possible deviation from the average, that is, the variation from the normal. The actual annual total for a station may be far above or below the annual statistical average. There may also be a considerable deviation from the normal regime. Generally

TABLE 3-2

World's Greatest Observed Point Rainfalls*

Duration	Amount (inches)	Location	Date
1 min.	1.23	Unionville, Md.	July 4, 1956
5 min.	2.48	Porto Bello, Panama	Nov. 29, 1911
8 min.	4.96	Fussen, Bavaria	May 25, 1920
15 min.	7.80	Plumb Point, Jamaica	May 12, 1916
20 min.	8.10	Curtea-de-Arges, Romania	July 7, 1889
42 min.	12.00	Holt, Mo.	June 22, 1947
2 hr. 10 min.	19.00	Rockport, W. Va.	July 18, 1889
2 hr. 45 min.	22.00	D'Hanis, Tex. (17 mi. NNW)	May 31, 1935
4 hr. 30 min.	30.8+	Smethport, Pa.	July 18, 1942
9 hr.	42.79	Belouve, Réunion	Feb. 28, 1964
12 hr.	52.76	Belouve, Réunion	Feb. 28–29, 1964
18 hr. 30 min.	66.49	Belouve, Réunion	Feb. 28–29, 1964
24 hr.	73.62	Cilaos, Réunion	Mar. 15–16, 1952
2 days	98.42	Cilaos, Réunion	Mar. 15–17, 1952
3 days	127.56	Cilaos, Réunion	Mar. 15–18, 1952
4 days	137.95	Cilaos, Réunion	Mar. 14–18, 1952
5 days	151.73	Cilaos, Réunion	Mar. 13–18, 1952
6 days	159.65	Cilaos, Réunion	Mar. 13–19, 1952
7 days	161.81	Cilaos, Réunion	Mar. 12–19, 1952
8 days	162.59	Cilaos, Réunion	Mar. 11–19, 1952
15 days	188.88	Cherrapunji, India	June 24–July 8, 1931
31 days	366.14	Cherrapunji, India	July 1861
2 mo.	502.63	Cherrapunji, India	June–July 1861
3 mo.	644.44	Cherrapunji, India	May–July 1861
4 mo.	737.70	Cherrapunji, India	April–July 1861
5 mo.	803.62	Cherrapunji, India	April–Aug. 1861
6 mo.	884.03	Cherrapunji, India	April–Sept. 1861
11 mo.	905.12	Cherrapunji, India	Jan.–Nov. 1861
1 yr.	1041.78	Cherrapunji, India	Aug. 1860–July 1861
2 yr.	1605.05	Cherrapunji, India	1860–1861

° *Daily Weather Map*, Dec. 13, 1962; J. L. H. Paulhus, "Indian Ocean and Taiwan Rainfalls Set New Records," *Monthly Weather Review*, 93, 5, May 1965, p. 335.

speaking, dependability of precipitation is relatively high in humid climates and decreases toward the regions with lower annual averages. The dependability of rainfall is a matter of great concern to farmers in subhumid and semiarid lands, where negative departure from the average annual rainfall—or even from the monthly means in certain critical months —can cause crop failure.

Frequency of rainfall is usually expressed as the number of precipitation days per year. Whether a station's total falls in a few heavy thundershowers or as light rain over a great number of days is of vital importance in many economic activities. Comparison of the amount of precipitation with the time during which it fell yields precipitation *intensity*. This ratio may be expressed for an individual storm or for longer periods.

ADDITIONAL READINGS

Day, John A., "The Building Blocks of Clouds," *Natural Hist.*, 74, 1 (1965), 36–43.

International Cloud Atlas, 2 vols. Geneva: WMO, 1956.

Ludlam, F. H., and R. S. Scorer, *Cloud Study.* London: John Murray, 1957.

Ludlum, David M., "Extremes of Snowfall in the United States," *Weatherwise,* 15, 6 (1962), 246–62.

Mason, B. J., *Clouds, Rain and Rainmaking.* London: Cambridge University Press, 1962.

Nagel, J. F., "Fog Precipitation on Table Mountain," *Quart. Journ. Roy. Met. Soc.,* 82, 345 (1956), 452–60.

Ruskin, Robert E., "The Measurement of Humidity in Meteorology," *Weatherwise,* 16, 2 (1963), 55–61.

Smith, Walter J., and Nancy J. Hoeflich, "The Carbon Film Electric Hygrometer Element," *Bull. Am. Met. Soc.,* 35, 2 (1954), 60–62.

Soberman, Robert K., "Noctilucent Clouds," *Scient. Am.,* 208, 6 (1963), 50–59.

Sutcliffe, R. C., "Water Balance and the General Circulation of the Atmosphere," *Quart. Journ. Roy. Met. Soc.,* 82, 354 (1956), 385–95.

Vaughan, Harry C., "The Spontaneous Freezing Temperatures of Melted Snow and of Small Water Drops," *Bull. Am. Met. Soc.,* 35, 2 (1954), 52–55.

Ward, R. C., "Measuring Potential Evapotranspiration," *Geography,* 48 (1963), 49–55.

motion 4
in the atmosphere

The atmosphere is in a constant state of agitation as a result of the interaction of variable forces. One of the basic forces is air pressure. The mass of a column of air above a given point determines the atmospheric pressure at that point; at sea level under standard conditions the pressure is about 14.7 pounds per square inch, and it is exerted in all directions. Atmospheric pressure varies from time to time at a given place; it varies from place to place over short distances and on a worldwide scale; and it decreases with increasing altitude. Horizontal pressure differences result primarily from temperature differences that produce density contrasts and from dynamic causes arising from atmospheric circulation. An increased proportion of water vapor in the air can alter pressure slightly because water vapor is less dense than the mixture of other components of air. Differences from place to place in the force of gravity also affect air pressure slightly. Ordinarily we cannot perceive small changes in pressure, but they motivate the winds that transfer heat and moisture from one area to another, often in connection with storms.

MEASUREMENT OF ATMOSPHERIC PRESSURE

Measurement of pressure variations is essential to the understanding of winds, storms, and related atmospheric phenomena. The most accurate instrument used is the *mer-*

curial barometer, and most other pressure instruments are checked against it. The principle which operates the mercurial barometer is the balancing of the column of air against a column of mercury in a sealed glass tube. (See Figure 4–1.) Under standard conditions at sea level the atmosphere balances a column of mercury 29.92 inches high. Fluctuations in air pressure produce corresponding differences in the height of the mercury, and a graduated vernier is mounted along the tube to facilitate accurate reading to a thousandth of an inch. For determination of actual pressure values corrections are applied to adjust for the temperature responses of the mercury column and brass scale, errors in instrument construction, and the variation of gravitational force with latitude and altitude. The corrected reading is the *station pressure.* Obviously the station pressure on a high mountain will always be much lower than that at a nearby valley location, and a comparison of the two will be of questionable value in determining the lateral distribution of pressure. In order to make possible direct comparison of pressures at different altitudes station pressure is converted to *sea level pressure.* It is assumed that the atmospheric column above the barometer extends on downward to sea level and a figure to

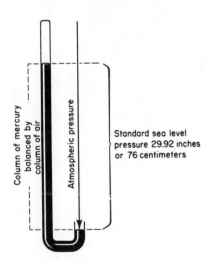

Column of mercury balanced by column of air

Atmospheric pressure

Standard sea level pressure 29.92 inches or 76 centimeters

Fig. 4-1 Principle of the mercurial barometer.

Courtesy U.S. Weather Bureau.

Fig. 4-2 Fortin-type mercurial barometer.

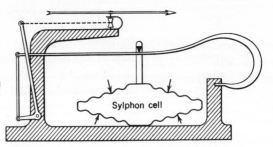

Fig. 4-3 Principle of the sylphon cell in the aneroid barometer.

Fig. 4-4 Microbarograph. Part of the assembly has been removed to show the sylphon cells. The pen arm traces a continuous record of pressure on a chart drum which sits on the clock at left.

represent the additional mass of air is added to the station pressure (or subtracted in those rare instances where the station is below sea level).

For certain purposes the mercurial barometer is too expensive or too cumbersome to move, so that a type of barometer known as the *aneroid* has been developed. The aneroid barometer indicates pressure using the principle of the *sylphon cell,* which is a partially evacuated metal wafer. When pressure in the outside air increases, the cell tends to collapse; when pressure decreases, the cell expands. This fluctuation with pressure changes is mechanically linked to an indicator on a calibrated dial. The common aneroid barometer found in many households usually has a dial calibrated in inches of mercury and such terms as *rain, windy,* or *fair*

72

printed along the circumference. Presumably the aneroid can forecast weather; actually pressure is only one of the weather elements, and it alone cannot be relied upon to indicate future weather with any certainty. The principle of the altitude barometer, or *altimeter,* is the same as that of the aneroid.

Another instrument employing sylphon cells is the *barograph.* It produces a continuous trace of barometric pressure on a clock-drum chart similar to that in the thermograph. Sylphon cells activate a pen arm which makes the ink record. Specially made *microbarographs* use several sylphon cells and a carefully constructed system of mechanical linkages to produce a more accurate record.

PRESSURE SCALES

Although laymen are probably most familiar with inches of mercury as the scale of pressure measurement, there are other scales in common use. The length of the mercury column may be measured using metric units, in which case sea level pressure is 76 centimeters or 760 millimeters of mercury. Measurements that employ the concept of force are especially useful in meteorological calculations. Meteorologists now use the *millibar* almost universally. The U.S. Weather Bureau instituted the use of the millibar scale in 1940. One *millibar* is the force exerted by 1000 dynes on a square centimeter. (A *dyne* is defined as the force which, act-

TABLE 4-1

Barometric Pressure Equivalents on Different Scales

Millibars	Inches of Hg	Centimeters of Hg	Atmospheres
940	27.76	70.51	.926
950	28.05	71.25	.937
960	28.35	72.01	.947
970	28.65	72.77	.957
980	28.94	73.51	.967
990	29.24	74.27	.977
1000	29.53	75.01	.987
1010	29.83	75.77	.997
1013.2	29.92	76.00	1.000
1020	30.12	76.50	1.006
1030	30.42	77.27	1.016
1040	30.71	78.00	1.026
1050	31.01	78.77	1.035

ing on one gram mass for one second, imparts to it a velocity of one centimeter per second.) In pressure measurements, one millibar is equivalent to .0295299 inch of mercury. One inch of mercury represents the same atmospheric pressure as 33.86395 millibars. The millibar value of mean sea level pressure is 1013.2.

Physicists use *atmospheres* in laboratory work, one atmosphere being the equivalent of 14.7 lbs. per sq. in., 29.92 in. of mercury, or 1013.2 mbs. Table 4–1 shows some equivalents of the different pressure scales used in recording atmospheric pressure.

PRESSURE-HEIGHT RELATIONS

Because air obeys the laws of gases and is compressible, its density is greatest at lower levels where it is compressed under the mass of the air above. Air pressure always decreases with an increase in altitude, but it does not decrease at a constant rate. Since about one-half of the mass of the atmosphere lies below 18,000 ft. the pressure at 18,000 ft. is about half that at sea level, although the atmosphere extends on upward for several hundred miles. Table 4–2 gives the average pressures at selected heights under standard conditions. The actual density of air depends upon the temperature, amount of water vapor in the air, and gravity. Because all these vary there is no simple relationship between altitude and pressure. As a general rule-of-thumb we can say that pressure decreases at the geometric ratio of about $\frac{1}{30}$ of its value for each increase of 900 feet in altitude in the lower atmosphere. Thus the pressure at 900 feet is about $\frac{29}{30}$ as great as at sea level; at 1800 feet it is $\frac{29}{30}$ of the value at 900 feet, and so on.

TABLE 4-2

Standard Pressure-Height Relationships*

Feet	Millibars	Inches of Hg
Sea level	1013.25	29.921
5,000	843.11	24.897
10,000	696.94	20.581
15,000	572.06	16.89
20,000	466.00	13.76
25,000	376.50	11.11
50,000	116.64	3.44
100,000	11.05	0.326
250,000	0.02	0.0006

* Adapted from United States Air Force, Geophysics Research Directorate, *Handbook of Geophysics*, Revised Edition, published by The Macmillan Company, 1960.

HORIZONTAL PRESSURE DISTRIBUTION

Comparison of pressure readings at different observing stations reveals small differences that are highly significant in the analysis of weather situations. On a worldwide scale average sea level pressure may vary from 29.00 to 30.50 inches of mercury or from about 982 to 1033 millibars. The world's highest observed sea level pressure was recorded at Irkutsk, Siberia, on January 14, 1893, when the barometer reached 1075.2 mbs. (31.75 in. of Hg). A record low of 877 mbs. (25.90 in. of Hg) was estimated by aerial reconnaissance in the eye of a typhoon west of the Marianas Islands on September 24, 1958.

In the same way that isotherms are used to show the distribution of temperature, *isobars* indicate pressure distribution. An isobar is a line connecting points with equal values of pressure. For surface conditions isobars of sea level pressure are ordinarily used, but they may also be drawn to show pressure distribution at a constant elevation in the upper atmosphere. In a general way isobars may be likened to contour lines on a relief map.

The underlying causes of most pressure differences at the bottom of the atmosphere are the same factors which affect the horizontal distribution of temperature, with latitude and land-water relationships being the most important. It should be remembered that the terms *high* and *low* as applied to temperature and pressure are relative. Low pressures in the hot equatorial zone are not necessarily as low in actual value as the low pressures associated with middle-latitude cyclonic storms. The effect of latitude, through temperature, upon pressure is to produce a more or less symmetrical pattern of pressure zones on the earth. Along the equator lies a belt of low pressure known as the *equatorial low* or *doldrums*. In the cold polar latitudes are the vaguely persistent high pressure areas, the *polar highs*. Centered at about 60° to 70° north and south latitude are the *subpolar low* pressure belts, and at 25° to 35° north and south latitude are the *subtropic highs*. These intermediate pressure zones result ultimately from temperature differences, but it is not possible to regard temperature alone as the direct cause of pressure distribution, since wind plays an important part in redistributing temperature characteristics from one latitude to another. Furthermore, the global circulation results in vertical motions that may cause dynamic pressure differences. For example, the piling up of air by winds blowing along convergent paths, as happens at upper levels over the subtropic highs, increases surface pressure. Nor should these pressure "belts" be regarded as permanent. They are greatly affected by differences in net radiation resulting from seasonal migration of the sun and from variations in heating of land and water surfaces. All

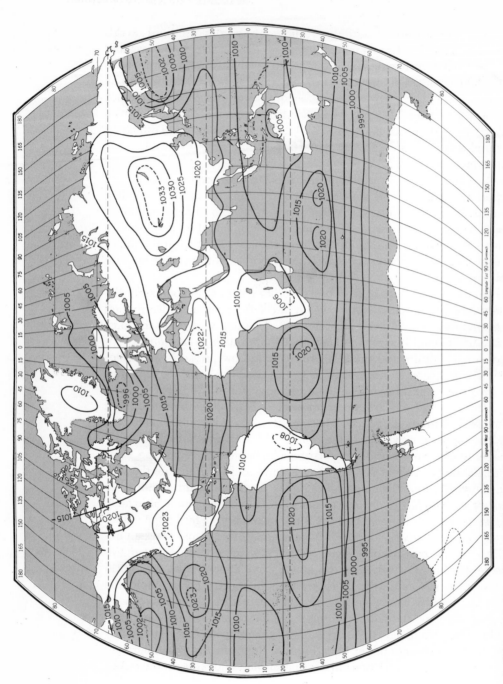

Van der Grinten projection, courtesy A. J. Nystrom & Co., Chicago.

Fig. 4-5 World distribution of mean sea level pressure in January.

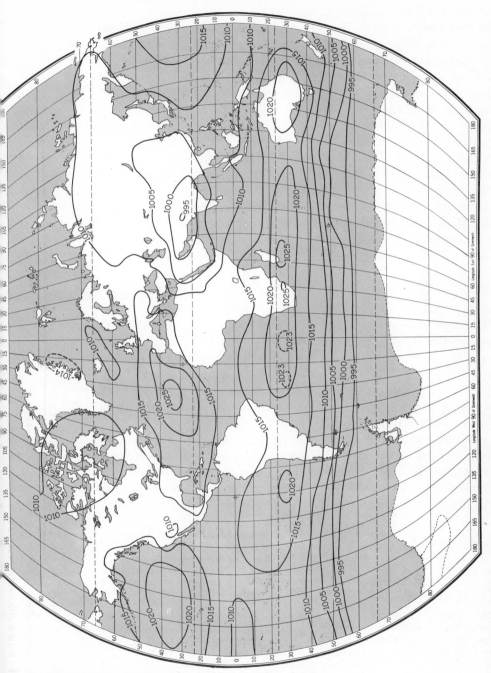

Van der Grinten projection, courtesy A. J. Nystrom & Co., Chicago.

Fig. 4-6 World distribution of mean sea level pressure in July.

are subject to incursions of air masses with contrasting temperature and density properties from other latitudes.

The effect of the irregular distribution of land and water upon pressure is best seen in seasonal contrasts, especially in the middle latitudes. In winter the continents are relatively cool and tend to develop high-pressure centers; in summer they are warmer than the oceans and tend to be dominated by low pressure. Conversely, the oceans are associated with low pressure in winter and high pressure in summer. By reference to Figures 4–5 and 4–6, which show the average sea level pressures for January and July, it can be seen that the North Atlantic, for example, is under the dominance of high pressure in summer and low in winter. In contrast, the Southern Hemisphere, which has a more homogeneous surface (mostly water) does not show such great seasonal differences. Note that the isobars in the latitudes 40°–70° South are nearly parallel and aligned along parallels of latitude. The tendency to greater persistence of the subtropic high and the more orderly arrangement of isobars in the Southern Hemisphere are both results of the smaller effect of land-water differences.

PRESSURE GRADIENT AND WIND

The rate of change in atmospheric pressure between two points at the same elevation is called the *pressure gradient* or *isobaric slope*. It is proportional to the difference in pressure and is the immediate cause of horizontal air movement. The direction of air flow is from high to low pressure and the speed of flow is directly related to the pressure gradient. The pressure gradient is said to be steep when the rate of change is great, and the steeper the gradient the more rapid will be the flow of air.

Vertical movements of air include eddies, convection currents, convergent ascent, and subsidence. Horizontal flow is called wind. In combination these movements comprise complete systems of circulation in the atmosphere. (See Figure 4–7.) Convection systems are analogous to the convectional distribution of heat in a room by hot radiators or hot air

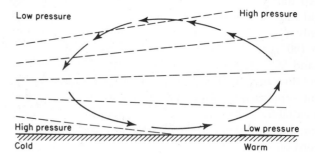

Fig. 4-7 Schematic relationship between pressure and winds. Dashed lines represent planes of equal pressure.

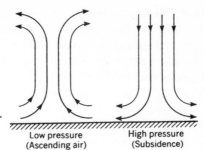

Fig. 4-8 Relationship between vertical air currents and pressure.

Low pressure
(Ascending air)

High pressure
(Subsidence)

vents. As long as sufficient differences in temperature, and therefore of air density, exist at different parts of the system air will continue to flow. Over low pressure areas, air will converge and rise, and over high pressure areas, the air will subside and diverge. Strong gradients between the two are indicated by closely spaced isobars on a pressure map, and the resulting winds will be of correspondingly high velocity.

WIND OBSERVATIONS

Wind direction may be ascertained quite simply by watching the movement of clouds, vegetation, smoke, waves on water surfaces, and so forth. This type of visual observation yields important information on winds, and, with some experience, an observer can also estimate the speed of surface winds. In 1805 Admiral Francis Beaufort introduced a wind force scale which was based upon the response of certain objects to the wind. In applying the Beaufort Scale the extent to which smoke is carried horizontally or to which trees bend before the wind is used as an index of speed. At sea the condition of waves, swell, and spray in addition to response of sails and masts is the basis for windspeed estimates.

Most weather stations are equipped with a wind observation unit which consists of a wind vane and an anemometer mounted at the top of a steel support column. The wind vane points into the wind, but it should be noted that winds are named for the direction from which they come. A wind blowing from north to south is a north wind. Meteorologists commonly use degrees of azimuth measured from north at 0°, around through east (90°), south (180°), and west (270°). North is represented by both 0° and 360°. Ordinarily the wind vane is electrically connected to show wind direction on an indicator inside the weather station, since the instrument support may have to be mounted at some distance from the roof immediately above the station. Adaptation of the movement resulting from changing wind direction to a pen arm makes possible a continuing record on the *wind register.*

In the United States and certain other countries the standard unit of wind velocity for observations is the *knot,* that is, one nautical mile per hour, although laymen may continue to think in terms of miles per hour. One knot equals 6080.20 feet, or about 1.15 miles, per hour; one mile per hour equals about 0.87 knots. The use of smaller units such as feet per second or meters per second is ordinarily restricted to research or micro-climatic observations.

For instrumental wind velocity observations several types of *anemometers* are used. The most common is the Robinson cup anemometer which is generally used by the United States Weather Bureau. Either three or four metal hemispheres are mounted on arms which rotate freely about a vertical axis. A system of gears similar to an automobile speedometer translates the rotation generated by the wind to an indicator or recorder for both speed and miles of wind that have passed the instrument. The *pressure-plate* anemometer is more satisfactory than the cup anemometer for measurement of gusts. A flat metal pendulum is mounted so that it swings freely and constantly turns perpendicular to the wind. The amplitude of the swing of the plate can be calibrated in terms of wind speed.

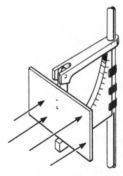

Fig. 4-9 Pressure-plate anemometer.

The *bridled anemometer* consists of a series of cups (usually 32) mounted somewhat as in the cup anemometer, but the vertical shaft is held, that is, bridled, by a spring. The rotation of the shaft against the spring represents wind force and is translated to an indicator which shows wind speed. This instrument is commonly used on ships. In order to determine wind velocity, however, allowance has to be made for the direction and speed of the ship.

The *pressure-tube anemometer* has the same principle as the *pitot tube* used on airplanes to determine air speed. It is mounted as a wind vane to keep the open end of the tube pointed into the wind. The difference between pressure due to the force of the wind and the atmospheric pressure activates a pressure gauge calibrated for wind speed. The dynamic principle employed in this instrument causes it to lag in registering gusts.

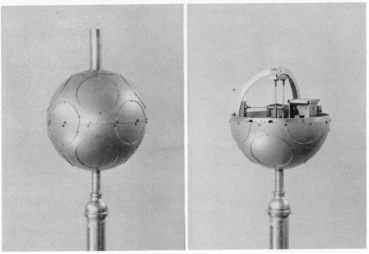

Fig. 4-10 Spherical transducer assembly of the wind vector indicator. On the right a hemisphere has been removed to show internal structure.

In microclimatological observations wind speed is often measured electrically. The rate of cooling of an exposed hot wire, a thermistor, or a thermocouple is a function of air movement and therefore an index of wind speed. Vertical as well as horizontal determination of speed and direction of air flow is accomplished by transducer assemblies. In this type of instrument wind pressure on different parts of a spherical probe activates electrical contacts to indicate both the force and the direction of the force. (See Figure 4–10.)

For purposes of analyzing storms and air masses as well as for planning air travel, observations of upper winds are as important as those of winds at the surface. Clouds are an obvious indicator of direction of winds aloft, and if their height is known their drift can be used to estimate their velocity. Several types of devices to track clouds employ principles of trigonometry and magnification by a telescope. They are not widely used and will not be treated in detail here. The disadvantage of using clouds as indicators of winds aloft is their relative confinement to certain levels. Moreover, the movements of low clouds may not indicate the most significant upper winds. Wind observations from airplanes can be useful additions to weather information, but they are available only at irregular times and at varying heights unless expensive special flights are made.

The most common method of obtaining upper wind data is by means of the *pilot ballon,* or "pibal." A balloon filled with hydrogen or helium is released from the earth's surface and as it floats aloft it rides the winds to reveal their direction and speed. The *theodolite,* a right-angled telescopic transit which is mounted so as to make possible reading of both azimuthal (horizontal) and vertical angles, is used to track the balloon. The latter's progress is plotted minute by minute on a special plotting board, and the direction and speed for successive altitudes can be computed. At night, a small flashlight is tied to the balloon so that it may be seen. When the sky is obscured by a low cloud cover, the pilot balloon is useless for upper air wind observations. Radar has provided the answer to this problem. A larger balloon with greater lift is employed to carry a metal radar target upwards. By means of a radar transceiver or radio theodolite, the target may then be followed until the balloon either breaks or travels out of range. This technique is known as a *rawin* observation.

MAPPING WIND DATA

Wind direction is ordinarily shown on maps by means of arrows pointing in the direction of flow, that is, flying with the wind. Where direction

Fig. 4-11 Pilot balloon theodolite.

Courtesy W. and L. E. Gurley.

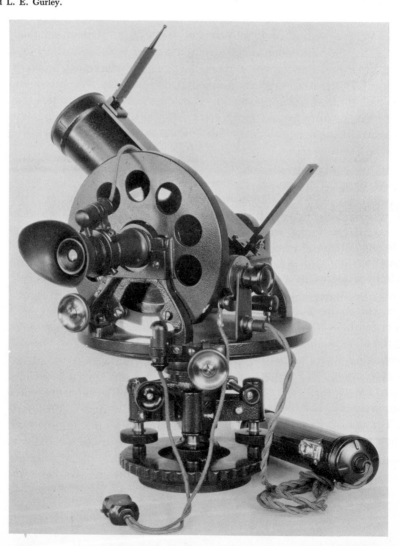

Symbol	Miles (Statute) Per Hour	Knots	Symbol	Miles (Statute) Per Hour	Knots
 ◎	Calm	Calm	 �	44 – 49	38 – 42
—	1 – 4	1 – 2	 �	50 – 54	43 – 47
⊥	5 – 8	3 – 7	 ⊾	55 – 60	48 – 52
⊾	9 – 14	8 – 12	 ⊾	61 – 66	53 – 57
 ⊾	15 – 20	13 – 17	 ⊾	67 – 71	58 – 62
 ⊾	21 – 25	18 – 22	 ⊾	72 – 77	63 – 67
 ⊾	26 – 31	23 – 27	 ⊾	78 – 83	68 – 72
 ⊾	32 – 37	28 – 32	 ⊾	84 – 89	73 – 77
 ⊾	38 – 43	33 – 37	 ⊾	119 – 123	103 – 107

Courtesy U.S. Weather Bureau.

Fig. 4-12 Wind symbols used on weather maps.

only is indicated, the arrow may be drawn through the point or circle representing the station location. Representation of actual observations is made by straight arrows; general air trajectories or theoretical flow patterns may be shown by means of curved *stream lines*. While wind speed may be entered in numerals, it is more commonly designated by short barbs or feathers attached to the tail of the arrow, the head of the arrow being the station circle. (See Figure 4–12) *Isotachs* are sometimes drawn connecting points with equal windspeed values.

Climatic aspects of wind are portrayed graphically on maps, charts and diagrams by *wind roses*. The relative lengths of lines radiating from the station circle indicate the percentage frequency of principal wind directions. The same data may be plotted as a polar graph to produce a *wind-direction frequency polygon.*

FACTORS AFFECTING WIND DIRECTION AND SPEED

Because wind results basically from the pressure gradient, the initial determinant of its direction is the force exerted by the pressure gradient. However, as soon as air begins to move along the earth's surface its direction is altered by certain other factors acting together. Most of the winds of the earth follow a generally curved path rather than a straight one because of these factors.

The deflective force due to the earth's rotation on its axis is one of the most potent influences upon wind direction. Known as the *Coriolis force,* it is, strictly speaking, not a force but an effect resulting from the rotational movement of the earth and the movement of air relative to the earth. But because we live on the earth and are a part of its rotation, the apparent effect is that of a force which turns winds from the paths initiated by the pressure gradient. The Coriolis effect causes all winds (indeed all moving objects) in the Northern Hemisphere to move toward the right and those of the Southern Hemisphere to move to the left with respect to the rotating earth. At the equator the effect has a value of zero and it in-

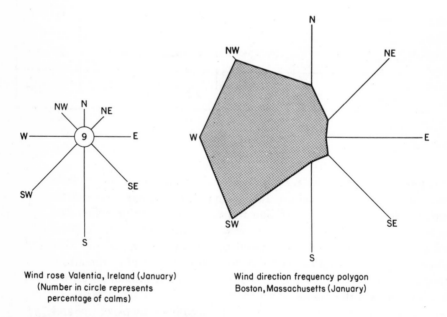

Wind rose Valentia, Ireland (January)
(Number in circle represents
percentage of calms)

Wind direction frequency polygon
Boston, Massachusetts (January)

Fig. 4-13 Methods of graphing mean wind directions.

creases regularly toward the poles. It acts at an angle of 90° to the horizontal direction of the wind and is directly proportional to horizontal wind speed. The Coriolis effect changes wind direction but does not change

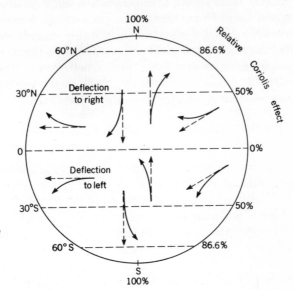

Fig. 4-14 Deflection of winds by the Coriolis effect.

wind speed. When the pressure gradient has initiated movement of air the resulting wind is deflected more and more to the right (left in the Southern Hemisphere) until it may be blowing parallel to the isobars, that is at right angles to the pressure gradient. If the motion of the air is along curved isobars, centrifugal force acts on it, tending to pull it outward from the center of curvature.

Along and near the earth's surface wind does not move freely in a horizontal plane. Irregularities in surface relief and local differences in thermal convection cause moving air to take on correspondingly irregular motion so that it undergoes abrupt changes in speed and direction. This fluctuating wind action, known as *turbulence,* is associated with lulls, gusts, and eddies and increases with increasing wind speeds. The effects of surface turbulence are not very great above 1500 ft., and at about 3000 ft. actual wind direction and speed are equivalent to the theoretical *gradient wind,* which may be calculated from the pressure gradient. The gradient wind is the resultant of the pressure gradient force, Coriolis effect, and centrifugal force. The effect of surface friction is to reduce wind speed. This results in a reduction of the Coriolis effect and centrifugal force and wind moves across the isobars at an angle toward lower pressure. (See Figure 4–15.) Other factors being equal, the difference in wind speed and direction between the surface and upper levels is greatest over rough land surfaces. Over water the surface wind more nearly approximates the gradient wind. On the average, low-speed winds cross the isobars over land at an angle of about 45° with a speed about 40 per cent of the gradient wind speed; over oceans the angle is about 30° and the surface speed about 65 per cent of the gradient wind speed. Recognizing the relationship of wind direction to pressure distribution, Buys-Ballot formulated the rule: If you stand with your back to the wind in the Northern Hemisphere, pressure is lower on your left than on your right. In the Southern Hemisphere, again with your back to the wind, lower pressure will be on your right and higher pressure on your left.

WINDS ALOFT

In free air the effect of increasing altitude is to reduce the kind of turbulence induced by surface friction. Ordinarily wind direction will change with altitude so as to become more nearly parallel to the isobars and wind speed will more nearly reflect the pressure gradient. Strong convection currents may cause turbulence at high levels, however. Along boundaries between air streams having converging directions or different speeds *wind shear* develops, sometimes creating violent turbulence. The swift passage of wind over the top of relatively calm air in a temperature inversion is likely to produce a turbulent layer.

Considerable variation of wind direction with altitude may result from convergence of two air masses, particularly if their temperatures are different. Along the boundary where cold air advances against warmer air the lighter, warmer air will rise and tend to spread out above the heavier, cold air so that winds in the upper air may be blowing directly opposite the cold surface winds. This phenomenon is commonly associated with the cyclonic storms of middle latitudes but it is by no means confined to those areas.

Because local winds are all comparatively shallow and have pressure gradients only vaguely related to the general circulation, vertical sound-

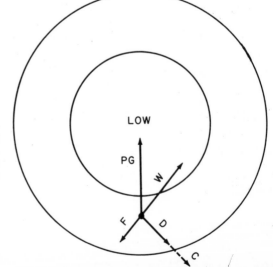

Fig. 4-15 Forces affecting surface wind around a low in the Northern Hemisphere. PG—pressure gradient; D—deflective force due to Coriolis effect; C—centrifugal force; F—friction; W—resulting surface wind.

ings through and above them often show great variation of both direction and speed. If the conditions responsible for the local wind create a pressure gradient in the same direction as the major circulation, the two will simply reinforce one another.

Although the considerations of upper winds so far have been chiefly with respect to free air, surface winds on hills and mountains are governed by most of the same principles. Rising above the maximum friction layer, mountain peaks are buffeted by the higher-speed winds of upper levels. The condition of trees near the timberline and the experiences of mountain climbers attest to this. The summits of mountains tend to increase further the speeds at upper levels. Air blowing across the top of a mountain is constricted between the summit below and the layers of air above; being thus funnelled, it increases in speed until it passes the summit. A dramatic example of wind force on a mountaintop occurred at Mt. Washington in northern New Hampshire on April 12, 1934. Wind speeds of more than 150 miles per hour were recorded for most of the afternoon and at one time reached 231 miles per hour.

DIURNAL VARIATION OF WIND SPEED

If we consider the air movement in an extensive wind system and disregard wind shifts or locally induced winds, we find a fairly regular daily variation of wind speed at the surface. The maximum speed usually occurs in the early afternoon and the minimum in the early morning hours just before sunrise. Probably everyone has experienced the phenomenon of

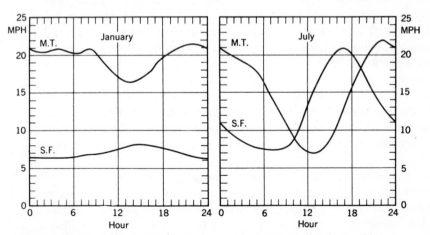

Data from Herbert H. Wright, "Characteristics of Winds at Mount Tamalpais, Cal.," *Mon. Wea. Rev..* 44, 9 (1916), 512–14.

Fig. 4-16 Hourly variations in mean wind speeds at Mount Tamalpais (2,604 ft.) and San Francisco (220 ft.) in January and July.

winds dying down in the evening only to rise again with renewed force in the morning. In order to find the reason for this it will be necessary to recall that wind speed increases with increasing altitude. During the daytime, convection caused by heating of the surface air layers brings about an exchange of air between lower and higher levels, and a more nearly uniform vertical distribution of speed exists. At night, the air near the ground is cooled and, being heavy, will tend to remain at the low levels, where because of the greater frictional drag it will resist being carried along by the fast-moving winds above. On high hills and mountains, especially if they are isolated, the effect may be the reverse. During the day the slowing effect of frictional drag is transferred to the upper levels by turbulence to produce a midday minimum of wind speed. At night the air rides above the cool layer lying in depressions and reaches its maximum speed for the 24-hour period. This is illustrated by the graphs in Figure 4–16, which compare wind speeds at San Francisco with those of nearby Mount Tamalpais. Note that in July, when daytime heating is much greater, the diurnal variation of wind speeds is greater. In the case of San Francisco fog often retards surface heating so that a westerly sea breeze does not reach its maximum speed until late afternoon.

GENERAL ATMOSPHERIC CIRCULATION

The net effect of the differential heating of the earth by insolation is to produce density differences that set the atmosphere in three-dimensional motion. Much of the energy for maintaining the global circulation comes from the tropical oceans, where evaporation transfers large amounts of latent heat to the air. Although the influence of latitude upon heating might be expected to create a simple circulation between tropical and polar areas, the effect of the earth's rotation diverts the winds into gigantic whirling systems that are aligned more or less in latitudinal belts. The resulting flow patterns have prevailing winds with strong easterly or westerly components and comprise the *general circulation*. If, for the time being, we neglect the influences resulting from differences in heat and moisture exchange over land and water surfaces we find an hypothetical arrangement of surface wind and pressure belts, as shown in Figure 4–17.

In the vicinity of the equator, where pressures are low, winds converge and rise, and the surface winds are light or variable. This belt is designated by several names. Among the more common are *doldrums, equatorial low, equatorial trough, belt of equatorial convergence,* and *intertropical convergence zone.* The last is the preferred term, for it best expresses the actual wind movements in the equatorial latitudes. On either side of the intertropical convergence, blowing into it (converging), are the *trades*. They are named the *Northeast* and *Southeast Trades* in the Northern and Southern Hemispheres respectively. Note that although the pressure gradient is directed from the subtropic high toward the intertropical convergence the winds are deflected by the earth's rotation so that they approach the equator at acute angles rather than at the perpen-

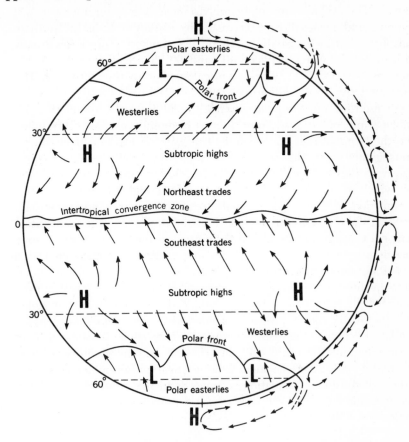

Fig. 4-17 Schematic arrangement of winds and pressure belts. The effects of differential heating of land and water surfaces are neglected.

dicular. The sources of the trades are the subtropic highs, sometimes called the *horse latitudes*, where much of the upper air that is moving from the equatorial zone converges and piles up, then subsides and diverges near the surface. The subtropic highs are not actually continuous belts, but are broken up into "cells," having their best development over the oceans. Because much of the air movement is downward a tendency to calms or variable winds characterizes these cells. A part of the diverging air becomes the trades; that which flows toward the pole forms the *pre-*

vailing westerlies. In the Northern Hemisphere the westerlies are from the southwest and in the Southern Hemisphere from the northwest. In each case the Coriolis effect accounts for the westerly component. The westerlies are zones of cyclonic storms, and although strong winds in these storms may blow from any direction of the compass, westerly winds predominate. The cyclonic storms themselves move in a general west to east direction. Land masses disrupt the westerlies considerably in the Northern Hemisphere, but in the Southern Hemisphere, where there is a virtually unbroken belt of water between 40° and 60° South, the westerlies are strong and persistent. They are often called the "roaring forties" in this zone, a carry-over from sailing days.

The westerlies and the *polar easterlies* meet and converge at the *subpolar lows*, or *polar fronts*. Here there is frequently a great contrast between the temperatures of the winds from subtropical and polar source regions, giving rise to the cyclonic storms or "lows" that are carried along in the westerlies. The polar easterlies carry air outward from the *polar highs,* which are regions of subsidence of air from higher levels.

Completion of the circulation pattern of the major wind systems requires that there be an exchange of air at the upper levels to compensate for any net transfer horizontally at the bottom of the troposphere. In spite of recent progress in the study of the upper atmosphere, much less is known about winds at great heights than at the earth's surface. Strong air streams in the upper troposphere, lower stratosphere, and possibly even in the mesophere help to achieve a balanced distribution in the global circulation. At the higher levels the mean flow is more nearly along parallels of latitude than is the case at the surface. Nevertheless there is a slight poleward flow in latitudes 0°–30° and 60°–90° and an equatorward flow in the middle latitudes. The small mean vertical motion which completes the three-dimensional circulation is upwards in the intertropical convergence zone and along the subpolar low; it is downward in the subtropical high pressure belts and near the poles.

THE JET STREAMS

In the latitudes of the westerlies in the Northern Hemisphere high-speed winds blow from west to east near the tropopause. These *polar front jet streams* achieve their maximum force and extent in winter, when there may be two or even three distinct currents. The main jet-stream system, also known as the *Ferrel westerlies,* undulates from north to south like a gigantic ribbon, often swerving far equatorward over the continents, and sometimes dividing into separates streams. Its position is closely related to the major fronts between tropical and polar air masses, suggesting that it may be a guiding mechanism for storms in the middle latitudes

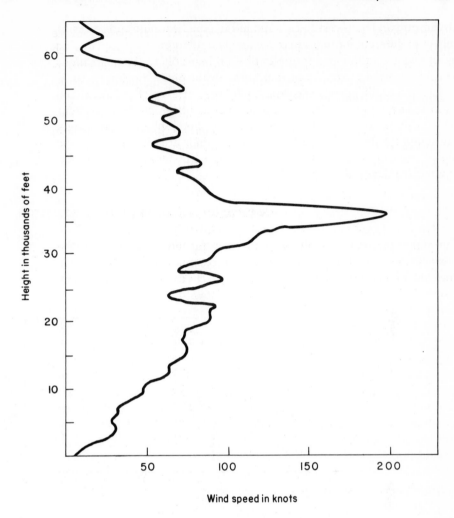

Fig. 4-18 Vertical variation of wind speed in a jet stream.

as well as the means of transporting vast quantities of air across the continents. Several thousand feet thick and as wide as 300 or 400 miles, it has
a middle core in which maximum speeds are often 200 knots and may
reach 300 knots or more. In summer it has a mean position at higher latitudes and its velocity and extent are reduced. A similar jet-stream system
in comparable latitudes of the Southern Hemisphere crosses South America, Australia, and New Zealand. Over the low-latitude margins of the
westerlies the *subtropical jet stream* persists through most of the year.
Speeds of more than 300 knots have been reported in both hemispheres,
for example, over Japan and the South Indian Ocean. The subtropical

jet streams travel from west to east and aid in equalization of pressures as air moves to different latitudes in the general circulation.

During winter in the high latitudes of each hemisphere the *polar night jet stream* is a strong westerly current in the stratosphere. Rocket observations have recorded speeds exceeding 330 knots at a height of nearly 50 miles in the arctic polar night jet stream. Still another jet stream system is the *easterly jet stream* of the tropical stratosphere, where wind speeds increase rapidly above about 12 miles. These winds are also known as the *Krakatoa easterlies* because they carried volcanic dust westward after the eruption of Krakatoa in 1883.

SEASONAL CHANGES IN THE GENERAL CIRCULATION

The apparent annual migration of the sun latitudinally between the Tropics of Cancer and Capricorn causes a corresponding migration of the patterns of temperature, pressure, and global circulation. The tendency

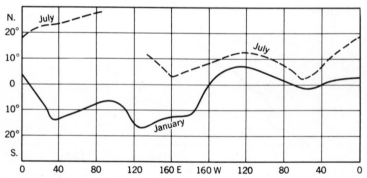

After Herbert Riehl, *Tropical Meteorology* (McGraw-Hill, 1954).

Fig. 4-19 Mean January and July positions of the intertropical convergence zone.

is for wind and pressure belts to shift northward a few degrees in the Northern Hemisphere summer and southward in winter. It should be emphasized, therefore, that the distribution of wind and pressure systems in the general circulation, outlined earlier in this chapter, represents idealized pressure distribution and prevailing air movements that are modified by several factors. It has been previously pointed out that pressures tend to be higher in winter over land and lower over adjacent waters. This is most evident in the middle latitudes. The result may be creation of complete reversals of pressure gradients over the continents with corresponding seasonal shifts in wind direction. The mean flow patterns of surface winds in January and July are shown in Figures 4–20 and 4–21.

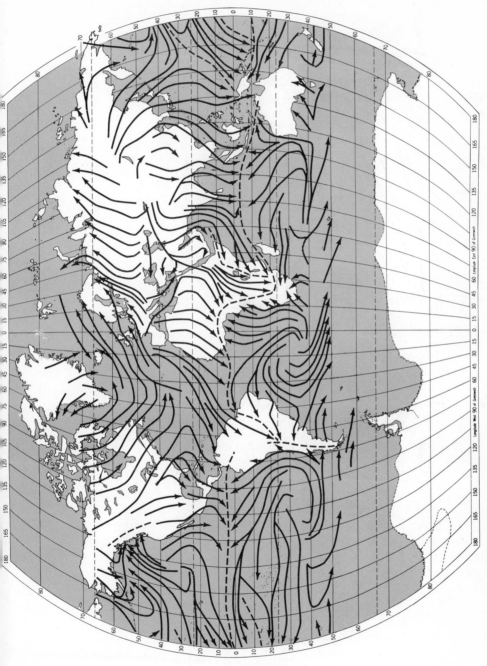

Van der Grinten projection, courtesy A. J. Nystrom & Co., Chicago.

Fig. 4-20 Mean flow patterns of surface winds in January.

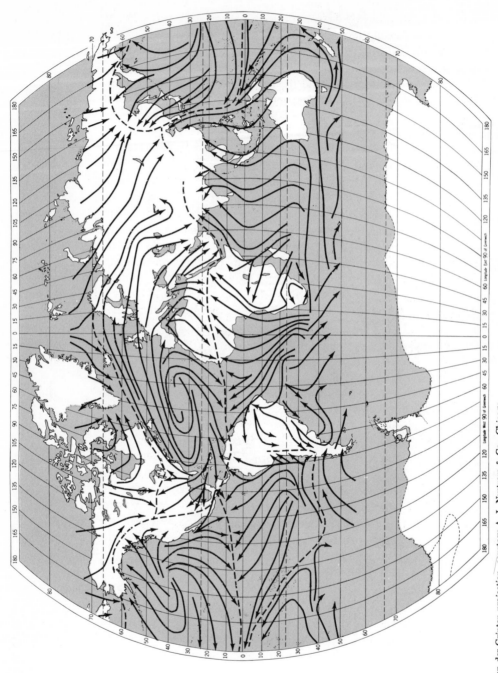

Van der Grinten projection, courtesy A. J. Nystrom & Co., Chicago.

Fig. 4-21 Mean flow patterns of surface winds in July.

OCEANIC CIRCULATION

There is a close relationship between the primary circulation of the atmosphere and the circulation of the oceans. Although the atmosphere is the chief agent for transfer of energy from the tropics to higher latitudes, the oceans also serve this function on a global scale. In addition, energy is exchanged between the oceans and the atmosphere by transfer of sensible and latent heat and by mechanical action along the ocean-air boundary surface. Ocean currents are motivated mainly by density differences due to variations in water temperature and salinity and by winds. Their direction is influenced by the Coriolis effect and by the configuration of ocean basins and shorelines as well as by the initial driving forces. Large-scale, slow movements of ocean water, resulting primarily from prevailing winds, are usually referred to as *drifts* rather than currents. These are best developed in the belt of prevailing westerlies in the Southern Hemisphere. (See Figure 4–22.) Examination of the map of world ocean currents reveals the close correlation between general atmospheric circulation and oceanic circulation in the middle and low latitudes. In the Northern Hemisphere the circulation is clockwise; in the Southern Hemisphere it is counterclockwise. The net effect of most of the surface oceanic circulation is to carry cold water toward the equator along the east margins of the oceans and warm water toward the poles along the west margins. At high latitudes the pattern of flow is broken up considerably by the arrangement of land masses. Cold water subsides in some of these areas and moves toward the equator at great depths.

Along some coasts prevailing winds skim the surface water away, producing a phenomenon known as *upwelling*. When the relatively warmer surface water is moved out by the action of wind the cooler water from below replaces it. Upwelling is especially important in influencing temperatures along the coasts of southern California, Peru and northern Chile, northwest Africa, and southwest Africa. In each of these areas the Coriolis effect turns the currents away from the shore. Since the surface water has a greater speed than that at greater depths, it is deflected at a greater rate, allowing upwelling of the colder subsurface water. As a result of the abnormally low temperatures at surface levels, moist air passing over the areas of upwelling frequently produces fog.

THE MONSOONS

In several parts of the world prevailing winds known as *monsoons* blow from approximately opposite directions in summer and winter. These seasonal wind systems are best developed in India and adjacent southeastern Asia, where there is a persistent flow from the Indian Ocean on to the land

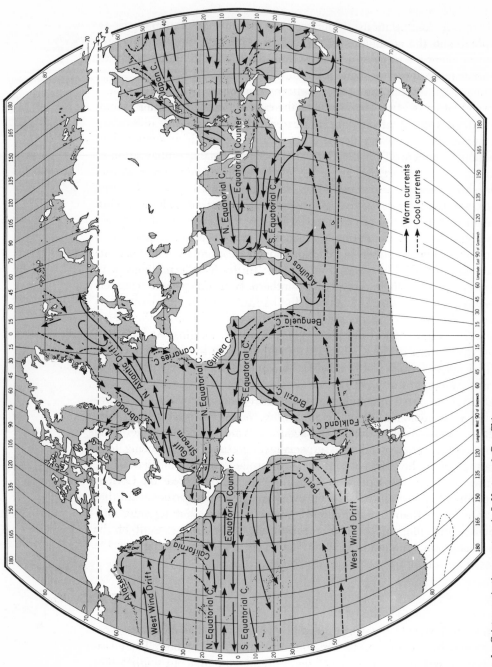

Van der Grinten projection, courtesy A. J. Nystrom & Co., Chicago.

Fig. 4-22   Major surface currents of the oceans.

in the summer half of the year and winds blow out from the continent in winter. The reversing circulation has traditionally been ascribed to the heating and cooling of the continent with the changes of season and a resulting change in the patterns of pressure distribution. Increased understanding of the jet stream in recent years has led to a modification of this simple explanation. In winter the high pressure over the Asian continent forces the westerly jet stream southward so that a portion of it lies south of the Himalayas. Subsiding air along the tropical margins of the jet moves toward the Indian Ocean, blocking incursions of maritime tropical air and producing the dry winter monsoon. In summer the jet stream shifts with the general circulation and lies north of the Himalayas, allowing moist tropical air of the wet summer monsoon to move onto the continent. Northern Australia experiences a similar, though less well-developed, monsoonal circulation which is related to seasonal migration of components of the general circulation.

Along the east coasts of Asia and North America there are other monsoonal effects which merge into the prevailing winds of the general circulation. Outbursts of polar air in the westerlies result in a predominantly westerly flow off the continents in winter, but in summer maritime air moves inland from the subtropic highs that lie over the adjacent oceans.

LOCAL WINDS

A number of winds of local importance develop as a result of local differences in temperature. These local winds affect relatively small areas and ordinarily are confined to the lowest levels of the troposphere. Their air movements may be generated either by heating or cooling of a particular area. Sometimes they represent virtually complete convectional circulation; in other cases they merge into the stronger wind systems of the general circulation or of major storms.

The *sea breeze* is one of the common local winds. Along seacoasts or large inland water bodies in summer the land heats much faster than the water on a clear day and a pressure gradient is established, directed from high over the water to the low over the land. The circulation which follows brings cool air onto the land, but the system is not entirely a self-contained unit because the air which returns to the sea at upper levels spreads out and does not necessarily all return at the surface. The sea breeze rarely has a depth of more than 1,500 feet and at its maximum strength does not extend inland more than 30 miles. (The distance is much less around lakes, where the wind is more properly called a lake breeze.) It begins offshore in the late morning hours and gradually moves inland to decrease afternoon temperatures. Toward evening it subsides. Because of the sea breeze, areas on the immediate coast in middle latitudes and the tropics may have cooler temperatures than a few miles inland.

At night a reversal of the sea breeze may occur but with somewhat weaker characteristics. The *land breeze* becomes established during the night as the land cools to temperatures lower than the adjacent water, setting up a pressure gradient from land to sea. Because temperature differences between land and water are rarely as great at night as in the daytime, the land breeze is less extensive both vertically and horizontally than the sea breeze. It usually attains its maximum intensity in the early morning hours and dies out soon after sunup.

Another combination of local winds which undergo a daily reversal consists of the *mountain* and *valley breezes*. On mountain sides on clear nights the higher land radiates heat and is cooled, in turn cooling the air in contact with it. The cool, denser air thus flows down the mountain slopes to drain into the valleys and lowlands. Since it blows from the mountain, this air flow is termed a *mountain breeze*. By morning it may produce temperature inversions in depressions so that the valley bottoms are colder than the hillsides. But, where the mountain breeze is funnelled into a narrow valley or a gorge, it may gain considerable velocity and generate enough turbulent mixing to break up the inversion. On warm sunny days, the heating of mountain slopes may generate an upslope flow of air called a *valley breeze*. As the warm air moves up the mountain, it is replaced by cooler air from above the valley, and surface temperatures are moderated slightly.

A type of wind known as a *gravity* or *katabatic wind* occurs in several parts of the world. Gravity winds result from the drainage of cool air off high plateaus or ice fields. The *mistral* flows onto the Mediterranean coast of France in winter from the higher lands and snow-capped mountains to the north. It is channelled somewhat by the Rhone Valley, and its coolness, dryness, and velocity sometimes detract from the otherwise attractive climate of the Riviera in winter. Along the northern coast of the Adriatic Sea, a cold, northeast wind known as the *bora* flows down from the plateau region in Yugoslavia onto the narrow coastal plain.

In numerous instances the winds associated with particular storm or pressure conditions occur with some regularity and are characteristic of the climate of a given locality. The Guinea Coast of Africa experiences the dry, dusty *harmattan* in winter when air from the relatively cool Sahara replaces humid tropical air. The harmattan has a marked cooling

Fig. 4-23 Principle of the mountain and valley breezes.

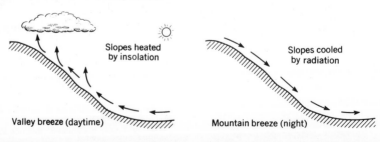

Slopes heated by insolation

Slopes cooled by radiation

Valley breeze (daytime)

Mountain breeze (night)

effect and is sometimes known as *The Doctor.* In spring, as the subtropic high moves northward, the *sirocco* blows from the south across the Mediterranean lands. In Egypt, where it is known as the *Khamsin,* and in other parts of North Africa, it is hot and dry. Along European coasts of the Mediterranean the sirocco has more moisture in its lower layers, but its high temperatures often have a withering effect on crops. *Leveche* is the name given to this wind in Spain. In the eastern Mediterranean northerly winds that persist at times during summer are known by the classical Greek name *Etesians.*

Winds that bring abrupt changes in temperature or moisture conditions are likely to take on local names. The *Norther* marks the onset of cold, stormy weather in winter over Texas, the Gulf of Mexico, and the western Caribbean. The *Pampero* is a squally wind from the northwest that blows over the Argentine pampas in winter. The *Chinook* of North America, the *Foehn* of the European Alps, and the *Nor'wester* of New Zealand are warm, dry, gusty winds induced by mountain ranges. They will be discussed in more detail in connection with special storm effects in Chapter 5.

ADDITIONAL READINGS

Batten, E. S., "Wind Systems in the Mesosphere and Lower Ionosphere," *Journ. of Met.,* 18, 3 (1961), 283–91.

Borchert, John R., "Regional Differences in the World Atmospheric Circulation," *Ann. Assoc. Am. Geogrs.,* 43, 1 (1953), 14–26.

Graham, Howard E., "The Columbia Gorge Wind Funnel," *Weatherwise,* 6, 4 (1953), 104–107.

Koteswaram, P., and N. S. Bhaskara Rao, "The Structure of the Asian Summer Monsoon," *Australian Met. Mag.,* 42 (1963), 35–56.

Lamb, H. H., "The Southern Westerlies," *Quart. Journ. Roy. Met. Soc.,* 85, 363 (1959), 1–23.

Ludlum, David M., "Extremes of Atmospheric Pressure in the United States," *Weatherwise,* 15, 3 (1962), 106–115.

McDonald, James E., "The Coriolis Effect," *Scient. Am.,* 186, 3 (1952), 72–78.

Namais, Jerome, "Interactions of Circulation and Weather Between Hemispheres," *Mon. Wea. Rev.,* 91, 10–12 (1963), 482–86.

Newell, Reginald E., "The Circulation of the Upper Atmosphere," *Scient. Am.,* 210, 3 (1964), 62–74.

Riehl, H., and Joanne S. Malkus, "On the Heat Balance and Maintenance of Circulation in the Trades," *Quart. Journ. Roy. Met. Soc.,* 83, 355 (1957), 21–29.

Serguis, Leo A., George R. Ellis, and Richard M. Ogden, "The Santa Ana Winds of Southern California," *Weatherwise,* 15, 3 (1962), 102–105.

Stommel, Henry, "The Circulation of the Abyss," *Scient. Am.,* 199, 1 (1958), 85–90.

Tyson, P. D., "Berg Winds of South Africa," *Weather,* 19, 1 (1964), 7–11.

Travelling along in the general atmospheric circulation are the air masses and storms that bring our daily weather and, by their cumulative effect, produce different climates. Fundamentally, most major weather changes consist of the advances and interaction of air masses and of processes within the air masses themselves. Precipitation over the continents is derived mainly from mass transport of moisture from the oceans, and air mass movements are largely responsible for the transfer of temperature properties and latent heat from one area to another. An adequate description of atmospheric conditions over an area must include air masses and storms as well as the individual elements of weather and climate that comprise those conditions.

PROPERTIES OF AIR MASSES

An *air mass* is defined as an extensive portion of the atmosphere having characteristics of temperature and moisture which are relatively homogeneous horizontally. In order for a large body of air to acquire temperature and moisture properties that are approximately the same at a given level, that air must rest for a time on a *source region*, which must itself have fairly homogeneous surface conditions. A large land or water area which has evenly distributed insola- **100** tion affords a good source region, but a second prerequisite is necessary if a distinctive air mass is to be developed, namely, large scale subsidence and divergence of air over the source region. Air that subsides over a homogeneous source region will become homogeneous itself and will tend to retain its characteristics when it moves away. The heat and moisture properties of the air mass will gradually change, however, as it moves over other surface conditions. Zones of convergence and rising air are inimical to the production of air masses because the general movement of winds is toward these areas at surface levels, bringing a constant renewal of air with heterogeneous temperature and humidity properties.

AIR MASS IDENTIFICATION AND ANALYSIS

Once an air mass has left its source region, it undergoes changes which often make it difficult to identify by ground observers. For example, if it is formed over a cold surface and subsequently passes over a warm ocean its temperature and moisture content will increase. Local surface conditions created by ocean currents, land relief, minor water bodies, or night-

Courtesy Friez Instrument Division, Bendix Aviation Corporation.

Fig. 5-1 Radiosonde in flight.

time radiation can produce quite different values of temperature and humidity at the bottom of an air mass. Consequently, it is necessary to analyze conditions in the upper air and to understand the processes that accompany the change in air mass properties.

Upper air observations to provide information for air mass analysis are carried out by means of the *radiosonde*. For the sake of convenience, radiosonde observations are called *raobs*. The radiosonde consists of a lightweight box fitted with a radio transmitter and sensing devices for pressure, temperature, and relative humidity. Although there are variations in the construction of radiosondes, they commonly employ a sylphon cell to indicate pressure, a thermistor for temperature, and a coated plastic strip for relative humidity. The instrument package rides aloft under a gas-filled balloon and descends on a parachute after the balloon bursts at an altitude of about 80,000 to 100,000 ft. At a ground station the signals are received, recorded, and translated into usable data. Analysis of raobs from a series of stations enables the forecaster to determine the kinds of air masses that prevail over a region. At some stations the radiosonde is followed by radar to obtain wind direction and speed at various levels as in the case of rawin. The combined technique is known as *rawinsonde*.

Another type of airborne instrument, the *transosonde*, was developed following experiments by the Japanese during World War II with constant-level balloons which carried incendiary bombs to the United States Pacific Coast. The transosonde is comprised of balloon-borne radiometeorological apparatus which can be controlled by releasing ballast or gas so that it floats along at a constant pressure level for several days. Its position can be determined at desired intervals by radio direction-finding techniques. Its advantage is that it can furnish data from positions over the oceans, where other sources of weather information are limited. Unfortunately, transosonde balloons create a hazard to high-altitude jet aircraft.

Identification of air masses is based upon three kinds of information: (1) the history of change in the air since it left its source region; (2) horizontal characteristics at certain levels in the upper air; and (3) the vertical distribution of temperature, winds, and humidity. Because the number of raob reporting stations is limited and because major changes in air masses may occur between the times of radiosonde observations, the historical approach alone is inadequate. Maps plotted with temperature, wind, and humidity values for one or more upper levels have the advantage of showing a minimum of the influences due to local surface conditions and of revealing moisture and energy components of the upper part of the air mass. They represent a horizontal "slice" through the atmosphere. Constant-level charts may be plotted either for a certain height or for a constant-pressure level, the latter being most often used by meteorological

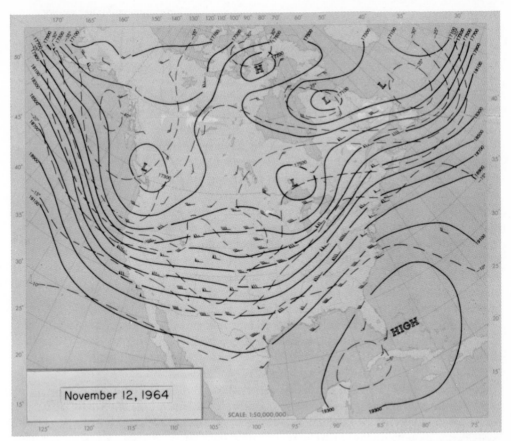

November 12, 1964

SCALE: 1:50,000,000

Courtesy U.S. Weather Bureau.

Fig. 5-2 A 500-millibar constant pressure chart for North America. Data for this map were gathered by radiosonde observations. Continuous lines show height of the 500-millibar surface above sea level. Dashed lines are isotherms for intervals of 5° C. Wind symbols show direction and relative speed at the 500-millibar level.

services. The National Meteorological Center at Suitland, Maryland, regularly prepares constant-pressure analyses for the 850-, 700-, 500-, and 300-mb. levels. Figure 5–2 is a constant-pressure chart for the 500-mb. level.

Just as charts showing the horizontal distribution of weather elements in the upper atmosphere help to identify air masses and their boundaries, so vertical cross sections based upon raob and upper wind reports make it possible to analyze vertical differences in the air. Wind direction and velocity in particular are useful in judging air mass movements and in flight planning. Temperature and humidity values from the raob are analyzed as a basis for forecasting temperature changes, cloudiness, storms, and precipitation.

STABILITY AND INSTABILITY

Vertical movements of air are of great significance because nearly all precipitation is associated with adiabatic cooling and condensation in rising air. The fundamental causes of rising air have been discussed. Let us now examine the factors within the air which affect its tendency to vertical motion, that is, its stability. If a mass of air tends to remain in its position, or to return to that position when displaced, it is said to be *stable*. If vertical displacement results in a tendency to further movement of the air from its original position, the air mass is termed *unstable*. If conditions in the air are such that it neither resists vertical motion nor aids it, the air mass is in a state of *neutral equilibrium*.

An air mass with colder, drier air in its surface layers than aloft is likely to be stable, and any process which cools the air at the bottom of an air mass tends to make it more stable. Radiational cooling at night, for example, produces a stable condition, that is, a temperature inversion. Advection of air over a cold surface will result in increasing stability, as when warm oceanic air passes over a cold ocean current or onto cold land. While these processes can produce condensation (fog or dew) in the lower layers of an air mass, they do not induce vertical currents and therefore are not likely to produce precipitation. Subsidence of air also increases its stability. As the bottom of a layer of subsiding air is compressed and diverges the top of the layer descends farther and is warmed more adiabatically than the base, thus producing a smaller difference in temperature between the top and base of the layer, that is, a decreased lapse rate. Upper-air inversions, which exhibit extremely stable lapse rates, are often caused by subsidence.

The vertical lapse rates of temperature and humidity determine the degree of stability of an air column. (See Figure 5–3.) If the actual temperature of the air increases with altitude, the colder, denser air below will tend to stay in place with the warmer, lighter air above—obviously a stable condition. If the actual temperature is exactly the same vertically through a layer of air, that layer is also stable. When an outside force causes stable air to rise, the air cools at the dry adiabatic rate as long as condensation does not take place. At a higher altitude (lower pressure), it will have a temperature lower than the surrounding air and will descend if the original lifting force is withdrawn. This effect is best seen by the comparison of the lapse rate of stable air with the dry adiabatic rate. (See Figure 5–3.) As long as condensation does not take place, air is stable if its lapse rate is less than the dry adiabatic rate. Because of its tendency to stay at or to return to its position, stable air does not move readily over mountain barriers but flows along them and pours out through passes and gorges. The weather associated with stable air is generally fair, but visibility is often

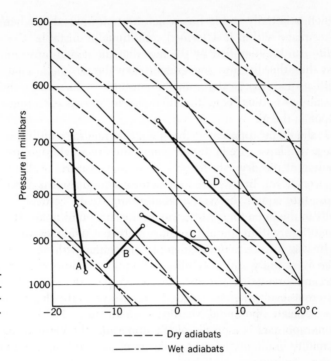

Fig. 5-3 Lapse rates showing different stability conditions. A—stable; B—stable (inversion); C—unstable; D—conditionally unstable.

poor owing to ground fog or concentration of smoke and haze near the surface. In winter stable air masses may be extremely cold in middle and high latitudes.

Instability in air occurs when its lapse rate is greater than the dry adiabatic rate of cooling. If air in an unstable layer is forced aloft it will be warmer than the surrounding air and will continue to rise. The initial force may result from heating at the earth's surface, from orographic lifting, or from convergence. As long as the actual lapse rate of temperature is greater than the dry adiabatic rate, the air will continue to rise and cool adiabatically. When its saturation temperature is reached, condensation produces clouds, and precipitation may result. Warm, humid air masses are unstable, especially when they lie over a warm surface. Instability may be developed in any air mass if it is warmed and if its moisture content is increased in its lower layers.

It frequently happens that air is stable while it rises and cools at the dry rate (that is, without condensation) but becomes unstable when condensation begins. Consider a mass of mildly stable air being forced aloft. It cools at the dry adiabatic rate until it reaches saturation. (See Figure 5-3.) The release of the latent heat of condensation gives added heat to produce further lifting and the air then cools at the slower wet rate. Strong convective activity and heavy precipitation is the probable result. Humid air which is initially stable but which becomes unstable when condensation takes place within it is termed conditionally unstable. *Conditional instability* can be identified by the fact that the actual lapse rate in the air is less than the dry rate and greater than the wet rate. That is, it is stable with respect to the dry rate but unstable with respect to the wet rate. Instability is thus "conditional" upon the presence of considerable water vapor in the air.

It should be apparent at this point that neutral equilibrium occurs when the actual lapse rate in dry air equals the dry adiabatic rate. Air rising and cooling at the dry rate has the same temperature as the surrounding air at every level. In saturated air neutral equilibrium is achieved when the lapse rate equals the wet adiabatic rate. Again vertical displacement results in the same temperature as in the surrounding air. In both cases the conditions within the air produce neither a tendency to sink nor to rise.

In view of their importance in connection with vertical motion in air masses, stability and instability are significant properties in air mass analysis and forecasting. By studying the temperature and humidity values for different levels the meteorologist can ascertain the degree of stability and the associated potential weather of an air mass. The lapse rate as plotted from raob data is a profile of the upper air; the vertical temperature and humidity gradients in various layers of air are fundamental clues to stability conditions.

AIR MASS SOURCE REGIONS AND CLASSIFICATION

An air mass source region has already been defined as a large area with approximately homogeneous temperature and moisture properties where there is a general subsidence and divergence of air. These conditions are found to be best developed in the semipermanent high pressure belts of the earth. In the belt of low pressure along the equator, however, the equatorial convergence may be weakly defined and stagnation of air will produce equatorial air masses. Where development of high pressure is seasonal, for example, over mid-latitude continental regions in winter, the source regions will likewise have seasonal maximum development.

Classification of air masses is based primarily upon their source regions and secondarily upon temperature and moisture properties. The two main categories are tropical or subtropical and polar or subpolar, because the great source regions are located at high and at low latitudes. Subdivision of these groups is made according to whether the source region is oceanic or continental, and further, according to what modifications the masses experience as they move from their source regions. Eventually, air masses become modified to such an extent that special designations are necessary. For climatological purposes this classification is of great importance be-

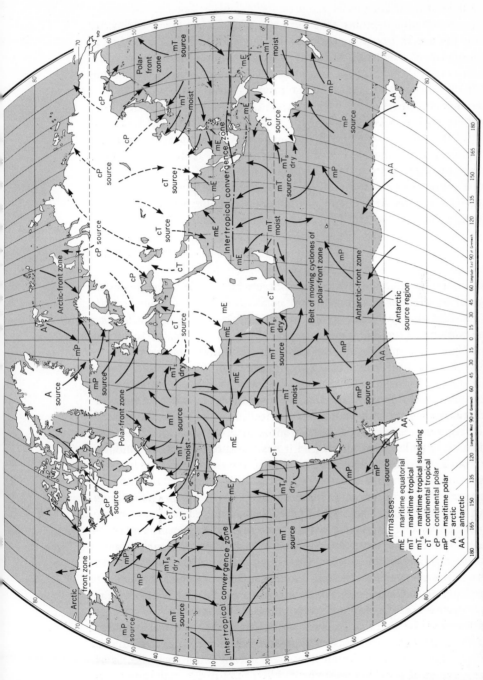

After Arthur N. Strahler, *Physical Geography* (John Wiley & Sons, Inc., 1951). Van der Grinten projection, courtesy A. J. Nystrom & Co., Chicago.

Fig. 5-4 Principal air masses and source regions of the world.

cause the extent to which air masses dominate different regions determines the climate of those regions.

In practice, letter symbols are used to designate air masses. Ordinarily *c* and *m* are used for *continental* and *maritime* and they are placed first in the designation. Following that the source region is indicated: *tropical (T), polar (P), equatorial (E), arctic (A),* and *antarctic (AA).* To indicate modifications of air masses due to transfer of heat between the bottom of the mass and the surface over which it passes, two letter symbols are appended: *k* (for the German *kalt*) for air colder than the underlying surface and *w* for air warmer than the surface. A generalized map of the principal world air masses is shown in Figure 5–4. Note that arctic air masses have their sources north of polar masses. This incongruity is explained by the history of air mass study. The term "polar" had already come into wide use to designate air masses in subpolar regions before the distinctive character of "arctic" air had been discovered.

THE EXTRATROPICAL CYCLONE

The general circulation of the atmosphere which favors divergence and air mass development in tropical and polar latitudes is characterized in the mid-latitudes by convergence of dissimilar air masses. When air masses having different temperature and humidity properties come together they do not mix readily but maintain a boundary surface of discontinuity for some time, the warmer, lighter air being forced aloft over the colder mass. The sloping boundary surfaces between contrasting air masses are called *fronts.* On the weather map a front is indicated by a line which represents the intersection of the frontal surface with the ground, but it should be remembered that a front is three-dimensional. It extends vertically as well as horizontally and it has thickness. Frontal boundaries vary from 2 or 3 miles to 50 miles in width. In the zone of contact between the prevailing westerlies and the polar easterlies there is a more or less permanent, undulating frontal discontinuity known as the *polar front.* Along this polar front the extratropical (mid-latitude) cyclones are developed. In much the same way that whirlpools are formed between adjacent currents of water moving at different speeds, giant waves or whirls form along the polar front. (See Figure 5–5.) In the typical Northern Hemisphere cyclone the cold air mass pushes southward along the ground under the warm air, which advances northward. The resulting convergence and rising air along the front is accompanied by low pressure, and it is for this reason that cyclones are often called lows or depressions. As the cyclonic wave develops, the pressure gradient is focused toward the center and the pattern of air flow takes on a counterclockwise, or cyclonic, circulation with winds making angles of 20° to 40° with the isobars.

Note that the Coriolis effect deflects the winds to the right of their intended path as they blow toward the low center. (In the Southern Hemisphere the Coriolis effect produces a clockwise circulation into the low center.) The "tongue" of warm air advancing from the south is known as the *warm sector*. Where the advancing warm air mass is replacing colder air at the surface the boundary is called the *warm front*. To the west of the warm sector the leading edge of the cold air is the *cold front*. Because air is being forced to rise along these fronts they are accompanied by appreciable cloudiness and usually precipitation. Conditions along the fronts are spoken of as "frontal weather," whereas "air mass weather" prevails in the areas away from the fronts.

Extratropical cyclones vary in diameter from 100 to as much as 2000 miles. Most are in the range of 500 to 1000 miles. Their form may be roughly circular or elongated and oval, or again they may be so broad and shallow that they are called weak depressions. Usually they travel in a

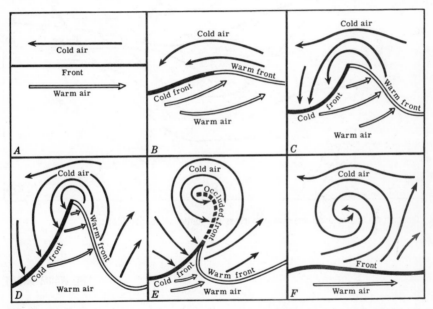

Courtesy U.S. Weather Bureau.

Fig. 5-5 Stages in the development and occlusion of a mid-latitude cyclone along the polar front. A—initial stage; B—beginning of cyclonic circulation; C—warm sector well defined between fronts; D—cold front overtaking warm front; E—occlusion; F—dissipation.

group whose movement is associated with waves in the pressure pattern at upper levels. Their general direction of movement is from west to east in the belt of prevailing westerlies, but specific paths are often curved and sometimes erratic. Some common paths are shown in Figure 5-6. Note that there is a tendency to curve toward the southeast into the Mississippi Valley and then toward the northeast. The speed of movement of cyclones, like the direction, may be variable; the average is about 20 to 30 miles per hour or from 500 to 700 miles per day. The rate of movement is greater in winter than summer. As long as the discontinuity in tempertaure and moisture conditions is maintained along its fronts the cyclone will persist. Some cyclones pass from central North America out across the Atlantic and enter western Europe; others lose their energy and dissolve because of modifications of their air masses.

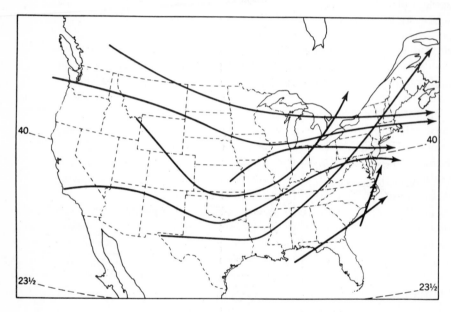

Fig. 5-6 Common paths of mid-latitude cyclones across the contiguous United States.

THE WARM FRONT

The warm front normally extends east and southeast from the low center of a cyclone, in the Northern Hemisphere. The wind shift at the warm front is not so pronounced as at the cold front. Maximum wind speed, perhaps with gustiness, is experienced slightly in advance of the front. Barometric pressure decreases gradually until the front passes and then tends to level off. The slope of the front is gradual; 200 miles ahead of its intersection with the ground it may be only 5000 or 6000 feet above the surface. The great areal expanse of rising air produces a vast cloud system with the highest clouds lying far in advance of the front. Since the vertical

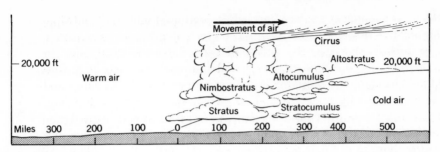

Courtesy U.S. Weather Bureau.

Fig. 5-7 The warm front.

movement along most of the warm front boundary is not violent the types of clouds are predominantly stratiform. High wispy cirrus, often in the form of "mares' tails" appear first. As the front moves in, the clouds lower and thicken progressively to cirrostratus, altostratus, and nimbostratus.

Precipitation from the warm front is light to moderately heavy and continuous, extending over a wide zone. Fogginess and poor visibility are common in the precipitation area. Sometimes the typical warm front precipitation is interspersed with heavy showers where convection takes place in unstable warm air as it rises rapidly over the cold air just ahead of the front. In winter, sleet or freezing rain may occur when rain falls from the warm air through the cold mass below. The succession of weather can include snow, sleet, and then rain as the front approaches, clouds lower, and temperature rises. Sometimes the temperature does not rise above freezing during the entire passage of a warm front. Nevertheless, an appreciable rise in surface temperature normally does accompany the passage of the front and the relatively warmer, moister air of the warm sector then begins to dominate the weather. The air which occupies the warm sector is likely to be unstable and therefore produce convective showers, especially in summer over land that is being heated.

THE COLD FRONT

The cold front is the leading edge of an intrusion of cold air into territory previously occupied by warmer air. It pushes under the warmer air after the fashion of a wedge, forcing it to rise. Frictional drag along the ground retards the advance of the cold air and it develops a relatively steep forward surface in contrast to the gentler slope of the warm front. Hence it is accompanied by clouds with vertical development and heavy, showery precipitation. At times, cold air in the upper levels overruns the warm air to create extreme instability and overturning. Convective clouds and showers then precede the surface advance of the front.

The most significant identifying feature associated with the cold front is the wind shift at its passage. In the warm sector ahead of the front, winds are generally southerly or southwesterly. As the front passes, the wind shifts to the northwest or north. The approach of the cold front is heralded by falling pressure; often there is a sharp drop just as the front passes. This is the basis for the popular association of a falling barometer with a coming storm. As the front moves on, the barometer rises again. A drop in temperature can ordinarily be expected with the passage of a cold front, but the surface temperatures are not so reliable as those in the upper air for detecting the transition from warm to cold air. Because of the lower temperatures and the probable polar origin of the air behind the cold front, it will have a lower moisture content. Therefore, humidity values also help in location of the front. The zone of precipitation along the cold front is ordinarily much wider than the discontinuities of wind, temperature, and humidity would seem to indicate, and yet it is narrower than in the warm front. A few hours after the front has passed, clearing weather can normally be expected. The following cold air mass moves over warmer ground which is probably also moist, so that instability may develop in its lower levels with resulting scattered showers. If the cold mass is unstable and moist itself, and especially if it is moving over mountainous terrain, intermittent cloudiness and showers may continue for several hours or for a day or two. In winter, when the precipitation is snow, the combination of low temperatures, high winds, and blowing snow along and following the cold front is called a *blizzard* in the central United States. A similar storm in Russia is known as the *buran*.

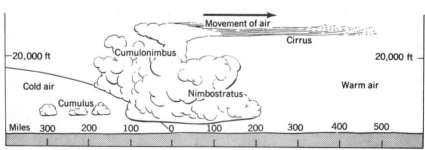

Courtesy U.S. Weather Bureau.

Fig. 5-8 The cold front.

THE OCCLUDED FRONTS

In the cyclonic storm, the cold front usually advances faster than the warm front, eventually overtaking it. When the air mass behind the cold

Official U.S. Navy Photo.

Fig. 5-9 Leading edge of a cold front at sea.

front comes into contact with the air in advance of the warm front, the air of the warm sector, being less dense, is pushed aloft. This process is called *occlusion,* and the new frontal surface thus formed is an *occluded front.* There are two ways in which an occluded front may form, depending upon the relative temperatures of the air masses within the cyclone. Over continents and east coasts of continents the air behind the cold front is normally colder than that ahead of the warm front because it has had a shorter path across relatively warm surfaces. As the occlusion develops, the cold front will run under the cool air to form a *cold-front occlusion* (See Figure 5–10.) Prefrontal weather ahead of the cold-front occlusion is similar to that of the warm front. The lifting of conditionally

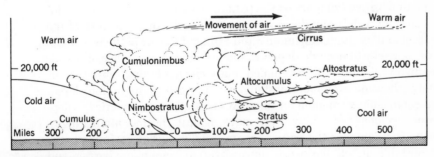

Courtesy U.S. Weather Bureau.

Fig. 5-10 The cold-front occlusion.

unstable air in the warm sector may be the "trigger action" to produce thunderstorms. At the front there is typical cold front activity, and after the occlusion has passed a marked improvement in conditions occurs. In their later stages, cold-front occlusions often become well-defined cold fronts. This results from the introduction of increasingly colder air behind the front and increasingly warmer air in the "cool" area ahead of the front.

Where the air behind the cold front is warmer than that ahead of the warm front, the former (cool) will run up over the latter (cold) when occlusion occurs, producing a *warm-front occlusion*. (See Figure 5–11.) In winter along west coasts where cool air flowing onshore is usually warmer than the cold air over the land, warm-front occlusions are especially prevalent. In its initial stage, this type of occlusion shows most of the characteristics of the warm front. Then follows moderate frontal activity in connection with the *upper cold front*. As the occlusion process continues, the whole system tends to dissipate because there is a lack of sharp, persistent differences in air mass properties.

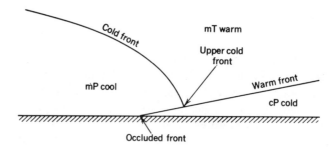

Fig. 5-11 Vertical section of a warm-front occlusion.

MOUNTAIN BARRIERS AND FRONTS

Mountain barriers lying across the path of a moving cyclone tend to induce occlusion by delaying the movement of the cold air in advance of the warm front and by promoting more rapid lifting of the air in the warm sector. The tendency to occlude depends upon the relative stability of the air masses involved. Stable air is dammed more effectively than unstable air, which may become even more unstable when forced up mountain slopes. This phenomenon is common on the west coast of North America, where numerous cyclones occlude as they move against the mountain ranges. When, as is frequently the case, a warm-front occlusion is formed, the moist, unstable air off the ocean moves over the mountain barrier and may continue for some distance to the leeward as an upper cold front,

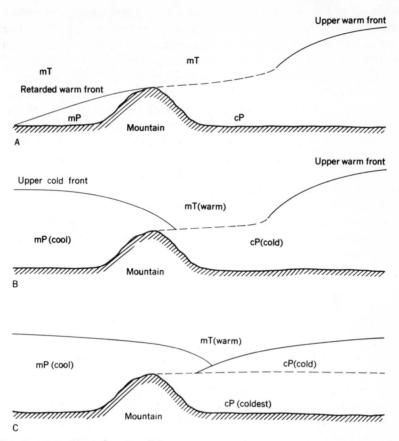

Adapted from Willett, *Descriptive Meteorology,* 1st edition.

Fig. 5-12 Stages in occlusion and formation of upper fronts induced by a mountain barrier.

riding above the cold continental air mass which preceded the original warm front. (See Figure 5–12.)

In addition to retarding the advance of frontal systems, mountains produce greater precipitation on their windward slopes than on the leeward as a result of the orographic effect.

ANTICYCLONES

The term anticyclone implies characteristics opposite those of the cyclone. Barometric pressure is highest at its center and decreases outward. Consequently the anticyclonic wind system blows out from the center, and because of the Coriolis effect it has a clockwise circulation in the Northern Hemisphere (counterclockwise in the Southern Hemisphere). (See Figure

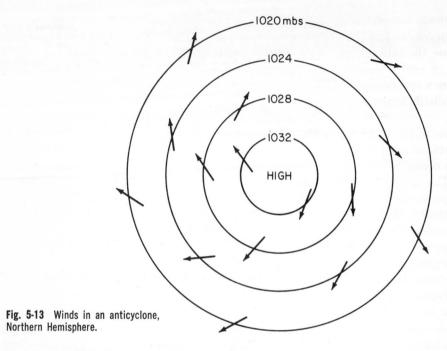

Fig. 5-13 Winds in an anticyclone, Northern Hemisphere.

5–13.) Further, the anticyclone is composed of subsiding air which renders it stable in contrast to cyclones or other low-pressure systems. It does not have fronts or definite wind-shift lines, but a gradual change in wind direction takes place as it passes. Except where surface instability is induced (for example, as the air moves over a warm surface) there is less cloudiness and therefore lack of precipitation in the typical anticyclone. Wind shear, convergence, and frontal activity often develop in the trough of low pressure between two anticyclones, however. (See Figure 5–14.)

In winter in middle and high latitudes anticyclones are essentially synonymous with the source regions of cold stable air masses which invade

Fig. 5-14 Cold front in a trough of low pressure between two adjacent anticyclones, Northern Hemisphere.

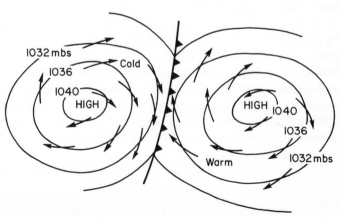

cyclonic systems in the form of cold fronts. These are known as "cold" anticyclones and they are confined to the lower troposphere. Like the cyclone, the anticyclone usually has a pressure pattern represented by circular or oval isobars, but it may assume various shapes. Diameters range from a few hundred to 2000 miles. On the average it travels at a rate appreciably lower than the typical cyclone, but it is even more erratic than the cyclone in its direction. The paths of highs are roughly similar to those of lows across North America except that they do not usually turn northeastward near the Atlantic Coast but proceed more directly out over the ocean.

The anticyclones of the subtropics are associated with the subtropic highs in the general circulation and are warmer than those of the higher latitudes. Their pressure results from the piling up of a great mass of air; subsidence accounts in part for their warmth. Although they tend to be more nearly stationary, portions sometimes break away to move along the margins of the westerlies. They are frequently reinforced by polar anticyclones that merge with them. Because of the difference in temperature between the two, a front may be formed in the trough of lower pressure that separates the high cells before they completely merge. Along their trade-wind margins waves may develop in the pressure pattern, leading to cloudiness and precipitation.

TROPICAL STORMS

Although they have certain features similar to those of mid-latitude storms, tropical disturbances generally do not exhibit sharp discontinuities of temperature. Many have weak pressure gradients and lack well-defined wind systems. Extensive, shallow lows occasionally bring long periods of overcast weather with continuous rain. In the intertropical convergence there may be convective activity and thunderstorms. Convergence tends to increase when the equatorial trough of low pressure moves poleward in summer, producing bands of cumulonimbus clouds and high overcasts of cirrus.

A common feature of tropical weather is the *easterly wave*, which normally forms in the trade winds and moves slowly from east to west. (See Figure 5–15.) Fair weather and divergent winds precede the wave, followed by convergent air flow and an extensive belt of towering clouds that may appear similar to a mid-latitude cold front. Squally weather and precipitation frequently accompany such a disturbance. Some easterly waves move poleward and curve toward the east to become extratropical cyclones. Others may develop vortices, become tropical cyclones, and even grow to hurricane intensity.

The violent and destructive forms of tropical cyclones are much better

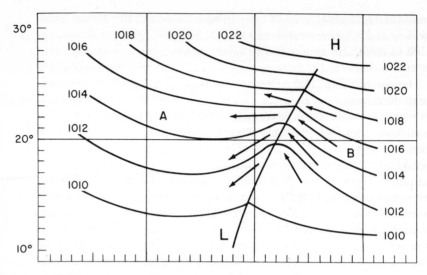

Fig. 5-15 Pressure distribution in an easterly wave in the Northern Hemisphere. Winds blowing from the direction of B converge toward the wave; in the region of A they diverge.

known than the weaker variety although the former are, fortunately, much less common. They originate over the tropical oceans only. In the Caribbean and off the Pacific Coast of Mexico they are known as *hurricanes;* in the seas off China, the Philippines, Japan, and the other islands of the western Pacific they are called *typhoons;* in the Indian Ocean they are simply called *cyclones,* a term which should not be confused with cyclones in general. In the Southern Hemisphere they occur east of the African coast and along the northwest and northeast coasts of Australia. Off northwest Australia the associated strong winds are locally known as *willy-willies.* Elsewhere the term *tropical cyclone* is generally applied. To avoid possible confusion with weak tropical cyclones and the extratropical cyclones, the term *hurricane* will be used in the following paragraphs unless otherwise specified. Hurricanes are apparently absent from the South Atlantic, presumably because the equatorial belt of convergence seldom moves far enough south of the equator in that region.

The energy of a hurricane depends upon an abundance of moisture in warm air along the intertropical convergence. It takes its whirling motion from the Coriolis effect and consequently is most likely to form when the zone of intertropical convergence is located at some distance from the geographic equator, that is, in late summer and autumn. At the equator there is inadequate deflective force to generate the violent whirling motion. Most hurricanes evolve from easterly waves or from weak tropical lows that become charged with warm, moist air and migrate poleward. Off the east coasts of Asia and North America they often move northwestward and then turn away toward the northeast, although the actual paths vary widely and may be erratic. The diameter of the typical hurricane is from 100 to 600 miles and increases as the storm moves away from the low latitudes. Some hurricanes, however, have diameters as small as 25 miles. The size of the disturbance has no direct relation to intensity, and its rate of movement appears to be unrelated to either its size or the wind speeds within the system. An advance of 10 to 20 miles an hour is typical, but hurricanes are erratic in their general rate of progress as well as in direction.

Several features distinguish tropical hurricanes from the cyclones of the mid-latitudes. The pressure distribution, which is represented by isobars, is more nearly concentric and circular and the isobars are closely spaced with very low values at the center, indicating the steep pressure gradient which produces the high velocity winds. (See Figure 5–16.) There are no fronts or wind-shift lines, but at the center of the whirl there may be a calm "eye" 5 to 30 miles in diameter in which air is descending and which, therefore, is comparatively clear and warm. The lack of introduction of contrasting air masses results in fairly even distribution of temperature in all directions from the center. Rainfall is also relatively evenly distributed, especially if the storm is stationary; in a moving hurricane, rainfall is slightly greater in the forward half of the storm. In either case rain is torrential. Because of the tropical nature of the air and the high freezing level in the latitudes of hurricanes, hail does not occur.

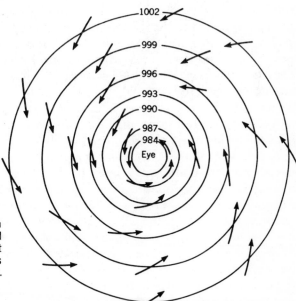

Fig. 5-16 The pressure distribution and winds in a hurricane. Toward the center the pressure gradient becomes steeper and surface winds blow more nearly along the isobars.

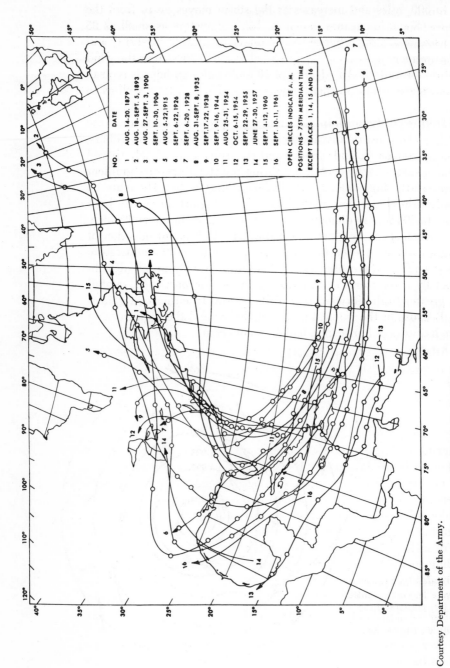

Courtesy Department of the Army.

Fig. 5-17 Paths of some destructive hurricanes in the North Atlantic.

The outstanding feature of the tropical hurricane is the wind force. At the outer edges of the system winds are only moderate, but their velocities increase rapidly toward the center. Technically, wind speed must reach 75 miles per hour to be classified as of hurricane force; speeds of 150 miles per hour have been observed, with gusts estimated as high as 250 miles per hour. The destructiveness of hurricanes is due to extreme wind force, which crushes frame structures, blows over standing objects, and sends huge pieces of debris flying through the air. Heavy rainfall and flooding also cause extensive damage. At sea, hurricanes produce a distinctive heavy swell that affects ocean shipping. Swells in advance of an approaching hurricane come at longer intervals than ordinary storm swells and are one of the most valuable warning signs to mariners because they appear before the winds of the hurricane are encountered. Heavy waves accompanying the hurricane swell can cause coastal damage even while the storm center is well out to sea. As the storm approaches a coast, the piling up of water by strong winds may produce a disastrous "storm tide."

When hurricanes pass inland, frictional effects and the loss of sustaining energy from warm water surfaces cause them to lose much of their force. Although of interest to the meteorologist, this phenomenon may be a small consolation to people in the affected region. Over land the hurricane often draws in air from poleward sources and may suddenly transform into an extratropical cyclone.

As a matter of convenience for tracking the paths of hurricanes in the western Atlantic and typhoons in the Pacific, the weather services use feminine names to designate the storms alphabetically as they are discovered.

THUNDERSTORMS

Thunderstorms are the most common kind of storm on earth; several thousand occur every day, mainly in the tropics. In polar regions they are virtually unknown. They are always associated with unstable air and strong vertical air currents, and, therefore, their cloud formations are of the cumulonimbus type. It is important to remember in this connection that an unstable lapse rate and overturning of air may result from either warming of surface layers or introduction of cold air aloft.

According to their origin, thunderstorms are classified broadly as *air mass* or *frontal* types. In both types a great deal of the energy for development comes from the release of the latent heat of condensation in rising humid air. Air mass thunderstorms may be produced by (a) heating and convection in moist air over a warm land surface; (b) passage of cold, moist air over warm water; (c) forced ascent of conditionally unstable air at mountain barriers; or (d) radiational cooling at upper levels. Moisture and rising air are the essentials for any thunderstorm. When the force of rising air is great enough, the storm can reach heights from 12,000 to over 60,000 feet. Cooling takes place at the dry adiabatic rate up to the base of the clouds and continues to be rapid as dry air is entrained in the violent updrafts. Inertia in the convective "chimney" may carry the air beyond the level where equilibrium is established between the convective mass and the surrounding upper air. The height of a thunderstorm is related to latitude and the season, greatest heights being developed in summer and in the tropics. Average diameters of thunderstorms vary from 5 to 25 miles. A well-developed cumulonimbus thunderhead has an anvil-shaped cirrus top which points in the direction of movement of the storm, and there are often shelves of clouds extending out in advance of the main thunderhead. Along its base the storm is dark and ominous and it may be preceded by a roll cloud, or *squall line*, created by air currents moving in opposing directions. Precipitation from the mature storm is characteristically heavy and composed of large drops of rain, literally a cloudburst. If the updrafts have sufficient force and penetrate well above the freezing level, hail may fall from the cloud, usually along its leading edge. Where the temperature conditions are favorable, snow or snow pellets can occur, although they are not common.

Thunderstorms caused by surface heating over land are most common in summer and in the afternoon or early evening. Over the oceans the temperature difference between the water and the cooler air ·above is greatest at night, and thunderstorm activity resulting from this cause is accordingly greatest at night. Over mountains the maximum occurrence is usually in the afternoon or early evening, when the combined effects of daytime heating and orographic lifting are at a maximum.

Frontal thunderstorms develop when air is forced up rapidly in zones of air mass convergence. They may be associated with the cold front, warm front, or upper fronts and are often accentuated by surface heating or orographic lifting. Those which form along the cold front are generally closer to the ground and more violent than the warm or upper-front types. In contrast with air mass thunderstorms, which tend to be spotted about in an erratic pattern, the frontal types are concentrated in a zone 15 to 50 miles in width and perhaps hundreds of miles in length. Because the upper portions of the cumulonimbus clouds are frequently obscured by lower clouds, frontal thunderstorms are difficult to identify. Pilots flying at high altitudes have some advantage in this respect. A line of air mass thunderstorms along the crest of a mountain range should not be confused with frontal thunderstorms, although it does represent convergence of air above ridges and peaks.

For purposes of meteorological observation and records, thunder must be heard at a station before a thunderstorm is reported. While thunder

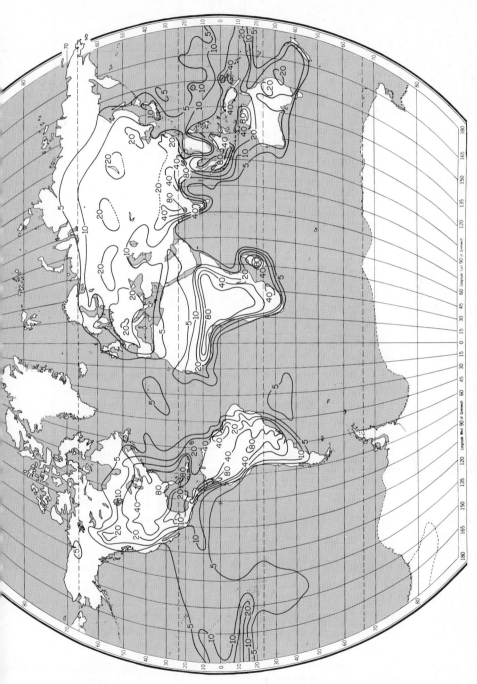

After Berry, Bollay, and Beers, *Handbook of Meteorology*. Van der Grinten projection, courtesy A. J. Nystrom & Co., Chicago.

Fig. 5-18 Mean annual number of days with thunderstorms in the world.

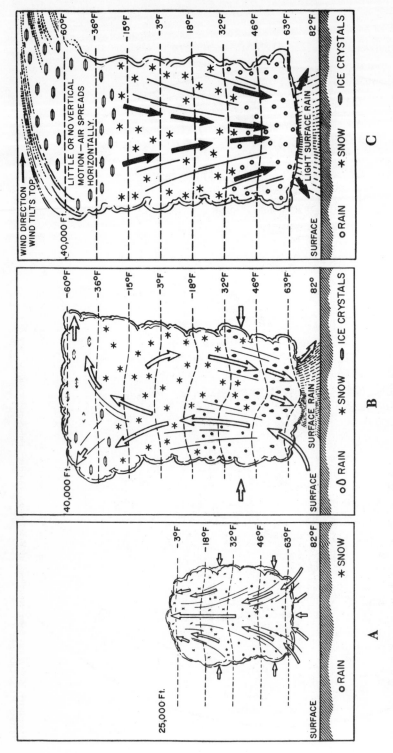

Fig. 5-19 Evolution of a thunderstorm. A—early (cumulus) stage; B—mature stage; C—Dissipating stage.

and lightning are associated with the typical thunderstorm and are often its most dramatic manifestations, they are in no way responsible for the development of the storm. Lightning results from the discharge of static electricity which is formed as drops of water are broken apart violently in rapid air currents. The discharge may take pace from cloud to cloud horizontally, between different levels in the cloud, or from the base of the cloud to the ground. In the latter case the "strike" can be fatal to persons and animals and it is especially dangerous as a cause of fires. Airplanes in flight occasionally suffer severe damage to the fuselage and radio equipment when struck, and pilots may be temporarily blinded by the flash unless they take special precautions. Thunder is the explosive sound created as the air expands suddenly with the great heat of the lightning discharge and then cools and contracts rapidly. Although it is often even more awesome than the lightning flash, it is not dangerous in itself.

TORNADOES AND WATERSPOUTS

Tornadoes are the most violent storms of the mid-latitudes. In the central United States they are sometimes mistakenly called cyclones, but should not be confused with the larger and much less violent extratropical cyclone. Another local name, *twister,* is more appropriate. The tornado consists of a tight cyclonic whirl (that is, counterclockwise in the Northern Hemisphere) around a center of extremely low pressure. Accurate wind observations are impossible in this maelstrom, but velocities of 200 to 300 miles per hour are probably common. A tornado can be distinguished by its writhing, funnel-shaped cloud, which extends downward from the base of a cumulonimbus or a turbulent cloud layer. If it reaches the ground, unbelievable destruction is suffered by anything in its path. Buildings seem to explode as a result of the wind force and the sudden decrease of outside pressure. A tornado which travelled through Missouri, Illinois, and Indiana on March 18, 1925, caused 689 deaths and property losses estimated at $16.5 million. Most tornadoes are only a few hundred yards in diameter at the ground, but widths of one or two miles have been recorded. They are formed in the warm sector of cyclonic systems just ahead of the cold front where cold air is overrunning aloft and sometimes along leading edges of intense thunderstorms. They are accompanied by thunderstorm activity, rain or hail, and lightning. Their cause is presumably a wind-shift discontinuity and abnormally strong convective turbulence. Paths of tornadoes are ordinarily parallel to the cold front and toward the center of low pressure, that is, from the southwest to northeast in the United States. This rule has exceptions, however, for tornadoes have been observed to make U-turns and even complete circles. Their rate of travel may reach 60 miles per hour or more or they may sometimes be stationary

Photos by Airman 1st Class Cecil W. Nichols, courtesy Air Weather Service.

Fig. 5-20 Stages in the development of a tornado at Shepard Air Force Base, Texas, on April 3, 1964.

for short periods. Tornadoes have been known to make contact with the ground and then lift, only to strike again several miles away. And, again, one may travel only a few yards before rising and dissipating. One of the longest paths on record is that of the tornado on May 26, 1917, which travelled from Louisiana, Missouri, for 293 miles to the east boundary of Jennings County, Indiana.

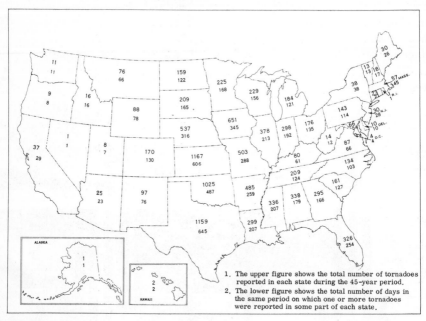

1. The upper figure shows the total number of tornadoes reported in each state during the 45-year period.
2. The lower figure shows the total number of days in the same period on which one or more tornadoes were reported in some part of each state.

Courtesy U.S. Weather Bureau.

Fig. 5-21   Tornado frequency by states, 1916–1960.

In the United States the greatest frequency of tornadoes is in the valleys of the Mississippi, Ohio, and lower Missouri Rivers, but they also occur in the Gulf States, Great Plains, and western Lake States. Indeed, every state in the contiguous United States has experienced tornadoes. (See Figure 5–21.) They are most likely to occur in spring and early summer, when contrasts of temperature and humidity in the air masses along cold fronts are at a maximum.

Tornadoes are comparatively rare in the rest of the world. One was sighted at Yellowknife, N.W.T., Canada, (Lat. 62° 28′N.), on June 19, 1962. Others have been reported in Japan, Australia, New Zealand, and West Africa.

At sea, tornadoes are known as *waterspouts*. They have much the same characteristics except that they are usually smaller in diameter. Frequency of occurrence is greatest where cold continental air pushes over warm water, as off the east coasts of the United States, China, and Japan. When in contact with the surface a waterspout picks up some spray, but its funnel is composed primarily of condensed water vapor in the low-pressure core. Along an embayed coast it is perfectly possible for a waterspout to move alternately over water and land surfaces, changing technically from waterspout to tornado.

In tropical waters, another type of waterspout is common in fair weather. Convection of warm, moist air and the resultant release of the latent heat of condensation lead to a small whirlwind which builds from the surface upward. Being little affected by deflective force it may whirl in either direction. It moves slowly as a rule and is not dangerous to large ocean vessels.

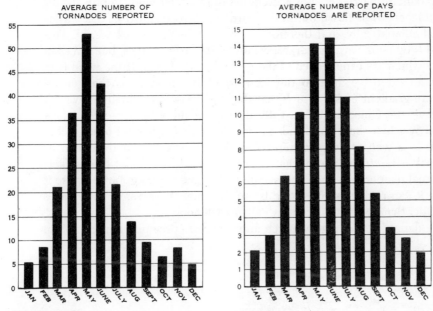

Courtesy U.S. Weather Bureau.

Fig. 5-22 Tornado frequency by months in the United States, 1916–1960.

SPECIAL AIR MASS AND STORM EFFECTS

There are a number of weather phenomena which do not possess the dramatic features generally considered to belong to storms and which are not accompanied directly by precipitation. Yet they incorporate distinctive "weather," and a few are referred to as storms, at least locally.

Perhaps the best-known of these phenomena is the *foehn effect,* which produces a warm, dry, and often gusty wind on the lee side of mountain ranges. The name *foehn* originated in Austria and Germany, where the foehn wind is frequently experienced on the north side of the Alps. In the western United States and Canada the same type of mountain-induced effect is called the *Chinook.* The explanation of the relative warmth of the typical Chinook rests upon two principles. Ordinarily a Chinook wind is accompanied by cyclonic activity which produces clouds and precipitation on the windward side of the mountain range (for example, the Rockies). The latent heat released to the air by the condensation process warms the air which passes across the range, and, because the air has lost some of its moisture, it will also be drier. However, the latent heat of condensation alone does not account for the temperatures which occur on the leeward. The mountain barrier creates a frictional drag which tends to pull the air from higher levels down on the leeward. Air forced down in this way is heated adiabatically, and therefore its relative humidity is lowered. This action is by no means regular, especially in its earlier stages, but comes in surges which are experienced at the ground as gustiness. If the wind is to affect an extensive area to the leeward of the mountains the general pressure gradient must be such that the cold air will gradually move out ahead of the Chinook. When fully developed the Chinook can remove snow cover in a short time, and it is in winter that it is most often recognized. It is well to keep in mind that the temperature of the foehn or Chinook is *relatively* warm, that is, it replaces colder air at the surface. Its actual temperature may occasionally be below freezing, but because it is dry it can remove snow or ice by sublimation; however, if it replaces air colder than itself, it is properly called a Chinook.

The danger of lending too much importance to precipitation and to the

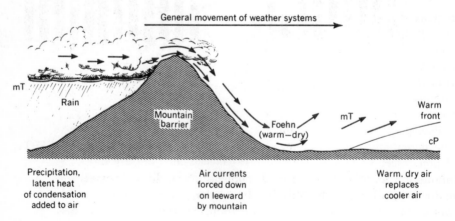

Fig. 5-23 Typical conditions which produce a foehn wind.

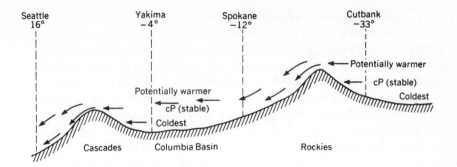

Fig. 5-24 Stable-air foehn induced by mountain barriers.

release of the latent heat of condensation on windward slopes as the cause of the foehn wind can best be illustrated by examining the *stable-air foehn effect.* Consider a mass of cold stable air moving against a mountain range, as might happen in winter when a polar air mass out of Canada travels along the eastern margin of the Rockies. (See Figure 5–24.) It is a characteristic of stable air that in its upper levels the air is potentially warmer, that is, if the upper air is brought down to lower altitudes it will be warmed adiabatically to temperatures greater than the surrounding air in the mass. When stable air lies against a mountain barrier it is this potentially warmer air which spills over. It warms as it descends, and, in the lowlands, has somewhat warmer temperatures than the surface air in the parent air mass. West of the Rockies it will normally replace warmer air and will therefore be experienced as a cold wave in contrast to the Chinook. Nevertheless, the temperatures on the west side of the barrier are not so low as those on the east. The stable-air foehn effect may be re-induced subsequently by the Cascade Range so that that portion of the cold air mass which reaches the Pacific Coast is further warmed. In making regional comparisons of temperature under such conditions it is, of course, necessary to take into account the different altitudes involved and the residual heat of the surface west of the mountains. Both tend to accentuate the temperature differences, although they can hardly be considered a part of the stable-air foehn effect.

In summer the stable-air foehn functions in the opposite direction along the Pacific Coast of North America. The relatively stable air blowing out of the Pacific high cell moves against the coastal ranges and the Cascades and the potentially warmer air of the higher levels crosses the barriers first. Upon descending on the lee side, it is warmed adiabatically and thus contributes to the higher temperatures of the interior.

The foehn wind unquestionably occurs in many mountainous areas of the world, but is best known and most easily recognized where high mountain chains lie approximately at right angles to prevailing winds.

Similarly, the stable-air foehn effect requires the proper juxtaposition of a mountain barrier and a stable air mass.

A large group of so-called storms are the *dust storms* of dry climates and drought-stricken areas. They are often actually associated with true storm conditions, for example, a mid-latitude cyclone, but all too rarely are they accompanied by subsequent precipitation. Dust storms result from the action of strong winds in picking up loose earth material and carrying it to great heights and perhaps for great distances as well. During the drought years of the early 1930's, dust storms ravaged a large area of the Great Plains of the United States as well as central Australia. Millions of tons of dust are transported by such storms. In desert regions, where there is little protective cover, dust or sand storms are common when sustained high velocity winds blow.

The much smaller *dust-devil,* or *whirlwind,* is an eddy that forms over hot, dry land as a result of intense local daytime convection and surface friction. It is a fair-weather phenomenon identified by the whirling column of dust, usually not more than a few yards in diameter and a few hundred feet in height. Ordinarily the dust-devil is not destructive, but it moves loose trash and is unpleasant for anyone caught in its path. Its whirling eddy of air operates on a small scale and may turn in either direction in response to the conflicting air currents that set it in motion. Dust-devils probably form in a manner similar to fair-weather waterspouts, but lacking the added energy due to condensation, they are generally somewhat smaller.

Electrical storm is a term applied variously to the lightning associated with thunderstorms and to disturbances in the outer atmosphere which affect radio transmission. The latter are frequently caused by displays of the aurora borealis or aurora australis, which in turn seem to show increased activity with the appearance of sunspots in great numbers. Their effect upon meteorological conditions in the troposphere is not fully understood, but they are believed to influence temperature, pressure, and winds in the stratosphere.

STORM AND AIR MASS OBSERVATIONS

A great deal of the information of value in forecasting weather and for climatic records comes from general storm observations. Details of temperature, pressure, humidity, wind, cloudiness, and so on, are essentially the symptoms of the storms; it is their peculiar combination that constitutes a specific disturbance. It is one thing to measure directly the various weather elements but quite another to undertake objective observation of an entire storm. Knowledge of areal extent, height, speed of movement, and intensity is desirable, however. Of these, intensity is the most difficult to express in quantitative terms. In connection with storm research, indices combining two or more measured quantities, such as wind force and rate of precipitation, have been established.

Radar storm-detection techniques make it possible to track clouds and precipitation at distances of 200 miles or more, and even to discern the size of water droplets or ice particles in the air. As a result, storms can be followed continuously and their evolution traced over areas where satisfactory ground observations are lacking.

Another adaptation of radio to storm observations is *spherics* (from *atmospherics*), a technique used in the detection and tracking of storms accompanied by electrical phenomena, thunderstorms in particular. Two or more stations about 100 miles apart are equipped with directional antennas and receivers which register the direction of electrical discharges. By means of triangulation the location of an electrical discharge can be determined. Spherics observations are especially useful in locating frontal thunderstorms that are otherwise obscured by cloud layers.

An obvious but expensive—and often dangerous—method of storm and air mass observation is aerial reconnaissance. Flights into the upper air often reveal a general storm or an air mass which is not evident from isolated radiosonde and winds-aloft reports. Furthermore, the flight path can

Fig. 5-25   Image of a hurricane on a radar storm-detection receiver.

Courtesy U.S. Weather Bureau.

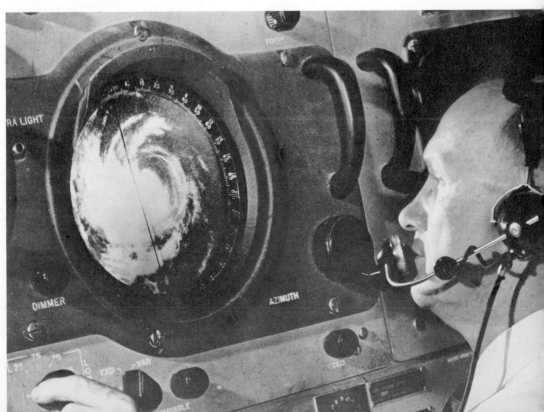

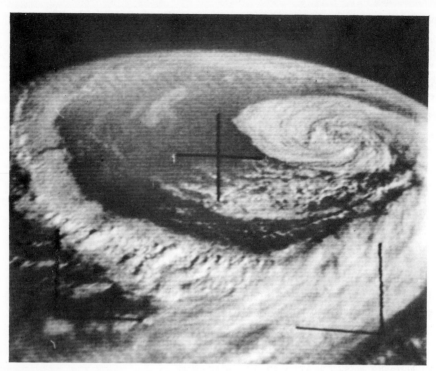

Courtesy U.S. Weather Bureau, Meteorological Satellite Laboratory.

Fig. 5-26 Spiraling cloud formations of an occluded cyclone over the North Atlantic southeast of Nova Scotia, photographed by TIROS VI on May 29, 1963. The top of the picture is toward the northwest. Note counter-clockwise circulation.

be altered to correspond to the location of a storm, and successive flights can follow the storm—an impossible maneuver for either ground stations or ground-based radiosondes. Instrumental and visual observations along weather reconnaissance routes have been especially valuable in weather research and forecasting. In both the Atlantic and Pacific areas, hurricanes (or typhoons) have been studied by means of airplane flights into the storms. Strong aircraft and careful navigation are necessary in the reconnaissance of a hurricane, but the information gained aids in forecasting the future path of the storm as well as in understanding the general principles which govern hurricanes. Weather planes are elaborately equipped with meteorological instruments, including radarscopes. Some planes periodically release *dropsondes* to obtain data on conditions in the air below the flight level. The principle of the dropsonde is the same as that of the radiosonde except that it is let down on a parachute instead of being carried aloft by a balloon, and the receiver is in the airplane.

Rockets and satellites, providing information from ever-greater heights,

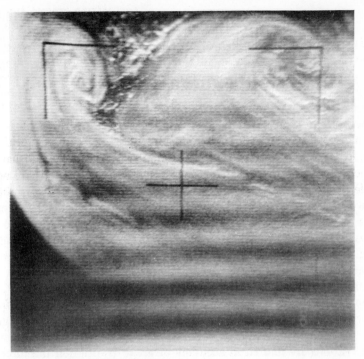

Courtesy U.S. Weather Bureau, Meteorological Satellite Laboratory.

Fig. 5-27 Two cyclonic systems photographed by TIROS V weather satellite over the far southern Indian Ocean on July 27, 1962. The pattern of clockwise circulation is indicated by the spiraling cloud formations. Centers of the two systems were about 450 miles apart and at approximately 55° S. latitude.

have opened up a new range of possibilities in storm observation. Satellites incorporating television and radar that can scan the atmosphere regularly from above furnish data on the extent and movement of storm centers as well as on certain associated phenomena. When the National Aeronautics and Space Administration launched *Nimbus* into a polar orbit in 1964 it became possible to photograph all parts of the earth twice daily. Satellite photographs show primarily the earth's cloud cover, which is interpreted by *nephanalysis* (cloud analysis) to follow the development of storms and indicate features of the atmospheric circulation. Weather satellites also have great potential in the measurement of radiation, albedo of the earth and cloud surfaces, and the extent of ice and snow cover, all of which have a direct bearing upon weather and climate. Rockets equipped with radiosonde instruments extend the range of upper-air observation considerably beyond that of conventional balloon ascents and thereby provide data at levels intermediate between the latter and satellites.

FORECASTING STORMS AND THEIR WEATHER

Two fundamental problems are encountered in weather forecasting. One is to forecast the movement of air masses and evolving storm systems; the other is to forecast the weather changes that will be associated with them as they travel and are modified by such factors as interaction along fronts or the surface over which they move. Certain air mass and storm types tend to typify the climate of a given region, perhaps with seasonal regularity. Knowledge of such facts constitutes the climatological aspect of forecasting. To cite an extreme example, hurricanes would hardly be expected over northern Canada. Where more direct methods are not possible, it is frequently useful to calculate the probability of certain types of weather on the basis of their occurrence in the past. Specific determination of what may be expected of a particular storm system in the future is based on developments in the immediate past and on the existing situation. Thus, the forecaster depends heavily upon accurate observations of weather at as many locations and for as many upper-air levels as are feasible. He must make an analysis of the current situation before he can prepare a prognosis. The observational data are plotted on maps and charts to enable him to "see" the prevailing weather over a large area and to estimate future movements and modifications. To the extent that observations are limited in accuracy or areal distribution the forecaster's task will be more difficult and his forecasts more subject to error. The absence of adequate coverage over the oceans causes large "blind spots" which hamper weather analysis. However, it must not be concluded that forecasts arise magically from an assemblage of observations. Whereas the observer's tools are his weather instruments, the forecaster's tools are maps, charts, diagrams, and mathematical formulae which aid in the analysis of weather patterns and their projection into the future. Especially in the middle latitudes, these tools are designed with two main principles as guides: (a) weather systems travel in the general circulation, and (b) weather processes act in three dimensions.

THE WEATHER MAP

The basic map for display of weather data is the *synoptic weather chart*, which shows the surface distribution of weather elements for a given time. That is, it gives a synopsis of the weather situation. The scale and area covered by the map depend on its intended use. Short-period forecasts for small areas can usually be made from maps covering an area only slightly larger than that included in the forecast. Sectional maps of this type for the local area are commonly used to supplement the larger synoptic map. Forecasts for a large area (such as a continent) or for a longer period require maps that extend well beyond the area in question, preferably to encompass en entire hemisphere.

Synoptic observations are taken simultaneously at many stations throughout the world by agreement through the World Meteorological Organization. Times for these observations are 0000, 0600, 1200, and 1800 Greenwich Mean Time. In addition, many airway stations take hourly observations which aid in making short-period forecasts for flights as well as in more detailed analysis of trends in the weather. Collection of weather data at forecasting stations requires efficient communications, including telephone, telegraph, teletype, radio, and radioteletype. Because a great deal of information must be transmitted in a short time, the observations are sent in the form of a numerical code known as the World Meteorological Organization Code. A sample coded message is shown in Figure 5-28. At the forecasting center the coded messages are decoded

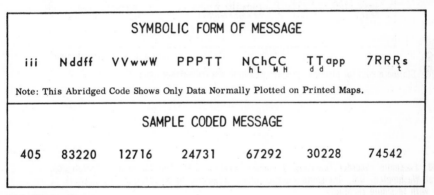

Courtesy U.S. Weather Bureau.

Fig. 5-28 Symbolic form of synoptic weather message and sample coded message.

and the data are plotted on the synoptic map as figures and symbols around the proper station circles. At the National Meteorological Center, Suitland, Maryland, computers and automatic plotting devices translate synoptic data directly onto maps, thus reducing the amount of hand plotting that would otherwise be necessary.

On the plotted map the analyst draws in lines to represent fronts, and isobars to indicate pressure distribution. Precipitation areas are shaded, and isotherms or other special information may be added. Other aids to forecasting, such as abbreviations of air mass types, are entered on the map after reference to upper-air charts. Since coded observations normally come in from nearby areas first and it may be two hours or more before data from distant stations are available, the analysis of a part of the map begins, ordinarily, even before all map data have been received and

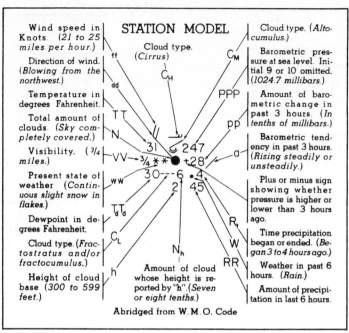

Fig. 5-29 Station model for plotting synoptic weather data on weather maps.

STATION MODEL

Wind speed in Knots. (21 to 25 miles per hour.) — ff

Direction of wind. (Blowing from the northwest.) — dd

Temperature in degrees Fahrenheit. — TT

Total amount of clouds. (Sky completely covered.) — N

Visibility. (3/4 miles.) — VV

Present state of weather (Continuous slight snow in flakes.) — ww

Dewpoint in degrees Fahrenheit. — T_dT_d

Cloud type. (Fractostratus and/or fractocumulus.) — C_L

Height of cloud base (300 to 599 feet.) — h

Cloud type. (Cirrus) — C_H

Amount of cloud whose height is reported by "h". (Seven or eight tenths.) — N_h

Cloud type. (Altocumulus.) — C_M

Barometric pressure at sea level. Initial 9 or 10 omitted. (1024.7 millibars.) — PPP

Amount of barometric change in past 3 hours. (In tenths of millibars.) — pp

Barometric tendency in past 3 hours. (Rising steadily or unsteadily.) — a

Plus or minus sign showing whether pressure is higher or lower than 3 hours ago.

Time precipitation began or ended. (Began 3 to 4 hours ago.) — R_t

Weather in past 6 hours. (Rain.) — W

Amount of precipitation in last 6 hours. — RR

Plotted values: 31, 247, +28, 3/4 ** , 30, -6, .4, 2, 45

Abridged from W. M. O. Code

Courtesy U.S. Weather Bureau.

Fig. 5-30 Facsimile recorder receiving a surface weather map. The National Meteorological Center at Washington, D.C., transmits weather charts regularly to an international network of stations with facsimile recorders.
Courtesy Muirhead Instruments, Inc.

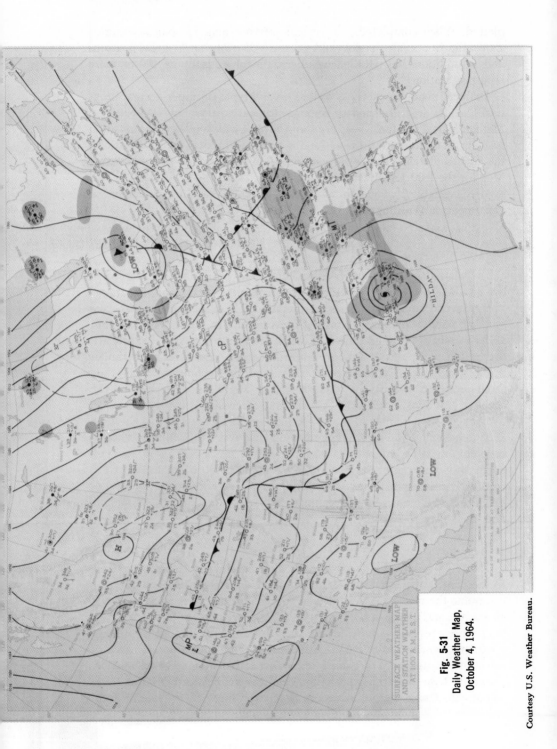

Fig. 5-31
Daily Weather Map,
October 4, 1964.

Courtesy U.S. Weather Bureau.

plotted. When completed, the typical weather map for North America shows the fronts, air masses, and pressure distribution as gross features and, in addition, has detailed weather data for as many as 400 or more reporting stations.

Analyzed synoptic charts as well as several types of upper-air and prognostic charts are furnished to regional forecast centers by the National Meteorological Center. These are transmitted by facsimile communication systems. In addition to these and maps prepared at local forecast stations, the United States Weather Bureau publishes an abridged *Daily Weather Map* for the 1:00 A.M. Eastern Standard Time synoptic observations. This map is available by mail to subscribers through the Superintendent of Documents in Washington, D.C. (See Figure 5–31.)

AIR MASS ANALYSIS AND AUXILIARY CHARTS

The plotted synoptic chart shows conditions primarily as observed at the ground. In order to provide a more complete picture of the atmosphere, several additional charts are prepared. These include vertical cross sections, winds-aloft maps, constant-pressure charts, lapse rate diagrams, and a variety of other graphic aids which are adapted to specific forecasting problems. Upper-air data are transmitted in a numerical code similar in structure to the synoptic code. Details of the techniques of plotting these data on the charts and analyzing their significance are beyond the scope of this book. Suffice it to say that the forecaster is eager to have all the aids he can assemble and bring to bear on his forecast within the time limit imposed by the forecast deadline. Many types of information have been combined experimentally with the aim of improving upon air mass and weather analysis and the subsequent forecasts. Meteorologists are constantly seeking mathematical relationships between air mass properties and weather as a basis for more objective forecasting.

THE FORECAST

The actual weather forecast is made after careful consideration of both surface and upper air charts. Computations and estimates are made to determine the rate of movement and future position of pressure systems, air masses, and fronts as well as the associated weather. A forecaster with long experience in a certain locality may become quite adept at judging a synoptic situation and making a somewhat subjective forecast. To this extent forecasting may be considered an art rather than an exact science. However, basic research on the physics of the air is improving the methods of calculation. Recent advances have been made in the use of high-speed electronic computers to digest and analyze large quantities of information and thereby furnish a basis for the forecast more rapidly.

One school of forecasting theory makes use of weather maps which show synoptic situations in the past that are analogous to the current situation. These maps are called *analogs*. Daily surface maps are available for the United States for the period since 1899, comprising almost 70 years of "memory" even for the inexperienced forecaster. For use in the analog system of forecasting they are classified into weather types in much the same way that fingerprint files are cataloged for efficient reference. The forecaster can quickly select the historical weather sequence which is most similar to the sequence he is working on and can study the succession of weather on the analog maps to see how the analogous situation developed in the past. Because no two synoptic situations are exactly alike, it has been found more fruitful to compare weather sequences or series rather than single maps. Furthermore, similar synoptic situations are not necessarily followed by the same weather patterns; it is up to the forecaster to weigh all the facts at his command to determine what nuances to expect in the current pattern.

The analog technique can also be employed with upper-air charts, but the historical files of upper-air data do not cover nearly as long a period as do surface maps. The accumulation of data for more stations and at higher altitudes makes upper air analogs increasingly valuable as forecasting aids.

Forecasts by the United States Weather Bureau are designed to serve as many interests as possible. They include information on expected storm and air mass movements, temperature, precipitation, cloudiness, wind, and special phenomena. Special forecasts are issued for violent storms such as hurricanes or tornadoes and for abnormally great weather changes. Forecasting for aviation and industry entails concentrated attention to one or more weather elements. For example, the airline pilot will be greatly concerned about upper winds or visibility, and, at the same time, the construction engineer or the fruit grower will be worried about possible freezing temperatures at the surface. In order to serve their "clients," both the government and private forecasters must prepare and issue forecasts as soon as possible after observational data have been received. Hours of study and calculations are worthwhile in research but in practical forecasting the results might not be available until the "forecast" had become a "hindcast."

With respect to time covered, forecasts may be divided into short-term forecasts for 24 to 72 hours, extended-period forecasts for several days to a month in advance, and long-range forecasts covering several months or even a year. Twice monthly the Extended Forecast Section of the U.S.

Weather Bureau publishes an *Average Monthly Weather Resume and Outlook,* commonly referred to as the "30-day forecast." The longer the forecast period the more complex is the forecaster's problem. Long-range weather forecasting merges into climatological forecasting, which will be discussed in Chapter 16.

ADDITIONAL READINGS

Atlas, David, "Indirect Probing Techniques," *Bull. Am. Met. Soc.,* 43, 9 (1962), 457–66.

Battan, Louis J., *The Nature of Violent Storms.* New York: Anchor Books, Doubleday & Company, Inc., 1961.

Cook, A. W., and A. G. Topil, "Some Examples of Chinooks East of the Mountains in Colorado," *Bull. Am. Met. Soc.,* 33, 2 (1952), 42–47.

Flora, Snowden D., *Tornadoes of the United States.* Norman: University of Oklahoma Press, 1953.

————, *Hailstorms of the United States.* Norman: University of Oklahoma Press, 1956.

Malkus, Joanne, "The Origin of Hurricanes," *Scient. Am.,* 197, 2 (1957), 33–39.

Myers, Robert F., "Vertical Soundings of the Atmosphere," *Bull. Am. Met. Soc.,* 43, 9 (1962), 467–74.

Nordberg, W., and Harry Press, "The Nimbus I Meteorological Satellite," *Bull. Am. Met. Soc.,* 45, 11 (1964), 684–687.

Petterssen, Sverre, *Weather Analysis and Forecasting,* 2nd ed., Vol. I, Motion and Motion Systems. Vol. II, Weather and Weather Systems. New York: McGraw-Hill Book Company, 1956.

Riehl, Herbert, "On the Origin and Possible Modification of Hurricanes," *Science,* 141, 3585 (1963), 1001–1010.

Tepper, Morris, "Tornadoes," *Scient. Am.,* 198, 5 (1958), 31–37.

part two

CLIMATES

OF

THE

WORLD

climatic 6
classification

The many variations in climate from place to place, as determined by different combinations of atmospheric processes, produce a correspondingly large number of climatic types. An area of the earth's surface over which the combined effects of climatic factors result in an approximately homogeneous set of climatic conditions, that is, a climatic type, is termed a climatic region. In order to facilitate description and mapping of climatic regions it is necessary to identify and classify the respective types. Regional climatology is concerned with this task and makes use of analytical and descriptive techniques in its search for order in the world climatic pattern.

APPROACHES TO THE CLASSIFICATION OF CLIMATE

There are numerous possible classifications of climate, for classification is a product of human ingenuity rather than a natural phenomenon. The value of a systematic arrangement of climates is determined largely by the purpose for which it is intended; a system that suits one purpose is not necessarily useful for another. For example, a classification based on the critical values of temperature and moisture for growth of a certain plant or animal organism might be satisfactory for detailed biological study, but it might not meet the requirements of weather forecasting, which is more concerned with factors such as the general circulation, storm types, or weather probabilities. Any of

145

the elements of climate can be used singly or in combination to establish criteria for climatic types. Relationships expressing the adequacy of heat and moisture have dominated climatic classification, although all elements are inherently significant in describing climate. Thornthwaite has stated that the purpose of climatic classification is to provide a concise description of the climatic types in terms of the truly active factors, primarily moisture and heat.* Other factors, such as wind, sunshine, or pressure changes are conceivably the active factors for specialized purposes.

A complete classification of climate should provide a system of pyramiding categories, ranging from the many microclimates of exceedingly small areas, through macroclimatic types, to major divisions on a world scale. But the description of world climates is not easily accomplished as the summation of a great number of microclimates, nor are microclimates readily fitted into the pattern of major world climatic regions.

In order to achieve objectivity in defining the categories of a system it is useful to have quantitative measurements of the climatic elements. To a large extent the selection must be made from available records. The lack of adequate records with respect both to periods covered and to world-wide distribution has presented a serious obstacle. There are more than 100,000 surface weather-observing stations of all types in the world, but they are by no means evenly distributed, and many record only one or two climatic elements during short or irregular periods. Although 3500 ships take meteorological observations that are of great value in weather forecasting, the transient nature of these stations limits the use of their records for climatological analyses. The small number of stationary weather ships in the North Atlantic and North Pacific provide only a token climatic record for huge expanses of water. This is a primary reason why so little has been done in the identification and mapping of climates over the oceans.

An "individual" climate is the synthesis of all the climatic elements in a unique combination resulting from interrelated climatic processes. Factors that determine atmospheric conditions may be used in classification, but the causes of climate are infinitely more difficult to measure than are the elements, and in many cases our understanding of their effects is still theoretical. Ideally, however, the criteria employed in the differentiation of climatic types should reflect the causes of climate if climatology is to be explanatory as well as descriptive. The ancient Greeks recognized a relationship between latitude and temperature and devised a system of *klima*, or zones (torrid, temperate, and frigid), that have persisted in writings to the present day. However, we know that net radiation does not vary

---

* C. W. Thornthwaite, "Problems in the Classification of Climates," *Geog. Rev.*, 33, 2 (April, 1943), 233–55.

solely with latitude and that other factors affect the distribution of temperature.

Outstanding among modern attempts at climatic classification are those of biologists and natural historians, who have sought a systematic relationship between climatic factors and the world pattern of vegetation. Natural vegetation integrates the effects of climate better than any instrument that has so far been designed, and it is thus an index of climatic conditions. By referring to the major plant associations, biologists have tried to determine the climatic factors that correspond with areal differences in vegetation. Numerous correlations between vegetation and heat or moisture factors have been discovered, permitting the use of temperature or moisture indices as criteria for climatic types. The resulting types and their regional boundaries approach reality in terms of the associated vegetation, while retaining a climatic basis. Commonly, classifications of this kind employ vegetation terms. Rain forest, desert, steppe, and tundra are names that have a climatic connotation. In each case there are climatic limits beyond which the characteristic plant association (or a specific indicator species) does not occur naturally. Fluctuations in climate lead to problems in the delineation of boundaries, however.

An improvement upon the use of simple rainfall or temperature limits in climatic classification recognizes the relationship between heat and moisture factors. Under high temperatures plants require more precipitation to meet the needs of evapotranspiration. Ten inches of rainfall annually may support but little plant life in a hot, tropical desert, but that amount may be sufficient for coniferous forest in the cool higher latitudes. Thus natural vegetation is an expression of the adequacy of moisture under a given set of temperature conditions. Precipitation–evaporation ratios and the concept of potential evapotranspiration have been introduced to indicate this more complex relationship and establish criteria for climatic types. Variability and seasonal distribution of precipitation and temperature are additional factors which influence plant growth and must be taken into account in any classification that derives from climate-vegetation relationships.

Human health and comfort suggest another possible approach to defining climatic types, with potential applications in clothing design, housing, physiology, and medicine.* In much the same way that heat and moisture data are used to determine critical boundaries for natural vegetation or crops, optimum and limiting values of climatic elements afford a basis for classification in terms of human response. Everyone is aware that the reaction of the body to a given air temperature is conditioned by wind,

* W. J. Maunder, "A Human Classification of Climate," *Weather*, 17, 1 (Jan., 1962), 3–12.

humidity, and sunshine. An individual's state of health, emotional outlook, style of clothing, degree of acclimatization, and a host of other factors also influence personal reaction to climate. One's own reaction to a climate is perhaps a satisfactory basis for a "personal" classification, but as a scientific approach to the problem it is attended by great complexity. The human body appears to be a far less dependable instrument for integrating climatic elements than is a plant. Nevertheless, there have been fruitful studies in the field of applied climatology which have related climate to health, clothing, diet, etc. Maps which show the regional distribution of such relationships are in effect very specialized climatic classifications.

Some knowledge of the common classifications of climate is necessary for an understanding of the methods and objectives of regional climatology. The more widely used systems are outlined in the following sections.

KOEPPEN'S CLASSIFICATION

The most used system of classification in its original form or with modifications is that of Wladimir Koeppen (1846–1940), a German biologist who devoted most of his life to climatic problems. Koeppen aimed at a scheme which would relate climate to vegetation but would provide an objective, numerical basis for defining climatic types in terms of climatic elements. Using the world vegetation map of de Candolle, a French plant physiologist, he devised his first classification (1900) largely on the basis of vegetation zones and later (1918) revised it with greater attention to temperature, rainfall, and their seasonal characteristics.

The Koeppen system includes five major categories which are designated by capital letters as follows:

A Tropical forest climates; hot all seasons.
B Dry climates.
C Warm temperate rainy climates; mild winters.
D Cold forest climates; severe winters.
E Polar climates.

In order to represent the main climatic types additional symbols are added. Except in the dry climates the second letter refers to rainfall regime, the third to temperature characteristics, and the fourth to special features of the climate. Table 6–1 shows the main climatic types of a modified Koeppen system and Table 6–2 explains the symbols and boundary criteria used in designating the subdivisions.

In actual application of the system to climatic statistics a great number of subdivisions are possible using the symbols noted in the tables. The numerical limits for certain of the subdivisions are different for each of

TABLE 6-1*

Main Climatic Types of the Koeppen Classification

Af	Tropical rain forest. Hot; rainy in all seasons
Am	Tropical monsoon. Hot; seasonally excessive rainfall
Aw	Tropical savanna. Hot; seasonally dry (usually winter)
BSh	Tropical steppe. Semiarid; hot
BSk	Mid-latitude steppe. Semiarid; cool or cold
BWh	Tropical desert. Arid; hot
BWk	Mid-latitude desert. Arid; cool or cold
Cfa	Humid subtropical. Mild winter; moist all seasons; long, hot summer
Cfb	Marine. Mild winter; moist all seasons; warm summer
Cfc	Marine. Mild winter; moist all seasons; short, cool summer
Csa	Interior Mediterranean. Mild winter; dry summer; hot summer
Csb	Coastal Mediterranean. Mild winter; dry summer, short warm summer
Cwa	Subtropical monsoon. Mild winter; dry winter; hot summer
Cwb	Tropical upland. Mild winter; dry winter; short, warm summer
Dfa	Humid continental. Severe winter; moist all seasons; long, hot summer
Dfb	Humid continental. Severe winter; moist all seasons; short, warm summer
Dfc	Subarctic. Severe winter; moist all sasons; short cool summer
Dfd	Subarctic. Extremely cold winter; moist all seasons; short summer
Dwa	Humid continental. Severe winter; dry winter; long, hot summer
Dwb	Humid continental. Severe winter; dry winter; warm summer
Dwc	Subarctic. Severe winter; dry winter; short, cool summer
Dwd	Subarctic. Extremely cold winter; dry winter; short, cool summer
ET	Tundra. Very short summer
EF	Perpetual ice and snow
H	Undifferentiated highland climates

* The data included in Tables 6–1, 6–2, and 6–3 are based on W. Koeppen, *Grundriss der Klimakunde* (Berlin: Walter de Gruyter Company, 1931); W. Koeppen, "Das geographische System der Klimate," Vol I, Part C, of W. Koeppen and R. Geiger, *Handbuch der Klimatologie* (Berlin: Gebruder Borntraeger, 1936); and modifications by R. Geiger, R. J. Russell, Glenn T. Trewartha, and others.

the higher categories, making the detailed use of the system rather complicated. Several climatologists and geographers have made modifications of the Koeppen classification. The German climatologist, R. Geiger, collaborated with Koeppen on revised editions of the world climatic map. He and others continued to modify it after Koeppen's death. It is inevitable that boundary revisions will need to be made as new climatic data become available. One of the best-known modifications of the Koeppen system in the United States is that by Glenn T. Trewartha, who has simplified the world climatic map, placing primary emphasis upon the cores of climatic regions.*

* Glenn T. Trewartha, *An Introduction to Climate*, 3rd ed. (New York: McGraw-Hill Book Company, 1954), Plate I.

TABLE 6-2

Criteria for Classification of Major Climatic Types in Modified Koeppen System
*(Based on mean annual and mean monthly values of precipitation in inches
and temperature in °F)*

Letter symbol			Explanation
1st	2nd	3rd	
A			Average temperature of coolest month 64.4°F or higher
	f		Precipitation in driest month at least 2.4 inches
	m		Precipitation in driest month less than 2.4 inches but equal to or greater than 3.94 — $r/25$*
	w		Precipitation in driest month less than 3.94 — $r/25$
B			70% or more of annual precipitation falls in warmer six months (April through September in the Northern Hemisphere) and r less than .44t — 3.5
			OR
			70% or more of annual precipitation falls in cooler six months (October through March in Northern Hemisphere) and r less than .44t — 14
			OR
			Neither half of year with more than 70% of annual precipitation and r less than .44t — 8.5
	W		r less than ½ upper limit of applicable requirement for B
	S		r less than upper limit for B but more than ½ that amount
		h	t greater than 64.4°F
		k	t less than 64.4°F
C			Average temperature of warmest month greater than 50°F and of coldest month between 64.4° and 32°F
	s		Precipitation in driest month of summer half of year less than 1.6 inches and less than ⅓ the amount in wettest winter month
	w		Precipitation in driest month of winter half of year less than ¹⁄₁₀ of amount in wettest summer month
	f		Precipitation not meeting conditions of either **s** or **w**
		a	Average temperature of warmest month 71.6°F or above
		b	Average temperature of each of four warmest months 50°F or above; temperature of warmest month below 71.6°F
		c	Average temperature of from one to three months 50°F or above; temperature of warmest month below 71.6°F
D			Average temperature of warmest month greater than 50°F and of coldest month 32°F or below
	s		Same as under **C**
	w		Same as under **C**
	f		Same as under **C**
		a	Same as under **C**
		b	Same as under **C**
		c	Same as under **C**
		d	Average temperature of coldest month below —36.4°F (**d** is then used instead of **a**, **b**, or **c**)
E			Average temperature of warmest month below 50°F
	T		Average temperature of warmest month between 50° and 32°F
	F		Average temperature of warmest month 32°F or below
H			Temperature requirements same as **E**, but due to altitude (generally above 5000 feet)

* In formulae t is the average annual temperature in °F; r is average annual precipitation in inches.

TABLE 6-3

Supplementary Subdivision Symbols and Criteria in Koeppen Classification

g	Ganges type of temperature regime; maximum before the summer rainy season
i	Annual temperature range less than 9°F
k'	Same as **k** but average temperature of warmest month less than 64.4°F
l	Mild; average temperature in all months between 50° and 71.6°F
n	Frequent fog
n'	Infrequent fog; high humidity, low rainfall, warmest month temperature below 74.2°F
p	Same as **n'**, except warmest month between 74.2° and 82.4°F
p'	Same as **n'**, except warmest month above 82.4°F
u	Coolest month after summer solstice
v	Warmest month in autumn
w'	Rainy season in autumn
w''	Two distinct rainfall maximums separated by two dry seasons
x	Maximum rainfall in spring or early summer, dry in late summer
x'	Same as **x** but with infrequent heavy rains in all seasons

THE THORNTHWAITE CLASSIFICATIONS

The American climatologist C. W. Thornthwaite (1899–1963) introduced his first classification of climates in 1931, when he applied it to North America; in 1933 he extended the system to the world.* The classification is like Koeppen's in that it attempts to define boundaries quantitatively, it is based on vegetation, and it employs combinations of symbols to designate climatic types. It departs from the Koeppen system primarily in its use of expressions for *precipitation effectiveness* and *temperature efficiency*. The effectiveness of precipitation is regarded as a function of precipitation and evaporation and is calculated by dividing the monthly precipitation by the monthly evaporation to find the *P/E ratio*. The sum of the twelve monthly P/E ratios becomes the *P–E index*. Faced with a widespread lack of data on evaporation, Thornthwaite developed a formula to express the P–E index in terms of precipitation and temperature. Applying the formula to world stations, he determined numerical limits for five humidity categories that correspond to five major vegetation types: rain forest, forest, grassland, steppe, and desert. Similarly, the sum of twelve monthly *temperature–efficiency ratios* (*T/E*), computed as functions of monthly temperatures, yields a *T–E index*. Temperature efficiency categories are designated as tropical, mesothermal, microthermal, taiga, tundra, and frost. Further subdivisions result from the use of a term to

* "The Climates of North America According to a New Classification," *Geog. Rev.*, 21, 4 (Oct., 1931), 633–55; and "The Climates of the Earth," *Geog. Rev.*, 23, 3 (July, 1933), 433–40.

express the seasonal distribution of precipitation. Combinations of symbols representing the P–E index, T–E index, and seasonal distribution of precipitation, in that order, denote thirty-two actual climatic types. (See Table 6–4.)

In 1948 Thornthwaite proposed as a basis for climatic classification the concept of *potential evapotranspiration,* that is the amount of moisture

TABLE 6-4

Structure of the First Thornthwaite Classification of Climate*

PRECIPITATION EFFECTIVENESS

P-E Index: $I = $ sum of twelve monthly values of $115 \left(\dfrac{P}{T - 10} \right)^{\frac{10}{9}}$

   $P = $ mean monthly precipitation in inches

   $T = $ mean monthly temperature in °F

Humidity Province		Vegetation	P–E Index
A	(Wet)	Rain forest	128 or above
B	(Humid)	Forest	64-127
C	(Subhumid)	Grassland	32-63
D	(Semiarid)	Steppe	16-31
E	(Arid)	Desert	Less than 16

TEMPERATURE EFFICIENCY

T-E Index: $I' = $ sum of twelve monthly values of $\left(\dfrac{T - 32}{4} \right)$

   $T = $ mean monthly temperature in °F

Temperature Province		T-E Index
A'	(Tropical)	128 or above
B'	(Mesothermal)	64-127
C'	(Microthermal)	32-63
D'	(Taiga)	16-31
E'	(Tundra)	1-15
F'	(Frost)	0

SEASONAL DISTRIBUTION OF PRECIPITATION

r	Rainfall adequate in all seasons
s	Rainfall deficient in summer
w	Rainfall deficient in winter
d	Rainfall deficient in all seasons

CLIMATIC TYPES

AA'r	BA'r	CA'r	DA'w	EA'd	D'	E'	F'
AB'r	BA'w	CA'w	DA'd	EB'd			
AC'r	BB'r	CA'd	DB'w	EC'd			
	BB'w	CB'r	DB's				
	BB's	CB'w	DB'd				
	BC'r	CB's	DC'd				
	BC's	CB'd					
		CC'r					
		CC's					
		CC'd					

* Adapted from C. W. Thornthwaite, "The Climates of North America According to a New Classification," *Geog. Rev.,* 21, 4 (Oct., 1931), 633–55.

that would be evaporated from soil and transpired by plants if it were available.* He rejected the idea of a classification based only on temperature and precipitation and their seasonal distribution, maintaining that potential evapotranspiration is a climatic factor equal in importance to precipitation. If more water were available in a hot desert there would be more vegetation, and more water would be used in evaporation and transpiration. The water need is greater in summer than in winter and greater in hot climates than cold. By comparing the amount of water available from precipitation with the water need, it is possible to assess

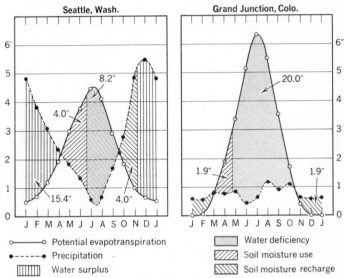

From C. W. Thornthwaite, "An Approach Toward a Rational Classification of Climate," *Geog. Rev.*, 38, 1 (Jan., 1948).

Fig. 6-1 Graphs of potential evapotranspiration and precipitation for Seattle and Grand Junction.

the moisture conditions to determine the seasonal distribution of water surpluses or deficiencies and whether a climate is truly wet or dry. (See Figure 6–1.) Inasmuch as potential evapotranspiration represents a transfer of both heat and moisture to the atmosphere and is primarily a function of energy received from the sun, it is an index of thermal efficiency as well as of water loss, combining both the moisture and heat factors in climate. Thus, a climate may be considered as the existing balance between incoming and outgoing heat and moisture at the earth's surface.

Actual measurements of potential evapotranspiration are still inadequate in number and duration for regional classification of climate. Cal-

* "An Approach Toward a Rational Classification of Climate," *Geog. Rev.*, 38, 1 (Jan., 1948), 55–94.

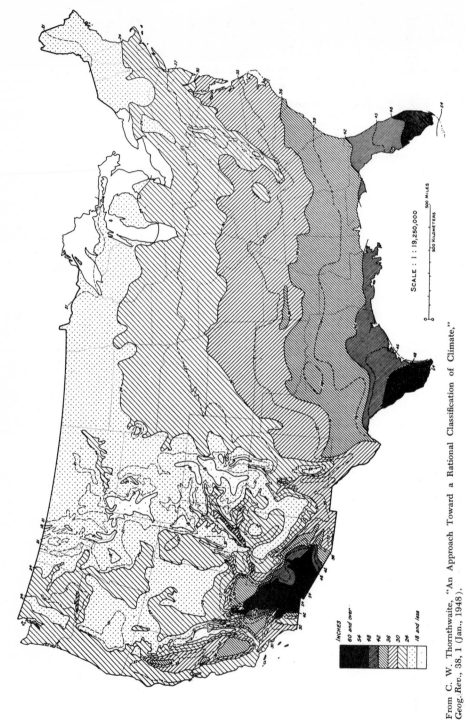

From C. W. Thornthwaite, "An Approach Toward a Rational Classification of Climate,"
Geog. Rev., 38, 1 (Jan., 1948).

Fig. 6-2 Average annual potential evapotranspiration in the contiguous United States.

culations of average potential evapotranspiration values have been made for a great many places in the world, using temperature and length of day as variables. Using computed indexes of moisture and heat, Thornthwaite delimited categories of moisture and thermal "provinces," and in his 1948 paper presented maps of the United States showing average potential evapotranspiration, average annual thermal efficiency, seasonal variation of effective moisture, and summer concentration of thermal efficiency. Maps prepared by Thornthwaite and others have depicted, in addition, average annual water deficiencies and surpluses for various parts of the world.

Perhaps the most significant applications of the potential evapotranspiration concept have been in practical studies of the water balance in relation to problems of water use. Some of these applications will be treated in Chapter 12, Climate and Agriculture.

OTHER CLASSIFICATIONS

Among the world classifications of climate many have been general and qualitative. They have tended to emphasize one or two climatic elements, especially temperature and precipitation, or one or more correlated factors such as latitude or the effects of land and water surfaces. Usually they employ words or phrases to designate the main climatic types. They make little provision for distinguishing climates in the lower categories or for mathematical determination of climatic boundaries. Several generalized world classifications have been developed by geographers with the primary objective of establishing world regions as a framework for study of patterns of human settlement or land use.

Some authors have made valuable contributions to the description of world climates without systematic classification of climatic types. Notable among them was the British climatologist, W. G. Kendrew, who described climates of the continents in terms of the distribution of elements and related causes.[*] His treatment delineates no specific climatic boundaries, but the continents are subdivided into geographic regions for the purposes of organized description.

CLIMATIC REGIONS OF THE WORLD

Inasmuch as the world distribution of climatic types is primarily the result of heat and moisture regimes, climate may be classified into broad categories based upon the interrelated effects of heat and moisture upon

[*] W. G. Kendrew, *The Climates of the Continents,* 5th ed. (London: Oxford University Press, 1961).

air masses, which in turn dominate the climates of different regions. The climatic types thus defined are (I) Climates dominated by equatorial and tropical air masses, (II) climates dominated by tropical and polar air masses, and (III) climates dominated by polar and arctic-type air masses. The final group in this basic category is (IV) the highland climates, which have distinctive features arising from the effects of altitude. Subdivisions of these four climatic groups into climatic types is based upon the regional distribution of climatic elements—especially temperature and precipitation—and their seasonal variations. The following outline lists the principal climatic types to be considered in the remaining chapters of Part Two. It follows the customary organization of world climates, beginning at the equator and proceeding toward the poles.

I. *Climates dominated by equatorial and tropical air masses*
1. Rainy tropics
2. Monsoon tropics
3. Wet-and-dry tropics
4. Tropical arid climate
5. Tropical semiarid climate

II. *Climates dominated by tropical and polar air masses*
6. Dry summer subtropics
7. Humid subtropics
8. Marine climate
9. Mid-latitude arid climate
10. Mid-latitude semiarid climate
11. Humid continental warm summer climate
12. Humid continental cool summer climate

III. *Climates dominated by polar and arctic-type air masses*
13. Taiga
14. Tundra
15. Polar climate

IV. *Climates having altitude as the dominant control*
16. Highland climates

This system of climatic types is designed to facilitate the explanatory description of world climates. It will be evident that it follows the Koeppen classification in its basic approach to major categories, relying heavily on temperature and precipitation, their seasonal distribution, and their relation to natural vegetation as criteria for the climatic types. The schematic relationship of climatic types to the temperature and moisture factors is diagrammed in Figure 6–3.

This system is in no sense a rational classification arrived at by mathematical computation. Nor is it readily susceptible to refinement to define the many climatic subtypes. Rather, it is intended to aid our examination of the major climates of the earth while introducing a minimum of departure from terminology one is likely to encounter in readings in geography, climatology, or other sciences dealing with the world patterns of spatial distribution. Classifications of this kind have been widely used by geographers and climatologists, and though they may not always be in agreement as to specific boundaries and subdivisions, the fundamental pattern of climates recurs in all for the reason that a fairly well-ordered system of climates does exist on the earth.

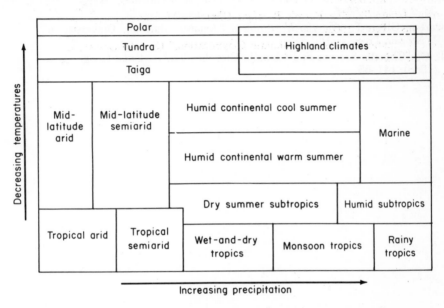

Fig. 6-3 Schematic relationship of the major climatic types to temperature and precipitation.

ADDITIONAL READINGS

Brooks, C. E. P., "Classification of Climates," *Met. Mag.,* 77, 911 (1948), 97–101.

Bailey, Harry P., "Toward a Unified Concept of the Temperate Climate," *Geog. Rev.,* 54, 4 (1964), 516–45.

Castelli, Joseph, "A Flow Chart for Climate Classification," *Journ. of Geog.,* 63, 1 (1964), 19–23.

Chang, Jen-Hu, "An Evaluation of the 1948 Thornthwaite Classification," *Ann. Assoc. Am. Geogrs.,* 49, 1 (1959), 24–30.

Curry, Leslie, "Thornthwaite's Potential Evapotranspiration Term," *Canadian Geogr.,* 9, 1 (1965), 13–18.

Doerr, Arthur H., and Stephen M. Sutherland, "Variations in Oklahoma's Climate as Depicted by the Koeppen and Early Thornthwaite Classifications," *Journ. of Geog.*, 63, 2 (1964), 60–66.

Hare, F. Kenneth, "Climatic Classification," Chapter VII in *London Essays in Geography*, edited by L. D. Stamp and S. W. Wooldridge. Cambridge, Mass.: Harvard University Press, 1951, pp. 111–134.

Maunder, W. J., "A Human Classification of Climate," *Weather*, 12, 1 (1962), 3–12.

Sibbons, J. L. H., "A Contribution to the Study of Potential Evapotranspiration," *Geografiska Annaler*, 44, 3–4 (1962), 279–92.

Thornthwaite, C. W., "Problems in the Classification of Climates," *Geog. Rev.*, 33, 2 (1943), 233–55.

Trewartha, Glenn T., *The Earth's Problem Climates*. Madison: University of Wisconsin Press, 1961.

Troll, C., "Climatic Seasons and Climatic Classification," *Oriental Geogr.*, 2, 2 (1958), 141–65.

climates dominated
by equatorial and tropical
air masses

Climates under the influence of equatorial and tropical air masses experience high temperatures throughout the year. They lie in low latitudes in the zones of the intertropical convergence, the trade winds, and the subtropic highs. The year-round abundance of insolation at low latitudes accounts for the major features of this group of climates.

THE RAINY TROPICS

The rainy, tropical type of climate prevails in the lowland areas on and near the equator and along tropical coasts which are exposed to trade winds but backed by interior highlands. The principal areas of the world having this type of climate are the Amazon Basin of South America, the windward coasts of Central America, the Congo Basin of Africa, Indonesia, New Guinea, the Philippines, and the east coast of Madagascar. The combination of constantly

Climatic Data for Rainy Tropical Stations
Nouvelle Anvers, Republic of the Congo

	J	F	M	A	M	J	J	A	S	O	N	D	Yr.
Temp.	79	80	79	78	79	78	76	76	77	77	78	78	78
Precip.	4.1	3.5	4.1	5.6	6.2	6.1	6.3	6.3	6.3	6.6	7.6	9.3	72.0

Santos, Brazil

	J	F	M	A	M	J	J	A	S	O	N	D	Yr.
Temp.	78	78	77	74	70	68	67	66	69	70	74	76	77
Precip.	11.0	9.8	12.3	7.3	6.1	5.7	4.3	4.1	5.7	6.4	7.7	7.8	88.1

high temperatures with heavy rainfall well distributed throughout the year makes this a climate literally without seasons. Monthly temperatures average nearly 80°F, and because there is a net gain of radiation throughout the year, the annual temperature range is small.

In the rainy tropics the diurnal range of temperature is normally much greater than the annual range between the maximum and minimum monthly means. Annual ranges are commonly less than 3° or 4°, whereas diurnal ranges may be 15° or 20°. Nighttime cooling of moist air under clear skies is frequently sufficient to produce saturation and heavy dew or perhaps fog, since the relative humidity is always high. These condensation products are soon evaporated into the warmed air after sunup. Average daytime maximums are usually below 90°F. Singapore has an average annual range of 3°. The considerably greater daily range is illustrated by the mean daily maximum and minimum temperatures given below for each month. Record high temperatures are lower than for many mid-latitude stations, rarely reaching above 100°. Again Singapore serves as an example. Another feature of temperatures is the small interdiurnal variation. That is, the change in temperature from day to day is small, with the result that the climate tends to be monotonous. Whereas in the higher latitudes there is a more or less regular seasonal rhythm to the climate, in the rainy tropics the cycle is the day.

Mean Daily Maximum and Minimum Temperatures at Singapore

	J	F	M	A	M	J	J	A	S	O	N	D
Mean Dly. Max.	86	88	89	89	89	88	88	88	88	88	87	86
Mean Dly. Min.	73	73	74	75	75	75	75	75	75	74	74	73

Highest and Lowest Temperatures on Record at Singapore

	J	F	M	A	M	J	J	A	S	O	N	D
Extreme Max.	93	94	94	95	97	95	93	92	93	93	92	93
Extreme Min.	67	66	67	70	70	71	70	69	70	69	69	69

Annual precipitation in the rainy tropics exceeds 60 in. at most stations. No month is exceptionally dry, yet a graph of the precipitation regime is by no means as smooth as the annual march of temperature. (See Figure 7–1.) Some stations have a definite maximum of precipitation in one month; a few have regimes with two maximums during the year, resulting from the seasonal migration of the intertropical convergence. Most rainfall is of the convectional type and comes with thunderstorms. The convergence of moist tropical air and the intense daytime radiation create ideal conditions for thunderstorm formation. Usually the thundershowers are concentrated in small areas and are of short duration. In many areas

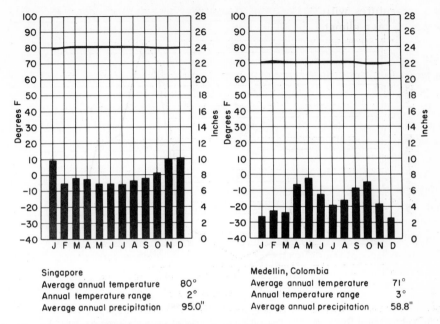

Fig. 7-1 Climatic graphs for Singapore and Medellin, rainy tropics.

their maximum occurrence is in the afternoon, and they are frequently preceded and followed by clear, sunny weather. Coastal locations and islands near the poleward margins of the rainy tropics may experience hurricanes, but these violent tropical cyclones do not occur along the equator nor in interior areas. Hurricanes may account for a considerable proportion of the autumn rainfall of coastal areas visited by this type of storm.

Although thunderstorms are the dominant storm type, shallow cyclonic circulation sometimes develops in the rainy tropics. Two air masses of equatorial or tropical origin are not likely to differ greatly in temperature characteristics, and zones of convergence accordingly tend to be broad troughs of low pressure accompanied by overcast skies and protracted periods of rain. On rare occasions, air masses from middle latitudes invade the tropics and produce frontal rainfall and lowered temperatures, but, for the most part, the storm lines of the tropics which seem to resemble extratropical fronts are zones of convergence within tropical air masses. In this connection it should be remembered that convergence can result from either different wind directions or wind speeds or both. Therefore, a close study of winds is necessary for prediction of weather in the tropics, for tropical weather is primarily of the air mass variety rather than the frontal.

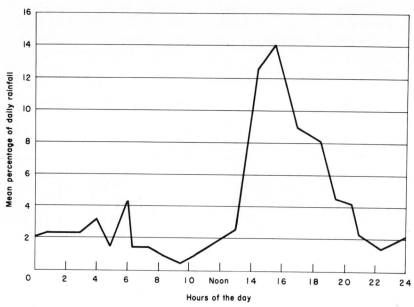

After OOI Jin-bee, "Rural Development in Tropical Areas," *Journal of Tropical Geography*, Vol. 12, March, 1959.

Fig. 7-2 Diurnal distribution of rainfall at Kuala Lumpur, Malaya.

Where mountain ranges lie athwart trade winds which have travelled across warm water, the average annual precipitation of the rainy tropics is greatly exceeded. Examples of these trade-wind coasts are found in the Caribbean Sea, southeastern Brazil, eastern Madagascar, and on the numerous volcanic islands of the tropical Pacific. Wherever the orographic effect is a factor inducing heavy rainfall, leeward sides of the mountains show small annual totals in striking contrast to the heavy rainfall on the windward sides.

Quite as important as the total annual precipitation and its regime is the effectiveness of precipitation. Owing to the constantly high temperatures in the equatorial regions the rates of evaporation and transpiration are high and a correspondingly greater amount of rain is required to maintain satisfactory conditions for plant growth. Thus, the monthly precipitation amounts which might seem adequate in the latitude of the Great Lakes may actually result in drought in equatorial latitudes. Although there is a marked variability of precipitation from year to year in this climate, there are ordinarily no droughts of serious proportions.

The air masses which dominate the rainy tropical climate are associated with the subtropic high and with stagnated air in the equatorial convergence. (See Figure 5–4.) The trade winds originate in the subtropical cells of high pressure and flow equatorward. They constitute the most dependable wind systems of this type of climate but are found chiefly along its margins on east coasts. Owing to their effect the rainy tropics reach their farthest poleward extensions. Some authors refer to these areas as the "tropical eastern littorals" or the "tropical windward coasts." Not all trade-wind coasts have the true characteristics of the rainy tropics, however. An example station in the poleward extension of the rainy tropics is Belize, British Honduras, for which climatic data are given below. Belize has an autumn maximum of precipitation, which can be accounted for at least in part by its location in a belt of hurricanes.

Climatic Data for Belize, British Honduras

	J	F	M	A	M	J	J	A	S	O	N	D	Yr.
Temp.	76	77	79	81	82	83	82	83	82	80	77	76	80
Precip.	7.4	3.2	2.5	2.2	4.9	7.9	8.2	8.3	9.4	10.6	13.3	6.7	84.5

The intertropical convergence dominates by far the greater part of the rainy tropics, and associated weather accounts for most tropical precipitation. Because it is essentially a belt of shallow depressions, convection, and convergence, it does not have strong prevailing winds but rather light, erratic air movement except along some trade-wind coasts. The best-developed horizontal temperature gradients in the rainy tropics are between land and sea, where the resulting pressure gradients produce daily land and sea breezes that alleviate daytime heat for many coastal locations.

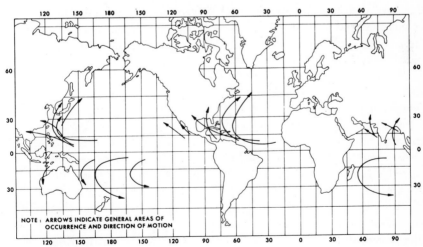

NOTE : ARROWS INDICATE GENERAL AREAS OF OCCURRENCE AND DIRECTION OF MOTION

Courtesy Department of the Army.

Fig. 7-3 Principal world regions of violent tropical cyclones.

The monsoon tropics are found in close association with the rainy tropics, generally along coasts where there is a seasonal onshore flow of moist air. The principal areas are the west coasts of India and Burma, the east coast of Vietnam, the northern Philippines, the western Guinea Coast of Africa, the northeastern coast of South America, and the northern coasts of Haiti and Puerto Rico. The monsoon tropical climate differs from the rainy tropics in that it has a distinct dry season. However, the storage of soil moisture is sufficient to maintain a forest through the rainless period. It may be regarded as transitional in nature from the rainy tropics to the wet-and-dry tropics, having annual rainfall totals comparable to the former and a regime of precipitation similar to the latter. It is well to remember that the term monsoon tropics does not apply to all climates affected by a monsoonal wind circulation. Its use stems from the characteristic climates of monsoon Asia, but the designation wet-and-dry tropics is applied to those regions with less annual precipitation and a distinct season of drought.

Mean monthly temperatures in the monsoon tropics are not greatly different from those in the rainy tropics, with typical values ranging well above 70°F. These climates extend farther poleward, however, and the annual range is greater in some cases. The outstanding feature of the annual march of temperature for a number of stations in the monsoon tropics is the occurrence of the maximum before the high-sun period, that is, in May or June rather than in July in the Northern Hemisphere. Maximum temperatures are usually reached in the period of clearer skies, increasing insolation, and deficient precipitation just before the onset of more persistent cloudiness and heavy rainfall.

Climatic Data for Monsoon Tropical Stations
Colombo, Ceylon

	J	F	M	A	M	J	J	A	S	O	N	D	Yr.
Temp.	80	80	82	83	83	82	81	81	81	81	80	80	80
Precip.	3.2	1.9	4.3	9.7	10.9	7.3	4.4	3.2	4.8	13.4	11.8	5.1	80.0

Port of Spain, Trinidad

Temp.	75	75	76	78	79	78	78	78	78	78	78	76	77
Precip.	2.7	1.5	1.8	1.8	3.6	7.9	8.8	9.6	7.4	6.6	7.0	4.7	63.4

Diurnal variation of temperature in the monsoon tropics is, on the average, slightly greater than in the rainy tropics. It is greatest in the drier months and least in the rainy season. During winter there may be some influence from cyclonic disturbances which pass on the poleward margin with resulting short periods of comparatively low temperatures.

Annual precipitation averages above 60 in. in most areas of the monsoon tropics. Where a strong onshore flow of moist air meets a coast backed by a mountain barrier exceptional rainfall totals are achieved.

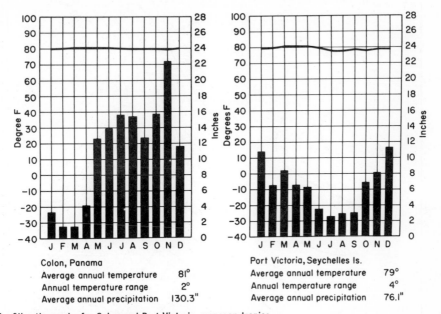

Colon, Panama
Average annual temperature   81°
Annual temperature range   2°
Average annual precipitation   130.3"

Port Victoria, Seychelles Is.
Average annual temperature   79°
Annual temperature range   4°
Average annual precipitation   76.1"

Fig. 7-4 Climatic graphs for Colon and Port Victoria, monsoon tropics.

Precipitation which accounts for most of the total in the monsoon tropics is of the showery type, with the orographic effect often playing an important part, but certain areas are visited by tropical depressions. Summer weather, that is, the rainy season, is similar to that of the rainy tropics, usually with greater monthly rainfall totals. Winter is slightly cooler and somewhat drier, having protracted sunny periods with occasional thundershowers. Remnants of polar fronts sometimes invade these climates above the level of the trades in winter, producing overcast skies and light rainfall but no very great temperature decreases at the surface.

In southeastern Asia the characteristic pattern of circulation is monsoonal. Air trajectories from the Indian Ocean meet the easterly trades to produce a belt of convergence in summer over the east coast and offshore islands. Much of the moisture precipitated along the east Asian littoral is transported aloft from the Indian Ocean. In winter a southern arm of the westerly jet stream lies south of the Himalayan divide, allowing little moisture into the area. Surface winds are from a northerly direction.

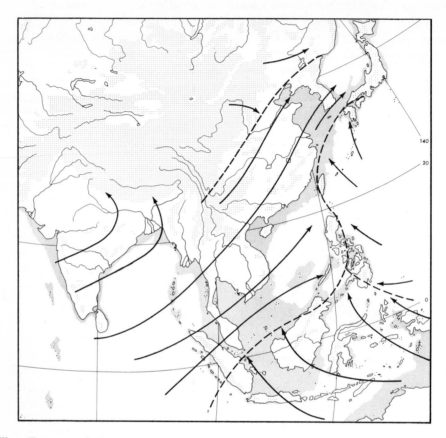

After Watts, Thompson, and others.

Fig. 7-5 Mean air trajectories over Southeast Asia in July. Dashed lines represent zones of convergence.

In other regions where the monsoon tropical climate prevails, the seasonal variation in strength and persistence of the trades combines with the effect of contrasting land and water surfaces to produce a "monsoon tendency." Although essentially easterly winds, the trades at times play a part in onshore flow of west winds, notably on the Guinea Coast of Africa and the Malabar Coast of India. As the world pattern of the general circulation migrates northward in the Northern Hemisphere summer the southeast trades take a position astride or even slightly north of the equator. Blowing into the Northern Hemisphere they come under the opposite influence of the Coriolis effect and curve to the right to become southwest winds as they approach these coasts. In the case of India they merge into the monsoon circulation. (See Figure 7–6.)

Wherever the trades are found they vary not only with the seasons, migrating to some extent with the general circulation, but also their strength varies periodically in what has been called the "surge of the trades." Periods of greater velocity in the trades are caused by disturbances from higher latitudes which create a steeper pressure gradient away from the subtropic high centers. When these surges are developing a wind discontinuity, or *shear line*, exists between the strong winds of the surge and the weaker winds of the trades nearer the equator. Convergence along the shear line results in clouds of the cumulus type and showers.

Climatic Data for Stations of the Wet-and-Dry Tropics
Bamako, Mali

	J	F	M	A	M	J	J	A	S	O	N	D	Yr.
Temp.	76	82	87	90	89	84	80	79	80	82	80	77	82
Precip.	T	T	0.1	0.6	2.9	5.4	11.0	13.7	8.1	1.7	0.6	T	44.1

Darwin, Australia

	J	F	M	A	M	J	J	A	S	O	N	D	Yr.
Temp.	83	83	84	84	82	78	77	79	82	85	86	85	82
Precip.	15.2	12.3	10.0	3.8	0.6	0.1	T	0.1	0.5	2.0	4.7	9.4	58.7

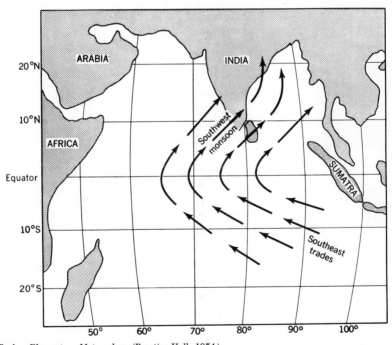

After George F. Taylor, *Elementary Meteorology* (Prentice-Hall, 1954).

Fig. 7-6 Trade winds and the summer monsoon in the Indian Ocean.

In areas of the monsoon tropics where the monsoon circulation is well defined, winter weather is controlled to a large extent by air moving off the land and hence is somewhat drier. There may be brief local reversals of the typical winter outflow and accompanying showers. Where the winter is not dominated by a strong offshore monsoon, the mere lessening of onshore movement of warm, moist air results in lower monthly precipitation averages.

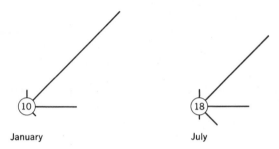

January　　　　　　July

Fig. 7-7 Wind roses for Georgetown, British Guiana.

Some stations which show the general characteristics of the monsoon tropical climate depart from the rigid pattern of "wet summers and dry winters." The northeast coast of South America, for example, has its heaviest rains in December and January, when onshore trades are strongest, and in May through July, when dominated by the intertropical convergence, but the August-through-October period is relatively dry. Total precipitation is generally above 80 in. Cayenne, French Guiana, with precipitation maximums in January and May, illustrates these features.

Mean Monthly Temperature and Precipitation at Cayenne, French Guiana. (5°N.)

	J	F	M	A	M	J	J	A	S	O	N	D	Yr.
Temp.	79	80	80	80	80	80	80	82	83	83	82	80	81
Precip.	14.4	12.3	15.8	18.9	21.9	15.5	6.9	2.8	1.2	1.3	4.6	10.7	126.3

Along the east coast of Brazil, south of Cape São Roque, the onshore flow of the southeast trades is stronger and more nearly perpendicular to the coast in late autumn and early winter. Bahia thus has a distinct autumn maximum of precipitation rather than the typical dry winter.

Mean Monthly Temperature and Precipitation at Bahia (Salvador), Brazil (13°S.)

	J	F	M	A	M	J	J	A	S	O	N	D	Yr.
Temp.	80	80	80	79	77	75	74	74	75	77	78	78	77
Precip.	2.6	5.3	6.1	11.2	10.8	9.4	7.2	4.8	3.3	4.0	4.5	5.6	74.8

WET-AND-DRY TROPICS

As the name implies, the wet-and-dry tropical climate has alternating wet and dry seasons. It is transitional between the rainy and monsoon tropics on the one hand and the tropical arid and semiarid climates on the other. There is a distinctly dry period of two to four months, usually coinciding with the winter, and annual rainfall totals are less than in the rainy tropics. Mean monthly temperatures range from 65° to above 80°F. The wet-and-dry tropics differ from the monsoon tropics most significantly in the effect of the dry season on vegetation and crops.

The climate occurs between the latitudinal limits of approximately 5–10° on the equatorial side to 15–20° on the poleward, that is, between the average locations of the equatorial low and the subtropic highs. The principal areas having this climate are in western Central America, northwestern South America, the interior uplands of Brazil and adjacent Bolivia and Paraguay, south-central and eastern Africa, western Madagascar, parts of India and Southeast Asia, and northern Australia.

Owing to a net excess of insolation over outgoing radiation the wet-and-dry tropics have generally high temperatures throughout the year, although on the higher plateaus of South America and eastern Africa altitude produces lower averages. As in the monsoon tropics, there is a tendency toward a maximum temperature in late spring or early summer just before the season of greatest cloudiness and heavy rain. There may be a secondary maximum again just after the rainy season. Along the poleward margins annual ranges are greatest, and, in general, the annual ranges are greater than in the rainy tropics.

Diurnal ranges of temperature are greatest in the dry season and at higher elevations and are somewhat greater than in the rainy tropics. Nighttime temperatures may drop below 60°F in winter. The daytime temperatures of 80–90° in winter are offset to some extent by the lower relative humidity. In summer, on the other hand, the diurnal range is small, temperatures are high, and these factors, combined with the rain and high humidity, produce oppressive conditions similar to the rainy tropics. Relief from the heat and humidity can be found only along coasts with strong sea breezes or at high altitudes.

The outstanding feature of precipitation (indeed of the climate) in the wet-and-dry tropics is the marked seasonal contrast. Many stations have one or more months with no precipitation recorded over a period of several years, whereas the wettest month has an average of 10 in. or more. Annual totals generally range from 40 to 60 in., appreciably lower than in the rainy tropics. On the margins of the climatic region nearest the equator, the dry season is short and it is difficult to define the boundary between the wet-and-dry type and the monsoon tropics or the rainy tropics.

Along the poleward margins the dry season is prolonged and conditions grade into the tropical semiarid climate, where potential evapotranspiration exceeds precipitation even in the wet season. Normally winter is the dry season, but along the Coromandel Coast of India spring is the dry period. Madras has a precipitation maximum in late autumn and early winter, when the monsoon circulation brings air across the warm Bay of Bengal from the northeast.

Mean Monthly Temperature and Precipitation at Madras, India

	J	F	M	A	M	J	J	A	S	O	N	D	Yr.
Temp.	76	78	81	86	91	90	87	86	85	82	78	76	83
Precip.	1.4	0.4	0.3	0.6	1.0	1.9	3.6	4.6	4.7	12.0	14.0	5.5	50.0

Reliability of precipitation is less than in the rainy tropics. A year with destructive floods may also have drought with serious economic consequences. Unseasonable rain or drought can be as disastrous as abnormal rainfall totals. The graph of annual rainfall over a forty-year period at Nagpur, India, illustrates the variability from year to year.

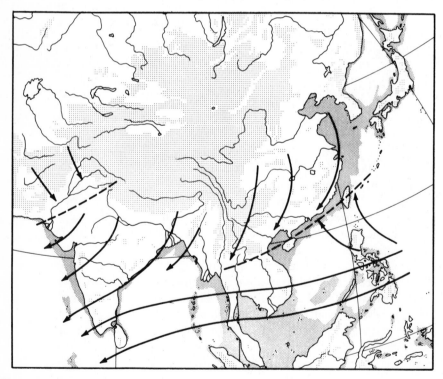

After Watts, Thompson, and others.

Fig. 7-8 Mean air trajectories across southern Asia in January.

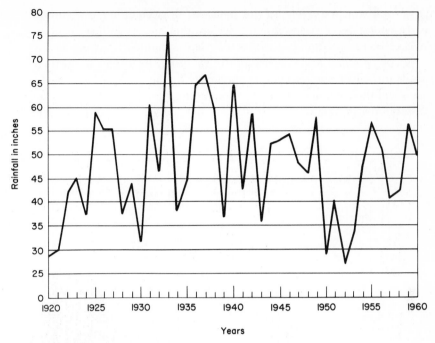

Data from Government of India Meteorological Department.

Fig. 7-9 Variations in annual rainfall at Nagpur, India, 1920–1960.

Precipitation in the wet-and-dry tropics is associated with thunder-storms and weak tropical lows. Thundershower activity is greatest at the beginning and end of the rainy season, when violent storms are inter-spersed with sunny periods. As the rainy season becomes established, shallow tropical lows of the type found in the rainy tropics bring long periods of rain and cloudiness. The dry season weather is essentially like that of the tropical deserts, with only erratic showers.

Although tropical air masses exercise the principal control over the wet-and-dry tropical climate, a marked seasonal alternation of dominant types is evident. In the wet season the equatorial trough and equatorial air masses control the climate, bringing weather not far different from the rainy tropics. This results directly from the poleward migration of the wind and pressure belts of the primary circulation in summer, when the sun is at or near the solstice. Although the effects of the sun's apparent poleward migration lag behind the noon sun's latitudinal position by a month or six weeks, they are nevertheless associated with the summer half of the year and indirectly produce rainy weather which gradually moves pole-ward until after the reversal of the sun's migration at the tropic. Even in India and parts of southeastern Asia, where the monsoon circulation is strong, the equatorial trough lies north of the equator in summer and plays a complementary role to the monsoon in accounting for summer rains. In winter the wet-and-dry tropics are dominated by the subsiding air masses of the subtropic highs, which have gradually moved toward the equator, bringing arid conditions. In "monsoon Asia" and in northern Australia this effect is again complementary to the monsoon, which in winter blows off the continent. Thus the climatic region is under the influence of unstable maritime air through most of the rainy season and of stable continental air in the dry season.

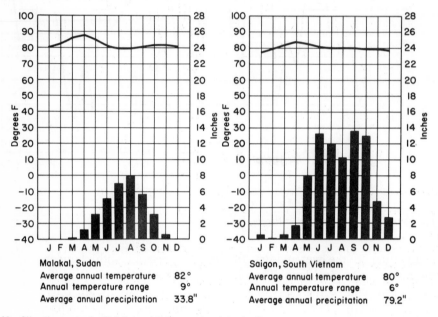

Fig. 7-10   Climatic graphs for Malakal and Saigon, wet-and-dry tropics.

TROPICAL ARID AND SEMIARID CLIMATES

The arid and semiarid climates of tropical latitudes have numerous features in common, their differences being more in degree than in kind. The semiarid types are essentially a transition zone from the very dry regions to the bordering moister climates. The distinctive characteristic of these climates is the lack of sufficient rainfall to sustain dense vegetative growth. They are differentiated from the mid-latitude counterparts by their higher average temperatures and the consequent need for more rainfall to offset evaporation and transpiration.

The tropical arid and semiarid climates are centered approximately on the latitudes 20° to 25° N. and S., where the prevailing air masses are those which subside in the subtropic highs. The process of subsidence results in adiabatic heating and low relative humidity and thus dries land surfaces over which it occurs. The effects of upper air subsidence inversions extend the arid conditions well into the zones of the trades. The trade-wind inversion (an upper air subsidence inversion) tends to suppress vertical cloud development. The chief areas of tropical arid (or desert) climate are in northwestern Mexico and southwestern United States, along the west coast of Peru and northern Chile, the Sahara and Somalia in north Africa, portions of southwestern Asia from Arabia to West Pakistan, the west coast of southern Africa, and in central Australia. With certain exceptions, notably along west coasts, the core areas of arid climates have transitional semiarid belts situated more or less concentrically around the wetter margins. On the Deccan Plateau of India an elongated area of semiarid climate occurs without a contiguous area of true arid climate. Where tropical arid climates are located along west coasts of continents, ocean currents modify desert conditions. The four principal instances are as follows:

Region	Ocean Current	Desert Name
Lower California and Sonora	California	Sonoran
Coastal Peru and Chile	Humbolt or Peru	Peru and Atacama
Northwest African Coast	Canaries	Sahara
Southwest Africa	Benguela	Namib

Upwelling associated with these currents produces cool temperatures along the immediate coasts and increases stability in the lower air layers, thereby reducing the tendency to cloud formation and precipitation. Advection fogs, stratus, and even drizzle are common along the coasts thus affected, however. In combination with lower temperatures they reduce the water need from precipitation.

Comparison of the climatic data for Walvis Bay, a coastal station of Southwest Africa, and Windhoek, inland but at an elevation of 5669 ft., reveals the influence of the cold Benguela Current. In view of its altitude, Windhoek might be expected to have cooler summer temperatures. Instead, it is both warmer and drier than Walvis Bay.

Climatic Data for Southwest African Stations
Walvis Bay

	J	F	M	A	M	J	J	A	S	O	N	D	Yr.
Temp.	66	67	66	65	63	61	58	57	57	59	62	64	62
Precip.	T	0.2	0.3	0.1	0.1	T	T	0.1	T	T	T	T	0.9

Windhoek

	J	F	M	A	M	J	J	A	S	O	N	D	Yr.
Temp.	74	72	69	66	60	56	55	60	65	71	71	74	66
Precip.	3.0	2.9	3.1	1.6	0.3	T	T	T	0.1	0.4	0.9	1.9	14.3

Another influence upon arid and semiarid climates of the tropics is the mountain barrier effect. There is no arid area which can be ascribed primarily to mountain barriers, although the Andes in South America and the Atlas Range in northwestern Africa form rather definite rainfall boundaries. A more important effect of mountains in these climates is to induce slightly greater rainfall on their slopes. Examples are to be found in the Ahaggar Mountains in the Sahara, the highlands of Yemen, and along the ranges of Iran and Afghanistan. Not only is the precipitation greater along the mountain slopes, but the temperatures are lower owing to altitude, and potential evapotranspiration is therefore less.

The arid and semiarid areas of East Africa and eastern Brazil must be regarded as atypical locations of these climates in view of their position in latitudes frequently visited by the intertropical convergence. In parts of northern Kenya average annual rainfall is less than 6 in. This is presumed to result from subsidence, divergence, and consequent stability of air that reaches the area, especially at upper levels, from the Indian Ocean. In far eastern Brazil the stable air of an offshore anticyclone produces a dry summer. In winter the moist Southeast Trades which bring rainfall to the coast south of Cape São Roque do not penetrate strongly beyond the uplands in most years.

Temperatures in the tropical arid climate are the highest in the world. The highest instrument shelter temperature ever recorded officially was 136°F at Azizia, Libya, on September 13, 1922. The United States extreme maximum of 134° was recorded at Greenland Ranch in Death Valley, California, on July 10, 1913. Ground temperatures far exceed these values. Monthly means of the hottest months are over 90°F for many tropical desert locations. Insalah, Algeria, with a July average of 98°, is an extreme example of stations having high temperatures. On the other hand, stations on coasts (for example, Walvis Bay) or at higher elevations (Windhoek) have lower summer mean temperatures.

Climatic Data for Tropical Arid Stations
Insalah, Algeria

	J	F	M	A	M	J	J	A	S	O	N	D	Yr.
Temp.	56	61	68	77	84	95	98	97	91	80	67	58	78
Precip.					Negligible								

Jacobabad, Pakistan

	J	F	M	A	M	J	J	A	S	O	N	D	Yr.
Temp.	58	63	76	86	94	99	97	93	89	82	70	60	80
Precip.	0.2	0.3	0.2	0.2	0.1	0.3	0.9	0.9	0.2	T	T	0.2	3.5

Annual range of temperature in the arid tropics is far greater than in the rainy tropics. This is due in part to the generally higher latitudes of the former but results primarily from the clear skies that permit high net radiation in the summer and considerable loss of heat by radiation in winter. The annual ranges for Insalah and Jacobabad are 42° and 41° respectively. Compare these with rainy tropical stations, for example, Nouvelle Anvers or Singapore. Coastal stations have smaller annual ranges. Just as the annual range is increased over dry lands and under clear skies, so is the diurnal range greater. Diurnal ranges of 25° to 50° are common. A daytime maximum of 120° may be followed by a nighttime minimum in the 80's. Insalah has mean diurnal temperature ranges as follows:

J	F	M	A	M	J	J	A	S	O	N	D	Yr.
26	28	30	30	30	30	30	29	28	28	27	26	29

The extremely high temperatures of summer account primarily for the large annual ranges in the tropical deserts, for winter cannot be called truly cold. Nevertheless, temperatures below freezing occur occasionally on winter nights when long-wave radiational losses through the atmosphere are rapid. These nocturnal frosts are particularly trying because of the contrast with the warm days.

Temperatures in the semiarid tropical climate are fairly comparable to those of the arid type. (See climatic graphs for Lahore and Cairo in Figure

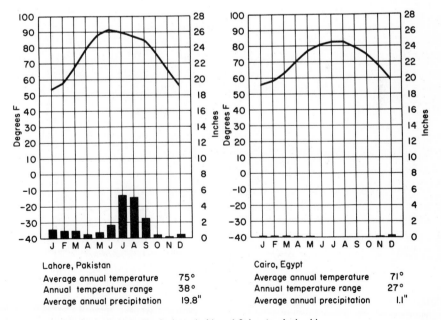

Lahore, Pakistan
Average annual temperature   75°
Annual temperature range   38°
Average annual precipitation   19.8"

Cairo, Egypt
Average annual temperature   71°
Annual temperature range   27°
Average annual precipitation   1.1"

Fig. 7-11   Climatic graphs for Lahore, tropical semiarid, and Cairo, tropical arid.

7–11.) As would be expected, the averages for semiarid climates on the high-latitude borders of the deserts are generally lower and the ranges greater than on the savanna margins nearer the equator.

Precipitation in the tropical arid climates is not only low in amount but it is also erratic. There is no definite seasonal regime that could be termed characteristic of tropical arid stations; the climate is identified by lack of effective precipitation rather than a unique seasonal distribution. For example, stations near the margin of the monsoon tropics have a monsoonal regime, whereas those on west coasts bordering the dry summer subtropics have a winter maximum. The stations with no significant precipitation in any month can hardly be said to have a regime of precipitation. Arica, in northern Chile, has the record minimum average annual rainfall—only 0.02 in. over a 43-year period. Iquique, on the coast south of Arica, had no rain for fourteen years, but has a statistical average of about 0.6 in. annually. In the semiarid climate the seasonal distribution becomes better defined as a rule and is more important in its effect on vegetation and land use. On the other hand, the variability of precipitation is a more critical factor in the semiarid climate than in the true desert. In wetter-than-average years settlers may venture into the semiarid grasslands only to find that the succeeding years are too dry for their type of land use.

Most of the precipitation of the tropical deserts is of the thunderstorm type. It comes in downpours that rapidly exceed the absorptive capacity of the soil, and because there is little vegetative cover the runoff is great, often of flood proportions. Thus a relatively small part of the rain is retained as soil moisture. In the semiarid climates there may be longer periods of rain associated with weak lows. In the poleward locations of the semiarid climate, winter rain comes with the mid-latitude cyclones which occasionally reach into these areas. On the margins toward the equator the intertropical convergence may bring limited summer rain.

The fogs and lower temperatures associated with the cold currents and upwelling along the coastal deserts modify the moisture conditions sufficiently to permit growth of some low forms of vegetation in spite of almost complete lack of rainfall. On the coast of Peru fog is so heavy at times that it is virtually a drizzle and is locally referred to as the *garua*. It is along the Peruvian coast that an interesting and unusual feature of variability in desert precipitation occurs. When the subtropic high moves abnormally seaward and the Peru Current flows at some distance from the coast, warm water from the north, known as the *El Niño*, spreads out over the cold water along the shore. If the intertropical convergence has moved southward, as may happen in the Southern Hemisphere summer, there may be heavy rains typical of the rainy tropics. The combination of conditions necessary to produce this phenomenon ordinarily prevails for only a short period. One of the worst occasions was in 1925, when ruins of sun-dried bricks that had stood for centuries in the vicinity of Trujillo were nearly washed away.

ADDITIONAL READINGS

Carter, Douglas B., *Climates of Africa and India According to Thornthwaite's 1948 Classification.* Publications in Climatology, 7, 4. Centerton, N.J.: Laboratory of Climatology, 1954.

Chang, Jen-Hu, "Comparative Climatology of the Tropical Western Margins of the Northern Oceans," *Ann. Assoc. Am. Geogrs.,* 52, 2 (1962), 221–27.

Davies, H. R. J., "Khartoum Weather," *Journ. of Geog.,* 58, 6 (1959), 286–91.

Garbell, Maurice A., *Tropical and Equatorial Weather.* New York: Pitman Publishing Corp., 1947.

Portig, W. H., "Central American Rainfall," *Geog. Rev.,* 55, 1 (1965), 68–90.

Riehl, Herbert, *Tropical Meteorology.* New York: McGraw-Hill Book Company, 1954.

Sellers, William D., "Potential Evapotranspiration in Arid Regions," *Journ. Appl. Met.,* 3 (1964), 96–104.

Thompson, B. W., "An Essay on the General Circulation of the Atmosphere over South East Asia and the West Pacific," *Quart. Journ. Roy. Met. Soc.,* 77, 334 (1951), 569–97.

Thornthwaite, C. W., "The Water Balance in Tropical Climates," *Bull. Am. Met. Soc.,* 32, 5 (1951), 166–73.

Watts, I. E. M., *Equatorial Weather.* London: University of London Press, 1955.

climates dominated by tropical and polar air masses

8

In the middle latitudes of both hemispheres lie the battlegrounds of contrasting air masses, where warm tropical air meets cold polar air along the ever-fluctuating polar fronts. Seasons are primarily warm and cold rather than wet and dry as in the tropics; the changing temperatures from season to season and with the advance and retreat of air masses play a much larger part in influencing man's activities. Instead of the monotony of the tropical climates there are both periodic and erratic weather changes, making these latitudes "intemperate" rather than temperate as they are commonly designated. These are the belts of the extratropical cyclones, where most of the precipitation is associated with fronts. All the climates of this group are subject to frost and all experience snow, although the amount and duration of snow cover vary widely. The principal air masses that dominate this group of climates are the cT, mT, cP, mP and their modifications. The interactions of these air masses produce the six major climatic types discussed in this chapter.

THE DRY SUMMER SUBTROPICS

The dry summer subtropical climate prevails on the west coasts of continents in the lower middle latitudes where the controlling air masses are mT out of the eastern margins of the subtropic highs. Only in the Mediterranean Basin does this climate extend far eastward from a major ocean. From this region the climate has taken another common name, the Mediterranean type. Other locations are central California, central Chile, the southern tip of Africa, southwestern Australia, and an area in the southeastern part of South Australia and adjacent Victoria.

The chief features of the climate are a hot, dry summer and a mild, rainier winter. During the summer the climate comes under the influence of stable air which flows out of the oceanic subtropic high cells to the west. (In the case of the Mediterranean Basin the zone of subsidence in the subtropic high extends far into the eastern end of the Mediterranean Sea.) Under these conditions the climate is very much like that of the tropical arid and semiarid types. In winter the migration of the global circulation brings to these regions the tropical margins of the westerlies with their cyclonic passages and occasional invasions of modified polar air masses.

Annual temperature averages are somewhat lower than in the tropical climates; this is a *sub*tropical climate in terms of latitudinal location and temperature. Monthly averages in summer do not often exceed 80°F, although extreme maximums of over 100° have been recorded at numerous stations. Coastal locations have much cooler summers because of a

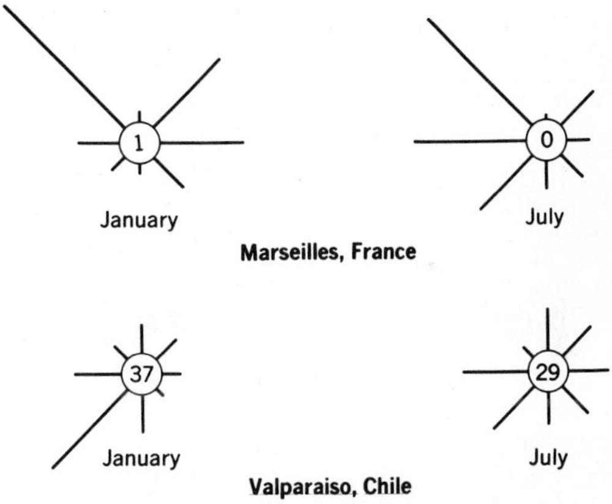

January   July

Marseilles, France

Fig. 8-1 Wind roses for Marseilles and Valparaiso.

January   July

Valparaiso, Chile

marine effect which is increased by cool ocean currents. An exception is found on Mediterranean shores, where the absence of cool currents and the generally warmer water temperatures cause higher summer temperatures than in other areas having this type of climate. A comparison of Sacramento and San Francisco affords an illustration of the influence of the ocean. Sacramento has a July mean of 76°F, whereas San Francisco on the coast has only 59°. Note that San Francisco does not achieve its maximum mean monthly temperature until September, when the coastal waters are warmer and there is less fog.

Climatic Data for Dry Summer Subtropical Stations
Sacramento, California

	J	F	M	A	M	J	J	A	S	O	N	D	Yr.
Temp.	47	51	55	60	66	72	76	75	73	65	55	48	62
Precip.	3.6	3.5	2.5	1.6	0.6	0.1	T	T	0.2	0.8	1.5	3.6	18.0

San Francisco, California

	J	F	M	A	M	J	J	A	S	O	N	D	Yr.
Temp.	51	53	55	56	57	59	59	59	62	61	57	52	57
Precip.	4.6	3.7	2.9	1.4	0.6	0.1	T	T	0.2	0.9	2.0	4.3	20.8

The summer temperatures of the interior locations are reminiscent of the deserts. Daily maximums are high, frequently above 90°, but the nighttime low may be below 60°. With clear skies and low relative humidity, daytime heating is intense, but nocturnal cooling is rapid. Along the coasts, however, diurnal temperature ranges are much lower. The mean daily maximum for January at Valparaiso on the coast of Chile is about 70°, whereas at Santiago in the interior it is 86°. Yet Santiago has a lower mean daily minimum in the same month. Winter is a distinctly cooler season in the dry summer subtropics, the coolest month having a mean temperature usually below 50°. As in summer, the diurnal ranges are greatest in the interior. Winter frosts occur but they are rarely severe. On the few occasions when night temperatures drop well below the freezing point there is great damage to citrus and other crops. Freezing temperatures in the dry summer subtropics are ordinarily the result of rapid nocturnal radiation and air drainage in the lower layers of a polar continental air mass that has invaded the subtropical latitudes, but sometimes freezing temperatures prevail throughout such air masses.

Katabatic, or gravity, winds sometimes plague the coastal regions in winter. The *mistral* in southern France and the *bora* along the Adriatic coast of Yugoslavia flow seaward from interior plateaus to create unpleasantly cool, dry conditions. In Southern California a hot, gusty wind known as the *Santa Ana* blows toward the coast in winter when a high pressure center is developed over the western United States. Wind speeds sometimes reach 60 miles per hour, and because of low relative humidity, the air becomes dusty and forest fire danger is often critical.

Annual precipitation totals in this climate generally fall within the range of 15 to 35 in., the amount being least on the semiarid margins and increasing poleward toward the marine climate. The summers have little or no rain, and this feature combined with the high temperatures results in extremely low soil moisture content. (See Figure 8-2.) The meager summer rainfall consists largely of scattered showers attended by rapid runoff. Typical summer weather is an unbroken series of hot, sunny days. Along the immediate coasts, the modified temperatures are accompanied by a tendency to fogginess, especially where the effect of cold ocean currents is extended poleward from the desert coasts. Fog and dew are important factors in plant growth along these coasts. Winter precipitation comes from cyclonic storms, the moisture sources, for the most part, being maritime tropical and maritime polar air masses. Frontal rainfall associated with cyclones is frequently light and scattered because the low centers normally pass by on the high-latitude side of the climatic regions. Occasionally a low passes directly over the region, bringing frontal conditions approximating those which are regular occurrences in the marine west coast climate, but with rainfall concentrated in fewer rainy days. Stations with little or no rain in the driest summer month commonly have 3 to 5 in. in the wettest winter month. Snow is rare at lower elevations. Both snow and total precipitation increase on the slopes of mountains, which at their greater heights are properly classified with the highland climates.

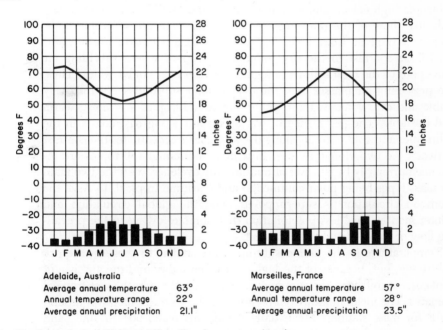

	Adelaide, Australia		Marseilles, France	
Average annual temperature	63°		57°	
Annual temperature range	22°		28°	
Average annual precipitation	21.1"		23.5"	

Fig. 8-2 Climatic graphs for Adelaide and Marseilles, dry summer subtropics.

THE HUMID SUBTROPICS

The humid subtropics are located approximately in the same latitudes as the dry summer subtropics, but they are on the eastern sides of the continents, where they come under the influence of unstable maritime tropical air out of the western margins of the subtropic highs. Annual precipitation is greater than in the dry summer subtropics, but in summer amounts may be inadequate to meet the needs of potential evapotranspiration.

World distribution of the humid subtropical climate is chiefly in the following areas: southeastern United States, a belt along northern India, southern and eastern China, Formosa and southern Japan, northeastern Argentina and adjacent areas, the Natal Coast of South Africa, and the eastern coast of Australia. A smaller area is found at the eastern end of the Black Sea. Note that although the poleward boundaries of these climates are essentially at the same latitude as the dry subtropics, they extend farther toward the equator and merge into one of the humid tropical types.

During the summer, the humid subtropics are dominated by maritime tropical air which flows inland from the anticyclonic circulation of the subtropic high cells. Summer temperatures and humidity are uncomfortably like those of the rainy tropics, for the air from the subtropic highs flows onto the land from the lower latitudes with a path over warm water. This is in contrast to the dry summer subtropics, where subsiding air moves out of the high cells from higher latitudes over colder water. Thus, the prevailing air masses over the dry summer subtropics are relatively stable and dry, whereas those of the humid subtropics are moist, warm and unstable. The prevalence of warm currents along east coasts in the subtropics and cold currents along the west coasts accentuates the contrast between the two climatic types. In winter, the humid subtropics are influenced primarily by the belt of mid-latitude cyclones, with the two main air mass types being polar continental and maritime tropical. In Asia, the monsoon circulation is superimposed upon the global circulation and winter months have less precipitation than summer owing to the prevailing flow of stable air off the continent.

Temperatures in the humid subtropics are similar to those in the dry subtropics, but, because of the high relative humidity and the absence of cool currents offshore, the summers are more like those in the wet tropical climates. The mean monthly temperature of the warmest month is around 80°F for most stations. Mean daily maximums reach 90° to 100°, and extremes exceed 100°. Diurnal ranges are small, the nights being much more oppressive than in the dry summer subtropics. Furthermore, temperature variations from day to day are not very great. The growing season is long, but relief from summer conditions of heat and high relative humidity comes with the autumn as the first salients of polar air reaches into these latitudes. Then the humid subtropics suddenly lose their similarity to the rainy tropics. Temperatures of the cold month average between 40° and 55° for most areas in the climatic type. The major exceptions are in monsoon Asia. Hong Kong, has, as its lowest monthly mean,

59° in February. Allahabad, India, has a January average of 61°. These stations would be classified with the tropical climates but for their distinctly cooler winter seasons. The greater proportion of water in the Southern Hemisphere causes annual ranges to be generally lower than in the Northern Hemisphere in this climate. In both cases coastal stations show smaller annual ranges than those in the interior. Compare the temperature data for New Orleans with those for Buenos Aires and Memphis. Memphis, an interior station, has an annual range of 40° as compared with 27° at New Orleans, whereas Buenos Aires has a lower summer maximum and a 25° annual range.

Climatic Data for Humid Subtropical Stations
Buenos Aires, Argentina

	J	F	M	A	M	J	J	A	S	O	N	D	Yr.
Temp.	74	73	69	62	55	50	49	51	55	60	66	71	61
Precip.	3.1	2.8	4.3	3.5	3.0	2.4	2.2	2.4	3.1	3.4	3.3	3.9	37.4

Memphis, Tennessee

	J	F	M	A	M	J	J	A	S	O	N	D	Yr.
Temp.	42	45	52	62	71	79	82	81	74	64	51	44	62
Precip.	6.1	4.7	5.1	4.6	4.2	3.7	3.5	3.0	2.8	2.7	4.4	4.9	49.7

New Orleans, Louisiana

	J	F	M	A	M	J	J	A	S	O	N	D	Yr.
Temp.	56	58	63	70	77	82	83	84	80	73	62	57	70
Precip.	4.4	4.7	6.2	5.4	5.1	5.5	7.9	6.3	6.0	3.2	3.7	4.9	63.2

Day-to-day variation in temperature becomes much greater as polar and tropical air masses alternately advance and retreat in their battle for supremacy in the succession of cyclones. While the winters can best be described as mild, frosts are normal in the higher latitudes and occasionally plague the tropical margins. Extreme minimums of 10–20° have occurred along the United States Gulf Coast. Severe frosts are a hazard to crops and orchards in Florida just as they are in California.

Typical annual averages of precipitation in the humid subtropics vary from 30 to 65 in. The lower averages are found in the regions bordering the semiarid climates, the greater amounts along mountain ranges and in the tropical extensions of the climatic type. Most areas have a fairly uniform distribution of rainfall throughout the year; 3 to 6 in. are typical monthly averages. Nevertheless, great variety can be found in precipitation regimes. In the southeastern United States the primary monthly maximum occurs in March at Vicksburg, in May at Little Rock, and in July at Mobile. Miami has a primary maximum in September owing to hurricane activity.

In India and eastern Asia the monsoon effect produces a distinctly dry winter, when air masses from the interior are dry. The graph for Chung-

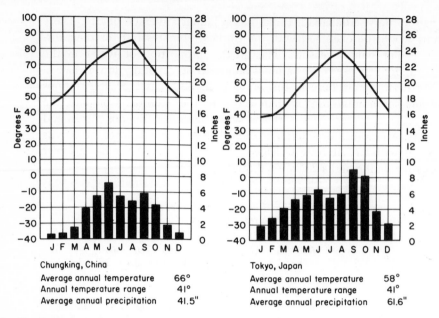

Fig. 8-3 Climatic graphs for Chungking and Tokyo, humid subtropics.

king illustrates. (See Figure 8-3.) Tokyo's regime represents the blending of a monsoon effect with winter cyclonic storms and an island location. Its secondary maximum in early summer results from a southwesterly stream of warm, moist, unstable air of equatorial origin. The rains of this season are known as the *Baiu* in Japan.

For the climate as a whole, summer precipitation is primarily from air mass thunderstorms. (See Figure 8-4.) Hurricanes or typhoons (or their remnants) visit the coasts occasionally in late summer and autumn and increase the monthly rainfall totals. (See Figure 8-3.) As the polar front moves into these regions, frontal precipitation and thunderstorms of the frontal type are common in the converging poleward flow of air drawn into the warm sectors of cyclones. Chungking has two monthly rainfall maximums, in June and September, which appear to be associated with greater thunderstorm activity as the frontal conditions retreat in the spring and reappear in the autumn.

Winter precipitation is mostly related to fronts and sometimes comes in the form of snow. Rainfall is lighter and more continuous; rainy days are greater in number, and cool, overcast days are more frequent. Frontal and ground fogs both occur in the humid subtropics, primarily in winter. Coastal fogs of the advection type are generally lacking because of the absence of cold currents in the adjacent oceans.

Mountain barriers have a significant effect on the distribution of pre-

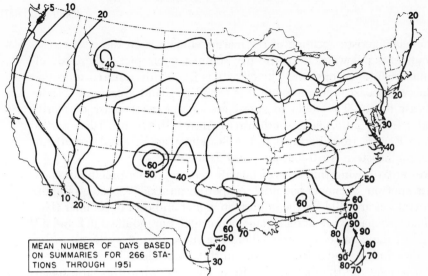

Courtesy U.S. Weather Bureau.

Fig. 8-4 Average annual number of days with thunderstorms in the contiguous United States.

cipitation in the humid subtropics just as in every other climate. One of the most unusual climatic stations in the world is Cherrapunji, India, to which allusion has already been made in Chapter 3. Cherrapunji is located at 4309 ft. above sea level on the south side of the Khasi Hills in northeastern India. It is almost 200 miles from the Bay of Bengal, but when the summer monsoon blows strongly the large area of lowlands allows moist air to pass inland, where it is forced upward in a funnel-shaped depression. Flood waters in the lowlands are warmer than the sea and probably contribute a share of the moisture that reaches the uplands. The dividing effect of the Khasi Hills acting as a mountain barrier is shown by the fact that Shillong, at 4920 ft. but on the northern slope 25 miles away, had only 95 in. mean annual rainfall in the period 1931–60. Were it not for the lower monthly temperatures and the relatively high annual range of temperature, Cherrapunji would be classified as a monsoon tropical station.

Climatic Data for an Unusual Humid Subtropical Station*
Cherrapunji, India

	J	F	M	A	M	J	J	A	S	O	N	D	Yr.
Temp.	53	57	62	66	67	68	69	69	69	67	61	55	63
Precip.	0.8	1.5	7.0	23.8	67.2	115.0	96.7	71.9	46.0	17.6	1.8	0.2	449.6

* These data are for the period 1931–60 and therefore do not include the record totals which occurred in the nineteenth century.

MARINE CLIMATE

The characteristic location of the marine climate is on the west coasts of continents poleward from the dry summer subtropics, where air of oceanic origin flows onshore. The climate is frequently referred to as the marine west coast type, although it is found in island areas and certain southeast coasts. The main locations are on the west coast of North America from California to southeastern Alaska; the British Isles; northwestern Europe from Portugal to the Scandinavian Peninsula; southern Chile; southeastern Australia; and New Zealand.

Most areas having this type of climate receive ample precipitation in winter, but in summer potential evapotranspiration exceeds rainfall. Temperatures are mild for the latitude in winter and cool in summer. The dominant air masses are of maritime polar origin, but modified mT and cP also affect the climate. In winter there is a succession of cyclones as the westerlies and the polar front prevail in these latitudes. There are fewer frontal passages in the marine climate in summer, when the subtropical oceanic high cells reach their highest latitudes, diverting cyclonic storms poleward. Along the eastern margin of the Pacific high an outflow of stable, subsiding air brings distinctly drier conditions to the North American Pacific Coast.

Climatic Data for Stations in the Marine Climate
Seattle, Washington

	J	F	M	A	M	J	J	A	S	O	N	D	Yr.
Temp.	41	44	46	52	57	61	66	65	61	54	47	44	53
Precip.	5.2	3.9	3.3	2.0	1.6	1.4	0.6	0.7	1.6	3.3	5.0	5.4	34.1

Melbourne, Australia

	J	F	M	A	M	J	J	A	S	O	N	D	Yr.
Temp.	67	67	65	59	54	50	49	51	54	57	61	64	58
Precip.	1.9	1.8	2.2	2.3	2.1	2.1	1.9	1.9	2.3	2.6	2.3	2.3	25.7

Mean annual temperatures in the marine climate are mostly in the range of 45° to 55°, unless modified by altitude. The mean monthly temperature of the warmest month is usually 60° to 65°. Daily maximum temperatures do not often exceed 75°, but extreme maximums of over 100° sometimes occur when continental air temporarily invades a coastal area. Nights are cool, partly owing to nocturnal radiation and partly because of the generally low temperatures produced by winds off the sea. The marine influence is seen in low diurnal ranges as well as low annual ranges of temperature, but the effect decreases inland. Horizontal temperature gradients are greater from the coasts toward inland locations than in north–south directions, because the transport of heat from ocean sources is more significant than latitudinal variation of net radiation in this climate. Wintertime anomalies are even greater than in summer, temperatures being from 10° to 30° warmer than the normal for the latitudes. Long periods with overcast skies and the prevailing onshore flow of maritime air in winter keep diurnal ranges small. Off northwest Europe and the British Isles, the Gulf Stream and the North Atlantic Drift carry the abnormally warm winter temperatures into high latitudes. Mean monthly temperatures of the coldest month are above freezing throughout the climatic region. Extreme minimums below zero occur at the higher latitudes and at inland and upland stations, but prolonged periods of continuous freezing weather are unusual at the coasts. Outbreaks of polar continental air are responsible for periods of clear, freezing weather. At such times the wind is from an easterly direction, blowing out of a continental high center (chiefly cP or A air masses). The North American Pacific Coast is protected to some extent from the cold continental air by the mountain barriers of the Rockies and Cascades. Even when the air pushes to the coast, the stable-air foehn effect modifies its chilling effects appreciably. In northwest Europe, the marine climate extends farther inland than on any other continent, largely because of the absence of an effective mountain barrier. Not only do the maritime effects reach farther eastward, but the occasional polar outbreaks of northern Europe cover a much larger area, often including the coasts. Boundaries between marine and continental climates are sharply defined by mountains in North America and in southern Chile but are transition zones in Europe.

There is a wide range of annual precipitation in the marine climate, with variations from less than 20 to more than 100 in. (See Figure 8-5.)

Although the marine climate as a whole must be characterized as having a deficiency of precipitation in summer, its dry season is neither so long nor so pronounced as that of the dry summer subtropics. As would be expected, the margins of the marine climate lying adjacent to the dry summer subtropics have the lowest summer rainfall averages. The absence of high summer temperatures is accompanied by reduced potential evapotranspiration so that natural vegetation does not show a marked influence of seasonal drought. Comparison of the water balance graphs for Birmingham, England, and Athens, Greece, shows the greater summer water need at the latter station.

At places in the lee of mountain barriers annual precipitation may be less than 20 in. Extreme southern Chile, the Otago Basin in southern New Zealand, and the lowlands about the Strait of Juan de Fuca in Washington and British Columbia are examples. The dry summer regime along the North American coast extends farther poleward than in any comparable area in the world. Under the Koeppen classification much of the Puget Sound-Willamette Lowland and southwestern British Columbia would be

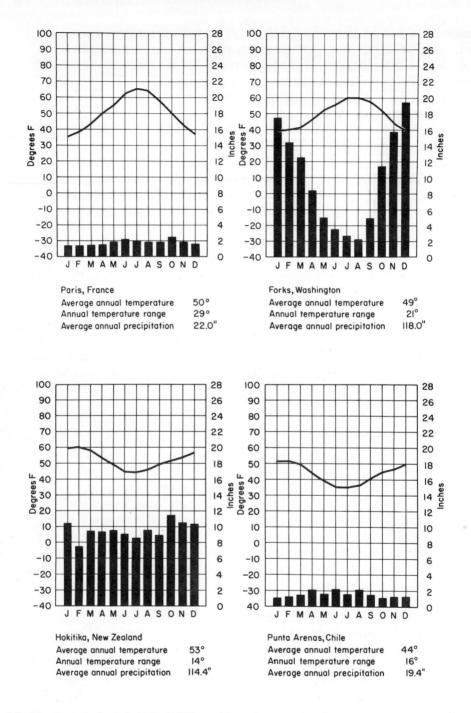

Fig. 8-5 Climatic graphs for Paris, Forks, Hokitika, and Punta Arenas, marine climate.

classified as dry summer subtropical in view of the low summer rainfall and a winter month maximum more than three times that of the driest summer month. Some agricultural land in this area is drained by tiles and ditches in winter and irrigated in summer. Cooler temperatures, a shorter dry season, and a location within the marine regional pattern possibly justify inclusion of these low rainfall areas as anomalous subregions of the marine type.

Some stations near the poleward margin of the climatic type have a precipitation maximum (or a secondary maximum) in autumn. The graph for Punta Arenas, Chile, illustrates this phenomenon. Glasgow, Scotland, has a primary maximum in December and a secondary maximum in August. October is the rainiest month at Sitka, Alaska. Autumn maximums are attributable to the fact that at that season the maritime air masses

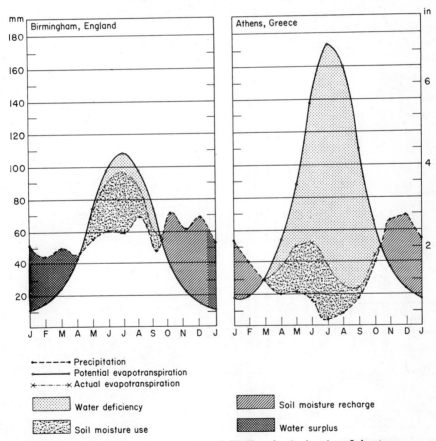

- - - - Precipitation
———— Potential evapotranspiration
×—·—·—× Actual evapotranspiration

[▓] Water deficiency   [▨] Soil moisture recharge

[▒] Soil moisture use   [▓] Water surplus

After method of Thornthwaite, based on data computed by C. W. Thornthwaite Associates, Laboratory of Climatology.

Fig. 8-6 Graphs of potential evapotranspiration and precipitation for Birmingham and Athens.

come from warmer water and have a higher moisture content than in late winter and spring.

The precipitation is reliable as well as comparatively effective in the marine climate. Great departures from the average annual or monthly means are uncommon. Two features of the climate are the reliability of the precipitation and the large number of rain-days, especially in winter. Many stations have more than 150 rain-days a year. (See Figure 8-7.) Bahia Felix, Chile, near the Straits of Magellan, has an average of 325 rain-days per year; in 1916, rain fell there on 348 days! In such a climate gray, overcast skies with light rain or drizzle are the rule. There may be a number of consecutive days with precipitation, but the total rainfall during such periods is small. Dull, drizzly weather is the price paid by inhabitants of the marine climatic regions for mild winter temperatures. (See Figure 8-8.) The parade of cyclonic storms brings maritime air with relatively warm temperatures, but it also brings moisture, and often strong winds. Stationary and occluded fronts are common, the occlusion process often taking place along coastal mountain ranges. On the other

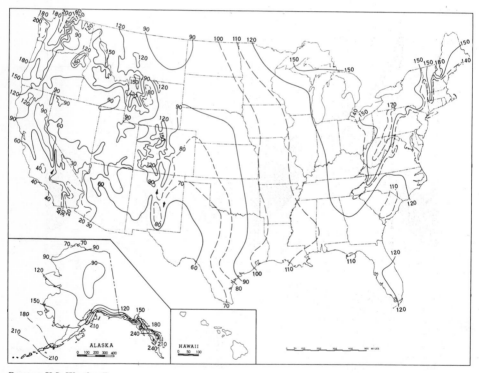

Courtesy U.S. Weather Bureau.

Fig. 8-7 Mean annual number of days with precipitation of 0.01 in. or more in the United States.

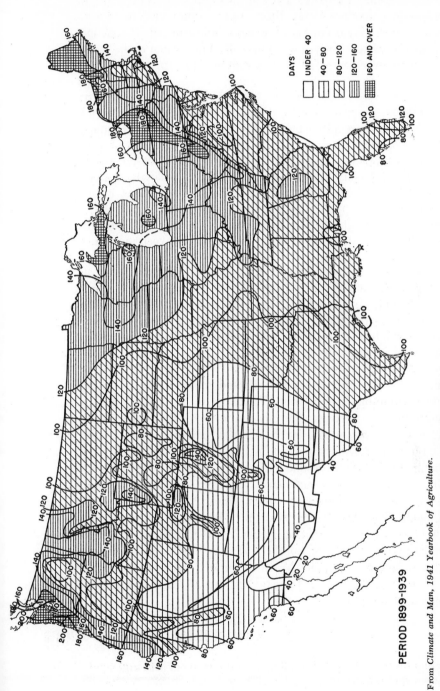

PERIOD 1899-1939

From Climate and Man, 1941 Yearbook of Agriculture.

Fig. 8-8 Average annual number of cloudy days in the contiguous United States.

hand, several fronts may pass over a region in rapid succession without a single rainless day. Needless to say, there are few sunny days in winter. In the lowlands, snow may occur on a few days, but ordinarily it remains for only a short time. Frequently it is "rained off." Only when an invasion of cold polar air follows a snowfall is there a snow cover for more than a day or two.

Summer precipitation is also largely of cyclonic origin. It is more showery and falls on fewer days and yet may reach monthly totals equal to those of winter, the exception being those coasts which come under marked influence of the oceanic highs. Thunderstorms are far less numerous than in the subtropical or the continental climates, for the air which moves in from the high cells tends to be more stable. Most lowland areas average fewer than ten thunderstorms a year. At higher elevations, in the mountain areas, total precipitation is, of course, greater and thunderstorm activity is more common. Quite often, conditionally unstable maritime air is cooled sufficiently by orographic lifting to set off convective storms along mountain ranges. In company with the showery precipitation and smaller number of rain-days in summer, there is more sunshine. One of the outstanding seasonal differences in the marine climate is the greater percentage of possible sunshine in summer. In the United States Pacific Northwest, summer is popularly defined as being synonymous with the sunny period. Though of short and variable duration, these "summers" have weather as pleasant as any on earth.

Fog frequency is high in the marine climate. The fogs of London have become legendary, but other areas are affected to some degree. Vancouver, British Columbia, has an annual average of 37 days with fog; Eureka, California, has 51 days. The maximum incidence of fog is in autumn and winter, when warm, stable maritime air drifts across land which has undergone considerable cooling. Industrial smoke reinforces the unpleasant effects of fog around cities, increasing the density and duration. The marine climate is remarkably free from violent storms such as hurricanes or tornadoes. However, winter winds of gale force are frequent, and, along the coasts, heavy seas are a hazard to shipping and shore installations. The name "roaring forties," used to indicate the fury of the prevailing westerlies in the Southern Hemisphere, is nearly as apt in the Northern Hemisphere. The North Atlantic, Irish Sea, Straits of Magellan, Australian Bight, and Tasman Sea are all infamous in the annals of merchant shipping.

MID-LATITUDE ARID AND SEMIARID CLIMATES

The dry climates of mid-latitudes differ from the tropical arid and semiarid climates in two important respects: average temperatures are lower, and subsiding air masses are not the chief controlling factors. A major factor influencing the arid and semiarid climates of middle latitudes is their location in the continents, far-removed from the windward coasts. Mountain barriers on the windward accentuate the aridity of several areas. The arid and semiarid phases of the dry mid-latitudes differ primarily in the degree of aridity, and they can conveniently be treated together here. This is not to say, however, that the differences in amount or effectiveness of precipitation are unimportant in their effects on crops and vegetation. Three continental regions comprise the principal distribution of these climates: the intermontane basins and Great Plains of western United States and Canada, southern U.S.S.R. and northern China, and western and southern Argentina. It should be noted that, in the Northern Hemisphere, the mid-latitude dry climates merge into their tropical counterparts. Temperature is the differentiating criterion and makes itself felt in the demands of evapotranspiration. It is well to remember that the transitions between tropical and mid-latitude dry climates are gradual and that boundaries drawn on the basis of temperature values alone are necessarily arbitrary.

The lower annual temperature averages are a response to the effects of higher latitude, and in some cases of altitude as well. Appreciable differences occur within the mid-latitude dry climates as a result of the latitudinal spread. The characteristic temperature curve shows a large annual range, a reflection of continental location. In summer the temperatures are high as continental tropical air masses develop over the heated land surfaces. Because there is a deficiency of moisture little heat is used in evaporation, most of it being used to further warm the subsiding air mass. In winter the prevalent air masses are again continental, but they are

Climatic Data for Mid-Latitude Semiarid Stations
Denver, Colorado

	J	F	M	A	M	J	J	A	S	O	N	D	Yr.
Temp.	30	32	38	47	57	67	73	72	64	52	39	33	50
Precip.	0.6	0.7	1.2	2.1	2.7	1.4	1.5	1.3	1.1	1.0	0.7	0.5	14.8

Ulan Bator, Mongolia

	J	F	M	A	M	J	J	A	S	O	N	D	Yr.
Temp.	−14	−6	9	30	42	56	61	57	46	30	9	−8	26
Precip.	T	T	0.1	0.2	0.4	1.1	3.0	2.0	0.9	0.2	0.2	0.1	8.2

Climatic Data for Mid-Latitude Arid Stations
Lovelock, Nevada

	J	F	M	A	M	J	J	A	S	O	N	D	Yr.
Temp.	30	36	43	50	58	66	74	72	62	51	40	31	51
Precip.	0.7	0.5	0.4	0.4	0.4	0.3	0.2	0.2	0.3	0.4	0.3	0.4	4.5

Santa Cruz, Argentina

	J	F	M	A	M	J	J	A	S	O	N	D	Yr.
Temp.	59	57	55	48	41	35	35	38	43	49	53	56	47
Precip.	0.6	0.3	0.4	0.6	0.4	0.5	0.4	0.6	0.3	0.3	0.4	0.7	5.4

primarily associated with outbreaks of polar air. Denver and Ulan Bator are representative of the mid-latitude semiarid climate; Lovelock and Santa Cruz typify the arid phase.

Note the contrasts in temperature as shown by the representative stations. Ulan Bator, deep in the Asian continent, has an annual range of 75 F°, whereas Santa Cruz, on the southern Argentina coast, has a range of only 24°. Patagonia lies to the leeward of the Andes and has a marine temperature regime, but it receives little moisture from the prevailing westerly flow of air. Only occasionally does cyclonic activity bring easterly winds, and the continent is too narrow to induce a thermal low-pressure center with monsoonal circulation onto the land in summer. The modified marine influence of southern Argentina is unique in the dry mid-latitude climates.

Extreme temperatures range from well below −50°F in winter to over 100° in summer in these climates. The lowest minimums are recorded in the northern Great Plains and in Siberia. The highest maximums occur at the lower-latitude margins of the climates. With respect to temperature, a summer day in certain parts of the dry mid-latitudes may be uncomfortably like the tropical deserts. Diurnal ranges are great, however, and especially at the higher elevations the nights can be pleasantly cool. Daytime heating and nocturnal cooling effect a large diurnal range, just as in the tropical arid and semiarid climates. Although the same is true to some extent in winter, the mid-latitudes have much lower monthly averages, and invasions of polar continental air bring severe freezing temperatures not found in the tropics. Compare the graphs of the daily march of temperature in January and July for Yuma and Salt Lake City, in Figure 8-9.

In common with the dry climates of the low latitudes the mid-latitude arid and semiarid climates have deficient precipitation. The minimum amount of precipitation that will support a vegetation association of a given density is, however, lower than in the tropics, for the temperatures and the consequent evaporation and transpiration are lower. Annual rainfall of 6 to 8 in. may support steppe vegetation in the cool mid-latitudes but would be adequate only for desert scrub in the tropics. It is ultimately on the basis of the ratio of precipitation to potential evapotranspiration that the arid and semiarid phases of the dry mid-latitude climates are best differentiated. Desert vegetation is characteristic of the arid climate and steppe grassland predominates in the semiarid regions. Accordingly, the climates are also well known by their associated vegetation as mid-latitude desert and steppe, respectively.

As in the dry tropical climates, in the mid-latitude counterparts there is no general rule governing the regime of precipitation. The margins near the dry summer subtropics have winter maximums; toward the humid continental climates summer maximums prevail, and where marine influences are marked, as on the east coast of Argentina, there is no great variation from month to month. The graph for San Juan, Argentina, illustrates the winter maximum in the arid type. (See Figure 8-10.) Lovelock also has a winter maximum. Williston, North Dakota, and Ulan Bator have summer maximums. Absence of a distinct seasonal maximum is shown in the data for Santa Cruz.

A characteristic of precipitation in all dry climates is the great variability. Conrad has computed the percentage of variability from the normal to show that, in general, variability increases with a decrease of mean annual precipitation. (See Table 8-1.)

Fig. 8-9 Diurnal variation of temperature in January and July at Salt Lake City, Utah, and Yuma, Arizona.

Adapted from Mark Jefferson, "The Real Temperatures Throughout North and South America," *Geographical Review*, 6, 3 (Sept., 1918).

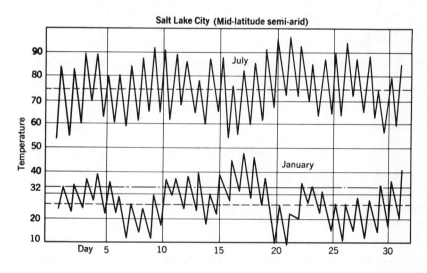

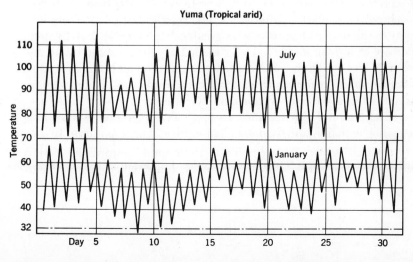

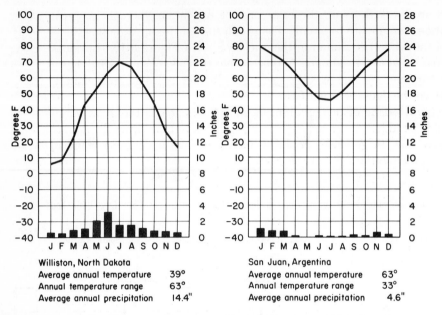

Fig. 8-10 Climatic graphs for Williston, mid-latitude semiarid, and San Juan, mid-latitude arid climate.

TABLE 8-1

World Average Variability for Given Amounts of Rainfall*

Average annual rainfall (inches)	5	10	15	20	30	60
Expected percentage variability	31	24	20	18	17	15

 ° V. Conrad, *Monthly Weather Review*, Vol. 69, 1941, p. 5.

In a study which has become a classic in geographic literature, Henry M. Kendall pointed out that, on the Great Plains in the period 1915–1924, humid years were experienced as far west as the Rocky Mountains and dry years occurred as far east as Minnesota. The significance of precipitation variability in the semiarid climate is far greater than in the arid. A 100 per cent increase of rainfall in a given year at an arid climate station with an average of 3 in. is not likely to revolutionize vegetation and human settlement. Agriculture is geared to irrigation, if practiced at all. In the steppe regions, however, a series of wetter-than-average years gives a false impression of agricultural potentialities, and settlers are tempted to institute land uses not actually suited to the long-term climatic pattern. In no climate is there more danger in the use of statistical averages than in the mid-latitude semiarid type. The dry years are as important as the "normal" years, if not more so, in determining the vegetation association and the optimum patterns of land use.

The meager winter precipitation in the dry mid-latitudes is frontal and comes with occasional cyclones, which replace the continental high pressure centers. It may come as snow, and high winds accompanying polar outbursts in the wake of a cold front produce blinding snowstorms, known as blizzards on the Great Plains. The infrequent cyclonic disturbances are sandwiched between periods of cold and generally clear weather. The Chinook, or foehn wind, is experienced over the northern Great Plains in winter and spring. A similar wind which descends from the Andes into western Patagonia is known as the *Zonda*. Surface wind speeds are generally high in these climates because of the large expanse of plains and plateaus. Immediately at the surface, the absence of trees is also a factor permitting free flow of air.

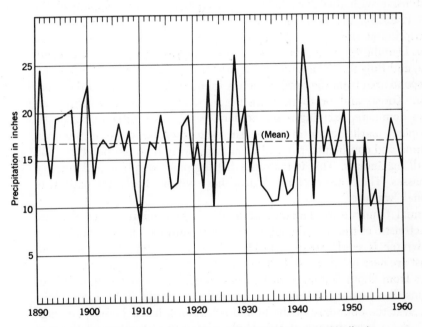

Fig. 8-11 Variations in annual precipitation at a station in the mid-latitude semiarid climate near Springfield, Colorado, 1890–1960.

Summer weather is influenced by thermally induced low-pressure centers over the continents. Although this may tend to produce monsoon-type winds blowing onto the continent from water bodies, mountain barriers and the distance of the dry climatic regions from the sea limit the amount of moisture that reaches to the interior. Summer rainfall comes with scattered thundershowers. All too often a dry period is broken by a violent cloudburst-hailstorm which does as much damage to crops as drought. In the United States, tornadoes sometimes form along belts of frontal thunderstorms, especially in the warmer half of the year.

HUMID CONTINENTAL WARM SUMMER CLIMATE

Extensive areas with humid continental climates occur only in the Northern Hemisphere; the Southern Hemisphere has mostly a water surface at these latitudes. As indicated by their names, the two types of humid continental climate differ primarily with respect to the length and intensity of the summer season. They are considered separately here to facilitate emphasis on their differing temperature characteristics.

The humid continental warm summer climate lies in three areas between latitudes approximately 35–45°N. In the United States it is roughly co-extensive with the Corn Belt, bordering the semiarid climate of the Great Plains on the west and running eastward to the Atlantic with an interruption at the Appalachians. In southeastern Europe it is centered on the Danube Basin and includes portions of Hungary, Romania, Yugoslavia, and Bulgaria. The long belt of dry climate in central Asia separates the second area from the third, which is found in Manchuria, northeastern China, Korea, and northern Honshu. In winter, polar continental air masses dominate, bringing much colder weather with intervening surges of tropical maritime air in the warm sectors of cyclones; in summer, maritime and continental tropical air masses bring high temperatures and rainfall maximums. This is truly the battleground of polar and tropical air masses. There are cyclonic "skirmishes" within the larger pattern of seasonal "warfare."

Annual temperature averages mask the large annual ranges that are characteristic of the humid continental warm summer climate. Summer is hot; winter is cold. Mean monthly temperatures for June, July, and August are near or above 70°F. The average length of the frost-free season ranges from about 200 days in the south to 150 days along the northern margins. Yet January averages are typically below 32°F. St. Louis, Missouri, near the boundary of the humid subtropics, has a January average of 32° but a July average of 80°. Harbin, near the boundary of the cool summer phase in Manchuria, has −1° as a January average and 72° as a July average.

A characteristic of continental climates is a great annual range of temperature. This is expressed in the warm summer type not only by high monthly means in summer but also by extreme maximums above 100°. Furthermore, diurnal ranges are small in summer so that the nights are often uncomfortably warm. Conditions of high humidity and high temperature are similar to those in the humid subtropics. A day and night in

Climatic Data for Humid Continental Warm Summer Stations
St. Louis, Missouri

	J	F	M	A	M	J	J	A	S	O	N	D	Yr.
Temp.	32	35	43	55	66	76	80	79	70	59	44	35	56
Precip.	2.0	2.0	3.0	3.7	3.7	4.3	3.3	3.0	2.8	2.9	2.6	2.0	35.3

Harbin, Manchuria

Temp.	−1	5	23	42	56	66	72	70	58	40	21	4	38
Precip.	0.2	0.2	0.4	0.9	1.7	3.7	4.4	4.1	1.8	1.3	0.3	0.2	19.2

Belgrade, Yugoslavia

Temp.	32	34	44	54	63	68	72	71	65	56	45	35	53
Precip.	1.6	1.3	1.6	2.2	2.6	2.8	1.9	2.5	1.7	2.7	1.8	1.9	24.6

Des Moines, Iowa, may be much like the same period in New Orleans, Louisiana, or Montgomery, Alabama, for temperatures do not decrease rapidly with latitude in this climate in summer. Winter is quite another matter. Not only are the monthly averages and the extreme minimums much lower, but the decrease in these values with increasing latitude is appreciable. The cold continental polar outbursts which bring the very low temperatures to the northern parts of the climatic region may not reach the southern margins, or, if they do, they are modified somewhat as they move to lower latitudes. Thus, typical annual minimum temperatures in northern Iowa are on the order of −25°, whereas in southern Missouri the average annual minimum is −5°. Note the maps of average temperatures for January and July for the United States. The isotherms, drawn for intervals of 5°, are much more closely spaced in the eastern United States in winter than in summer, indicating a steeper temperature gradient. The influence of the large continental land mass in Asia results in even lower winter temperatures in the humid continental warm summer climate of Manchuria. Harbin has already been noted. Mukden has a January average of 8°.

Annual precipitation in this climate varies from 20 to 50 in. In general, the amount decreases toward the northern latitudes and toward the continental interiors. Spring or summer is the season of maximum rainfall. There are occasional frontal passages, but convective showers account for most of the warm season rain. Scattered thunderstorms and a high percentage of possible sunshine produce summer weather similar to the humid subtropics. A maximum of rainfall in the summer half of the year is most marked in the interior areas and in eastern Asia, where the monsoonal influence is an important factor. For example, in July Harbin has 4.4 in. but in January only 0.2 in. A characteristic of the precipitation regimes of interior locations in this climate is the spring or early summer maximum, usually in May or June. (See Figure 8-14.) In spring the air

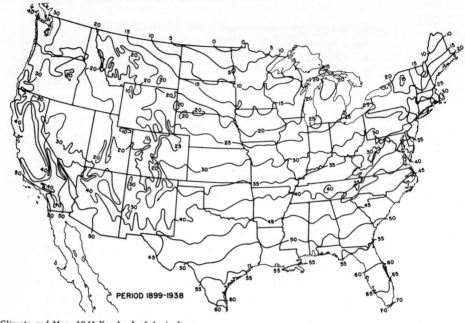

From *Climate and Man, 1941 Yearbook of Agriculture.*
Fig. 8-12 Average January temperatures in the contiguous United States in °F.

Fig. 8-13 Average July temperatures in the contiguous United States in °F.
From *Climate and Man, 1941 Yearbook of Agriculture.*

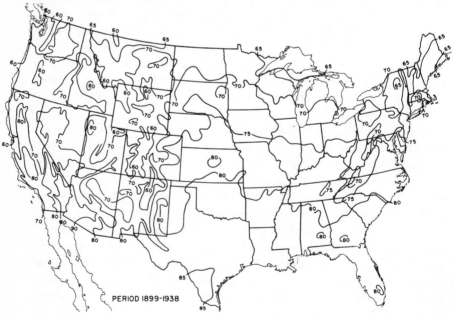

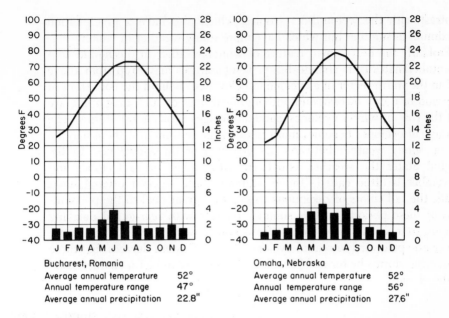

Fig.8-14 Climatic graphs for Bucharest and Omaha, humid continental warm summer climate.

masses are still cold from the north and the contrasting tropical maritime air comes from water that has reached its lowest temperature for the year. The land heats rapidly, however, and the consequent warming of lower layers of advancing maritime air increases instability and leads to numerous convective showers. Although thunderstorms continue throughout the summer the differences in temperature between the land and the upper air become less and the degree of instability is therefore lessened. Sometimes hail accompanies thunderstorms in this climate. In the Mississippi Valley tornadoes are an additional hazard, primarily in the warm months.

Except on the east coast of the United States, the winter months usually have much less precipitation, a feature which is particularly evident in eastern Manchuria and northern China, where a monsoonal regime prevails. A part of the winter precipitation comes as snow, the proportion increasing with latitude and altitude. It is primarily of frontal origin, and the blizzards behind the cold fronts may extend into the humid continental warm summer climate from the west or north. Average annual snowfall varies from 10 to 40 in. Frontal weather in winter may also bring rain, occasional fog, and sometimes sleet or freezing rain. Air mass thunderstorms can develop in the warm sectors of cyclones whose paths follow the southern margins of the climatic type. In general, winter is much less sunny than summer, a fact taken for granted by residents in the areas with humid continental climate. Nevertheless, conditions are in marked contrast with the wet-and-dry tropics, which also have a precipitation maximum in summer but which have more sunny weather in winter.

Probably the best-known feature of winter weather in the humid continental climates is its changeability. Temperatures may drop from above 60° in the warm sector of a cyclone to below zero behind the cold front in a period of a day or two, and, although extremes of such magnitude are not the rule in winter cyclones, sudden changes typify most storms. The passage of cyclones becomes more frequent in autumn, but there may be warm, sunny weather between the first two or three cyclones. In the United States the weather associated with stable air in October and November is often called "Indian summer," and since it often follows frosts, the fall colors of deciduous trees add a great deal to the pleasantness of these periods. Just as summer retreats with rear-guard delaying actions, so in spring there are late frosts and snowstorms which punctuate the erratic poleward retreat of cyclonic storms. Custom decrees that these late spring storms be termed "unseasonal"; they are in fact a characteristic of the climate.

HUMID CONTINENTAL COOL SUMMER CLIMATE

The humid continental cool summer climate is like the warm summer type in so many ways that it can be discussed by comparing the two. The most obvious distinguishing features have already been mentioned, the cooler summer and shorter growing season, which result from location in higher latitudes. The climatic region lies north of the warm summer type in North America, eastern Europe, and the far east of Asia. In each case it has wider longitudinal extent than the humid continental warm summer type. In North America it roughly straddles the Canadian-United States border, with a poleward extension into central Alberta on the west and an eastern limit at the Atlantic Coast in the Maritime Provinces and New England. In Europe and the U.S.S.R. it takes the shape of a long isosceles triangle with southern Scandinavia, Poland, and Czechoslovakia at the base and the vertex deep in central Siberia. In Asia it extends from northern Manchuria out to Hokkaido and southern Sakhalin.

Being in higher latitudes, the cool summer type of humid continental climate is affected by polar air masses for a longer season. Incursions of tropical continental or tropical maritime air are more frequent in summer. On the east coasts, maritime air is drawn onto the continents as cyclones approach the sea.

Temperatures are generally lower both in winter and summer than in the warm summer type. Summer extremes may reach 100° under a "heat wave" of tropical continental air, but these are offset by cool periods, often with cloudiness. Winnipeg and Moscow have July means of 68° and 65°F respectively in contrast with July means of 78° at Omaha and 73° at Bucharest.

Climatic Data for Humid Continental Cool Summer Stations
Winnipeg, Manitoba

	J	F	M	A	M	J	J	A	S	O	N	D	Yr.
Temp.	1	4	19	38	52	62	68	66	55	43	23	8	37
Precip.	0.9	0.8	1.1	1.2	2.1	2.6	2.7	2.5	2.3	1.4	1.1	0.9	19.7

Moscow, U.S.S.R.

	J	F	M	A	M	J	J	A	S	O	N	D	Yr.
Temp.	15	16	24	39	54	62	65	62	52	40	27	18	39
Precip.	1.5	1.4	1.1	1.9	2.2	2.9	3.0	2.9	1.9	2.7	1.7	1.6	24.8

The frost-free season is generally less than 150 days in length, except for coastal locations, and it decreases in the higher latitudes. It is significant, however, that with the increase of latitude the summer daylight periods are longer; this tends to offset the short season to some extent insofar as crop production is concerned. Thus the longest day at Edmonton, Alberta (Lat. 53°45′N.), is over 17 hours, compared with less than 15 hours at St. Louis, Missouri (Lat. 38°35′N.), in the warm summer climatic type.

In the winter the days are increasingly shorter as one proceeds northward and the contrast between the seasons is correspondingly accentuated. Annual ranges of temperatures are even greater than in the humid continental warm summer climate. Winnipeg has a range of 67°; at Moscow the range is 50°. These large annual ranges result from a combination of latitude and interior continental location. Winters are severe; typically the January average is well below 32°, and for some interior stations it is below 0°. Note, however, that the climate is identified primarily by its summer rather than its winter temperature characteristics. Harbin, Manchuria, for example, has a January mean temperature of −1° but a warmer and longer summer than in the humid continental cool summer type of climate. Extreme minimums in the cool summer type fall to −50° or −60°, but they are not an annual occurrence. A series of several days with temperatures below 0° can be expected in most winters as polar air masses lie over the continents. Short-term changes of temperature are greatest in winter, and they are more marked in connection with the nonperiodic cyclonic disturbances than with the diurnal cycle of insolation.

Annual precipitation in the humid continental cool summer climate is usually less than in the warm summer type. The areas within the climatic region are farther from the sources of maritime tropical air and they are influenced for a greater part of the year by drier polar air masses. Annual amounts for most stations range from 15 to 25 in., but the temperatures are lower and a given amount of summer precipitation is more effective than in the warm summer type. Regimes of precipitation are similar to those of the warm summer type, the maximum coming in summer in the interiors. Toward the east coasts of North America and Asia and in Japan, the summer maximums become less pronounced and autumn maximums are more characteristic. Summer thunderstorms are not so common, but summer frontal passages occur more frequently. In the winter season the proportion of snow is greater and snow lies for longer periods. Prolonged snow cover is a factor which inhibits the warming of southward-moving air masses, and, consequently, contributes to the severity of winter conditions.

Along the east coasts of North America and Asia the humid continental climates are considerably modified by the proximity to oceans. Southerly and easterly winds in the circulation of cyclones bring maritime air onto these regions, resulting in increased precipitation and moderated temperatures, especially in winter. Portland, Maine, has 43 in. of precipitation fairly well distributed throughout the year. Nemuro, on Hokkaido in northern Japan, has 38 in. and a September maximum. (See Figure 8-15.) The peculiar features of the humid continental cool summer climate on the east coasts have led some authors to classify it as a distinctive climate under the names "modified humid continental" or "New England-Hokkaido" type. On the coast of New England and the Canadian Maritime Provinces precipitation is much more evenly distributed than in the interior. At St. John's, Newfoundland, there is a November maximum. Mean

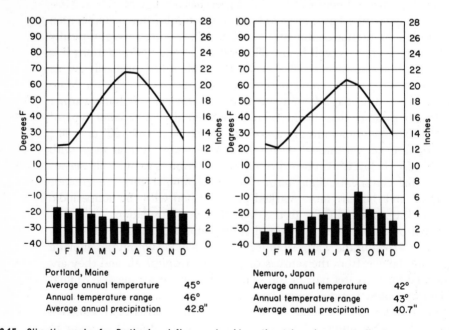

Portland, Maine		Nemuro, Japan	
Average annual temperature	45°	Average annual temperature	42°
Annual temperature range	46°	Annual temperature range	43°
Average annual precipitation	42.8"	Average annual precipitation	40.7"

Fig. 8-15 Climatic graphs for Portland and Nemuro, humid continental cool summer climate.

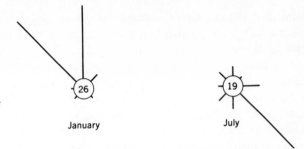

Fig. 8-16 Wind roses for Vladivostok, U.S.S.R.

January   July

temperatures in summer and annual ranges are both appreciably lower than inland. The Maine coast has an exceedingly steep gradient of annual temperature ranges away from the coast. At Eastport the range is 40°, whereas at Woodland, only 30 miles inland, the range is 54°. The ocean not only modifies temperature ranges, but also produces a longer frost-free season. A further characteristic of the coast of New England and the Maritimes is the frequency of gales associated with the succession of cyclones. On rare occasions tropical hurricanes reach this area. Off the coast of Canada the tropical water of the Gulf Stream meets the cold Labrador Current and fogs are frequent in the overlying air. Light winds carry the fog onto the coasts, but it rarely penetrates far inland. The greatest fog frequency is in summer months and over the Grand Banks east of Newfoundland.

Maritime effects in northern Japan are basically similar to those in New

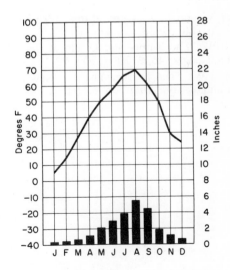

Fig. 8-17 Climatic graph for Vladivostok, humid continental cool summer climate.

Vladivostok, U.S.S.R
Average annual temperature   40°
Annual temperature range   63°
Average annual precipitation   23.6"

England, but the persistent continental air masses act as a barrier to oceanic air in winter, resulting in an extension of the continental characteristics to the east coast of mainland Asia. The mountainous islands receive moisture in winter from the Sea of Japan and thus do not exhibit the usual dry winter regime of the mainland. Note that Nemuro has a September maximum of rainfall which coincides with the typhoon season. Comparison of the graphs for Nemuro and Vladivostok reveals the effect of an island location in producing a smaller annual temperature range and a more even distribution of precipitation. The winter climate of Vladivostok is essentially continental; in the month of January winds are almost entirely from the north or northwest.

ADDITIONAL READINGS

Garnier, B. J., *The Climate of New Zealand*. London: Edward Arnold (Publishers) Ltd., 1958.

Kendall, Henry M., "Notes on Climatic Boundaries in the Eastern United States," *Geog. Rev.*, 25, 1 (1935), 117–24.

Kendrew, W. G., and B. W. Currie, *The Climate of Central Canada*. Ottawa: Queen's Printer, 1955.

Kimble, George H. T., *Our American Weather*. New York: McGraw-Hill Book Company, 1955.

Lydolph, Paul E., "The Russian Sukhovey," *Ann. Assoc. Am. Geogrs.*, 54, 3 (1964), 291–309.

Taylor, James A., and R. A. Yates, *British Weather in Maps*. London: Macmillan & Co., Ltd., 1958.

Villmow, Jack R., "The Nature and Origin of the Canadian Dry Belt," *Ann. Assoc. Am. Geogrs.*, 46, 2 (1956), 211–32.

Wahl, Eberhard W., "The January Thaw in New England (An Example of a Weather Singularity)," *Bull. Am. Met. Soc.*, 33, 9 (1952), 380–86.

climates dominated 9
by polar and arctic air masses;
highland climates

The most widespread variations in temperature on the earth are those resulting from latitudinal and altitudinal variations in the net gain of heat. An increase in either latitude or altitude is normally accompanied by decreasing temperatures, and distinctive features of the climates of high latitudes or high altitudes arise primarily from the low temperatures. Temperature and precipitation characteristics differ between the two climatic groups, however. We shall consider first the cold climates of high latitudes.

TAIGA CLIMATE

The term *taiga* is of Russian origin and refers to the northern continental forests of North America and Eurasia. It has been used also to designate the distinctive climate that prevails in these forest regions. Names such as "subarctic" or "boreal forest" have been applied to the taiga climate.

Two large world regions embrace the taiga climate. In North America it extends in a broad belt from western Alaska to Newfoundland; in Eurasia from Norway to the Kamchatka Peninsula. In both regions the climatic type reaches farther south on the eastern margins of the continent than on the west, reflecting the effect of the large land masses. These regions are the sources of polar air masses, and for most of the year their weather is dominated by cold, dry, stable air. As a result, annual temperature ranges are high and precipitation is meager.

The mean July temperature at Yakutsk, in east central Siberia, is 67°F, but the January average is −45°, giving an annual range of 112°. Ranges of 60° or more are typical in the interior locations; conditions are moderated somewhat near the oceans, particularly on west coasts. Tromso, Norway, has a mean annual range of only 27°.

Climatic Data for Stations in the Taiga Climate
Fairbanks, Alaska

	J	F	M	A	M	J	J	A	S	O	N	D	Yr.
Temp.	−11	−4	9	30	47	58	60	54	44	27	3	−9	26
Precip.	0.9	0.5	0.4	0.3	0.8	1.5	1.9	2.5	1.0	0.9	0.6	0.6	11.9

Tromso, Norway

	J	F	M	A	M	J	J	A	S	O	N	D	Yr.
Temp.	26	25	26	32	39	47	52	51	44	36	30	27	36
Precip.	4.3	4.4	3.1	2.3	1.9	2.2	2.2	2.8	4.8	4.6	4.4	3.8	40.7

Yakutsk, U.S.S.R.

	J	F	M	A	M	J	J	A	S	O	N	D	Yr.
Temp.	−45	−35	−8	22	43	60	67	59	43	20	−19	−43	14
Precip.	0.3	0.2	0.2	0.2	0.6	1.3	1.1	0.9	0.9	0.6	0.4	0.2	6.9

In the short summer the days are long and maximum temperatures frequently rise above 80°. Yakutsk has recorded a temperature of 102°; Fairbanks has an official extreme maximum of 93°. At such stations a small diurnal range might be expected as a result of the long daylight periods, but even where there is 24 hours of daylight an appreciable difference exists between the amount of effective insolation at noon and that received at midnight, when the sun is at a very low angle with the earth's surface. Thus diurnal ranges are commonly on the order of 20° or 30°. As usual, marine influences moderate the diurnal range considerably. The frost-free season in the taiga varies with the latitude and with distance from the sea. Inland it lasts for 50 to 90 days, but there is always the risk of summer frost. The short duration of the frost-free season is balanced to some extent by the longer days, so that certain hardy crops can mature in a shorter calendar period in the taiga than in lower latitudes. Not only is the summer short, but it also ends abruptly. Autumn is often said to begin with a hard freeze, last a few days, and end with the first snow of winter.

Winter is the dominant season. Except on favored coasts, six to eight months have mean temperatures below 32°, and many stations have three or four months with means below 0°F. Furthermore, average daily *maximum* temperatures in winter are generally well below freezing. Under the dominance of the continental anticyclones the weather is usually clear, but the daylight periods are short or entirely absent and outgoing radiation far exceeds insolation. The lowest official surface temperature on record in the climatic type is −90°F at Verkhoyansk in eastern Siberia. It occurred on the 5th and again on the 7th of February, 1892. At Oimekon, about 400 miles to the southeast, the temperature record is shorter, but in recent years it has been colder than Verkhoyansk. An unofficial −108°F was reported at Oimekon in 1938, but details of the date and exposure of the thermometer are unknown. In North America the lowest official temperature is −81°F, recorded at Snag, Yukon Territory, on February 3, 1947. Although these are exceptional temperatures, they indicate the extreme cold which frequently envelopes the taiga in winter. Under the calm conditions that sometimes accompany the extremely low temperatures the dry air does not produce the same physiological chilling as moister air would at appreciably higher temperatures. With wind, however, chilling effects rapidly increase and powdered snow may pervade the air, reducing visibility to zero in a "whiteout."

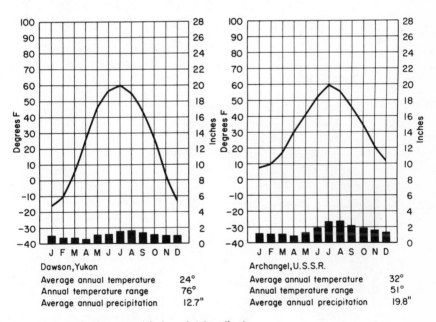

Dawson, Yukon		Archangel, U.S.S.R.	
Average annual temperature	24°	Average annual temperature	32°
Annual temperature range	76°	Annual temperature range	51°
Average annual precipitation	12.7″	Average annual precipitation	19.8″

Fig. 9-1 Climatic graphs for Dawson and Archangel, taiga climate.

Except along the seaward margins, precipitation in the taiga climate is generally under 20 in. annually. It is mostly of cyclonic origin and has a definite summer maximum, again with the coasts excepted. (Compare the data for Tromso and Fairbanks.) At interior locations rainfall is often inadequate to meet the demands of potential evapotranspiration during

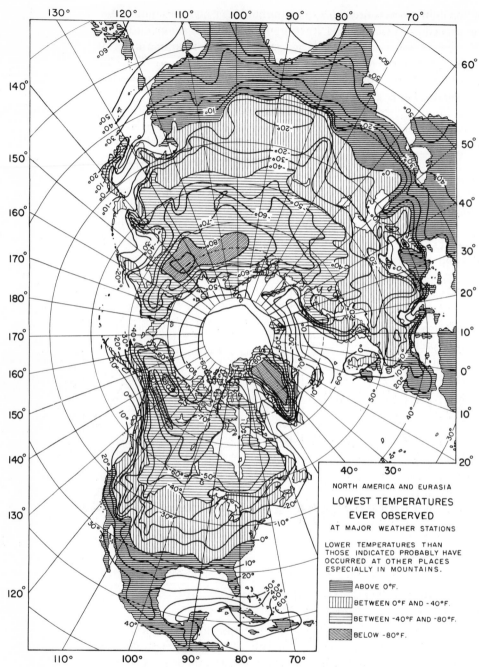

From United States Air Force, Geophysics Research Directorate, *Handbook of Geophysics,* Revised
Edition, published by The Macmillan Company, 1960.

Fig. 9-2 Lowest temperatures ever observed in the Northern Hemisphere.

the long daylight periods of summer, so that dust forms and irrigation may even be necessary in the few areas where crops are raised. Winter snow actually accounts for the smaller part of annual precipitation in most of the taiga, although it may accumulate for several months.

Fog and low stratus clouds are fairly common along the coasts of this climatic region, being especially prevalent in the Aleutian Islands. Ice fogs may form over snow surfaces in winter when temperatures are extremely low.

TUNDRA CLIMATE

Like taiga, *tundra* is a vegetation term which has also been applied to the associated climate. The tundra climatic region lies north of the taiga and extends along the arctic coasts of North America and Eurasia. For the most part it is found north of the Arctic Circle, but in eastern Canada and in eastern Siberia it extends into lower latitudes in keeping with the continental influence. Northern Iceland, coastal Greenland, and many islands in the Arctic Ocean also have this type of climate. The climate does not occur in the Southern Hemisphere except on a few islands in the Antarctic Ocean and small areas on Antarctica, because of the predominance of water surface in the corresponding latitudes.

For most of the year the tundra climate is under the influence of continental polar or continental arctic air masses. In summer the air may have maritime characteristics as a result of the melting of sea ice and more frequent advances of air from oceanic sources in lower latitudes. Even in winter, islands and coasts experience limited marine influences. These effects are the basis for a possible subdivision, the polar marine climate.[*] Although the long periods of ice cover on the Arctic Ocean render it less effective as a moderating influence than oceans at lower latitudes, it nevertheless does affect the tundra climate. Even in winter, when entirely frozen over, the Arctic Ocean has enough heat to modify temperatures slightly. For this reason the extreme minimum temperatures occur farther south within the continents, where loss of heat by radiation is great, rather than at the higher latitudes on the coast. The boundary between sea-ice and water is probably one of the most significant factors in the weather of the arctic. Along this boundary the greatest horizontal temperature gradients occur, and it is consequently a zone of frequent storms.

Mean annual temperatures in the tundra are normally below 32°F, and the annual range is large. Point Barrow, Alaska, has an annual mean of 10°, but the July average is 40° and that for February is −19°. The range

[*] James A. Shear, "The Polar Marine Climate," *Ann. Assoc. Am. Geogrs.*, 54, 3 (Sept., 1964), 310–17.

of 59° shows the marked continental nature of the climate in spite of the station's location on the coast. Vardo, Norway, at a comparable latitude, experiences a greater maritime influence, having à July mean of 48°, a February mean of 21°, and an annual range of only 27°. The more moderate temperatures at Vardo are due in part to the effects of the North Atlantic Drift, which creates positive temperature anomalies in the far northern Atlantic. Prevailing southerly and westerly winds in winter augment the marine influence. (See Figure 9-3.) There is no comparable movement of warm water through the Aleutian Island chain and Bering Strait into the Arctic Ocean north of Alaska.

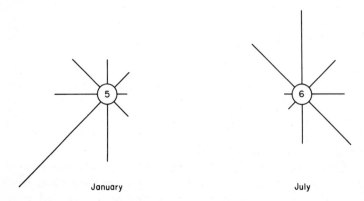

January   July

Fig. 9-3 Wind roses for Vardo, Norway.

Climatic Data for Stations in the Tundra Climate
Barrow, Alaska

	J	F	M	A	M	J	J	A	S	O	N	D	Yr.
Temp.	−16	−19	−15	0	20	35	40	39	31	17	1	−10	10
Precip.	0.2	0.1	0.1	0.1	0.1	0.3	0.9	0.8	0.5	0.5	0.3	0.2	4.1

Vardo, Norway

	J	F	M	A	M	J	J	A	S	O	N	D	Yr.
Temp.	22	21	24	30	35	42	48	48	43	35	28	24	33
Precip.	2.7	2.6	2.1	1.6	1.4	1.5	1.8	2.0	2.4	2.5	2.5	2.6	25.7

Summer temperatures in the tundra are reminiscent of mild winter weather in the mid-latitudes; the average temperature in the warmest month is below 50°. The extremely long daylight period is not enough to overcome the negative effects of low sun altitude and the ice-choked polar seas. On rare occasions maximum temperatures of over 80° have been recorded, but a more representative maximum is 60° or 65°. On the other hand, frosts may occur in any month. Most stations record only two to six months with average temperatures above 32°. The exceptions are those stations in especially favored coastal locations near the southern margin of the climatic types.

The long, cold winters of the tundra do not differ greatly from those in the taiga. Six to ten months have mean monthly temperatures below freezing. The high latitude results in a long period when the sun appears above the horizon each day for only a short time or not at all. During this period, the loss of heat by radiation is far in excess of insolation, but the region is not as dark as might be supposed. Cold weather is accompanied by clear skies, and the long nights are illuminated by the moon, stars, twilight, and displays of the aurora borealis. Extreme minimum temperatures are slightly higher than in the taiga because of the adjacent sea, although the difference between, say −60° and −70°, is of doubtful importance to human beings in the two regions.

Annual precipitation is less than 15 in. over most of the tundra, and it comes largely with cyclonic storms in the warmer half of the year. In the extreme northern reaches of the Atlantic, however, the warmer sea temperatures and a persistent upper-level trough of converging air streams combine to produce greater amounts of precipitation. (See map of world distribution of precipitation, in Chapter 3.) Thus Ivigtut on the southwest coast of Greenland and Angmagssalik on the east coast have 48 in. and 34 in. respectively. On the west coast Upernivik has 9 in., Jacobshavn, 12 in., and Godthaab, 18 in.

Snow contributes a greater proportion of the precipitation in the tundra than in the taiga. Wet summer snows are common along the poleward margins. Winter snowfall ordinarily does not exceed 60–80 in. and is prob-

Fig. 9-4 Climatic graphs for Upernivik and Ivigtut, tundra climate.

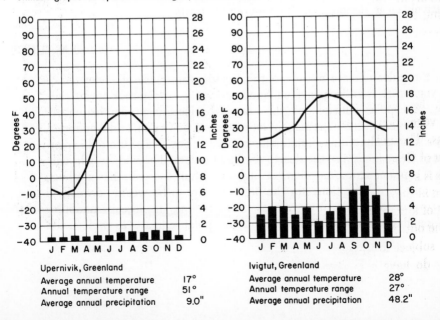

Upernivik, Greenland

Average annual temperature	17°
Annual temperature range	51°
Average annual precipitation	9.0″

Ivigtut, Greenland

Average annual temperature	28°
Annual temperature range	27°
Average annual precipitation	48.2″

ably not more than 25 in. in the northern areas. Snow depths in winter are somewhat greater in northeastern Canada and the lands bordering the North Atlantic than in northern Alaska, northwestern Canada, and Siberia. In the former areas, wintertime cyclonic storms are more common. With the low temperatures, the snow is powdery and drifts easily and is consequently difficult to measure accurately. In the regions of scanty snowfall, large areas may be swept bare while others are covered by deep drifts. Blowing snow frequently reduces visibility to a few yards.

Maximum storminess in the tundra occurs in autumn and in spring. In autumn there are appreciable differences between temperatures of the land and the unfrozen sea, and in spring the zone of cyclonic storms is best developed over the region. Some maritime stations have late summer or autumn precipitation maximums that are related to this seasonal distribution of storms. The precipitation graph for Ivigtut illustrates this feature. Bulun, in north-central Siberia, has more than one-half of its annual precipitation in the third quarter of the year.

Climatic Data for Bulun, U.S.S.R.

	J	F	M	A	M	J	J	A	S	O	N	D	Yr.
Temp.	−41	−35	−18	1	22	43	51	47	33	10	−23	−35	5
Precip.	0.3	0.2	0.3	0.3	0.5	1.0	1.5	1.6	1.5	0.9	0.4	0.3	8.8

No general statement can be made about cloudiness and fog in the tundra, the amount varying with storm activity and location with respect to water bodies. Fog and low stratus are prevalent along the seacoasts in the warmer months. Where cold water and drift ice move southward underneath warmer humid air, as along the Labrador Coast and in the Bering Strait, summer fog reaches its maximum. Winter skies are comparatively clear, although ice fog sometimes occurs.

POLAR CLIMATE

In the polar climate mean monthly temperatures are all below 32°F and vegetation is entirely lacking. Snow and ice or barren rock covers such areas. The polar climate and the associated icecaps predominate over most of Greenland, the permanent ice of the Arctic Ocean, and Antarctica. Less is known about this climate than any other because of limited exploration in these areas and the dearth of climatic data. The widely held concept of a permanent anticyclone or high at each of the poles has not been borne out by observations, for the high appears to be weakly developed and subject to invasion by cyclones. Nevertheless, the icecaps undoubtedly do have a marked influence on the polar climate as well as on climates of adjacent regions. The cold air masses formed by cooling over the icecaps play an important part in cyclonic activity along the border zone between ice and water and occasionally move into lower latitudes in winter.

The lowest mean annual temperatures on earth are those on the polar icecaps of Greenland and Antarctica. Amundsen-Scott Station at the South Pole recorded a mean temperature of −55.7°F in 1957. Annual ranges are large, although not so striking as at some continental locations in lower latitudes. In Antarctica the annual range is greatest in the interior and least on the coasts, reflecting the effects upon the heat budget of latitude and continentality. McMurdo Sound, on the Ross Sea, has an annual range of 39° compared with 68° at Vostok on the interior plateau. Monthly means in summer are normally well below freezing. In addition to pro-

Temperature Data for Polar Climate Stations
McMurdo Sound, Antarctica

	J	F	M	A	M	J	J	A	S	O	N	D	Yr.
Temp.	23	14	8	−8	−13	−14	−15	−16	−14	−5	13	23	−1

Vostok, Antarctica (Lat. 78° 27′ S., Long. 106° 52′ E.; 11,440 ft.)

	−26	−47	−71	−84	−85	−87	−85	−94	−87	−70	−47	−27	−68
Temp.	−26	−47	−71	−84	−85	−87	−85	−94	−87	−70	−47	−27	−68

viding a cold surface, the ice cover reflects much of the meager solar radiation. Nevertheless, thawing does occur on the ice pack of the arctic near the North Pole. Mushy ice and pools of water are a hazard to explorers travelling over such areas. Antarctica is much colder than the North Polar area in summer. January (Southern Hemisphere summer) temperatures of less than −50°F have been recorded.

Winters in the polar climates are colder still, with monthly means ranging −15° to −80°F. A temperature of −87°F was recorded at 9820 ft. on the Greenland icecap in 1949. Eismitte, at 9941 ft., has a February mean of −53°. A record minimum of −127°F occurred at the Soviet antarctic base, Vostok, at 11,440 ft. above sea level on August 24, 1960. A feature of temperature trends in the arctic basin, on Greenland, and in Antarctica is a flat curve during the winter months with the minimum at the end of the dark period. This phenomenon has been called the *kernlose* winter. Its occurrence in Antarctica has been explained as follows: After the sun sets at the end of summer the difference between temperatures of the continent and the surrounding oceans brings about instability and initiates cyclones that move maritime air inland to "ventilate" the lower troposphere above a thin layer of cold air, thus slowing the normal decline of surface temperature. By late winter ice covers a much wider belt around Antarctica and reduces the temperature of southward-moving air masses. The result is a secondary drop in temperature to the seasonal minimum.*

Diurnal variations of temperature are small throughout the year in polar climates. In summer they decrease generally toward the poles, where the change in altitude of the sun during the day is least.

Cyclonic storms penetrate the polar icecap regions, bringing cloudiness, some snow, and often fierce winds. Precipitation records are fragmentary; possible concentrations of snowfall in a particular season have not been clearly established. Studies of accumulated snow layers on Greenland have confirmed the short-term records of small annual totals. Estimates based on snow and ice profiles in Antarctica indicate annual values ranging from less than 2 in. on the high interior plateau to more than 20 in. on parts of the coastal periphery. When humid air reaches the maritime fringes of the icecaps, formation of frost and rime may contribute to ice accumulations. One principle is certain: as long as an icecap maintains its depth and extent there must be accretions of snow to compensate for losses by sublimation, melting, and break-off around the margins.

Strong, steady, katabatic winds are a marked feature of weather along the icecap coasts. Intense radiational cooling forms a shallow layer of cold surface air that flows downslope, sometimes at great speeds and with local gusts that fan the snow into a blizzard. In the interior of Antarctica milder katabatic winds produce unusual snowdrift patterns known as *sastrugi*.

HIGHLAND CLIMATES

The outstanding feature of highland climates is the great diversity of actual climates which prevail, resulting in large differences over short horizontal distances. The principal regions designated as having highland climates are the main mountain chains and high mountain basins of the middle and low latitudes. These are the Cascade–Sierra Nevada and Rockies in North America, the Andes in South America, the Alps in Europe, the Himalayas and associated ranges as well as Tibet in Asia, the Eastern Highlands of Africa, and mountain backbones in Borneo and New Guinea. It will be noted at once that these are by no means all the world's upland areas. Altitude influences climate everywhere, but where other factors overshadow its influence or where the affected areas are small, the highlands have been included in other types of climate for the purposes of regional description. Near the poles, for example, climates are cold at both low and high elevations, and a detailed examination of the differences is hardly warranted in a world view of climates. The Ahaggar Mts. in the central Sahara most certainly have a modified form of the tropical

* H. Wexler, "Seasonal and Other Temperature Changes in the Antarctic Atmosphere," *Quart. Journ. Roy. Met. Soc.*, 85, 365 (July, 1959), 196–208.

arid climate, but again the differences represent detail beyond the scope of this book.

There is no single, widespread highland climate with a reasonably distinctive combination of elements analogous to, for example, the rainy tropics or the marine climate. Regions with highland climates are mosaics of innumerable microclimates fitted intricately into the pattern of relief and altitude. It would be quite impossible to represent them adequately on an ordinary small-scale map of the world or even of a continent. It is necessary, therefore, to indicate the factors which produce the many small climatic differences and to generalize about the characteristics common to the regions included in this climatic type. The regions considered here as having highland climates are those which have considerable areal extent and which have features distinguishing them from other climatic regions at comparable latitudes. The dominant factors which affect highland climates are: (1) altitude, (2) local relief, and (3) the mountain barrier effect.

The normal lapse rate of temperature entails an average decrease of about 3.3 F° per thousand feet increase of elevation. There are important exceptions to this in actual lapse rates (see Chapter 2, Vertical Distribution of Temperature), but, on the whole, higher altitudes are associated with significantly cooler temperatures. Barometric pressure always decreases with altitude. The atmosphere above areas at high elevations is ordinarily much freer of clouds, dust, smoke, and other nongaseous material, and the air is accordingly more transparent to the passage of both incoming and outgoing radiation.

The influence of local relief is most pronounced in connection with the effectiveness of insolation on slopes with varying exposures and with the modification of wind direction and speed. Every difference in degree of slope with respect to the sun's rays produces a different microclimate. In the Northern Hemisphere, the southern slopes of hills and mountains receive more direct insolation, whereas northern slopes are less favored. Many deep valleys and steep northern slopes are exposed to the direct rays of the sun for only a short time each day; in rare cases they may be forever in the shade. Variations in exposure to winds also produce local climates. Wind speeds at high altitudes are generally greater because of less friction with the earth's surface; the higher a site is above the maximum effect of surface friction, the more nearly wind direction conforms to broad patterns of circulation. Winds tend to be gusty in rugged terrain. Locally they may be funnelled through constrictions in canyons or valleys, forced over ridges, or routed around mountains. Under conditions of fair weather, mountain and valley breezes are generated by the relief itself. Thus the direction and speed of wind in mountain valleys may be quite at variance with the air movement aloft or over adjacent plains. Prevailing winds in mountains are often conditioned more by the trends of valleys than by global or continental circulation.

The barrier effect of mountains has previously been treated in connection with several of the climatic elements. Stable air masses of major proportions can be dammed by a mountain range with the result that temperatures differ markedly from one side of the range to the other. In this manner in winter the east–west mountain chains of Europe hold much of the polar air away from the northern Mediterranean coast, the North American Rockies and Cascades protect the Pacific Northwest, and the Himalayas decrease the southward flow of cold air masses from central Asia. Whatever air does overflow these barriers is subject to the stable-air foehn effect and is therefore not so cold when it descends the slopes at the continental margins. (See Chapter 5, Special Air Mass and Storm Effects.) Mountains in the path of moist winds receive considerably more precipitation on the windward side than on the leeward. The accumulations of snow and ice at the higher elevations have their own effect upon temperatures and consequently upon air drainage. In general, mountain barriers tend to differentiate the climates of the windward and leeward wherever they lie in belts of prevailing winds of the major circulation systems.

Since highland climates are distributed through a wide range of latitudes, no specific temperature values can be said to characterize all such climates. Under clear skies, insolation is intense at high altitudes and there is a greater proportion of the shorter wave lengths (violet and ultraviolet), which do not penetrate well to lower elevations. As a result, one's skin burns or tans more readily. Temperature differences between daylight and darkness and between sunshine and shade are great. One can almost literally "burn on one side and freeze on the other." The same clear air that permits easy transmission of insolation also allows rapid loss of heat by radiation and large diurnal ranges of temperature. Night frosts are common even where daytime temperatures rise well above freezing. A distinctive feature of highland climates in the tropics is a larger diurnal than annual range of temperature. Monthly means and the annual march of temperature are determined primarily by latitudinal variations in insolation and in the transport of air from land or water source regions. Quito, Ecuador, virtually on the equator, has an insignificant annual range appropriate to its latitude, but the daily range normally exceeds 20°. Pikes Peak has a much greater annual range (38°) in response to the variation in insolation through the year.

Whereas temperatures are markedly lower with an increase in elevation, precipitation tends to increase, at least up to altitudes of several thousand feet. Above a zone of maximum precipitation it again decreases, for the orographic effect has already exhausted most of the precipitable moisture. On mountainous trade-wind islands, there is heavy rainfall on

Climatic Data for High-Altitude Stations
Pikes Peak, Colorado (Lat. 39°N.; 14,111 ft.)

	J	F	M	A	M	J	J	A	S	O	N	D	Yr.
Temp.	2	4	8	13	23	33	40	39	32	22	11	6	19
Precip.	1.6	1.5	2.0	3.5	3.8	1.6	4.2	3.8	1.7	1.4	1.9	2.6	29.6

Quito, Ecuador (Lat. 0°10'S.; 9350 ft.)

	J	F	M	A	M	J	J	A	S	O	N	D	Yr.
Temp.	55	54	54	54	55	55	55	55	55	55	54	55	55
Precip.	4.2	4.3	5.2	7.4	5.0	1.5	0.9	1.5	3.0	3.7	3.8	3.8	44.1

Leh, Kashmir (Lat. 34°N.; 11,503 ft.)

	J	F	M	A	M	J	J	A	S	O	N	D	Yr.
Temp.	19	21	33	43	47	56	63	62	56	45	33	24	42
Precip.	0.4	0.3	0.3	0.2	0.2	0.2	0.5	0.6	0.3	0.1	T	0.2	3.3

low windward slopes, but at higher elevations an upper-air subsidence inversion (the trade-wind inversion) produces arid conditions. As in the case of temperature, no general statement can be made about average amounts of precipitation. Average annual totals are related to the dominant air masses and to the moisture characteristics of prevailing winds. Fogginess is generally greater in mountains than on nearby plains or valleys. A great deal of mountain fog is simply clouds formed by one or more of the lifting processes, but radiation fogs are common in calm air on clear nights and in the early morning hours. Table 9-1 compares the number of fog days per year for some adjacent mountain and valley stations.

TABLE 9-1

Comparison of Number of Days with Fog per Year at Neighboring Mountain and Valley Stations*

Station	Elevation (feet)	Fog Days Per Year
Mt. Washington, N.H.	6,284	318
Pinkham Notch, N.H.	2,000	28
Pikes Peak, Colo.	14,140	119
Colorado Springs, Colo.	6,072	14
Mt. Weather, Virginia	1,725	95
Washington, D. C.	110	11
Zugspitze, Germany	9,715	270
Garmisch, Germany	2,300	10
Taunus, Germany	2,627	230
Frankfurt, Germany	360	30

* From Landsberg, *Physical Climatology*, 2nd ed. (1958), courtesy Gray Printing Co., Inc.

With increased elevation there is an ever greater proportion of precipitation in the form of snow, and the snow cover remains for a longer period. The elevation of the lower limit of permanent snow or ice is determined by air temperature, by slope exposure to the sun, and by depth of snowfall.

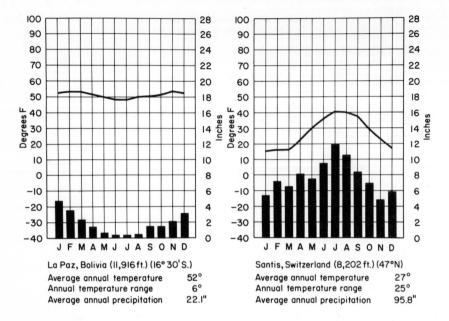

Fig. 9-5 Climatic graphs for La Paz and Santis, highland climate.

In general the snowline is highest in the tropics and becomes lower with increasing altitude. It is evident from Table 9-2, however, that the snowline is not highest at the equator but rather in the two drier belts which roughly correspond with the tropical arid and semiarid climates. A scanty accumulation of snow obviously can be melted away in a short time under cloudless skies. This also explains the generally higher level of permanent snow on the leeward sides of mountains and uplands far removed from

TABLE 9–2

Mean Altitude of Permanent Snowline at Various Latitudes*

Latitude	Elevation (feet) Northern Hemisphere	Elevation (feet) Southern Hemisphere
0–10	15,500	17,400
10–20	15,500	18,400
20–30	17,400	16,800
30–40	14,100	9,900
40–50	9,900	4,900
50–60	6,600	2,600
60–70	3,300	0
70–80	1,650	0

* From Landsberg, *Physical Climatology*, 2nd ed. (1958), courtesy Gray Printing Co., Inc.

the oceans. The snowline in the Rockies of Montana is higher than that of the Cascades, which, in turn, is higher than that on the Olympics in the same latitude. Foehn winds account for a more rapid removal of snow on leeward slopes. Other variations from the averages indicated in the table occur on shaded slopes, where snow will remain much longer than on slopes exposed to the sun. Where there is a winter maximum of precipitation the snowline will tend to be lower than in areas at the same latitude with a summer maximum. In any particular location the actual lower limit of snow results from these various factors working together or in opposition.

The causes of precipitation in a highland climate are much the same as elsewhere in the general geographic area in question, except for the intensification by the orographic effect. In the belt of cyclonic storms, for example, the characteristic frontal storms prevail and the annual regime of precipitation is similar to that of the surrounding lowlands, but the annual amount and the total falling in a given storm is likely to be somewhat greater in the highlands.

ADDITIONAL READINGS

Gordon, A. R., Jr., and W. C. Woodworth, "Some Inter-Relationships of Snow and Ice Conditions and Weather in the Arctic," *Bull. Am. Met. Soc.*, 31, 8 (1950), 271–78.

Rubin, M. J., "The Antarctic and the Weather," *Scient. Am.*, 207 (1962), 84–94.

Shear, James A., "The Polar Marine Climate," *Ann. Assoc. Am. Geogrs.*, 54, 3 (1964), 310–17.

Wexler, H., "Seasonal and Other Temperature Changes in the Antarctic Atmosphere," *Quart. Journ. Roy. Met. Soc.*, 85, 365 (1959), 196–208.

WEATHER
CLIMATE
AND LIFE

climate 10
and the world pattern
of vegetation and soils

The world distribution of three elements of man's natural environment show a remarkable coincidence because one, climate, is the dominant factor in shaping the other two, vegetation and soils. Thus climate ultimately affects all forms of life. An earlier discussion of vegetation as an indicator of climatic types treated the influence of climatic elements on plant life in terms of broad correlations. The interrelationship of climate, vegetation, and soils will now be examined in greater detail.

CLIMATIC FACTORS IN PLANT GROWTH

All plants have certain environmental requirements that must be met if they are to thrive. These may be broadly classified under the headings: (1) climatic, (2) physiographic, (3) edaphic, and (4) biotic. The first is of primary concern here, although influences of terrain or relief, soils (the edaphic factor), and the interrelations of plants with other plants and with animals cannot be neglected in the study of plant ecology. Climate does not act alone to set limits to plant growth but rather it exerts its influence in conjunction with the other factors. Yet its role is always important directly in its effects upon plants and indirectly in its influence on edaphic and biotic factors.

The principal direct influences of climate on plants are exerted by precipitation and soil moisture, humidity, temperature, sunlight, and wind. Variation in one of these factors can change the significance of the others in producing different rates of evapotranspiration and photosynthesis. The moisture factors are the most important over large areas of the earth. Water not only goes into the composition of plant cells; it also serves as a medium for transport of nutrients to growing cells and through evapotranspiration acts as a temperature control. For most land plants the immediate source of moisture is the soil. The amount and availability of soil moisture is not necessarily a simple function of precipitation, but is affected by surface drainage conditions and by the ability of the soil to retain moisture as well as by the losses due to evapotranspiration. Thus swampy areas occur in the midst of deserts and sandy or gravelly soils in rainy climates may be entirely devoid of vegetation. Just as deficient moisture limits plant growth, so excess amounts restrict certain plants by limiting aeration and the oxygen supply in the soil. Excessive soil moisture tends to develop unfavorable soil characteristics and to increase disease damage.

Plants that live in water or in a very moist climate are *hygrophytes;* those adapted to drought are called *xerophytes.* In climates with distinct seasons vegetation must be adapted to alternating cold-hot or wet-dry conditions. Plants with the ability to make the required adjustments are known as *tropophytes.*

The humidity of the air in which plants grow has varying significance depending upon the type of plant as well as upon the soil moisture available to it. Low vapor pressure of the air induces increased losses of moisture through transpiration. Many plants can withstand low humidities so long as their roots are supplied with adequate moisture. The xerophytic vegetation of dry climates is adapted to limited moisture in several ways. Thick waxy bark and leaves inhibit loss by transpiration. Certain plants have root systems that extend deep into the soil as well as over a wide radius to gather moisture from a large volume of soil. Some plants of the desert, notably certain species of cacti, store water during relatively wet periods to be used in dry times. Many desert annuals avoid the prolonged dry spells by passing rapidly through the life cycle from seed to seed after a rain. These are better classified as drought-escaping than drought-adapted.

Whereas moisture provides the *medium* for the processes of plant growth, heat provides the *energy.* Plants can grow only within certain temperature limits, although the limits are not the same for all plants. Certain algae live in hot springs at 200°F, and arctic mosses and lichens survive −90°F. For each species and variety there is a minimum below which growth is not possible, an optimum at which growth is best, and a maximum beyond which growth stops. Most plants cease growth when the soil temperature drops below about 42°F. If the soil temperature is low the rate of intake of moisture through the roots is decreased and the plant may not be able to replace water lost by transpiration. Freezing temperatures can thus damage the plant cells by producing chemical changes and desiccation. Alternate freezing and thawing are especially damaging. Species differ a great deal in their adaptation to temperature conditions, however, and many plants can endure long periods of below-freezing temperatures although they do not grow. The effect of high temperature is generally to speed up the growth processes. Under natural conditions high temperatures are rarely the direct cause of death in plants. Rather, the increased evapotranspiration induced by the heat causes dehydration of the plant cells. Up to a point this can be forestalled if the moisture supply is adequate. Consequently, the temperature–moisture relationships are quite as important as temperature alone.

The moisture requirements of plants become higher as temperature increases. A given amount of precipitation may result in a moisture deficit in a hot climate, but under cooler temperatures the same amount may exceed potential evapotranspiration and create a moisture surplus. If the demands of evaporation from soil and transpiration from plant surfaces are not met, wilting and eventual death occur. Both evaporation and transpiration are cooling processes that tend to offset the effects of high temperature. Hot winds increase potential water loss and hasten damage to plant tissues; they may be disastrous even when there is abundant soil moisture. Where growing conditions become cooler, as with increasing altitude or latitude, species of plants are successively eliminated from vegetation formations and ultimately all plant life is prohibited regardless of the amount of moisture available in snow, ice, or the frozen soil.

The sunshine factor in plant growth has several aspects. Sunlight has a direct role in photosynthesis and in the production of chlorophyll. Without it most plants fail to develop properly, whereas others are adapted to dark or shaded conditions. Light is also a factor in the time required for certain species to flower and produce seed. Ordinarily the amount of light available to growing native plants is sufficient for normal development so that light is not of major importance as a factor affecting geographical distribution of vegetation. However, for an individual plant in a specific environment, light conditions can be critical. Sunshine also is closely related to the temperature factor. Direct radiation combined with atmospheric heat can drive the temperature above the maximum limit permitted by the moisture supply. In moderate intensity it can stimulate plants to their optimum development.

Wind influences vegetation directly by its physical action upon plants and indirectly by accelerating moisture loss. The rending and tearing action of high or gusty winds is a familiar process. Trees are blown over or stripped of leaves and branches; leaves of bushes are shredded; stems of plants are twisted or broken. Abrasion by windblown sand, gravel, or ice particles can also be quite damaging to plants. These are, however, local effects. There is no direct worldwide correlation of wind belts with the vegetation pattern. Extensive wind damage is common on exposed mountains, where it is combined with the effects of poor soil, low temperatures, and ice or snow cover.

Although mean values of the climatic elements may have broad application in determining the suitability of an area for plant growth, the variations from the normal and the extremes are frequently vital considerations. Occasional droughts, floods, heat waves, or frosts can prove fatal to plants otherwise adapted to the normal conditions. Only those plants which escape the disaster or which are able to withstand it survive. Hence climatic anomalies play a leading part in plant adaptation and natural selection.

Duration of minimum conditions for vegetative growth is another consideration which involves the seasonal distribution of the climatic elements. Whether precipitation is well distributed throughout the year, concentrated in a short season, or is erratic sets broad limits for plant associations. Thus, moisture-loving species of the rainy tropics are not adapted to the hot, dry season of the dry summer subtropics. The duration of temperature conditions is likewise restrictive or permissive relative to the plant association in question. Length of growing season is usually defined as the period between the last killing frost of spring and the first killing frost of autumn. It has its widest usage in connection with crop plants, but short growing seasons set limits to natural vegetation as well. As pointed out in the discussion of climates dominated by polar air masses, the longer daily duration of sunlight in summer at high latitudes intensifies the growing season so that plants are able to concentrate their annual growth into a shorter period than at lower latitudes. Furthermore, plants differ in their susceptibility to frost damage; some are simply hardier than others.

All species of vegetation have climatic optima under which their growth is most efficient. The fact that these optima as well as the extreme climatic limits are different for various plants accounts for the distribution of plant associations on earth. Although the other environmental factors may be favorable they can be negated by adverse climatic conditions.

In summary, heat and moisture are the great determiners of where plants will grow naturally, and precipitation and temperature largely set the world pattern of vegetation.

WORLD DISTRIBUTION OF VEGETATION

The close relation between climate and vegetation is a fundamental relationship in the natural environment. The correlation is in the broad groupings rather than in details and is possible only where undisturbed natural vegetation has reached an approximate equilibrium with the climatic environment. Blumenstock and Thornthwaite diagrammed these broad relationships effectively, as shown in Figure 10-1. Under constantly frozen conditions there is an ice and snow cover or barren rock with no vegetation. Toward progressively warmer climates tundra and taiga prevail, and since even meager precipitation may equal potential evapotranspiration under the low temperatures, moisture is subordinate to temperature as a limiting factor. In warmer regions adequate moisture becomes the dominant factor and there is a succession of desert, steppe, grassland, forest, and rain forest ranging from arid to very wet climates.

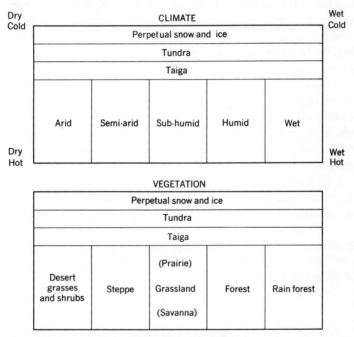

After Blumenstock and Thornthwaite, *Climate and Man, 1941 Yearbook of Agriculture.*

Fig. 10-1   Schematic diagrams of the relationship between climate and vegetation.

Each of these vegetation categories has its cool and hot subdivisions. Thus there are cold deserts and hot deserts, prairie grasslands and savanna, subarctic rain forests and tropical rain forests. In each climatic region there is a characteristic vegetation formation consisting of associated plant species which, through the centuries, have become adapted to that climatic region. These dominant forms are the *climax vegetation*. Other species may exist and the climax forms may be locally absent because of soil factors, fire, or human interference, but generally the climax formation reflects climatic influences.

FORESTS

In the rainy tropics the climax vegetation is the tropical rain forest, characterized by many species of tall broadleaved evergreens with spreading, interlocking crowns. Pure stands of a single species are found only rarely. Life seems to be concentrated largely in the treetops. Monkeys and many types of birds are representative animal life. In the densest rain forests, the canopy of overhead growth inhibits the lower plants, but vines push into the treetops in search of light. Epiphytic and parasitic plants also grow in the upper story. Where the tall trees are more widely spaced a dense under story of smaller trees and bush forms fills the openings. On the other hand, the forest floor is relatively clear of vegetation because of the absence of light. Leaves, twigs, and fallen trees are rapidly returned to the soil by insects, bacteria, and the chemical action attending the hot, wet climate. Some species have special requirements which restrict their distribution. The coconut, for example, is found only on or near tropical coasts, and the mangrove is confined to tidal flats. Tropical rain forest, or selva, is found in the Amazon Basin, Congo Basin, and on most of the islands off Southeast Asia. Smaller areas occur along several stretches of wet equatorial and tropical coasts. In each region the demands for high temperature and abundant moisture must be met throughout the year, although there are modifications as in the monsoon tropics, where there is a short dry season.

On its drier margins, the tropical rain forest grades into lighter forest associations or scrub and thorn forest. Plant growth is not so luxuriant and

Fig. 10-2 Myall scrub and salt bush near the arid fringe of the dry summer subtropical climate in South Australia.

Courtesy South Australian Government.

the individual species are adapted to lower effective precipitation or seasonal drought. Dense forests are found mostly along watercourses. Typical semideciduous forest has a more open stand of trees than the selva, and sunlight penetrates to the ground to support a thick, impenetrable undergrowth known as jungle. Many of the trees shed their leaves in the cooler dry season and take on drab colors. This seasonal rhythm of vegetation is less evident in the selva. The scrub and thorn forests do not have as many species as either the selva or the semideciduous forests. Trees are relatively small and spaced far enough apart to allow grasses on the forest floor. In some areas, thorns cover the trees as a protective adaptation. Most characteristic of the animal life of the semideciduous and scrub forests are the many insects, notably ants and spiders. The large, so-called "jungle" animals really belong to the adjacent savannas but invade the forests, especially in the dry season when their normal habitat cannot meet the demands for food.

The mid-latitude forests are divided into three broad classes: Mediterranean scrub, broadleaf and mixed broadleaf-coniferous, and coniferous. Mediterranean scrub forest is made up of broadleaf evergreen scrub types that are adapted to the hot, dry summers and mild, wetter winters. It is also sometimes called the sclerophyllous forest because of the small, thick, waxy leaves and thick bark which enable the plants to resist the desertlike summer. Species vary in the different continents but the forest has the same general open appearance. In southern Europe and California oaks are common trees. The commercially important cork oak of Mediterranean Europe is valuable because of its very thick, spongy bark. Dense thickets of shrubs and bushes are common in Europe, where they are known as *maquis,* and in southern California, where a similar association is called *chaparral.* The Mediterranean scrub forest coincides remarkably well with the dry summer subtropical climate and therefore has virtually the same worldwide distribution.

The broadleaf and mixed broadleaf-coniferous forests of the middle latitudes flourish where there are moderate temperatures and generally plentiful summer rainfall. They are also known as the temperate or *mesophytic* forests. They have a wealth of species but not as great a variety as in the tropical forests. In North America they are found chiefly in the eastern third of the United States, where humid continental climates prevail, but they extend into the humid subtropical climate of the South also to grade into the coniferous belt. Representative trees are the oak, ash, hickory, magnolia, gum, pine, and spruce. Lower forms of natural vegetation are ferns, shrubs, and creeping vines. A similar vegetation group was native to a belt stretching from the British Isles through Europe into central U.S.S.R. In eastern Asia the principal regions are eastern Manchuria, Korea, Japan, and eastern China. Throughout the Northern

Hemisphere, these forests have been heavily cut over. In China the original forest has been so completely denuded that its character and extent can be determined only approximately by inference. In the Southern Hemisphere, the mesophytic forests occur in southern Brazil, southern Chile, along the Natal Coast of South Africa, on the southeastern margin of Australia, and in Tasmania and New Zealand. In southern Chile and southwestern New Zealand there are dense subantarctic rain forests.

The coniferous forest coincides fairly well with the taiga climate. There are important exceptions, however, on the Pacific Coast of North America, in the Rocky Mountains, New England, and the southeastern United States. The latter area belongs to the humid subtropical climatic region, and pines are the dominant species. Along the Pacific Coast of Canada and the United States the abundant rainfall has permitted an extratropical rain forest, but conifers predominate. In the taiga the chief species are fir and spruce with some pine and larch. Enclaves of deciduous birch and aspen also occur. In general, the density, size, rate of growth, and number of species in the coniferous forest decrease with latitude, and their commercial value likewise diminishes.

GRASSLANDS

The major grassland formations are *savanna, steppe,* and *prairie.* The tropical scrub and semideciduous forests are transitional to the savanna, where tall grasses are dominant, but scattered drought-resistant trees and shrubs nevertheless occur. The general appearance is that of an open park with small umbrellalike trees dotted about. The savanna coincides closely with the wet-and-dry tropical climate. Where the wet-and-dry tropics merge into the tropical semiarid climate the short-grass steppe becomes dominant. Outstanding examples of savanna are the *llanos* of the Orinoco Valley and the *campos* of south-central Brazil in South America and the Sudan in northern Africa. There are also savanna belts in southern Africa and northeastern Australia.

In general, the proportion of trees in savannas varies with the amount of effective precipitation. Along stream courses, dense growths of trees extend into the savanna to form *galerias* (from the Italian word *galeria,* meaning tunnel). Away from permanent water supplies trees must be adapted to a dry winter season lasting from two to four months. Some are thorny whereas others have thick, leathery leaves which help control moisture losses, and still others are deciduous. The tall, thick-stemmed grasses dry up in winter but revive again with the rainy season. Various large animals feed on the savanna grasses or on tree leaves, being especially numerous in Africa. On other continents there are different animal communities, but the principle of interdependence of elements of the animal kingdom relying on the savanna still pertains. The dry season is a critical period for plants and animals alike.

The steppes consist of a more or less continuous mat of grasses only a few inches in height with shrubs (for example, sagebrush) sometimes dominant. They occur in the mid-latitudes as well as the tropics. Along the dry boundaries xerophytic shrubs are common, and the desert is distinguished more by the open spaces between plants than by the species present. All the great steppe regions are contiguous to desert along at least a part of their dry borders. The tropical steppes have their widest distribution to the north and south of the Sahara, in an irregular strip from Asia Minor eastward to India, in the Kalahari region of South Africa, and around the periphery of the Australian desert. The principal mid-latitude steppes are the North American Great Plains, a belt extending eastward from the Black Sea to Manchuria, and the wetter Patagonia of Argentina. The desert-steppe boundary has been the subject of much study concerning both vegetation and the associated climate. It appears likely that extreme drought years are a factor in determining the boundary zone and resisting the spread of grasses into the desert.

Distinctive grasslands known as prairies border the steppes on their wetter margins in some areas. Tall-grass prairie plants are deep-rooted and reach heights of three to ten feet under natural conditions. Short-grass prairies merge into the steppes. The drier edges of the prairies, like the steppes, are probably delimited by dry years. Where they merge into forest the transition is usually narrow, although galeria forest may extend along streams. Most of the world's prairies have been plowed up so that few examples of the natural plant associations remain. The principal areas in which prairie grasses were the native vegetation are east of the Great Plains in North America, north of the steppes in U.S.S.R., central Manchuria, the pampas of Argentina, and a small area east of the steppe lands of South Africa. The prairies are associated with both humid continental and humid subtropical types of climate.

DESERT

To many minds the term *desert* conjures up visions of dry, open expanses entirely devoid of vegetation. Such a concept would limit use of the word to very small areas. From the point of view of plant geography, desert vegetation consists of many species widely spread over the ground and not making a continuous cover. The adaptations which characterize the steppe are even more pronounced in the desert. Hard surfaces to prevent water loss, fleshy stems and leaves to store moisture, or extensive root systems are the means by which xerophytic desert plants exist for long, rainless periods. Annuals must complete their life cycle after a

By courtesy of the South African Information Service.

Fig. 10.3 The Quiver Tree (**Aloe dichotoma**), an example of adaptation to a tropical arid climate. This plant grows in the Namib Desert of Southwest Africa. Note the thick bark and leaves.

chance rain. All species must be adapted to a climate where potential evapotranspiration far exceeds precipitation.

TUNDRA

Tundra as a vegetative region lies between the poleward limits of the taiga and the polar climatic region, which has no vegetation. It represents the forward line of vegetation in its attempt to clothe the earth to the highest latitudes. Low temperatures and permanently frozen subsoil inhibit growth of any but the lower forms of plants. The southern limit of the tundra coincides fairly well with the 50° isotherm for the warmest month. In the areas with warmer summers the chief vegetation forms are mosses, lichens, sedges, stunted willows, and occasional birches and aspens. Farther poleward there are few, if any, bush forms, and, under the most severe climatic and edaphic conditions, expanses of bare rock, boulder fields, or gravels have practically no vegetation. These latter areas are known as *desert tundra* in contrast to the *grass tundra* and *bush tundra* in the more favorable environments. The annual freezing and thawing of the surface soil causes much heaving and separation, resulting in a distinctive pattern of hummocks or knobs that make the terrain difficult for travel. During summer the surface waters are held in small depressions between these knobs, for the permafrost does not allow downward percolation. Because there is only slow loss by evaporation, such waters provide breeding places for myriads of mosquitoes. The economic value of tundra plants is limited, but they do furnish forage for animals such as the

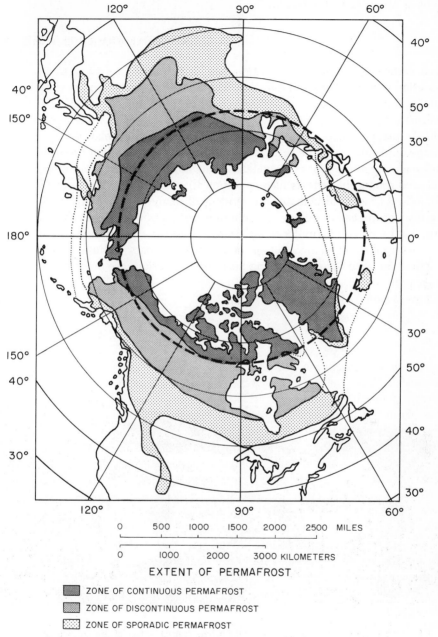

Fig. 10-4 Distribution of permafrost conditions in the Arctic.

EXTENT OF PERMAFROST

- ZONE OF CONTINUOUS PERMAFROST
- ZONE OF DISCONTINUOUS PERMAFROST
- ZONE OF SPORADIC PERMAFROST

From United States Air Force, Geophysics Research Directorate, *Handbook of Geophysics*, Revised Edition, published by The Macmillan Company, 1960.

reindeer, caribou, and the few remaining musk oxen. Fur-bearing animals and birds also inhabit the tundra.

VERTICAL DIFFERENTIATION OF VEGETATION

The vertical zonation of vegetation has already been referred to in connection with the highland climates. The altitudinal range and variety is greatest in the tropics, but, wherever vertical differences in climate occur, corresponding changes in vegetation are likely—unless the climate prohibits plant growth at all altitudes as it does on the polar icecaps. Altitude duplicates, in some respects, the effects of latitude upon the heat balance and upon the types of vegetation; but slope, exposure, cloudiness, wind, and orographic effects also condition the climatic environment of highlands. As highland climates are mosaics of many microclimates with a vertical arrangement, likewise mountain vegetation falls into broad altitudinal belts with many local variations. Thus, the concept of vertical life zones applies regionally, but—in detail—the plant associations vary a great deal. Some of the most striking horizontal variations are on opposite

Photo by author.

Fig. 10-5 Vertical zonation of vegetation in southern New Zealand. A belt of evergreen beech forest lies between the tussock grassland (foreground) and the alpine plants and rock outcrops of the higher alpine slopes.

sides of mountains and result from differences in amount of orographic rainfall or in the amount of effective insolation.

Since temperature generally decreases with altitude, whereas precipitation ordinarily becomes greater, the combined result is a rapid increase in the ratio of precipitation to potential evapotranspiration as elevation increases. At the higher levels, the upper limits of plants are more likely to be set by low temperatures than by lack of moisture. On the lower slopes (at least in low and middle latitudes), moisture is the critical factor. On some slopes with relatively sparse rainfall the moisture demands of a forest are partly met by fog and clouds which reduce evaporation and deposit quantities of water droplets upon the plant surfaces.

Although a given level on a tropical mountain may have annual temperature and precipitation averages like those of a place at a higher latitude, it does not have the same climate. Seasonal rhythm in the climatic elements, especially temperature and precipitation, changes with latitude, and the rhythm of plant growth changes with it.

In the tropical highlands of Latin America, four vertical life zones are commonly recognized in relation to vertical differences in temperature and precipitation effectiveness. The lowest is the *tierra caliente* (literally, hot land), extending from sea level up to 2000 or 3000 feet and having vegetation typical of the tropical lowlands. Annual temperature averages are generally above 75°F. Above the *tierra caliente*, the *tierra templada* (temperate land) rises to elevations of 6000 to 6500 feet and embraces a modified form of tropical forest. Temperatures range between 75° and 65° on the average. Higher still is the *tierra fria* (cold land) from 6000 to 11,000 feet. There the forest becomes less dense and grades into bushy types. The upper limit of the *tierra fria* coincides with the upper limit of cultivated crops, which is at about the 54°F annual isotherm. The *tierra helada* (frost land) extends on upward to the permanent snowfields. It is a zone of alpine meadows, whose character depends upon the amount and seasonal distribution of precipitation. Where there is adequate moisture throughout the year the grasses are relatively dense and perpetually green. Farther from the equator, there is a short dry season and the alpine meadows are dry for a part of the year. Toward the regions of subsidence in the subtropic highs, conditions become drier and the associated vegetation grades into thorny and desert forms.

In the middle latitudes, the *tierra caliente* is absent and there is actually nothing akin to the *tierra templada*. Altitudinal limits to vegetative types are lower, but moisture conditions still have much influence on both horizontal and vertical distribution of plants. Figure 10-6 illustrates with a specific example the vertical zonation of vegetation in the Central Sierra Nevada region of California.

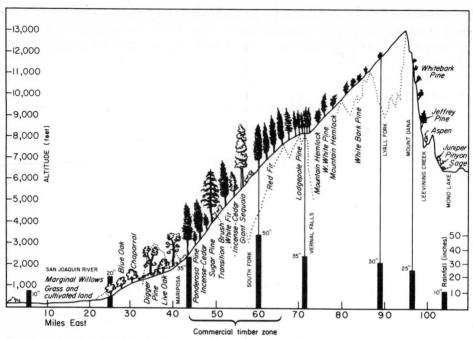

From *Trees, 1949 Yearbook of Agriculture.*

Fig. 10-6 Vertical zonation of forest types in the central Sierra Nevada.

CLIMATE AS A FACTOR IN SOIL FORMATION

Five natural factors influence the formation of soils: (*1*) climate, (*2*) plant and animal life, (*3*) relief, (*4*) parent material, and (*5*) time. Of these climate is the most active. Soils are affected by climate directly throughout their evolution from parent rock to their current state of development. Their character is shaped indirectly by climate acting through vegetation and animal life. Many of the effects of varied relief are ultimately climatic as a result of local microclimates produced by exposure, slope, drainage, or altitudinal differences.

Soil is a layer of earth material which undergoes constant change and development, not merely an inert mass of finely divided rock. The dynamic processes which form soils are of three broad classes: physical, chemical, and biological. Physical breakup of parent rock, termed *disintegration,* is induced climatically through the action of rain splash, rainfall and snow-melt runoff, glacier movements, freezing and thawing, and abrasion or transport by wind. Chemical weathering, or *decomposition,* results from chemical interaction of various compounds, and it takes place more rapidly under warm, humid conditions than in cold or dry climates. Rocks softened by chemical action are more easily worn away by physical processes and become more suitable for plant growth. Once the weathered parent material begins to support life, plants, bacteria, worms, and so on speed up the chemical and physical changes and add organic matter. Within certain limits, chemical and biological activity increase with increased temperature and moisture; neither is possible without water. The transport of small colloidal solids is called *eluviation,* whereas *leaching* is the term given to removal of mineral or organic compounds in solution. Both tend to impoverish the top layers of the soil. On the other hand, where there is lack of moisture there is accordingly limited downward percolation and capillary water tends to leave concentrations of dissolved salts at the surface when it evaporates. The salt flats and alkaline soils of arid climates are examples of soils formed in this way. Broadly speaking, the soils of deserts and steppe grasslands are formed where evaporation exceeds precipitation, whereas forest soils are associated with the reverse conditions. Thus total precipitation is not the sole control of moisture in soil formation. Cloudbursts tend to puddle the surface soil and seal it off to downward water movement so that there is excessive surface runoff. Gentle rains have time to soak into the soil and are more significant in soil-forming processes requiring moisture. Obviously the degree of permeability of the soil will also affect water percolation. Whether the rate of percolation is rapid, as in sands and gravels, or slow, as in clays, greatly affects the usefulness of precipitation. Wind is a drying agent as well as an agent of erosion. By increasing evaporation from the soil it increases the water need of plants.

In the processes of soil formation the climate within the soil is quite as important as that of the air above. Temperature changes are conducted downward slowly in soil so that at a depth of two or three feet diurnal variations are not experienced. Seasonal variation lags considerably at the greater depths, and at about 50 feet below the surface there is little or no seasonal temperature change. The structure of the soil and its moisture content help to determine its conductivity; dry, loose soil conducts heat slowly, whereas wet, compact soil and solid rock are much better conductors. Air, being a very poor conductor, reduces heat transfer in porous soils. Similarly, snow or a mantle of plant litter inhibits heat conduction. Rain water and snowmelt tend to carry heat downward as they penetrate into soil pores, however.

Except in the very dry deserts, the air in the soil below the immediate surface is ordinarily saturated, a fact of considerable importance in both chemical and biological processes so long as temperatures are favorable. The relative humidity within the soil is sometimes determined by the relative humidity of the atmosphere. If the average relative humidity of the air is close to saturation (90 to 100 per cent), the soil climate is moister than in regions of low humidity even though rainfall may be less.

Assuming that the weathered parent material is not eroded away (as is likely on a steep slope), the various soil-forming processes combine to produce layers, or *horizons,* in the soil and over a period of time a distinctive *profile* is developed. The soil profile is the most useful feature for soil identification and classification. The characteristics of color, texture, structure (arrangement of soil particles), and the chemical and organic matter content vary downward through the profile and afford a basis for study of the origin of the soil. Figure 10-7 is an idealized soil profile. Not every soil should be expected to have all of the horizons, but it will have some of them. The degree to which soil profiles are related to the major soil-forming factors is the basis for classification of soils into three broad orders:

Zonal soils have well-differentiated horizons resulting from strong climatic and biological influence. Their distribution shows a close correlation with climate.

Intrazonal soils reflect the dominance of relief or parent material in their formation. Microclimatic effects or soil climate induced by relief may be expressed in their profiles. For example, bog soils are often formed in depressions where there is excessive soil moisture, even though the atmospheric climate is relatively dry.

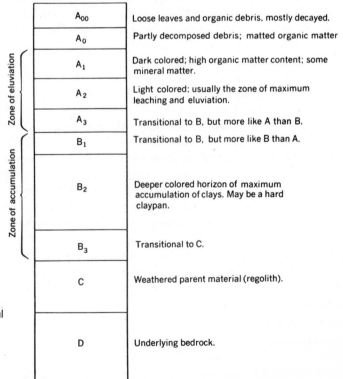

Fig. 10-7 The hypothetical soil profile.

Azonal soils have poorly developed profiles, usually reflecting the short time during which they have undergone the soil forming processes. Recent deposits of alluvium or loess, sand dunes, and partially weathered bedrock are examples of azonal soils.

WORLD DISTRIBUTION OF SOILS

The importance of climate as a soil-forming factor makes itself felt in world soil regions which correspond, in a general way, to the world climatic regions and, therefore, to the world distribution of vegetation. Because the soils of the zonal order are most influenced by the climatic and biological factors it follows that they are more closely correlated with those factors than are the intrazonal or azonal soils. In the same manner that vegetation formations are related to temperature and moisture conditions in the diagram, Figure 10-1, the major zonal soils have been represented in Figure 10-8. Under perpetual snow and ice zonal soils cannot

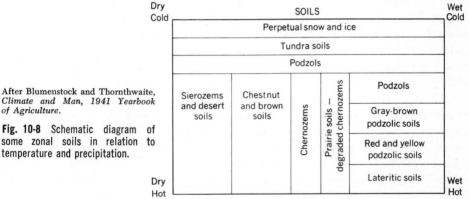

After Blumenstock and Thornthwaite, *Climate and Man, 1941 Yearbook of Agriculture.*

Fig. 10-8 Schematic diagram of some zonal soils in relation to temperature and precipitation.

develop. In the tundra the poor vertical drainage and low temperatures result in distinctive shallow, acidic, and often peaty soils of little agricultural value. In the higher temperatures and longer summers of the taiga climate, the characteristic cold-forest podzols form. Podzolization occurs at the greatest rate where there is a soil moisture surplus in cold winter climates, that is, in the taiga. It is less significant in warmer forests, and the resulting profiles are not as acidic or as well developed. True podzols are ordinarily associated with the coniferous forests.

The gray-brown podzolic soils form primarily under deciduous and mixed forest, where the temperatures are somewhat higher than in the taiga. They are not as acidic as the podzols and lack the concentrated horizon of organic matter at the surface. As a result of less intense leaching they do not have the light-colored A_2 horizon. Their distribution roughly approximates that of the humid continental climates, although they are also found in the marine climate of western Europe and in the dry summer subtropics in limited areas of Italy and South Africa. Under still warmer, humid conditions, the decomposition of organic matter and leaching of bases and other soluble materials takes place even more rapidly to produce the acidic red and yellow podzolic soils. The red and yellow colors in the subsoil are caused by stains of iron compounds. The surface soil is deficient in organic matter and in mineral plant nutrients. The yellow podzolic soils are the more strongly leached. They are associated with the pine forests in the southeastern United States, whereas the red podzolic soils are identified with mixed broadleaf-conifer forests. Red and yellow podzolic soils are approximately co-extensive with the humid subtropics and are transitional between the podzolic soils of cooler climates and the latosolic soils of the tropical humid climates. They are often classed with the tropical latosolic soils because the processes of laterization account for certain of their characteristics.

Zonal soils of the humid tropics are called latosolic soils. Bacterial activity and rapid chemical action, combined with excessive leaching, keep humus to a bare minimum. Latosolic soils are found only in warm regions where there is heavy rainfall. Their distribution, therefore, coincides fairly well with the rainy tropics, monsoon tropics, and wet-and-dry tropics. The red and yellow podzolic soils previously mentioned represent conditions where laterization is in evidence but is not so far advanced.

In subhumid climates the native vegetation is primarily grassland. The representative zonal soils are the prairie soils and chernozems in order of progression toward drier conditions. Surpluses of soil moisture are uncommon, and the processes of leaching and eluviation are accordingly slowed. The abundance of organic matter from grass roots and decayed leaves makes the A horizon much darker than in the forest soils. Prairie soils are transitional from the podzolic or latosolic groups to the chernozems. Their characteristics often show the effect of fluctuations in rainfall from year to year appropriate to the associated climate. Thus they mark the boundary zone between the humid soils, which are leached and eluviated, and the soils of drier regions, which experience far less percolation of salts and colloids. They may have a calcium carbonate accumulation in the lower profile, especially in the C horizon, but they never have a "lime layer" in the upper horizons as do the arid-land soils. Prairie soils occur in the western Corn Belt of the United States, east central Europe and adjacent U.S.S.R., central Africa, northern Argentina and Uruguay, and parts of northeastern Australia. On their drier borders they grade into the chernozems, or black earths, which are associated with the prairie-steppe boundary.

Chernozems have a very dark topsoil two to four feet in depth and containing large amounts of organic matter. In contrast to the humid climate soils, there is no leached A_2 horizon. The B horizon has a concentration of colloidal particles and base minerals percolated from the A horizon above. Soil reaction may be either slightly acid or slightly alkaline, but deep in the profile there is a definite accumulation of "lime" in the form of small nodules. The level at which accumulation takes place is approximately the average depth to which water percolates below the surface and is therefore related to moisture conditions. Chernozems occur in the eastern Great Plains of North America, south-central U.S.S.R., the central Indian Peninsula, north-central Argentina, on the wetter margins of the steppes in both hemispheres in Africa, and in northeastern Australia.

On the steppe grasslands of semiarid climates, representative soil groups are the chestnut and brown soils. In these soils, the lime accumulation is much nearer the surface than in the chernozems, and, since the amount of organic matter is progressively less with drier conditions, they are lighter in color and have a shallower A horizon. Plants which require large amounts of base minerals tend to aid in the concentration of the calcium salts near the surface by bringing them up to replenish the losses due to leaching. The prairie, chernozem, chestnut, and brown soils tend to be banded more or less concentrically in that order as rainfall decreases toward the deserts. The sierozems and desert soils are the extremes in soil formation under lack of moisture. Their horizons are poorly developed, and they have little or no humus. In the mid-latitude deserts they are typically gray in color; in the tropical deserts a reddish color resulting from certain iron compounds is more characteristic. The accumulation of soluble salts may be immediately at the surface. Under conditions of poor drainage, as in depressions or flat basins, surface waters evaporate to leave saline deposits.

The effects of altitude and relief upon climate are reflected in the soils of highland regions. Just as highland climates are mosaics of many local climates, so soils of mountains and valleys vary greatly over short distances. Their complex arrangement makes it impossible to represent them on a small scale map. Many are azonal as a result of the steep slopes and rapid erosional processes. Others are formed under local conditions of climate induced by relief and drainage and are classed as intrazonal. Only on gentle slopes, on plateaus, or in broad valleys are zonal soils likely to be extensive. The altitudinal zonation characteristic of mountain vegetation is repeated in general in the distribution of soils, the effect of altitude being something like that of latitude. Alpine soils, for example, can be roughly compared to tundra soils, although the former are classified as intrazonal because relief and drainage factors rather than climate are considered to be dominant in their formation. Acting directly and through the dominant vegetation associations, the lower temperatures, heavier precipitation, and the consequently greater precipitation effectiveness produce a succession of soils corresponding to the life zones of plants. An example of the gradation of soils with altitude is illustrated in the diagram, Figure 10-9, which represents the soils on the eastern slopes of the Rocky Mountains and the High Plains in Colorado.

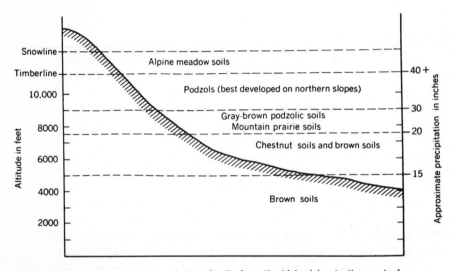

Fig. 10-9 Generalized diagram showing gradation of soils from the high plains to the crest of the Rocky Mountains in Colorado.

SOIL EROSION

We have already seen that the natural processes of erosion are active in the development of soils and that they are closely associated with climate. Our present concern will be with accelerated erosion, which tends to destroy soils that are more or less in harmony with natural conditions. The immediate climate-connected causes of accelerated erosion are the same as those which weather and transport parent rock in the early stages of soil formation; consequently, the distinction between "natural" and "accelerated" erosion is not always clear. But in one way or another, man is usually an indirect agent in accelerated erosion. Where there is excessive precipitation and hence a great potential danger of erosion due to surface runoff, a dense vegetation cover ordinarily exists to inhibit soil erosion. In arid climates vegetation is sparse, but running water is not such a great threat to the soil. Thus, there is a semblance of equilibrium between the forces that form the soil and those that would erode it. Man's contribution is essentially a negative one. Cutting forests, cultivation, grazing of herds, or burning of the plant cover all serve to upset the natural equilibrium and to accelerate erosion. Once the protective cover of vegetation and the organic matter in the topsoil are reduced, erosion proceeds at a more rapid rate. Cultural practices in land use have all too rarely provided for a compensating acceleration of soil-forming processes. Many soil-building practices are known, but they are beyond the scope of this book.

The world distribution of actual accelerated erosion does not show the close correlation with the patterns of climate and vegetation that zonal soils do, being in part the result of land-use practices. Rather it is the potential erosion, or what might be called the "erosion hazard," which is closely related to climatic conditions and to the associated soils. The fact that some soils erode more easily than others is traceable, in part, to the effect of climate upon their formation. In the regions of heavy rainfall, running water readily attacks exposed soils. In the humid tropical climates the soils are generally deficient in humus so that, although the clay sub-

Courtesy U.S. Department of Agriculture, Soil Conservation Service.

Fig. 10-10 Steep slopes without plant cover are readily eroded by rainfall and snowmelt run-off. This scene is in the Palouse region of eastern Washington, where fine textured loess soils are easily removed by both wind and water.

soils are quite resistant to erosion, the topsoil washes away easily. Where the rainfall is seasonal, where the soil is frozen for a part of the year, or where there is a snow cover for an extended period, the forms and intensity of erosion on exposed soils are altered but may be none the less disastrous. When frozen soil begins to thaw, melting usually takes place at the top first, and, until thawing is complete, vertical drainage of water is impeded. Under these conditions, moving surface water can rapidly carry away layers of mud. Snow affords a protective cover until it melts; thereafter the melt water from heavy snowpacks becomes a particularly active agent in sheet and rill erosion. The intensity of rainfall, as well as the amount, is important in determining the degree of erosion due to runoff. Thundershower precipitation does not penetrate the soil as well as light continuous rains, and the resulting runoff and erosion are much greater, especially in dry lands. One cloudburst can do far more damage than several months of gentle rains. Similarly, the concentration of a given amount of rainfall in one season creates an erosion hazard greater than that of an area with the same rainfall total more evenly distributed through the year. Heavy rains which break a period of drought commonly cause considerable loss of soil, for vegetative cover is at a minimum and the loose topsoil is easily removed.

Soils in regions of arid and semiarid climates are the most susceptible to the ravages of wind erosion. Soil water not only adds to the weight of the particles but is a cementing agent which reduces the tendency of soil to be blown about. When exposed to the wind, soils lacking in moisture are readily blown if the particles are small enough. Unfortunately, wind, like water, has a sorting action. It picks up and removes the finer particles

Fig. 10-11   Topsoil blown from the field on the right has nearly buried this fence.
Courtesy U.S. Department of Agriculture, Office of Information.

which are the basis of soil fertility and leaves the heavier material in
drifts or dunes. Its earth-moving capacity is not as closely related to slopes
as in the case of erosion by water. In the drought years of the 1930's in the
"Dust Bowl" of the United States, the loose topsoil was completely removed from large areas, leaving only the compact clays of the subsoil.
Semiarid grasslands are especially critical regions for wind erosion when
excessive disturbance of the plant cover (through overgrazing or over-
cultivation) coincides with unusually dry years.

Temperature has its maximum effect on accelerated erosion indirectly
through its influence on plant cover and the weathering processes. Freezing and thawing directly alter the structure of the soil and thus make it
more susceptible to the action of wind or running water. When frozen for
a continuous period, the soil is largely spared from erosion. The soils of
the tundra and taiga are singularly free from accelerated erosion, mostly
because of the lack of cultural disturbances but partly owing to the long
periods of freezing temperatures.

ADDITIONAL READINGS

Gates, David M., "The Energy Environment in Which We Live," *Am. Scientist,*
    51, 3 (1963), 327–48.

Hadlow, Leonard, *Climate, Vegetation, and Man.* New York: Philosophical
    Library, 1953.

Holdridge, Leslie R., "Determination of World Plant Formations from Simple
    Climatic Data," *Science,* 105, 2727 (1947), 367–68.

Major, Jack, "A Climatic Index of Vascular Plant Activity," *Ecology,* 44, 3
    (1963), 485–98.

Richards, P. W., "Plant Life and Tropical Climate," in *Biometeorology,* edited
    by S. W. Tromp. London: Pergamon Press, 1962.

Tosi, Joseph A., Jr., "Climatic Control of Terrestrial Ecosystems: A Report on
    the Holdridge Model," *Econ. Geog.,* 40, 2 (1964), 173–81.

climate 11
and water resources

Of all the earth's resources none is so fundamental to life as water. The properties of water in its three physical states make it by far the most useful of compounds. We can breathe it, drink it, bathe in it, travel on it, or see beauty in it in one or more of its forms. It is a raw material, source of power, waste disposal agent, solvent, medium for heat transfer, or coolant as the needs of modern industry may require. The high specific heat of water, its ability to exist in gaseous, liquid, or solid forms under natural conditions, and its capacity for storing and releasing latent heat with changes of state give it immense influence over atmospheric processes. The availability of water at different times and places is ultimately related to weather and climate. The restless atmosphere is the most active agent in the constant redistribution of water on the earth's surface—a fact that becomes all the more striking when we realize that only a minute fraction of one per cent of the earth's water is contained in the atmosphere at any one time. If all the atmospheric moisture were precipitated it would create a layer averaging only about one inch in depth over the entire globe. About 97 per cent of all the earth's water is contained in the seas and oceans; 1 per cent is in the snowfields and glaciers; and fresh-water bodies and ground water account for nearly 2 per cent.

THE HYDROLOGIC CYCLE

The constant circulation of water from oceans to air and back again to the oceans—with temporary residence in life forms, fresh-water bodies, ice accumulations, or as ground water—is called the *hydrologic cycle,* or simply the water cycle. It has no "beginning" or "end." Figure 11-1 shows that it is an intricate combination of evaporation, transpiration, air mass movements, condensation, precipitation, runoff, and ground-water movements. While the greater part of moisture which eventually falls as precipitation comes from the oceans, some water takes a short cut in the cycle and enters the air directly through evaporation and transpiration from soil and vegetation. But only a small part of precipitation over land can be traced back to evapotranspiration from the same area. Precipitation over the oceans is another form of hydrologic short cut. Other water completes the cycle with fresh-water bodies taking on the function of the oceans. A slowdown in the cycle for various periods is brought about when plants and animals use water for cell building, when icecaps and snowfields detain it in a solid state, when chemical action incorporates it in other compounds, or when ground water is trapped. But, sooner or later, virtually all terrestrial water appears elsewhere in the hydrologic cycle.

The part of the hydrologic cycle concerned with atmospheric moisture has been treated in Chapter 3. The processes of evaporation, condensation, and precipitation are essentially climatic; their functions in the water cycle would be simple indeed if it were not for the constant motion in the atmosphere. Thus, the patterns of atmospheric circulation have a bearing upon the regional manifestations of the hydrologic cycle. Dry air masses assume a part of the task of removing water from the continents. When they warm in moving toward the equator, they are especially effective in speeding up evapotranspiration. Their moisture content may also be increased by mixing with maritime air or by evaporation of rain falling from overriding maritime air. Water gained in this manner is precipitated again in storms over land or sea, or the air masses are further modified over oceans to become maritime. Maritime air masses carry water onto the land. Wherever they undergo the lifting processes—convection, orographic ascent, or convergence—precipitation is likely to result. The hydrologic cycle requires heat as well as moisture. Where heat and moisture are abundant, as in the rainy tropics, the cycle is active. In dry climates an essential part of the cycle, atmospheric moisture, is lacking. In very cold climates, the energy to operate the cycle is limited. Were it not for the encroachment of warm maritime air masses into high latitudes, there would be far less precipitation in polar regions. Insolation, through its effects on the atmospheric processes, provides the "fuel" to operate the hydrologic cycle. The flow of water vapor across boundaries of watersheds or continents is just as much a part of the cycle as the flow of liquid water down a river to the sea.

The practical value of an understanding of the hydrologic cycle comes from the fact that it is the means by which water is made available on

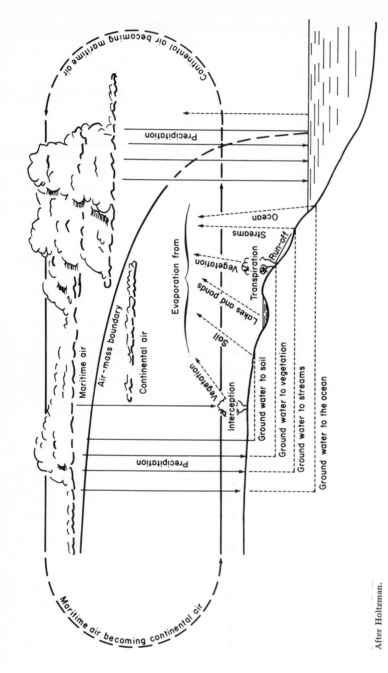

After Holtzman.

Fig. 11-1 The hydrologic cycle.

the land for the many uses to which man puts it. A great deal of mental and physical energy is expended in trying to control the hydrologic cycle to our better advantage. The conservation of water resources, and for that matter of most natural resources, is intimately related to one or more of its phases. Where we cannot control it we must adjust to its peregrinations.

RUNOFF AND FLOODS

Runoff is that portion of precipitation that returns to the oceans and other water bodies over the land surface or through the soil and water table. It may involve the direct return of rainfall or the flow of melted snow and ice fields which have temporarily stored the water. The significance of runoff to soil erosion has been discussed in Chapter 10. Floods differ from simple runoff only in degree, the distinction between the two depending for the most part upon how they affect surface features. River floods result whenever the channel capacity is exceeded by the runoff. Excessive runoff of rainfall or snowmelt is the fundamental cause, but the channel capacity may also be affected by barriers to flow (such as dams or ice jams), sudden changes of direction of the stream, reduced gradient, siltation of the stream bed, or sudden release of water due to a broken dam. On many rivers, floods are defined in relation to arbitrary gauges placed at important points along the stream. Not all floods are "bad." Many of the features of the earth's surface have been sculptured by running water. Since antiquity agricultural areas like the lower-Nile flood plain and Mesopotamia have depended upon annual river flooding and the accompanying deposits of fertile silt. What is gained in this way in the lowlands must be lost at higher levels in the watershed.

The amount of runoff in a given region is conditioned by several factors: the amount and intensity of precipitation, temperature, character of the soil, vegetative cover, and slope. If precipitation occurs as rain, the proportion that runs off will depend upon the capacity of soil and vegetation to absorb it. Plants have the ability to retain some rainfall on their external structures and to slow the velocity of raindrops. They also detain water in its horizontal movement. They improve soil structure and their roots provide channels to divert excess soil water into the ground water at greater depths. The high humus content of soils with a dense grass cover makes for better absorption, for it acts something like a sponge. Porous soils absorb more water by infiltration than dense clays or rock. If already saturated or if sealed by the intense pounding of raindrops, however, their absorptive capacity is limited. Similarly, impervious subsoil reduces the amount of water that can be taken in. When frozen in a wet condition, soils can absorb very little rain, but if frozen when porous and nearly dry they have a high capacity for water.

Surface runoff varies with the character of an individual storm. Long-continued rains charge the soil to its full capacity and the proportion which runs off becomes progressively greater. Loose sands and gravels constitute an exception, if they are not underlain with impervious material. In the case of snow or hail, infiltration must await melting. When the soil and plant cover are warm, some melting begins at once. If the surface and the air above are too cold, there is a delay of hours, days, or even months in the runoff. Ultimate surface flow is determined by the various surface and soil characteristics, the rate of melting, and the amount of snow lost by sublimation. Sometimes snow and ice are removed principally by sublimation, or by melting and evaporation, so that the runoff phase of the water cycle is assumed partly by the air. This removal process is referred to as *ablation*.

CLIMATIC CAUSES OF FLOODS

The predisposition of a climate to storms producing excessive precipitation is the fundamental basis of the flood hazard. In some climates flood-producing storms occur irregularly; in others they follow a seasonal pattern. Two types of storm are the initiating agents for most rain-caused floods: the violent thundershower, which is of short duration and produces flash floods, and the prolonged, general rain which, through sheer quantity of water, creates extensive flooding over entire watersheds. The flash flood is common only in those regions which experience heavy thunderstorms, that is, where unstable maritime air masses are frequent visitors. However, the occasional thunderstorms of arid climates also lead to destructive floods. The thunderstorm may be of convective, frontal, or orographic origin; so far as flooding is concerned, the important feature is its intensity not its origin. In general the less a flash flood is expected the more disastrous it is likely to be. In the desert it is a decided anomaly; in the rainy tropics it is anomalous to the extent that the normal stream channels may be unable to carry away the excess runoff. While scattered convective storms or a line of frontal thunderstorms often contribute to extensive flooding in large river systems, such floods are usually the result of long-continued, warm, rainy weather. This type of weather is most common in the humid climates of middle latitudes when frontal systems occlude or remain stationary for protracted periods. As long as the storm system is fed by moist maritime air, rain can continue. Once the water-holding capacity of soil and vegetation is exceeded, the foundation is laid for a major flood. Such conditions are typical of the Ohio Valley in spring, when neither the wet soil, the swollen tributaries, nor the high ground-water table can absorb even a moderate fall of rain.

If the precipitation falls as snow, the flood is not necessarily avoided. It is merely delayed. The most effective instrument for snow removal is a warm wind. If it is dry (for example, the foehn wind), it carries much of the water away in the air and is not a likely cause of flooding; if it is moist as well as warm, it produces rapid melting and runoff. Direct sunshine is not a major factor in rapid melting, unless the snow surface is darkened by dust or soot. Clean snow reflects most of the radiation, whereas dirty snow absorbs it better. Thus sunlight becomes a more effective agent as the season wears on. Rainfall upon snow does not at once produce runoff of flood intensity, for a snow cover has considerable capacity to hold water. When prolonged rains come in combination with warm winds, however, ideal flood conditions prevail. Another factor in snowmelt runoff is the temperature of the soil under snow cover. If the soil is frozen there is very little melting and runoff under the snow, but melting due to other causes is likely to produce a high proportion of runoff. Unfrozen soil causes some melting throughout the winter, and a large part of the water enters the soil to become ground water rather than runoff, because the melting process is slow.

The seasonal distribution of precipitation is the principal determining factor in the regimes of rain-caused floods. In the arid climates the thundershowers and resulting flash floods are both erratic. Concentrations of rainfall in one season (for example, as in the monsoon tropics) are likewise accompanied by seasonal floods. In mountainous areas of mid-latitudes and at high latitudes, flooding due to snowmelt runoff occurs with the onset of the warm season and is not always directly related to the precipitation regime. For example, in the dry summer subtropics the precipitation maximum is in winter, but the maximum runoff of melted snow is in spring or early summer. On the other hand, spring and summer snows in the mountains of marine climates contribute to the runoff in those seasons, often being removed by subsequent rains. In humid continental climates seasonal floods come at the end of the period of soil moisture accumulation, that is, in spring.

Destructive floods occur in every month in the United States, often with loss of life and damage to property running into many millions of dollars. In the United States, as a whole, loss of property and deaths due to floods have been great in all months, with winter and spring the worst seasons. The normal maximum of runoff of streams shows a distinct seasonal pattern. Figure 11-4 shows the normal annual distribution of runoff for representative rivers in the United States and southern Canada. Note the influence of late snowmelt on the regimes of northern rivers. In Florida snow is not a factor in runoff and the runoff is greatest in autumn in response to the rainier season and decreasing evaporation.

A unique variation in the normal runoff regime for snow-fed rivers occurs in rivers like the Mackenzie, Ob, or Yenesei, which flow northward

Courtesy Missouri-Kansas-Texas Lines.

Fig. 11-2 Flooded railway tracks along the Missouri River near St. Charles, Missouri. Washouts of the railway embankment resulted in flooding of farmlands on the left.

Fig. 11-3 The aftermath of a flood. Silt washed from adjoining fields has buried the trunks of these apple trees, which are likely to die if the sediment is not cleared away. Flood damage of this type is not so dramatic as that in heavily settled areas but, nevertheless, adds to the great economic loss caused by flooding each year.

Courtesy U.S. Department of Agriculture, Soil Conservation Service.

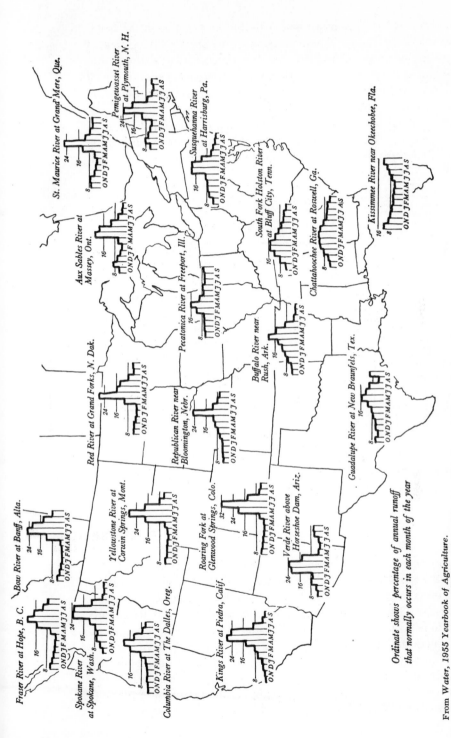

Ordinate shows percentage of annual runoff
that normally occurs in each month of the year

From *Water, 1955 Yearbook of Agriculture.*

Fig. 11-4 Normal distribution of runoff by months for representative rivers in the United States and Canada.

at high latitudes in North America and Asia. Melting begins in the head-waters and middle courses of these streams earlier in the spring than it does in the lower flood plains. Because the downstream channels are choked with ice there is extensive flooding until the thawing season is well underway. A contributory factor is permafrost, which allows little or no infiltration of surface waters.

In summary, floods are a temporary acceleration of the runoff phase of the hydrologic cycle. They can always be traced back to moisture in the atmosphere, but their intensity is affected by both natural and cultural features of the land surface.

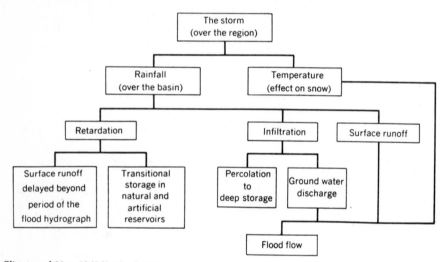

From *Climate and Man, 1941 Yearbook of Agriculture.*

Fig. 11-5 Factors involved in runoff forecasting.

RUNOFF FORECASTING

Runoff forecasting has two principal phases: One is concerned with forecasting the amount of rainfall or snowmelt that will be available to run off; the other attempts to predict the rate of flow in relation to stream capacity. Figure 11-5 summarizes graphically the main factors which are considered in flood forecasting for a particular storm. The techniques of forecasting quantitatively the precipitation to be expected from a storm are being refined, but, generally speaking, only qualitative indications of impending distaster due to heavy rainfall can be given in advance of the storm. For example, if a cyclone is drawing large quantities of tropical maritime air over a watershed which is already wet there is a distinct possibility of flooding. Extreme instability of the moist air may presage an even greater flood threat. Temperatures of the conflicting air masses within the storm, the temperature of air expected to follow the storm, and wind are factors which modify the meteorological aspects of the flood hazard. If the precipitation is snow, the threat is deferred until melting begins. Forecasts of snowfall are not of such immediate importance in flood warnings as forecasts of rainfall and potential snowmelt. When there is some question of whether rain or snow will fall generally over a watershed, the flood forecaster is in a delicate position. In mountainous areas, the lower level of snowfall will determine the area to be affected by rainfall runoff. Thus, a careful investigation of the probable upper-air temperatures is necessary. In regions visited by hurricanes, advance warning of the coming storm is a prerequisite to timely forecasts of so-called "tidal waves" along coasts as well as of excessive runoff inland.

In the United States, flood-forecasting services are coordinated by the United States Weather Bureau—a recognition of the importance of knowing as early as possible what the runoff will be. Numerous other agencies cooperate in taking observations and assembling data that may be brought to bear on forecasts. Measurements of rain even as it falls provide valuable data for flood prediction. Networks of precipitation-gauge stations have been set up in many watersheds of the United States. Correlated with subsequent stream flow, these measurements help to establish patterns of rainfall–flood relationships that are the basis for future flood forecasts as well as of immediate utility. *Hydrographs,* that is, graphs on which stream

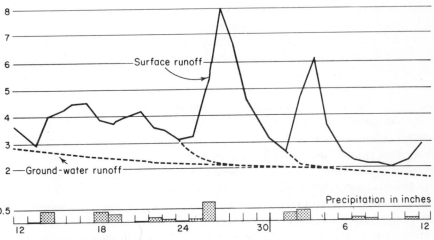

From *Water, 1955 Yearbook of Agriculture.*

Fig. 11-6 Hydrograph of stream flow in the Muskingum River at Dresden, Ohio, during a 31-day period. Values are in thousands of cubic feet per second. The lower graph shows daily precipitation in inches during the period.

flow is plotted as a function of time, have been useful devices for studying the effects of storms on flooding. The progress of storm centers across the river basins, the characteristics of air masses, the measured rainfall over the watersheds, and past stream behavior are the principal factors employed in making stream-flow forecasts.

After precipitated waters begin to flow from a watershed, much more accurate forecasts of stream discharge are possible. Such forecasts are based primarily upon a knowledge of the flow patterns of main streams and their tributaries. Reports of measured flow from upstream locations are collected to determine the amount of water that can be expected to pass specific points downstream. One swollen tributary does not produce a major river flood, but several together may. In the headwaters, the period of advance warning is shortest and reliance upon rainfall forecasts is greatest. Downstream forecasts are more accurate and there are usually several hours advance warning. Exceptions occur when torrential rains fall in lowlands or when major obstructions to runoff, such as flood-control dams, break.

SNOW SURVEYING AND RUNOFF FORECASTS

In the mountainous regions of the world, especially in middle latitudes, nature provides a reservoir for storage of water in the form of snow to be released with the rising temperatures of spring. This fact is of vital significance to water users in arid lands adjacent to snow-capped mountains. Efficient planning for water use (and control) during the season of peak flow is better carried out with a prior knowledge of expected stream flow. So far it is not possible to predict accurately far in advance how much snow will fall on mountain snowfields. The alternative is to measure the water content of the snowpack so that potential runoff can be determined.

Each winter several public and private organizations in the western United States cooperate in snow surveys with the Soil Conservation Service as the coordinating agency. The principle of snow surveying involves a sampling technique, since quantitative measurements of all the snow at upper levels is neither feasible nor necessary. Representative areas known as snow courses are selected in the snowfields which feed the major watersheds. Several snow courses may be necessary for a region to cover the differences in storm frequency and intensity which occur. Accessibility must be taken into account in the selection, and ordinarily it is undesirable to change the location of a course because continuity of records is disrupted. Measurements on the snow courses are taken on the first of each month throughout the winter and spring. Runoff forecasts are prepared early in the winter and revised monthly. The depth of snow alone is inadequate for snow surveys used in runoff forecasting. The water content is the important factor, for snow densities vary greatly. A snow sampling device permits measurement of water content as well as of depth. Coupled sections of lightweight aluminum tubing are thrust vertically downward through the snow to the ground beneath. A serrated cutting edge facilitates penetration through ice or hard snow layers. Snow weight, that is, water content, is determined by weighing the snow and tube on a simple spring scale, which is calibrated to make allowance for the weight of the tube. Ten or twelve samplings spaced 50 to 100 feet apart are taken along each snow course. Snow surveying is carried out by men from several cooperating agencies who reach the snow courses on skis, by snow tractor, or in light planes or helicopters. Successful experiments have been carried out using permanent remote-control measuring stations that incorporate the principle of radar. The radar transceiver is mounted on a pole with a target at its base. The rate of return of radio waves to the radar instrument is proportional to the water content of the snow and can be translated into snow weight. The information can be relayed to central recording stations by either wire or automatic radio.

The water equivalent of snow may also be measured by radioactive

Fig. 11-7 Weighing snow sampler to determine water content of snow on a snow course near Ketchum, Idaho.

Courtesy U.S. Department of Agriculture, Soil Conservation Service.

isotopes. The gamma rays from the cobalt-60 isotope, for example, are transmitted through snow in proportion to the water content of the snow. When the isotope is inserted to the bottom of a snow layer, measurement of the gamma-ray intensity at the surface yields an index of water content that can be converted into inches of water.

Through the correlation of the snow survey information with subsequent runoff from the respective watersheds, formulas and graphs to express the relationship have been established. These are fundamental to water supply forecasts—which, as a result, have become increasingly accurate. Such forecasts give a good indication of the amount of snow-melt which will enter the streams of a given watershed, but they cannot tell when the runoff will occur or whether there will be destructive floods. When full-scale runoff begins, because of high temperatures or storms, the flood forecaster must resort to the techniques described in the previous section, but information on the amount of water in the snowpack is invaluable in assessing the imminence of a major flood. Besides aiding in flood forecasting, the snow surveys provide information on the probable water supply for irrigation, hydroelectric power, navigation, fisheries, and a host of other water uses. An irrigation farmer, knowing in advance what the water supply will be, can plan his crops accordingly; power companies can compute future output and make firm commitments to consumers, and the industrial consumers of electric power can expand or curtail their production with the minimum of financial loss. City water departments are able to establish realistic sprinkling regulations; the Fish and Wildlife Service has been able to plan with greater accuracy for winter feeding and summer water supplies for fish and waterfowl on the basis of snow cover information. Snow survey data have even been used, with some success, to predict the ground-water supplies of certain river basins.

Special surveys in recreation areas gather supplementary data on conditions for skiing and avalanche forecasts. Unstable snowpacks on steep slopes can be a hazard to transportation and communication facilities, winter sports enthusiasts, and buildings. The danger is so acute each winter in Switzerland that a special Swiss Avalanche Commission has been organized. Avalanches are, in a sense, a flash flood of water in the solid form. While the angle of repose of the snow cover and the underlying surface features are basic considerations in avalanches, they are set off naturally by unfavorable conditions of snow structure, temperature, humidity, and wind. Any disturbance of an unstable snow cover is likely to cause an avalanche. *Moist* snow is relatively cohesive and does not avalanche readily, but snow *soaked* with water is predisposed to flow or slip. New snow, composed of light, interlocking snow crystals, is stable, as is granular snow, whose particles resist movement. The layering of the snow-pack also influences the tendency to avalanche. Generally, the layers reflect weather fluctuations. Some layers may be wet and compact; others loose and dry. Snow cores provide data on the strata in the snowpack. Meters to measure the pressure of the snow, and rams to test the resistance and coherence, are also used to determine the avalanche hazard. In the light of the weather conditions which prevail or are expected, avalanche forecasts are prepared.

Wind blasts known as *avalanche winds* frequently accompany severe avalanches. They are caused by the mass movement of the snow against the air and by greatly reduced pressure behind the moving snow mass. Trees have been broken off by the more violent blasts, although several yards removed from the path of the avalanche.

Whether they are concerned with runoff forecasts or matters pertaining to the snowpack *in situ,* snow surveys have been of great benefit. They have been extended to the eastern United States and Canada as well as to many other nations with water supplies depending on mountain snows.

RAINMAKING AND THE WATER SUPPLY

In subhumid, semiarid, and arid climates practically every class of water user has at one time or another experienced frustration as clouds drifted by overhead without precipitating needed water. Large quantities of water vapor often pass above temporarily parched humid lands that could be brought to life if the moisture were only condensed and precipitated. Much can be and has been done to husband water supplies on the surface and in the ground, but atmospheric moisture has not proven amenable to control by man. The first thing usually brought to mind at the suggestion of weather modification is rainmaking, but the control of air masses, winds, and temperature can be included theoretically as well. Rainmaking is by no means a new idea. Among primitive civilizations in dry lands there is a fairly persistent thread of attempts to induce rainfall, generally tied in with pagan religion. In modern times, as light began to dawn in the fields of meteorology and climatology, less emphasis has been placed on spiritual assistance and "rainmakers" have turned to methods based upon theories of precipitation. In the nineteenth century, professional rainmakers attempted to induce rain scientifically on the Great Plains. Large fires, chemicals, and cannon fire were tried without dramatic success. The few qualified successes were probably coincidences resulting from storms that were already developing. When performed under cloudy skies, especially with thunderheads present, the percentage of success was somewhat greater, but usually, nonetheless, coincidental. The final chapter in the theory of precipitation has not been written, however. The effects of compression waves, fires, smoke, or chemicals upon the processes of condensation and precipitation cannot be summarily dismissed.

A belief held widely in the last century was that most of the rainfall in the interior of North America came ultimately from water evaporated from the land. If in some way the land could be made to hold—and therefore yield—more water, precipitation would be increased. Some learned men suggested that if the Great Plains were plowed, the broken soil could hold more water and thus have more to evaporate. It happened that in the 1870's and early 1880's increased rainfall over much of the Great Plains did accompany a wave of settlement, giving some credibility to the theory. In the late 1880's and early 1890's droughts brought an end to another coincidence. Closely allied to the notions of a relationship between cultivation and rainfall were the beliefs that planting trees widely on the plains would increase rainfall. Many "tree claims" were planted with this in mind; few remain today. Their values as windbreaks and shelters for livestock and wildlife far exceeded their rainmaking potential.

Recent experiments in rainmaking have dealt with that part of the hydrologic cycle which precedes the precipitation process. Thoughts of increasing water vapor in the air or of controlling the movement of moist air masses have been largely shelved in favor of attempts to bridge the gap between condensation and precipitation. Clouds from which no rain is falling are a common phenomenon. The problem is to get these clouds to release their water. Immediately there arises a need to examine the theory of natural precipitation. When the processes that cause a cloud to release rain are known, the next step is to try to duplicate them artificially in clouds that appear to have rain potential but nevertheless are not yielding rain. The low and middle clouds are composed of very small droplets which do not fall as rain until they grow to a size too large to be buoyed up in the air. How can the droplets be caused to form large drops? A ridiculously simple answer is to provide the larger drops by spraying water into the cloud. In nonfreezing clouds of the warmer latitudes, rain is thought to begin with abnormally large droplets which fall through the others, growing by collision into full-fledged raindrops. Water sprayed from airplanes has produced rain from warm clouds, but the cost is prohibitive and flying in storms is dangerous.

CLOUD SEEDING

In November, 1946, Vincent J. Schaefer sprinkled six pounds of powdered dry ice from an airplane into a cloud at 14,000 feet near Schenectady, New York. Snow subsequently fell from the cloud, although it did not reach the ground. *Cloud seeding* became a standard procedure in rainmaking experiments as a result. Although the effects of cold materials on clouds had been known for several years, no one had ever followed experiments to the extent of relating the fact to possible rainmaking. Schaefer's discovery of the effect of extreme cold upon supercooled water droplets grew out of laboratory research intended to determine the nature of sublimation nuclei which could start the formation of ice crystals. None of a great number of powdered materials dropped through supercooled droplets in an ordinary home freezer brought about the desired crystallization. (Later silver iodide was proved effective by Bernard Vonnegut.) But when dry ice was put into the freezer to lower the temperature, crystals began to form at once. The cause was the extremely low temperature of the dry ice, not its ability to furnish sublimation nuclei. Whenever the droplets were cooled below $-39°C$ (about $-38°F$) ice crystals resulted. In 1945 a British scientist, Bohdan M. Cwilong, had made the same discovery of the critical temperature by cooling small quantities of moist air under laboratory conditions. Because he did not use cold substances added to the air he did not discover the possibility of seeding clouds under natural conditions.

Most convective clouds of mid-latitudes are composed of supercooled water droplets at altitudes above the freezing level. Under temperatures of about $-38°F$ or lower these droplets will freeze into ice crystals which

Courtesy Irving P. Krick Associates, Inc.

Fig. 11-8 Silver iodide generator used for cloud seeding. The hopper contains coke impregnated with silver iodide solution. The coke is burned to vaporize the silver iodide, which is forced into the air by a fan. The resulting crystals of silver iodide act as sublimation nuclei in the atmosphere.

grow and fall out as rain or snow, depending upon the temperatures at lower levels. Dry ice, with a temperature of −110°F, easily meets the requirements to initiate the action. It has been found to produce similar results in warm clouds in the tropics, presumably because it forms ice crystals which attract water droplets and start a chain reaction of coalescence in the cloud.

A related technique in cloud seeding is *artificial nucleation,* whose purpose is to provide the larger drops that will set off precipitation without necessarily lowering the temperature. Natural nuclei will begin the process in supercooled clouds at temperatures between −40° and 5°F. Certain dust particles from the Great Plains are effective at temperatures as high as 18°F. Crystals of silver iodide introduced into the air start ice crystal formation at temperatures between 8° and 25°. Ice appears to have an affinity for silver iodide crystals because the crystalline structures of both are hexagonal and they are of comparable size. Thus, silver iodide can be effective in warmer clouds or at lower (warmer) levels in a cloud. It can be introduced into a cloud from below in a vapor form which is carried upward by convective currents, or it can be dropped from above by airplane or rocket. The latent heat released when freezing takes place aids the convectional development of the cloud. Ground generators to dispense silver iodide vapor have been placed in strategic upwind locations in experimental attempts to induce precipitation in specific regions. The success of artificial nucleation has been difficult to appraise. When a storm cloud is seeded from an airplane and precipitation follows, it may be more than mere coincidence, but the procedure is expensive and dangerous. Using the ground generator method, the operator cannot be sure where the nucleating agent is blown by the wind, how long it maintains its effectiveness, or what proportion of the rainfall in leeward areas is really due to its nucleating powers. Nor, unfortunately, can he know how much other seeding is being done by amateurs or other experimenters. It is impossible to know how much rain would have fallen from a particular storm if the clouds had not been seeded. Statistical comparisons with other storms, other seasons, or adjacent areas are always subject to the laws of chance.

The chief value in cloud-seeding experiments has been their contribution to the understanding of the nature and causes of precipitation. There is only so much water on Earth, and, although only a small part of it is being used by man and other life forms at any one time, it is used over and over again. Rainmaking cannot increase the total water supply, but it could speed up the hydrologic cycle so that at a specific time and place more water is available for immediate use. In its broadest sense, water conservation aims to slow down and use more effectively the runoff phase of the water cycle and to speed up and redistribute the atmospheric phase.

ADDITIONAL READINGS

Carter, Douglas B., *The Water Balance of the Mediterranean and Black Seas,* Publications in Climatology, IX, 3. Centerton, N.J.: Laboratory of Climatology, 1956.

Church, J. E., "Snow Surveying: Its Principles and Possibilities," *Geog. Rev.,* 23, 4 (1933), 535–63.

Huschke, Ralph E., "A Brief History of Weather Modification Since 1946," *Bull. Am. Met. Soc.,* 44, 7 (1963), 425–29.

Kuenen, P. H., *Realms of Water.* New York: John Wiley & Sons, Inc., 1955.

Miller, David H., "Insolation and Snow Melt in the Sierra Nevada," *Bull. Am. Met. Soc.,* 31, 8 (1950), 295–99.

United States Department of Agriculture, *Water, 1955 Yearbook of Agriculture.* Washington: Government Printing Office, 1955.

van Hylckama, T. E. A., *The Water Balance of the Earth.* Publications in Climatology, IX, 2. Centerton, N.J.: Laboratory of Climatology, 1956.

Vestal, C. K., "The Precipitation Day Statistic," *Mon. Wea. Rev.,* 89, 2 (1961), 31–37.

Work, R. A., *Stream-Flow Forecasting from Snow Surveys,* U.S.D.A. Circular No. 914. Washington: Government Printing Office, 1953.

Workman, E. J., "The Problems of Weather Modification," *Science,* 138, 3538 (1962), 407–412.

climate 12
and agriculture

One hardly needs to leave home to become aware of the enormous influence climate has on agriculture the world over. A casual inventory of the kitchen food cupboards will reveal agricultural products from a variety of climatic regions: cocoa from the rainy tropics, rice from the dry summer subtropics of California or the humid subtropics in Louisiana, flour from the semiarid wheat belts, or dates from the hot deserts. Whether one lives in Thule, Chicago, or Singapore, it is at once apparent that not all these items are local products. As climate largely defines the climax vegetation formations throughout the world, so it sets limits for crop production. Domestic animals, too, respond to climatic differences, both physiologically and by virtue of the feeds they require for economic production of food and fiber. In general, crops and animals have their optimum climatic conditions for production, although we must not lose sight of such other factors as soils, relief, insects and diseases, market, and transportation facilities which, singly or in combination, may modify the suitability of a particular area for a specific type of cultivation or animal husbandry. The actual distribution of crop plants is determined by the combined influence of physiological, economic, social, technological, and historic forces; but no crop can attain importance in an agricultural system unless it is adapted to prevailing environmental conditions.

General aspects of the relationship of climate to crops have been known for centuries; yet important details of the influence of climate on agriculture are still being revealed.

In examining the relationship, we are interested in two broad, overlapping problems. One is concerned with the effect of climate upon the distribution of crops and domestic animals; the other pertains to the more detailed influence of climatic elements upon specific crops or animals and their productivity. Agriculture is one of the riskiest of all enterprises. Not the least of the risks are those imposed by weather and climate.

CLIMATIC FACTORS IN CROP PRODUCTION

The principal climatic factors affecting crop production are the same as those influencing all vegetation—temperature, length of growing season, moisture conditions, sunlight, and wind—but they must be considered in a different light with respect to crops. Natural vegetation is, axiomatically, adapted to the climatic conditions with which it is associated as a climax formation. For economic reasons, man has domesticated crop plants and cultivated them in environments where they could not survive without his help. In other words, crop plants are less hardy than natural vegetation. Agriculture is essentially a combination of processes designed to promote, artificially, a favorable environment for growth. Its practices are so diverse as to include drainage and irrigation to control the moisture factor, artificial sheltering to control temperature, and shading or the use of electric lights to control light. In the extreme, any crop can be grown anywhere if labor and expense are not in question; in the realm of practicability, all crops have their climatic limits for economic production—limits which can be extended by plant breeding and selection as well as by cultivation methods.

In their influence upon crops, the climatic factors are closely interrelated. The effect of each is modified by the others. Daily, seasonal, or annual variations in any or all of the climatic elements are of importance in determining the efficiency of crop growth. In considering the climatic environment of plants it is important to keep in mind that the microclimate immediately around the plant is of vital significance. Critical conditions, whether they be at the maximum or minimum limits for the plant, may prevail in the air at plant level while at a few feet above the surface the temperature is well within the safe range. Similarly, moisture, light, and wind effects may be quite different at and near ground level from conditions in the free air above.

TEMPERATURE AND CROPS

The temperature of the air and of the soil affects all the growth processes of plants. Every variety of every crop plant has minimum, optimum, and maximum temperature limits for each of its stages of growth. Winter rye has relatively low temperature demands and can withstand freezing temperatures during a winter period of dormancy. Tropical crops (for example, dates or cacao beans) have high temperature requirements throughout the year. The upper lethal temperatures for active plant cells of most species ranges from 120° to 140°F but varies with species, stage of growth, and length of exposure to the high temperature. High temperatures are not as serious as low temperatures in arresting plant development—if the moisture supply is adequate and the crop is adapted to the climatic region. Crops ordinarily do not "burn up"; they "dry up." But, under very high temperatures, growth is slowed or even stopped regardless of the moisture supply, and premature loss of leaves or fruit is likely. Mid-latitude plants will *grow* structurally but *fruit* poorly in the tropics. Disaster to crops usually comes with the combination of dry and hot conditions. Winds that would be expected to produce evaporative cooling often only speed up transpiration and result in dehydration of plant tissues. The optimum temperature for the maximum rate of plant growth is not always the best for crop production. Temperatures that promote quick growth may also result in weak plants which are more easily damaged by wind, hail, insects, or disease. Some crops fail to produce their fruit or seed if forced under high temperatures. Within limits, the problem of high temperatures can be solved under field conditions by increasing the moisture supply through irrigation or moisture-conserving tillage practices. These practices permit the successful production of many different crops in hot desert oases. Delicate plants can be shaded from the direct rays of the sun by higher tree crops or artificial cloth or slat shades. Selection of planting sites on the less-exposed slopes of hills can also alleviate high temperatures if the crop demands it. Sometimes it is desirable to have low temperatures during the stages of germination or flowering of crops. This is achieved by planting early in the season or in a cooler location. Water bodies defer the rise of temperatures to the leeward in spring and thereby help to prevent blossoming in fruit orchards until the danger of killing frost is past. Such is the case in the fruit-producing areas east of the Great Lakes. Citrus fruits take on better coloring and become sweeter when subjected to short periods of near-freezing temperature.

Few crops are restricted in their worldwide distribution because of the direct effects of high temperatures alone, although many yield best when grown near their poleward limits. Since production of many crops has been pushed farther and farther into high latitudes, the effects of low temperature have had increasing significance. In discussing the effects of low temperatures on crops, we must distinguish between chilling and freezing. Prolonged chilling of plants at temperatures above freezing retards growth and can kill certain plants which are adapted only to constantly warm conditions. Chilling may not directly kill plant cells but reduces the vital flow of water from the roots so that transpiration losses cannot be regained. Yellowing of plant leaves sometimes results from this kind of physiological drought. Crops such as rice and cotton are killed by near-freezing temperatures of two or three days' duration; potatoes, maize, and many garden vegetables can "weather" such cold spells with little or no damage, although their growth is slowed. As would be expected, the warm-climate crops are most seriously affected by chilling. Application of cold irrigation water to a field retards growth by reducing temperatures in the soil and at the immediate surface. Evaporation of soil moisture also tends to decrease the temperature. Loss of heat due to evaporation may be serious in the case of flooded rice paddies. In northern Japan chemical solutions which act as evaporation suppressors are applied to the surface of flood waters in order to maintain higher daytime temperatures at the level of the growing rice plants. On the other hand, wet soils do not cool as rapidly at night, and irrigation water can actually help stave off chilling if its temperature is above that of the air.

The influence of low night temperatures varies greatly with different crops. Certain crops, such as potatoes and sugar beets, store carbohydrates more rapidly during periods with cool nights. Cotton, maize, and tobacco require warm nights for maximum development. In high latitudes, the greater length of the daylight period makes it possible for crops otherwise adapted to cool climates to condense their growing season into fewer days. Light as well as heat contributes to speeding growth during the long days.

Whenever growing plants are subjected to freezing temperatures, damage or even death is imminent. Some crops, notably fruit trees such as the apple, complete fruiting during the warm season and can withstand below-zero temperatures in the winter. Others have a hardy underground structure in the form of roots, bulbs, tubers, or rhizomes which maintain life while the upper parts of the plant die down during the winter. Annuals simply complete their full life cycle during the growing season, their hardy seeds being the medium for renewed life. Winter freezing can hardly be prevented in climates where it is the normal course of events. Crops adapted to the seasonal cycle of temperature must be selected. Hothouses can, of course, be used, but they are economically feasible for only certain high-value crops such as vegetables or flowers.

FROST

The greatest agricultural risk in connection with low temperatures is the threat of unseasonable frosts. Two kinds of frosts may be distinguished: (1) advection, or air mass, frost, which results when the temperature at the surface in an air mass is below freezing; and (2) radiation frost, which occurs on clear nights with a temperature inversion and usually results in formation of ice crystals on cold objects. The former, sometimes called *black frosts,* are more properly termed freezes. While air mass freezes are common in winter in middle and high latitudes, they are an agricultural problem primarily in relation to specific crops which are limited in their winter-hardiness. Actual plant damage may be the result of alternate freezing and thawing, frost-heave in the soil, or desiccation. Winter wheat, for example, can withstand freezing temperatures but is *winter-killed* if the roots are disturbed too much by frost-heave. If unusually severe, an air mass freeze can be disastrous in winter, but it creates a special hazard when it occurs in early autumn before plants have made the necessary physiological adjustments, or in late spring when field crops are in the seedling stage and trees and shrubs are budding or blossoming. In the subtropics a severe freeze is regarded as unseasonable at any time of year. Millions of dollars in crop damage have been sustained in the southern states as a result of cold air masses. The citrus industry is particularly vulnerable. Because the temperature of air masses cannot be controlled on a large scale, not much can be done to forestall the general hazard attending air mass freezes. High-value crops may justify the use of covers or mulches which reduce the loss of soil heat. Expensive shrubbery and small trees are often wrapped to prevent freezing and other types of damage. In spring, hotbeds and coverings can be provided to protect seedlings against moderate freezes. For production of most field crops, the only satisfactory solution to the problem of freezing is to avoid it as far as possible by planting after the danger is past in spring, and by selecting varieties which will mature before the renewal of the hazard in autumn. Even then the farmer may be taking a calculated risk.

Damage due to radiation frost differs from freeze damage in degree and in its spotty occurrence. Plants which are killed by a general freeze may be only partially damaged by frost, although the economic effects can be just as great. An entire fruit or berry crop may be wiped out by a single hard frost although the plants themselves are not necessarily killed. The hazard is greatest during critical stages of growth; for warm-climate crops, this means the entire growing season. Germinating seeds are not often affected by surface frost, but young seedlings may be killed unless they are of frost-hardy varieties. Crops like potatoes, tomatoes, and melons are vulnerable right up to maturity. The flowering stage is a critical period for most crops of field and orchard. In the spring-wheat belts of North America and Siberia, late summer frosts are destructive even after the kernels of grain have begun to form. Frosty nights followed by warm, sunny days produce a *sun scald* on orchard fruits, considerably reducing their value. Tree trunks are sometimes affected by the alternate freezing and warm sunshine also; orchardists whitewash the trunks so they will

not absorb so much heat during the day. In this way the range of temperature experienced by the bark is reduced.

Prevention of crop damage due to radiation frosts is more feasible than
thwarting a general freeze. Preventive measures are based upon a knowledge of the conditions for frost. These conditions are (1) a prevailing
stable air mass with cool surface temperatures, (2) clear skies to allow loss
of heat by radiation, (3) little or no surface wind to mix the cold air near
the ground with the warmer air above, (4) a relatively high dew point
temperature, and (5) topographic features which induce drainage of cold
air into depressions. It is this latter factor which accounts for the spotty
distribution of frost. Whether or not frost crystals will form on plant surfaces depends on the dew point of the air. If cooling takes place until the
dew point is reached at a temperature above freezing, the formation of
dew releases latent heat and retards further cooling. Below 32°F frost will
form. This process also releases latent heat, which explains why light frosts
of short duration may cause surprisingly little damage. Evaporation of
water from soil or plants, especially after a previous rain, also serves to
reduce the temperature at ground level, and it is frequently a contributory
cause of frost.

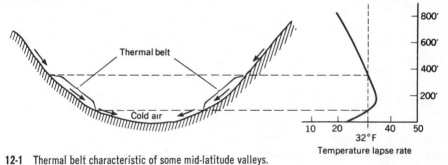

Fig. 12-1 Thermal belt characteristic of some mid-latitude valleys.

As with freezes, a logical adjustment to frosts is to avoid them. Selection
of frost-hardy plants is one way. Another is to grow delicate crops on
slopes above the level to which below-freezing air is likely to extend or
where air drainage or winds can be depended upon to stir the air throughout the night. North-south valleys are in the shade earlier in the evening
than those which open to the west and inversions therefore develop sooner
and have a longer period in which to concentrate freezing air in the valley
bottom. In mid-latitudes mountain slopes frequently exhibit a *thermal belt*
of maximum nighttime temperatures between fairly well defined levels.
Below the belt, frosts associated with radiation and air drainage are a
hazard; above the upper limit, low temperatures are related to the normal
lapse rate and are negative factors in plant development by day as well as
at night.

FROST PREVENTION

Direct frost prevention measures are largely aimed at breaking up the inversion which accompanies intense nighttime radiation. This is accomplished by stirring the air, heating it, providing a protective blanket of smoke, or by any combination of these. Obviously, the methods will work only in stable air. For many years smudge pots have been used to combat radiation inversions in citrus groves. Cheap oil or any fuel may be used, the objective being to create some heat at tree level and to form a dense pall of smoke which spreads out over the surrounding area and reduces the loss of heat by radiation in much the same way that a cloud cover does. In addition to raising slightly the temperature of the surface air, heat from the burners creates convection currents and brings about the desired mixing of air in the inversion layer. Of course, the soot settles on fruit trees and everything else in the vicinity so that it creates a problem in itself. By day a smoke cover retards warming at the surface. More

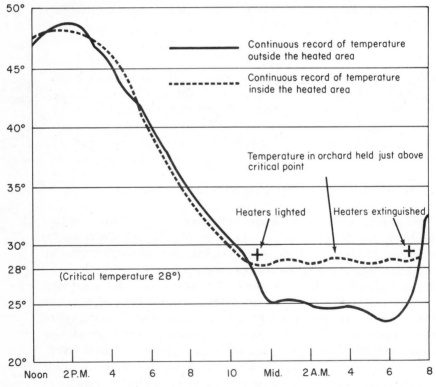

Courtesy U.S. Weather Bureau.

Fig. 12-2 Graph of temperature inside and outside an area using orchard heaters to prevent frost damage.

Sunkist Photo.

Fig. 12-3 Fan and heater for frost prevention in a lemon grove.

efficient heaters which give off less smoke are now more common, and, although they do not provide the smoke blanket, the direct heating and resulting convective activity often successfully alleviate the frost danger. Another method of stirring air is by means of huge fans, usually operated by electric or gas-driven motors. Carefully located in and around the area to be protected, they can be turned on when the critical stage is reached to mix the lower air layers. Fans cannot prevent damage from an invading air mass with freezing temperatures, whereas heaters may at least reduce the effect of the freeze if it is not too severe. Airplanes and helicopters have also been used to fan the air above crops, but this is an expensive procedure usually reserved for emergencies. Frost damage to wheat fields in northern states has been successfully prevented by the use of airplanes. The best known frost prevention activities are those in the citrus areas of California and Florida, where virtually every grove is equipped with thermometers and heaters or fans (or both). But these methods are widely employed in fruit orchards throughout the country, especially at the time of spring flowering. Where only a light frost is expected, water sprayed over fruit blossoms has proven effective in ameliorating the hazard. The water droplets tend to produce a protective cover of fog and maintain the temperature at or near the freezing point. In orchards and vineyards in Europe protection against temperatures as low as 23°F has been achieved by the use of fine sprays. Orchards are a long-term investment and expensive measures often prove economically sound. One heavy frost can mean the loss of a whole year's crop. Growers of winter or early vegetables can hardly afford to combat chance frosts by such methods, however. Even after a hard spring freeze, vegetables can usually be replanted; if it is too late for one variety, another can be substituted so that the financial loss is not complete. Tender plants are commonly covered with paper or straw for frost protection during the early stages of growth, an extension of the principle of cold-frame covers for seedlings. Some plants can be successfully covered with soil by plowing if there is advance warning, although the covering and uncovering processes cause a certain amount of damage. Flooding with water has also been employed as an emergency frost-prevention measure. Cranberry bogs are often saved from frost in this way. In certain circumstances, proper drainage of surface and soil waters can be equally important in frost prevention as a result of the reduction of evaporation. Cultivation practices, such as weeding and mulching, also can inhibit frost.

FROST WARNINGS

In order for frost-prevention methods to be effective, it is necessary to have advance warning of the danger. Forecasting of general freezing temperatures associated with a cold air mass is based upon analysis of air masses and predictions of their movements and modifications in local areas. While this is by no means a simple task, radiation frost forecasts are even more difficult because of the great local differences in the frost hazard. During the critical season, the United States Weather Bureau operates a special Frost Warning Service in conjunction with its other activities. Federal-state cooperation has made frost warnings especially valuable in the citrus-producing areas, where nightly reports are broadcast during the winter. Detailed forecasts of radiation frost are not feasible, but warnings of potential danger can be made. In a given locality the threat of damaging frost must be interpreted in relation to soil conditions and heat storage during the previous period, the stage of crop growth, topographic influences, the dew point, and wind, as well as the expected degree and duration of minimum temperatures below freezing. While it is usually "better to be safe than sorry," it is just as important to know that frost will not occur as to know that it will, if the needless expense of preventive measures is to be avoided. Because of the spotty nature of radiation frost, every efficient farmer who faces a frost hazard has his property equipped with instruments to register local temperature, humidity, and wind so that he can determine the degree of danger for all parts of his orchard or cropland. He is alerted by frost warnings for his vicinity, but the final decision to light heaters or to begin other procedures rests on purely local conditions.

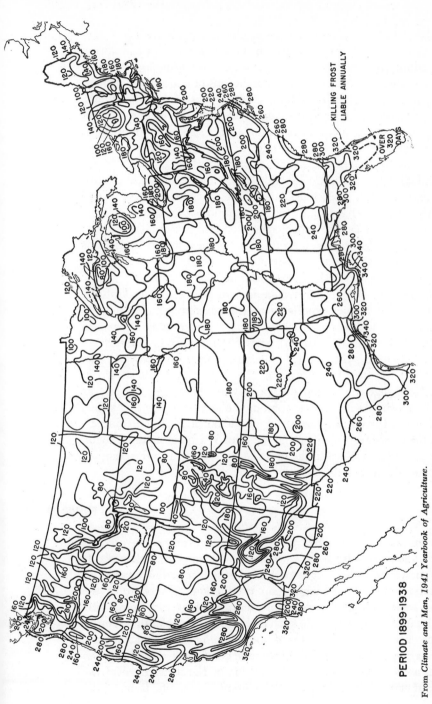

PERIOD 1899-1938

From *Climate and Man, 1941 Yearbook of Agriculture.*

Fig. 12-4 Average length of frost-free period in days in the contiguous United States.

THE FROST-FREE SEASON

Closely related to frost effects on crop production is the *frost-free season,* defined as the length of time between the last killing frost of spring and the first killing frost of autumn. As an index of the *growing season,* it is usually interpreted in terms of the principal crops of a locality, although it is actually different for crops with varying degrees of frost-hardiness. Statistically, the frost-free season is taken as the number of days during which the temperature is continuously above 32°F; the period between the mean dates of the last spring frost and the first autumn frost is commonly taken to be the *growing season* at a particular place.

The dependability of a certain length of growing season is of importance to farmers. It is the occasional, unexpected frost, especially in late spring or early autumn, that usually causes the most damage. Thus, it is the growing season that can be expected in a certain percentage of years that is most useful in planning crop production and in calculating risk. For many crops it is better to operate well within the average frost-free period to avoid the risks associated with departures from the normal.

In general, the frost-free season decreases with an increase in latitude. Large areas within the tropics experience no frost except at high altitudes. The other extreme is at the poles, where there is no growing season. In the mid-latitudes the growing season varies considerably in response to climatic controls. There is often a wide fluctuation from year to year. The average length of the frost-free season in the United States is shown in Figure 12-4. Note that the season decreases with increasing altitude as well as with increasing latitude. The combined effects of prevailing winds and the land–water relationship are strikingly demonstrated in a comparison between the frost-free season on the coasts of Washington and Oregon and on the New England coast in the same latitude. Note also the complex pattern produced by mountain ranges.

PHENOLOGY

Although temperature extremes that may damage crops are obvious climatic phenomena which affect agriculture, the rate at which plants develop in their various stages of growth is of equal importance in determining climatic limits of economic crop production. *Phenology* is the science which relates climate to periodic events in plant and animal life. Phenological data for crops include such facts as dates of planting, germination, and emergence of seeds; dates of budding, flowering, and ripening; and dates of harvest. These depend on climatic conditions preceding each event as well as on climatic factors at the time of the occurrence of the event. Their specific relationship to the climatic elements is not fully understood, but they nevertheless represent observed facts of plant growth that can be put to practical use. Generations of farmers have kept phenological diaries listing the dates of observed development of natural vegetation and crops as well as facts concerning the periodic reactions of birds and animals to climate and the seasons. Such information, recorded or not, has been the chief basis for denoting "signs of spring," "signs of autumn," and so on. When correlated with climatic observations, it is invaluable in studying the relation of agriculture to climate. Phenological maps can be prepared with *isophenes* connecting places at which a phenological event took place on the same date. For example, the winter wheat harvest begins in Texas in June and gradually proceeds northward to Nebraska by early July. The difference in dates of significant phases of plant development over a given distance is the *phenological gradient*. Phenological gradients of microclimatic proportions are common perpendicular to garden walls, fence rows, or hedges. On the sunny side, plants are likely to develop faster close to a wall which reflects heat. If shaded by the wall, however, the same variety may mature later. Similarly, differences occur on opposite exposures of hills or mountains, although complications are introduced if the higher temperatures of sunny slopes are accompanied by a moisture deficiency.

The rate of development of a plant variety is the resultant of all the environmental factors: climatic, physiographic, edaphic, and biotic. For a particular field under standard cultivation practices, it is primarily a function of climate, with temperature and light being the most important factors. A close relationship exists, therefore, between plant phenology and both latitude and altitude. It is well recognized that "spring moves northward" in the Northern Hemisphere and that "autumn moves southward." The growing season is progressively shorter with increasing latitude. In far northern latitudes the longer days in summer compensate for cooler temperatures to some extent so that certain crops can mature in approximately the same length of time as in mid-latitudes. Figure 12-5 shows graphically the phenology of the *Marquis* variety of wheat in several North American locations. The total time required from seeding to ripening of the wheat was 87 days at Fairbanks, Alaska (Lat. 64°N.), and 90 days at Lincoln, Nebraska (Lat. 41°N.). Obviously factors other than monthly temperature averages entered into the development of the wheat plants. Fairbanks has a mean July temperature of 60°F, whereas the comparable value for Lincoln is 78°. (Tlalnepantla, Mexico, represents a special set of conditions related to high altitude. There, 148 days were required from sowing to maturity for the same variety of wheat, but the longer frost-free season nevertheless permitted production of a crop.) The longer periods of daylight aided the maturity of the crop at the northerly latitudes and offset the lower temperatures. The importance of light in the

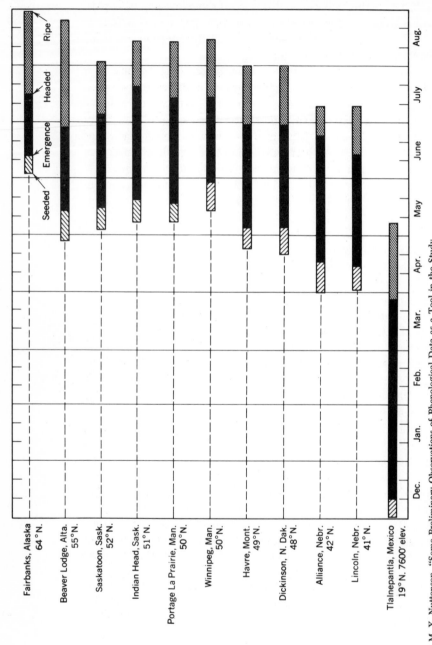

From M. Y. Nuttonson, "Some Preliminary Observations of Phenological Data as a Tool in the Study of Photoperiodic and Thermal Requirements of Various Plant Material," in A. E. Murneek, R. O. Whyte, *et al., Vernalization and Photoperiodism.* Copyright 1948, The Ronald Press Company.

Fig. 12-5 Chart of the phenology of Marquis wheat at selected North American locations.

development of *Marquis* wheat was shown in an experiment by Klages in which wheat plants were exposed to electric lights so placed as not to raise the temperature. The lights were turned on from 5 P.M. to 8 A.M. daily. Without artificial illumination the wheat in a control plot required 179 days from planting to heading. Under the lights, the period was only 48 days, a reduction by 73 per cent.[*]

At a given location the period between planting and harvesting is not a specific number of calendar days but rather a summation of energy units, which may be represented as *degree-days*. The duration of a certain temperature is quite as important as temperature averages. A degree-day for a given crop is defined as a day on which the mean daily temperature is one degree above the *zero temperature* (that is, the minimum temperature for growth) of the plant. Some representative zero temperatures are:

Spring wheat	32 to 40°F (Depending on variety)
Oats	43°
Field corn	54 to 57.°
Sweet corn	50°
Potatoes	45°
Peas	40°
Cotton	62 to 64°

The period required for achieving maturity is also a function of the length of day, or *photoperiod*. In general a crop planted early in the spring requires more calendar days to mature than the same crop planted later. In mid-latitudes the days are shorter in spring and temperatures are lower. For efficiency in the use of labor and equipment at planting and harvesting times it is expedient to make successive plantings of a crop so that the ensuing harvest can be spread across several days or weeks. In this way all the facilities for harvesting, processing, and marketing can be kept to a minimum and yet can be used for a maximum time each season. This is especially significant for vegetable crops which must be harvested immediately at maturity in order to maintain quality. Let us consider green peas as an example. Table 12-1 gives the phenological data for Alaska peas planted on different dates at College Park, Maryland, in 1926. Note that the peas planted on March 29 took 74 days to mature to the harvesting stage, whereas those planted on May 8 required only 51 days. The average length of the photoperiod was 14 hours during the entire period for the first planting and 14.6 hours for the last, and average daily temperatures naturally increased as the season progressed.

[*] K. H. W. Klages, *Ecological Crop Geography* (New York: The Macmillan Co., 1942), pp. 279–80.

TABLE 12-1

Phenology of Alaska Peas at College Park, Maryland, 1926*

Date planted	Date emerged	Date first blossom	Date of harvest	Total days
Mar. 29	Apr. 14	May 13	June 11	74
Apr. 3	Apr. 16	May 14	June 11	69
Apr. 9	Apr. 21	May 17	June 14	66
Apr. 16	Apr. 28	May 21	June 17	63
Apr. 24	May 4	May 27	June 22	61
Apr. 30	May 8	May 30	June 22	54
May 8	May 16	June 6	June 28	51

* Data selected from Victor R. Boswell, "Factors Influencing Yield and Quality of Peas," in *Biophysical and Biochemical Studies*, University of Maryland Agricultural Experiment Station, Bulletin No. 306 (College Park: March, 1929).

Careful studies of the phenology of crops over a number of years make it possible to establish planting schedules that are best adapted to local climate, availability of labor, and market demands. Sometimes it is also possible to avoid the periods of maximum hazard from insects, diseases, or seasonal weather phenomena. In irrigated areas phenological data can be the basis for determining the best time to plant in order to make the least demand on water supplies.

THE MOISTURE FACTOR

Within rather wide limits of temperature conditions, moisture is more important than any other environmental factor in crop production. There are optimum moisture conditions for crop development just as there are optimum temperature conditions. Because crop plants obtain their water supplies primarily through their root systems, maintenance of soil moisture is the most compelling problem in agriculture. Excessive amounts of water in the soil alter various chemical and biological processes, limiting the amount of oxygen and increasing the formation of compounds that are toxic to plant roots. The underlying cause of inadequate soil aeration may be poor vertical drainage as well as excessive rainfall. Therefore, conditions can be improved to some extent by drainage practices. On the other hand, a high rate of percolation of water through the soil tends to remove plant nutrients and inhibit normal plant growth. Cover crops and addition of humus to the soil help to alleviate this problem. Heavy rainfall may directly damage plants or interfere with flowering and pollination. By packing the surface soil, deluges make difficult the emergence of tender seedlings. Small grains are often beaten down, or *lodged,* by rain so that harvest is difficult. Lodged grain is susceptible to spoilage and disease.

The effect of rain on the harvesting and storage of grain and hay crops is a common problem. Special labor-consuming methods are employed to speed up drying and curing of hay to avoid rotting. Artificial drying of both forage and grain has been adopted as a method of combating damp conditions at harvest time. Wet weather during the later stages of maturity and harvest of cotton causes losses of both seed and fiber, often by providing favorable conditions for disease.

Snow, sleet, and freezing rain are threats to wintering plants. The sheer weight of ice and snow may be sufficient to break limbs on trees and shrubs. A thick ice cover on the ground tends to produce suffocation of crop plants such as winter wheat. Hail is a special case of "excessive moisture" which causes direct damage to plants. Locally it may be a disaster, although over large areas it is a minor hazard compared to drought or the effects of low temperatures. The degree of damage depends on the stage of growth of the crop and upon the intensity of the hailstorm. Because hail is most common in the warm season, it frequently catches crops at a critical stage, pounding young plants into the ground, shredding leaves, or shattering flowers and seed heads. Figure 12-7 is a map of the average annual number of days on which hail occurs in the United States. The areas in which hail normally causes the most damage are in eastern Wyoming, eastern Colorado, western portions of Nebraska, Kansas, and Oklahoma, and in northern Texas. Many farmers in these and adjacent areas carry hail insurance on their crops. Premium rates are determined on the basis of weather records and hail damage records of insurance companies that pool data through the Crop-Hail Insurance Acturial Asso-

Fig. 12-6 Hail damage in an Iowa cornfield.

Courtesy U.S. Department of Agriculture, Office of Information.

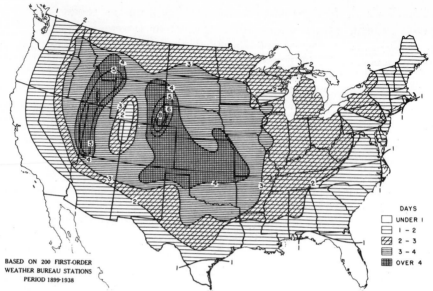

DAYS

☐ UNDER 1
⊟ 1 – 2
▨ 2 – 3
▤ 3 – 4
▦ OVER 4

BASED ON 200 FIRST-ORDER
WEATHER BUREAU STATIONS
PERIOD 1899-1938

From *Climate and Man, 1941 Yearbook of Agriculture.*

Fig. 12-7   Average annual number of days with hail in the contiguous United States.

ciation in Chicago. Figure 12-8 shows regional variations in hail insurance premiums for small grains in the United States.

Attempts at hail suppression have recently been incorporated in experiments designed to modify clouds and precipitation. Cloud seeding has been employed on the theory that an increase in the number of nuclei for ice crystal formation would result in many small hailstones rather than fewer large ones. If small enough, the hailstones would presumably melt before reaching the ground.

DROUGHT

Under natural conditions, excessive moisture is far less a problem than drought. Thornthwaite defines *drought* as "a condition in which the amount of water needed for transpiration and direct evaporation exceeds the amount available in the soil."* Three classes of drought may be differentiated: (*1*) permanent drought associated with arid climates; (*2*) seasonal drought, which occurs in climates with distinct annual periods of dry weather; and (*3*) drought due to precipitation variability. In every case, the underlying cause of drought is insufficient rainfall, although any

* C. W. Thornthwaite, "Climate and Moisture Conservation," *Ann. Assoc. Am. Geogrs.*, 37, 2 (June, 1947), 88.

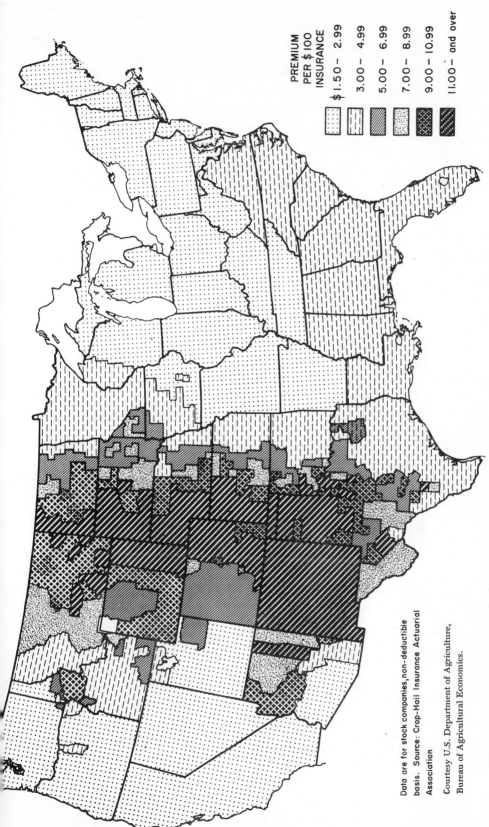

PREMIUM
PER $100
INSURANCE

$1.50 – 2.99
3.00 – 4.99
5.00 – 6.99
7.00 – 8.99
9.00 – 10.99
11.00 – and over

Data are for stock companies, non-deductible basis. Source: Crop-Hail Insurance Actuarial Association

Courtesy U.S. Department of Agriculture, Bureau of Agricultural Economics.

Fig. 12-8 Hail insurance rates for small grains in a typical year.

factor that increases water need tends to aid in causing drought. Low relative humidity, wind, and high temperatures are contributory factors because they lead to increased evapotranspiration. Soils which lose their moisture rapidly by evaporation or drainage also augment drought. Drought does not begin with the onset of a dry spell; it occurs when plants are inadequately supplied with moisture from the soil. Thus, crops growing on soils which have a high capacity for holding water are less susceptible to short periods of dry weather. Land-use practices which tend to increase runoff decrease vital soil moisture storage accordingly. Thornthwaite suggests that, on the average, the soil can store the equivalent of 4 to 6 inches of rainfall within the root zone of plants. The amount varies with soil characteristics and the arrangement of plant roots.

With these facts in mind, it is obvious that the incidence of drought cannot be determined alone from a map of average precipitation. In addition to the average amount, it is necessary to know the seasonal distribution, dependability, intensity, and the form of precipitation. Furthermore, different crop plants have different moisture requirements. Ultimately, then, drought must be defined in terms of the *water need* of a particular crop growing under a specific combination of environmental conditions. If the minimum water need is not met for those conditions the plants do not develop and mature properly.

The basic criterion for water need of plants is *potential evapotranspiration,* that is, the amount of water that would be evaporated from soil and transpired from plants if it were available. (See Chapter 6, Thornthwaite Classifications.) Only recently have attempts been made to measure potential evapotranspiration directly. The essential features of a measuring device known as an *evapotranspirometer* are shown in Figure 12-9. It consists of (*1*) a sunken field tank filled with soil in which crop plants like those of the surrounding area are grown and (2) a covered percolation tank sunk into the ground at a distance of several feet from the field tank to catch the surplus water which drains from the field tank through (3) a connecting underground tube. The field tank receives water only through precipitation or irrigation and loses it by downward percolation or by evapotranspiration. The soil in the field tank and the surrounding cropland

Fig. 12-9 Essentials of a field evapotranspirometer.

Adapted from John R. Mather, *The Measurement of Potential Evapotranspiration* (Johns Hopkins Laboratory of Climatology, 1954).

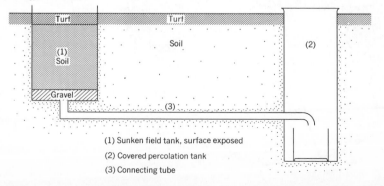

(1) Sunken field tank, surface exposed
(2) Covered percolation tank
(3) Connecting tube

are irrigated whenever necessary to maintain optimum soil moisture conditions. Since the amounts of water added to the field tank by precipitation and artificial watering are known, the potential evapotranspiration is determined by subtracting the water loss by percolation from the total amount received in the evapotranspirometer field tank. Soil moisture storage may vary from day to day, and the amount of water collected in the percolation tank varies with it, but over longer periods the fluctuation is insignificant.

Because of the rather elaborate equipment required for measurement of potential evapotranspiration, its theoretical value for numerous climatic stations has been computed mathematically from mean temperature values and the length of day, factors to which it is closely related. Details of the method are beyond the scope of this book.* Computed values have been found to agree fairly well with measurements made by evapotranspirometers. The use of net radiation values in the computation would produce even better agreement, since evapotranspiration is more closely correlated with net radiation received at ground level than with air temperatures. Humidity and wind speed also affect potential evapotranspiration. Further refinement of the basic formula will be possible as more and longer records of potential evapotranspiration measurements become available.

Some climates have rainfall equal to or greater than the potential evapotranspiration in all months. The water-balance graph for Zurich, Switzerland, Figure 12-10 (based on computed potential evapotranspiration), is representative of this. For most areas the monthly precipitation does not regularly exceed water need, however, and for part or all of the year there is a moisture deficiency. In the mid-latitudes the deficiency occurs in summer, when higher temperatures increase the rate of evapotranspiration. In the graph for Tokyo, Figure 12-10, note that during the first half of the year precipitation is in excess of water need. In the early summer, crops must depend upon stored soil moisture and actually may suffer from a small moisture deficit. With the seasonal decline of temperature and the approach of the autumn rainfall maximum there is a recharge of soil moisture and a return to conditions of water surplus. In climates having distinct summer maximums of precipitation there may, nevertheless, be summer water deficits. Such is the case at Irkutsk in south-central Siberia. (See Figure 12-10.) Although precipitation in the summer months is several times that in winter, the long summer days and higher temperatures create water need in excess of the amount provided by rainfall and stored soil moisture. Note that the meager winter precipitation never succeeds in charging the soil to its full capacity. A degree of drought thus prevails throughout the growing season.

* See C. W. Thornthwaite, "An Approach Toward a Rational Classification of Climate," Geog. Rev., 38, 1 (Jan., 1948), 89–94.

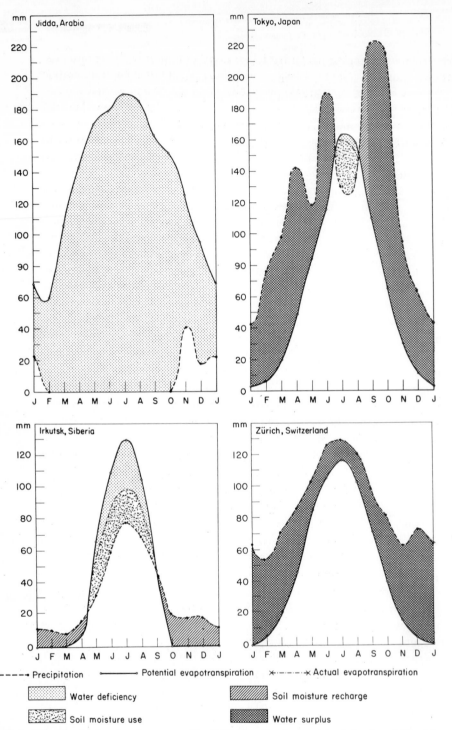

After method of Thornthwaite, based on data computed by C. W. Thornthwaite Associates, Laboratory of Climatology.

Fig. 12-10 Water balance graphs for selected stations having different temperature and moisture regimes.

There is a broad relationship between permanent and seasonal types of drought and the world pattern of climates. Arid climates experience permanent drought, as the water-balance graph for Jidda, Arabia, Figure 12-10, indicates. Climates with well-defined seasonal minimums of rainfall are likely to have corresponding seasonal droughts, although their economic significance depends to some extent on whether they coincide with the growing season. In the dry summer subtropics the dry season, unfortunately, comes in the warm months. In the wet-and-dry tropics winter is the dry season, and summer cropping can be carried on if soil moisture is built up in time. A delay in the onset of the rainy season can be disastrous, however. Some of the worst famines of southern Asia have resulted from failure of the summer monsoon to develop as early as usual. Variability of precipitation creates the greatest drought hazards. This is especially true in the semiarid climates, where a slight departure from the average may be the critical factor in crop failure. Even in humid climates there may be true drought which reduces the yield of crops, even though it does not wipe out harvests entirely. There are degrees of drought and consequently of drought damage; the effects of moderate drought are not always exhibited in such obvious forms as withering plant leaves but may appear instead in lowered quality or yield.

The water-balance graphs referred to above represent average conditions over a number of years. They cannot show the haphazard occurrences of dry weather which plague the farmer in normally wet seasons or in humid climates. Nor do they represent the year-to-year fluctuations which appear in precipitation and therefore in the drought hazard. These are, nonetheless, significant to agriculture. Several years of abnormally dry climate are usually accompanied by higher-than-average temperatures which accentuate the drought conditions. The cyclical nature of these fluctuations will be discussed in Chapter 16. Prolonged drought conditions serve to alter the pattern of agricultural land use on a major scale. In the past they have led to migrations from affected areas, for example, the exodus from the Great Plains in the 1930's.

COMBATING DROUGHT—IRRIGATION

As we have seen, drought is a condition where water need is in excess of available moisture. Prevention of drought damage to growing crops, then, is a matter of either (a) decreasing the water need of crops or (b) increasing the water supply, or possibly a combination of the two. Planting of crops that have low water demands helps reduce the water need. Cultivation practices which improve the soil structure and inhibit runoff are effective drought-prevention measures, although they have limitations. Weed control is especially important if the available water is to be used most effectively for crops, for weeds accelerate water loss by transpiration at the expense of soil moisture.

In subhumid and semiarid climates *dry farming* methods depend on the conservation and use of two—or sometimes three—years' rainfall for one year's crop. During the period when a field lies fallow it is cultivated to kill weeds and to create a soil structure that will retain as much moisture as possible. Thus, soil moisture storage accumulated during the fallow period supplements the meager rainfall in the crop season. In the case of seasonal droughts the planting schedule can sometimes be adjusted to permit maturity and harvest before the effects of the dry season become too great. This is possible only if the temperatures are high enough in the wetter season.

Wherever the water need of crops or grassland cannot be reduced to conform to the moisture supply, the only alternatives are to abandon agriculture or to provide water artificially. At best, the artificial stimulation of rainfall has rather narrow limitations for supplementing natural precipitation. Whatever else may be claimed for it, the fact is that it has not had any importance in combating drought in the past. On the other hand, irrigation is a widespread method for providing all or a part of the water need of crops. In arid regions, or where cropping must be confined to a warm, dry season, agriculture is possible only with irrigation. In semiarid and subhumid climates, irrigation makes possible larger yields and a greater variety of crops. It also lengthens the period during which land can be used productively. In humid regions its main value is supplementary in times of drought. The chief limitations on irrigation are the availability of water from surface or ground water sources and the cost of getting it to the fields.

Within these limits, irrigation has the advantage that it can be regulated to meet the variable demands of different crops, different seasons, or chance droughts. Ranging between the obvious necessity for irrigation in deserts and the almost total absence of need for it in constantly wet climates are the variable circumstances that determine the amount of irrigation needed and when it should be applied. The total amount of water required for crop production is equal to what is used in transpiration and evaporation, plus what is lost by percolation below the root zone and unavoidable forms of waste incurred in the irrigation process or in rainfall runoff. The proportion that has to be provided by irrigation depends on rainfall. In general, irrigation is desirable whenever the soil moisture storage in the root zone drops to about 40 per cent of capacity. In any case, to be effective, water must be applied before plants begin to wilt.

There are several methods of determining the moisture content of the soil. Many farmers simply make a qualitative inspection of the soil at different depths. More accurate methods involve actual measurement of water in soil samples. One of the most common procedures is to weigh the sample before and after drying in an oven, the difference in weights representing the proportion of water in the sample. Thornthwaite and Mather have suggested that soil moisture be regarded as a "balance between what enters as a result of precipitation and what leaves through evaporation and transpiration."* Since soil moisture sampling is time-consuming and expensive, evapotranspiration can be used as an index of the need for irrigation. The daily loss of water by evapotranspiration is budgeted against daily rainfall. Deficits are to be made up by irrigation.

> An irrigation schedule thus can be set up as a bookkeeping procedure. The moisture in the soil may be regarded as a bank account. Precipitation adds to the account; evapotranspiration withdraws from it. We merely need to keep track of the evapotranspiration and restore by irrigation whatever is not promptly returned by precipitation.†

The principal advantage in using either soil moisture measurements or evapotranspiration as an index of irrigation needs lies in the resulting efficiency of water use. It is wasteful to irrigate before water is needed or to apply too much water. The absence of rainfall for several days may or may not be an indication of the need for irrigation. Temperature is likely to be a more important factor, since it directly affects evapotranspiration.

In summary, irrigation may be feasible in any climate where water need exceeds precipitation for a long enough period to reduce crop yields. Irrigation is man's best answer to drought. Where irrigation water is made available, temperature becomes the dominant climatic factor controlling crop distribution and yields.

CROPS AND WIND

Wind has its most important effects on crop production indirectly through the transport of moisture and temperature properties in the air. Movement of air increases evapotranspiration. It may speed up chilling of plants or, on occasion, prevent frost. The action of the wind as an agent in the dispersal of pollen and seeds is natural and necessary for native vegetation and may be helpful for certain crops, but it is detrimental when weed seeds are spread or when unwanted cross-fertilization of plants occurs. Continuously strong winds interfere with the pollination activities of insects. Direct mechanical effects are the breaking of plant structures,

---

* C. W. Thornthwaite and J. R. Mather, "The Water Budget and Its Use in Irrigation," in *Water, 1955 Yearbook of Agriculture* (Washington: Government Printing Office, 1955), pp. 349–50.
† *Ibid.*, p. 350.

lodging of hay and cereals, or shattering of seed heads. Fruit and nut crops may be stripped from the trees in high winds. The unfavorable consequences of depletion of the soil by any form of erosion should be obvious. Low plants are sometimes completely covered by windblown sand or dust; abrasion of plant stems and leaves by sand particles is often associated with wind erosion. Along the shores of salt lakes and oceans, salts transported inland by the wind affect both plants and the soil.

Practices to avert the effects of wind on evapotranspiration are essentially those, including irrigation, employed to combat drought. Mechanical damage due to wind can be lessened somewhat by making use of natural or artificial shelter. Protected valleys and lee slopes are suitable for some types of crops which are easily damaged by wind. Windbreaks composed of trees, shrubs, hedges, or fences are widely used to protect both crops and animals from the wind. Some plants require only temporary protection which can be provided by screens or individual windbreaks. An example of the latter is the use of boards or metal cylinders to shelter young tomato plants. The best permanent windbreaks are rows of trees planted perpendicular to the prevailing winds. Their moderating effect is felt for a distance equal to several times their height. Where winter snow is common, they have the added advantage of inducing snowdrifts over the adjacent fields. As a widespread measure to combat wind, they have some disadvantages, however. They reduce the area of cultivated land, compete for soil moisture, and may produce harmful shade. The first of these objections can be overcome if the species can be selected and managed so as to provide a compensation in the form of harvest from the windbreak itself.

CLIMATE AND FORESTRY

In modern forestry, timber is regarded as a crop and, as such, it is subject to the influences of weather and climate just as field crops are. The relationships between climate and forests are at least partially reciprocal. The distribution and rate of growth of forest species are influenced by climatic conditions, and forests, in turn, affect the climate on a local scale. The major effect of trees on climate is felt in the area they occupy and is roughly proportional to the density of the forest cover, but forests modify the climate of adjacent areas as well. Temperature averages within a forest are slightly lower than in adjacent open areas and the ranges are not so large. In the mid-latitude lowlands the mean annual temperature within a forest is about 1F° lower than on the outside; at 3000 feet the difference is 2°.[*] The greatest average difference occurs

[*] Raphael Zon, "Climate and the Nation's Forests," *Climate and Man, 1941 Yearbook of Agriculture* (Washington: Government Printing Office, 1955), p. 479.

in summer, when it may reach 4°. In winter it is only about 0.1°. On the hottest summer days a forest may reduce the surface air temperature by more than 5°, whereas, in extremely cold winter weather, the difference is only about 2°. In low-latitude forests the influence of a tree cover on air temperature is even greater. In a dense forest the upper canopy shades the ground and acts as the primary absorbing surface during the day, thus retarding the rise of soil temperature. At night the canopy radiates heat more rapidly than the ground, which is slower to cool. The same principle holds true for seasonal variations. In spring and summer, the soil of the forest floor is slow to heat but in autumn and winter it remains slightly warmer than soil outside the forest, though the difference is less. Depending upon the density of the cover, forests may intercept up to 90 per cent of the sunlight which is incident at the treetop level. Anyone who has tried to take a photograph inside a forest can attest to this. The reduction in light is the primary cause of paucity of low plants under a dense forest canopy such as is found in the tropical rain forest.

There is no clear evidence that total precipitation over a forest differs appreciably from that over adjacent areas. Rain gauges placed in open spaces within the forest usually indicate greater rainfall than outside the forest, but this is probably due to their being protected from the wind so that they collect a more accurate sample. Tree crowns intercept a part of the precipitation which falls over a forest, and much of it is evaporated back into the air. The proportion thus withheld from the soil depends on the density of foliage and also on the duration and type of rainfall. A light rain of short duration may be almost entirely caught in the canopy of a dense forest, whereas in a driving rainstorm accompanied by wind most of the rain will reach the ground. Snow collected in the crowns of trees may be shaken out by the wind or it may melt and drip to the ground or flow down the trunks. On the other hand, a great deal of this potential soil moisture is lost by sublimation of the snow or by melting and evaporation. In general, coniferous forests intercept more precipitation than do hardwoods, and deciduous species prevent comparatively little precipitation from reaching the ground in winter. By thinning or clear-cutting portions of evergreen forest it is possible to reduce the interception of snow in treetops and admit more snow to the ground, where it can augment runoff with smaller losses due to sublimation. Conversely, reforestation may actually result in decreased stream flow from a watershed.

Relative humidity is 3 to 10 per cent higher within a forest on the average owing to the lower temperatures, lighter air movement, and transpiration from plants. Evaporation from the soil is considerably lessened as a result of the protective influence of the forest, and, if the ground is well covered with plant litter, it is reduced by one-half to two-thirds as compared to evaporation from soil in the open. During the growing season, trunks and branches have lower temperatures than the surrounding air and they are further cooled by radiation at night with the result that dew or fog is formed. The movement of air from a forest to adjacent open country often carries fog with it and aids in preventing frost.

Surface wind speeds are markedly reduced by trees; only a few hundred feet within a dense forest wind force is but a small fraction of that on the outside. Rows of trees planted at right angles to the wind afford shelter to the leeward for a distance of twenty times the height of the trees. Evergreen species are most effective throughout the year; deciduous species have limited value as shelter belts in winter. By restricting air movement, trees aid in reducing evaporation, lowering temperatures, and increasing relative humidity. Within the forest, the reduction in wind results in a more even distribution of snow cover; along its edges or on the lee of shelter belts, drifts accumulate to the benefit of adjacent cropland.

The influences of climate on forests, as well as those of forests on climate, must be taken into account in silvicultural practices. As a group, forest species have higher moisture demands than do most other types of plants, and forests are therefore associated with humid climates. On a smaller scale, the variations in climate associated with local differences in slope, exposure, or altitude influence the distribution and rate of growth of trees. (See Figure 10-6.) Individual tree species, like field crops, have optimum climatic requirements. Favorable conditions must be met by both the general atmospheric climate and the climate within the forest itself. In a climax forest dominated by one or more species, other trees equally adapted to the regional climate may not be able to gain a foothold because of shading or other environmental effects created by the existing forest. When burned or cut over, the climax forest species may be unable to regenerate without a favorable environment provided by intervening plant associations. Some species require protection from direct sunlight and the accompanying high soil temperatures when in the seedling stage but later become aggressive enough to crowd out trees that afforded the protection. In the practice of scientific forestry it is possible to control the forest microclimate by logging methods, for example, thinning and burning, in order to maintain a desired forest association, whether it be the climax formation or not. Primarily, this entails control of the amount of light reaching the forest floor. Dense stands tend to develop tall, straight trees of small diameter as the trees fight upward for sunlight. Subsequent thinning, whether natural or artificial, allows more light and space for growth as the trees approach maturity. Selective logging of large trees often "releases" smaller trees of the same age so that they begin to grow much more rapidly. Too-heavy cutting of certain species may expose the trees to wind damage, however. Windfall is especially common along the margins of clear-cut areas in dense coniferous forests. In the perpetuation

Fig. 12-11 Wind damage in a Douglas fir-hemlock forest in Oregon.

of a forest, reforestation, or the planting of a new forest, knowledge of the climatic environment which is best suited to growth at all stages is basic to most efficient management for timber production, watershed protection, and other forest values.

Since trees have a much longer life span than field crops, they are influenced much more by climatic fluctuation through the years. During a series of dry years their growth is limited; in wet periods they grow more rapidly. Extreme temperature fluctuations also influence growth; high average temperatures ordinarily accompany dry years and cool periods go with wetter climate. Increasing evidence of the fluctuations in climate during the life history of trees is being gained by inspection of their annual growth rings. This subject will be discussed in greater detail in Chapter 16 as it pertains to climatic changes and cycles.

FOREST-FIRE WEATHER

One of the greatest enemies of forests is fire, and forest-fire prevention and control constitutes one of the most expensive, albeit necessary, phases of forestry management. Innumerable fires are directly caused by lightning. It has been estimated that lightning sets 6000 fires annually in the

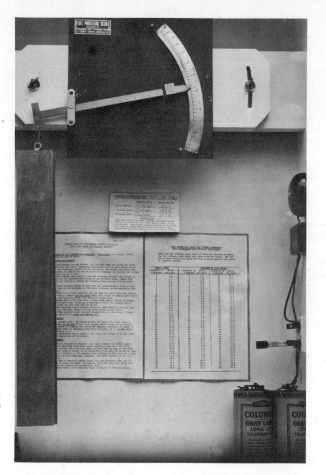

U.S. Forest Service.

Fig. 12-12 Fuel moisture stick being weighed to determine index of forest-fire danger.

forests of the western United States alone. Fortunately many of these are kept from spreading by rain. Others are fanned into disasters by high winds. Prevention of lightning-caused fires could conceivably begin with control of lightning. To whatever extent cloud-seeding techniques can moderate thunderstorms, this is a possibility. Control methods for fires started by lightning are essentially the same as those for other forest fires and include firebreaks, slashing, and direct attack on the fire with water or chemicals. Forecasts of possible lightning storms and a knowledge of forest conditions resulting from previous weather can be invaluable in determining the best techniques for arresting a fire. Because lightning strikes are more common on elevations, fires thus started are often much more difficult to reach than man-caused fires and their control calls for special methods and equipment.

The potential occurrence of forest fires and their rate of spread once started are both direct functions of weather conditions. The previous weather is quite as important as that currently prevailing, since it influences the degree of flammability of forest materials. Factors considered in determining the fire danger include relative humidity, temperature, wind

294

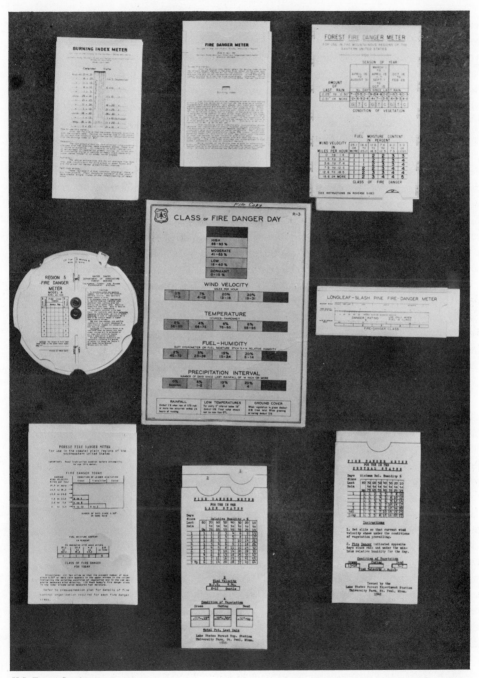

U.S. Forest Service.

Fig. 12-13 Forest-fire danger meters. Devices such as these are widely used in the United States to integrate fire-danger factors.

speed and direction, precipitation, and condition of the vegetation and litter. Extreme fire danger results from long periods of hot, dry weather, especially when associated with stable air masses. Wind aids in drying out the forest and considerably increases the rate of spread of a fire. During the fire season, observations of the weather elements are taken at numerous stations operated by various public and private agencies. These stations employ standard instruments and usually have in addition a device for determining the moisture content of forest litter. This *fuel moisture indicator* consists of wooden sticks that are mounted in the open where they are freely exposed to the weather. They are periodically weighed on a scale which is calibrated to give an index of fuel moisture content. Analysis of observational data in the light of general forest conditions is combined with the regional weather forecast in preparing fire-weather forecasts and warnings. In the United States, fire-weather forecasting is coordinated by the United States Weather Bureau through its Forest Fire Warning Service, which issues regular fire-weather reports during the period March to October. These reports are the basis for restrictions on logging and travel in forests and for the readying of fire-fighting crews. Mobile weather stations are also maintained to give local information at the scene of a fire. Only with complete knowledge of weather conditions can forest fires be prevented or controlled effectively.

CLIMATIC FACTORS IN ANIMAL HUSBANDRY

Since domestic animals are highly dependent on the availability of feed, the climatic factors which influence the growth of pastures or feed crops exert an indirect influence on livestock. The suitability of a particular breed of animal to a climate depends on the quality and quantity of feed which is available naturally or which can be grown in that climate quite as much as on the physiological adjustment of the breed to the climate. It is often feasible to transport feedstuffs into areas where grain or forage crops are inadequate, but this is subject to economic considerations. Generally it is satisfactory only where the demand for an animal product is very great or where there is a temporary shortage of feed because of climatic or other factors. Fluctuations in the output of animal products frequently result from variations in the feed supply rather than from the direct effects of climatic elements on the animals. Thus, there may be a decrease in milk production during a drought period because the amount and nutritive quality of pastures are impaired. Similarly, meat animals may not fatten in the normal length of time if unfavorable climate interferes with their feed supply. In general, animals are adapted to a wide range of climatic conditions provided that their feed and water requirements are met. There are, however, direct climatic effects on the normal body functions of animals. All breeds have optimum climatic requirements for the maximum of growth and development. When removed to a much different climate they do not ordinarily die as plants often do, but they may fall below minimum economic levels of production.

The climatic elements which affect livestock indirectly through the feed supply are those which influence plant growth or the spread of insects and diseases. Those which have direct effects are temperature, precipitation, relative humidity, atmospheric pressure, wind, storms, and light. Of these, temperature is the most important. High temperatures generally reduce production. It has been found that dairy cows produce less milk under high temperatures, the optimum temperature being about 50°F. Hens produce larger eggs in winter and at high latitudes. Many animal breeds reduce their ingestion of feed under hot conditions and therefore do not produce fat and flesh so rapidly. Under extreme heat, they experience discomfort just as humans do. The reproductive capacities of animals are generally reduced by high temperatures also; the fertility of both males and females is greater in cool seasons. Mid-latitude breeds show a marked decline in fertility when relocated in tropical climates. The effect of extreme cold is to lower production also, for too much body energy is required to combat the cold. Where seasonal contrasts are great, most domestic animals adjust to winter by undergoing certain physiological changes, notably the growth of thicker coats of hair. Long exposure to cold, especially if it is accompanied by wind, may cause frostbite or death. Another problem associated with cold weather is the water supply, for animals will not satisfy their water requirements from ice or snow.

Sunlight and the duration of daylight influence animals in several ways. Breeds of cattle and pigs with light-colored skins are occasionally sunburned under intense sunshine. The daily feeding period of most classes of livestock is determined in part by the length of day. Cattle will normally graze more in shaded locations than in the sun and they will rest during the midday periods of highest temperature and strongest sunlight. Fertility is also affected by the duration of daylight, especially in poultry. Commercial poultry farmers commonly extend the day by means of artificial lighting in order to increase egg production.

The primary influence of precipitation on livestock is through its effect on feed. If it is associated with cold weather, it tends to accentuate the detrimental effects of the low temperatures. Freezing rain can cause much discomfort to say the least. Heavy snow makes moving and grazing difficult or impossible for range animals. Crusted snow or ice may cut their feet and a heavy cover of snow over small animals can cause suffocation. In blinding snowstorms, cattle and sheep often pile up against barriers, where they are trampled or die of suffocation, or they may stampede over precipices. Ranchers who use mountain pastures in summer are well

Courtesy U.S. Department of Agriculture, Office of Information.

Fig. 12-14   Range cattle winter feeding on hay in Beaverhead County, Montana.

advised to move their livestock to lower elevations before the time of possible autumn snowstorms. By the same token, too-early grazing of mountain pastures in spring must be avoided. Hail, being restricted to the warm season, is not as great a problem as snow. It can be particularly disastrous to young poultry flocks, however, and has been known to cause range animals to stampede.

High relative humidity, whether associated with abundant rainfall or not, influences respiration and perspiration in animals. Very dry air may cause discomfort, but it is ordinarily of less importance than high temperature in a drought provided that feed and water are available. Low relative humidity, wind, and high temperatures all increase the water requirements of animals. Even the camel can go but a few days without water under the extreme heat and dryness of the tropical deserts in summer. Wind may have good or bad effects, depending on wind speed and the accompanying temperatures. Moderate breezes ameliorate discomfort and ill effects caused by high temperatures. On the other hand, high winds increase drying, may fill the air with dust and sand, or intensify the impact of precipitation. In extreme cases, the force of the wind may be sufficient to blow down the shelters or buildings intended for protection. Moving cold air produces chilling much more rapidly than still cold air of the same temperature.

Changes in atmospheric pressure appear to have some effect on animals. The relatively large pressure differences accompanying changes in altitude are especially significant. For example, the fur-bearing chinchilla had to be "acclimated" to higher pressures in successive stages in order to transfer breeding stock successfully from the high altitudes in the South

298

American Andes. Probably the lesser pressure changes which occur with cyclonic storms are felt to some degree by animals. It is believed that lowering pressure might be one of the stimulants to intensified feeding prior to the arrival of storm centers or fronts.

The climatic elements are combined in storms and they do not act separately on animals. Wind, temperature, and precipitation are the three most important elements. In thunderstorms, lightning may be added to the hazards.

Many of the practices in animal husbandry designed to lessen the negative effects of climate depend on the use of natural or artificial shelters. Specific problems such as the control of temperature can be solved to some extent by heating and air conditioning. Experiments with dairy cattle in the tropics have shown that milk production can be increased by cooling stables with an air-conditioning system. Heating is widely employed in farrowing pens for sows and in brooder houses for poultry. Well-built barns and sheds help to conserve animal body heat in cold climates and in winter; in many instances this is sufficient. Overheating of buildings generally has a detrimental effect. Heating of dairy barns in winter results in reduced milk production. It is usually impractical to provide buildings for large numbers of range livestock. They are best driven to sheltered locations where feed and water are available. Windbreaks of trees and shrubs afford shelter to animals kept in the open.

Some animals gain relief from high temperatures if their coats are clipped. The outstanding example is sheep, which are normally shorn in spring. Cows and horses also benefit from clipping.

SELECTION AND BREEDING FOR CLIMATIC ADAPTATION

Where a suitable environment cannot be provided economically for a specific breed, the alternative is to select breeds or to breed new types that are adapted to prevailing conditions. Numerous examples might be cited of the adaptation of animal breeds to a particular set of climatic conditions. The Merino sheep is well suited to the semiarid climates of mid-latitudes. The English mutton breeds, on the other hand, do best in cool, humid climates. Northwest European dairy breeds such as the Holstein and Guernsey produce best in the mid-latitudes. The Jersey is considerably better adapted to warm climates than other common dairy breeds. As an extreme example, one can point to the reindeer, which has achieved a natural adaptation to the Arctic environment. By selecting individuals that have, in some degree, the desired qualities of tolerance it is frequently possible to breed lines that are better adapted to a given range of climates.

Crossbreeding of animal types to combine the desirable qualities of the foundation stock has been successful among several classes of livestock. Since the heat tolerance of European cattle breeds is low, crosses with tropical breeds have been developed in the tropics and subtropics. The *Santa Gertrudis,* for example, is a cross between the Brahman and Short-horn breeds. Dual purpose sheep breeds such as the *Columbia* and *Corriedale* have been developed to produce high-grade mutton and good-quality wool under varied climatic conditions. Crossbreeding has also overcome, to some extent, the low lard-producing characteristics of hogs in hot climates.

INSECTS AND DISEASES

Many of the restrictions upon the productivity and regional distribution of both plants and animals are pathological, that is, they result from the effects of insects or diseases. Climate, nevertheless, exerts an indirect influence, for insects and diseases have rather narrow climatic limits for maximum development. A favorable season for enemies of crops can result in a major catastrophe. Even short-term weather conditions may determine the extent of development and spread of a plague. That the relationships of insects and disease to climate are complex can be seen from the fact that weather conditions sometimes favor parasites or maladies which make inroads on insects. Moreover, the food supply of insects is controlled to varying degrees by weather and climate. Various types of plant enemies, such as mildew, rusts, scabs, and blights, reproduce and spread most rapidly under conditions of warmth and high humidity. Spores of fungus diseases are spread by the wind, making control very difficult. Wheat, barley, and certain legumes are largely excluded from humid climates because of disease problems rather than direct climatic factors. Coffee is confined to cooler uplands in the tropics primarily because of disease problems in the hot, wet lowlands. A host of mid-latitude crops are unsuited to the tropics for pathological reasons, even though the climate might appear to be directly favorable. A great many diseases and insects which attack plants are kept in check by seasonal fluctuations in temperature or moisture or both. For example, in the areas of the South which are infested with the cotton-boll weevil, it has been estimated that 95 per cent of hibernating adults die during the winter. Thus, the winter has a marked bearing upon the incidence of boll weevil damage in the summer. The incidence of diseases and insects harmful to plants is considerably less in high latitudes; this is due to the absence of host plants as well as to low temperatures. In other words, the same climatic factors that restrict diseases and insects often limit crop production as well. Wind influences the migration of insects, especially if the air is warm. The direction of migration is with the prevailing wind, and upper winds may be dominant in the distribution, for flights of insects sometimes reach heights above the surface winds.

The density of airborne insects is much greater near the surface when the air is relatively calm, but turbulence carries them upward. In North Africa and Southwest Asia locust swarms are associated with the intertropical convergence zone. Rain along the convergence zone provides moisture required for breeding as well as for vegetation upon which the larvae feed. The northerly and southerly winds tend to carry the swarms toward the areas of most favorable ecological conditions. (See Figure 12-15.)

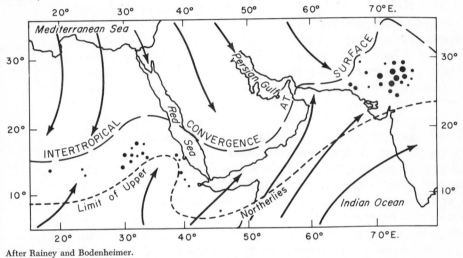

After Rainey and Bodenheimer.

Fig. 12-15 Locust swarms in relation to the intertropical convergence zone. Dot size is approximately proportional to number of swarms reported July 12–31, 1950.

Control of insects and diseases which damage plants belongs in the province of plant pathology rather than climatology. Any agricultural practice which provides an unfavorable environment for a crop pest has potential value for controlling it. Forced exposure to extremes of temperature, sunlight, or moisture conditions is one of the most practical approaches to the problem.

Insects and diseases which attack animals have a complicated relationship to climate and other environmental factors. Of the climatic factors, temperature and moisture are the most important, and as a result, there are broad correlations between infestation and both climatic regions and seasons. As in the case of crops, animals generally have fewer pathological enemies in the colder climates. Probably the largest class of malefactors in the livestock industries are internal parasites. Climate and daily weather have a marked influence on the distribution, rate of spread, and intensity of infestation of parasitic diseases. In the process of developing in that part of the life cycle which is outside the animal, most parasites have limiting ranges of temperature and moisture requirements. Exposure to direct sunlight is usually fatal to eggs and larvae. Thus, control can be achieved to some extent by measures which enhance the destructive effects of climatic conditions on the eggs and larvae of parasites or on their intermediate hosts. Chemical sprays, insecticides, vaccination, and drenches or other internal medication are widely used for direct control of both internal and external animal diseases. Rainfall, wind, and sunlight render valuable assistance in maintaining sanitary conditions in pastures and feedlots. Their aid can be put to the best advantage by rotating animals from one enclosure to another.

Development of resistant types through selection and crossbreeding has met with some success in combating animal diseases. Certain breeds have natural immunities, and it is often possible to combine qualities of disease resistance and high productivity by crossbreeding. Among tropical breeds of domestic animals, there is commonly some degree of immunity to tropical diseases as well as heat tolerance, so that crossbreeding has improved both climatic adaptation and disease resistance of high-producing mid-latitude breeds in the tropics and subtropics.

It is difficult to separate the discussion of insects from that of diseases because, very often, an insect species is the carrier of a disease. Numerous insects, of course, attack animals directly. One can cite those which sting, chew, suck blood, lay eggs in the hair or skin, or merely swarm menacingly about the animal. Among the many insects which infect animals with disease, an outstanding culprit is the tsetse fly, which is limited to tropical Africa. There are several species of tsetse, none of which can endure low temperature nor extremely hot, dry weather. They live solely on blood, and, since they are disease vectors, they infect the animals on which they feed.

PLANT AND ANIMAL INTRODUCTION

The adaptation of crops and livestock to certain climatic optima is of great significance in connection with the introduction of a particular variety or breed into a new area. To the extent that climate influences the productiveness of crops or livestock, transfer of plants or animals to another region with a similar climate is likely to be successful. Tropical tree crops have been transplanted literally around the world. Coffee, believed to have been native to the highlands of eastern Africa, is now widely grown in tropical Latin America. The native rubber tree of Brazil (*Hevea brasiliensis*), has met with more favorable circumstances for commercial production in Southeast Asia than in its original habitat.

Cacao, also indigenous to the Latin American tropics, is produced in the Guinea Coast region of Africa as well as in South and Central America. The introduction of such Mediterranean crops as citrus fruits, olives, and wine grapes into other dry summer subtropical regions is an example of migration of crops to similar climates. There is a huge list of crops which originated (or at least were acclimatized) in Europe, and which have been successfully carried into other mid-latitude climates by European emigrants. Nowhere is there a more striking example of wholesale transfer of plants and animals into a similar climate than the establishment of British agriculture in New Zealand. Breeding and selection play an important part in plant and animal introduction, as do economic and cultural factors. But the suitability of a climate for a particular crop or animal is a primary consideration which is not altered by the fact that many crops and animals have a wide range of adaptability to climate.

While many crop plants have been introduced into new areas in the past largely on a trial-and-error basis, recent efforts have been directed toward detailed study of agro-climatic relationships to improve yields, quality, or disease resistance. As world agriculture has expanded and the demands for food have increased, plant introduction has come to mean more than the establishment of a new crop; it entails new varieties which have better characteristics for productivity. Thus, for a given locality, varieties with desired characteristics are sought in areas with analogous climates. Nuttonson has developed a series of *agro-climatic analogs* for North America by comparing climatic factors in different parts of the world.* He defines climatic analogs as "areas that are enough alike with respect to some of the major weather characteristics affecting crop production, particularly during the growing period, to offer a fair chance for the success of plant material transplanted from one area to its climatic counterpart." Information used to determine agro-climatic analogs includes mean monthly and annual temperatures; mean monthly, seasonal, and annual precipitation; Thornthwaite's precipitation-evaporation ratios; length of frost-free season; latitude; and phenological data. Weather records are compared for numerous stations in similar climates to find the localities most nearly alike. Generalized agro-climatic regions are then delineated on the basis of the distribution of analogous characteristics. The practical value of this work lies in its use in the search for plant varieties which may be introduced into a specific area with the minimum of climatic difficulties.

Animals, being far more adaptable to variations in climate than plants, do not present so great a problem in connection with their introduction into a new region. Within broad limits climate influences animal intro-

* *International Agro-Climatological Series* (Washington, D.C.: American Institute of Crop Ecology, 1947).

duction more through its effects on feed supplies than by direct means. When climates with sharply contrasting temperatures are involved, however, failure to acclimatize and to maintain satisfactory production levels may present a serious obstacle to livestock introduction. As stated earlier, crossbreeding and selection have overcome this problem to some extent.

ADDITIONAL READINGS

Barton, Thomas F., "Rainfall and Rice in Thailand," *Journ. of Geog.*, 62, 9 (1963), 414–18.

Crawford, M., "Diseases of Livestock as Influenced by Weather," in *Biometeorology*. London: Pergamon Press, 1962, pp. 162–73.

Frisby, E. M., "A Study of Hailstorms of the Upper Great Plains of the North American Continent," *Weatherwise*, 17, 2 (1964), 68–74.

Fuquay, D. M., "Mountain Thunderstorms and Forest Fires," *Weatherwise*, 15, 4 (1962), 149–52.

Johnson, C. G., "The Aerial Migration of Insects," *Scient. Am.*, 209, 6 (1963), 132–38.

Penman, H. L., "Weather and Crops," *Quart. Journ. Roy. Met. Soc.*, 88, 377 (1962), 209–219.

Riley, J. A., "Moisture and Cotton at Harvest Time in the Mississippi Delta," *Mon. Wea. Rev.*, 89, 9 (1961), 341–53.

Schein, Richard D., "Biometeorology and Plant Diseases," *Bull. Am. Met. Soc.*, 44, 8 (1963), 499–504.

Tannehill, Ivan Ray, *Drought: Its Causes and Effects.* Princeton: Princeton University Press, 1947.

Ventskevich, G. Z., *Agrometeorology.* Jerusalem: Israel Program for Scientific Translations, 1961.

Wang, Jen-Yu, *Agricultural Meteorology.* Milwaukee: Pacemaker Press, 1963.

Went, Fritz W., "Climate and Agriculture," *Scient. Am.*, 196, 6 (1957), 82–94.

relations of weather and climate to transportation, communication and industry

Nowhere in the broad field of applied climatology are there more complex relationships than those which concern transportation, communications, and industry. With the exceptions of aviation, which has received wide attention in recent decades, and ocean transport, studies of climatic problems in these areas of economic activity have been scattered and are only now beginning to advance beyond the descriptive phase. Research involving the participation of entire industries offers opportunities to extend the practical application of information presently available through meteorological and climatological services.* The chapter that follows presents more problems than solutions: Perhaps its readers will be among those who will discover the "hidden" uses of weather information.

AVIATION

The acceleration of research in the field of meteorology in the twentieth century has been closely allied with the increase in air travel. Knowledge of weather processes is vital to safety and efficiency in aviation. As man ventures continuously farther into the upper atmosphere, knowledge of the processes is increased, but at the same time becomes more necessary in planning and executing air and space travel. Since aviation is based on the earth's surface, weather conditions in the lower levels are as important as those in the upper air. Nor can climatology be neglected, for the probability of occurrence of

* See Gerald L. Barger and John C. Nyhan, eds., *Climatology at Work* (Washington: Government Printing Office, 1960).

certain conditions enters into many decisions concerning both the functioning of air terminals and flight.

The application of climatology to aviation begins with the selection of an airport site. Assuming the need for an airport for either civilian or military use in a given area, the best site depends on a number of interrelated factors. Level land, absence of surrounding obstructions, and access to centers of population appear superficially to have little connection with climate. They may be factors affecting wind or visibility, however. Radiation fogs form more often in broad valleys, and if the site is to the leeward of industrial centers, smoke and other pollutants play a part in reduced visibility. Climatological studies make possible the selection of a site which experiences a minimum of weather hazards such as poor visibility, low clouds, turbulence, wind shifts, and thunderstorms. Air bases for training and experimentation are best located in regions having predominantly clear weather as well as sparse population. Commercial air terminals must be near cities but in locations which enjoy the maximum of good visibility, high ceilings, and favorable winds. The actual layout of runways is determined by prevailing winds and permits aircraft to take off and land into the wind. Figure 13-1 shows a wind frequency polygon for a hypothetical airport and the arrangement of runways. The primary landing strip is oriented to the prevailing wind direction. Average wind speeds

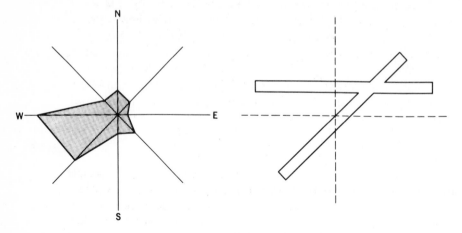

Fig. 13-1 Wind direction frequency polygon and corresponding airport runways.

as well as direction are taken into account; wind from some directions may be so light as to have little influence on takeoffs and landings. For operation from aircraft carriers, the ship is maneuvered to align the runway with the wind direction, and the speed of the ship becomes a factor in the relative wind speed along the flight deck. A flight cannot be judged by its speed and economy of operation in the air alone; weather conditions at takeoff or landing can nullify an entire flight. If poor weather conditions are confined to a particular locality, landings may be possible at an alternate field; or the conditions may be temporary so that a plane can circle the airport, awaiting improvement. These possibilities make it necessary to carry a reserve supply of fuel.

Of the weather elements affecting the use of airports, air currents, visibility, and ceiling are the most important. Unless they are unusually gusty or violent, wind effects can be overcome by proper selection of runway and direction of takeoff or approach. Severe turbulence caused by a storm, local relief, or differential heating of surfaces introduces a hazard. Light planes are most susceptible to these effects. Regardless of the number and accuracy of instruments in the aircraft or on the ground the pilot will prefer to see the landing field for as long as possible before he lands, and since any takeoff may need to be followed by an immediate landing the importance of good visibility applies to takeoffs as well. Under a low ceiling, the surface visibility may be good, but a pilot approaching the field may not establish visual contact with the ground until he descends to a dangerously low altitude. Various types of instruments and applications of radio have been devised to enable the pilot to "see" the ground from above a cloud layer. Still others are in the experimental stage. If visibility at the ground is obscured the danger is even greater, and it is generally considered wise to close an airport to traffic.

In order to provide continuous information on airport weather conditions, the United States Weather Bureau and the Federal Aviation Agency maintain an Airways Weather Service at airports throughout the United States. Hourly reports are gathered and transmitted to other stations, principally by teletype, and to aircraft in flight by radio. They include data on cloud height and coverage, visibility, sea level barometric pressure, temperature, dew point, wind direction and speed, altimeter setting, precipitation, and special or severe weather conditions. Special observations are taken when sudden changes in the weather occur. Weather observations at airport stations are classified on the basis of minimum ceiling and visibility conditions for takeoffs and landings. The main categories are as follows:

VFR: Visual flight rules. Basic minimums: ceiling, 1000 feet; visibility, 3 miles.

IFR: Instrument flight rules. Minimum ceiling and visibility conditions vary according to airport traffic control facilities, local terrain features, and other factors, but are generally lower than those for *VFR*.

Closed: Either ceiling or visibility below the minimums for *IFR* flight.

The Administrator of the Federal Aviation Agency prescribes these conditions as minimum for air safety. In addition to low ceilings and low visibilities, the pilot must, of course, take into account wind, icing, and other potentially dangerous conditions. Most major airlines maintain a special supplementary weather service for their pilots and dispatchers. Such a service makes use of Weather Bureau data and pilot reports in forecasting for airline operations.

Knowledge of weather and climate enters into the design of aircraft and engines. Stresses likely to be encountered in severe storms, the possibility of damage by hail or lightning, and icing must be taken into account in structural engineering. Temperature variations, precipitation, and icing conditions affect power plant efficiency. Engines must be able to function at high elevations where pressure is much lower and where the temperatures may be 100° or more below those at the point of takeoff. Aircraft flying from bases in winter or in high latitudes experience operational difficulties not found in the tropics. Special hangars or preheating devices are required to overcome certain problems arising from extremely low temperatures.

FLYING WEATHER

When in flight, aircraft are truly at the mercy of the weather. Contrary to popular belief, an arc of a great circle may not be the fastest nor the most economical route for air travel. Moreover, it may be far from the safest route if unfavorable flying weather intervenes. Wherever possible a flight path should take advantage of tailwinds and avoid headwinds. Since wind speeds vary with altitude, this suggests selection of the proper flight level as well as the best horizontal course. By climbing into the stream of strongest tailwinds, an airplane can reap full advantage in savings on fuel and gains in ground speed. The direct relationship of upper winds to pressure distribution forms the basis for *pressure pattern* flying. Consider a high-pressure system with strong winds blowing out from the center (clockwise circulation in the Northern Hemisphere). (See Figure 13-2.) A flight through the system from west to east can take advantage of the winds by passing to the north of the center. Going from east to west the strongest tailwinds will occur to the south of the center. Rarely, however, is wind direction parallel to an air route, and, consequently, an aerial navigator must know the true wind direction and speed in order to make adequate adjustments for drift. The extent to which it may be feasible to alter the flight path depends on the length of the flight, the position of the points of origin and destination with respect to the pressure system, wind speeds, and the possibility of encountering air mass weather. In a low-pressure system, it may be more expedient to avoid the worst of frontal weather than to take advantage of high winds. For long-range flight (for example, across continents or oceans) the pressure pattern principle can be applied to prevailing wind belts and pressure distribution

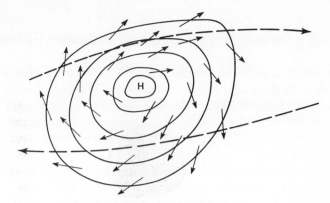

Flight paths for maximum tailwinds in
high pressure center

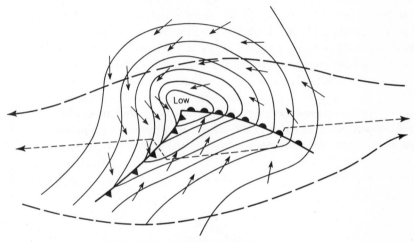

Flight paths through and around a low pressure
center with frontal storms

Fig. 13-2 Preferred flight paths in relation to high and low pressure centers, Northern Hemisphere.

at upper levels. The westerly jet streams have made it possible to achieve some remarkable records on west-to-east flights, even though an airplane may have deviated appreciably from the great circle route. Overseas flights often follow routes in winter different from those taken in summer in accordance with latitudinal shifts in wind and pressure systems.

For supersonic aircraft, winds are less significant on high-altitude flights of less than about 4000 miles. But the efficiency of supersonic jet engines is greater at lower air temperatures, and it may be feasible to deviate from the great circle route in order to travel through colder air and thereby reduce fuel consumption.

Although powered aircraft operate most efficiently with tailwinds, gliders (or sailplanes) depend upon headwinds and vertical air currents to maintain altitude, and they have a limited range. Rising air currents over slopes, heated surfaces, or along zones of converging winds are favorable for lifting a glider and often are useful to light airplanes as well. Downdrafts, on the other hand, are to be avoided. Downslope winds along the margins of uplands create especially hazardous flying conditions. A pilot of an airplane or glider approaching a mountain may find that he is unable to maintain a safe altitude to fly above the mountain if the downslope flow is strong.

The use of the aneroid altimeter makes it necessary to keep abreast of changes in barometric pressure in flight. If an altimeter is set at zero at an airport prior to takeoff it should read zero upon return to the field provided no change in atmospheric pressure has occurred. At another field it should indicate a value equal to the difference in elevation of the two fields, if the places have the same sea level pressure. Surface pressure readings vary with time and with the distribution of pressure systems, however, and it is necessary to make an altimeter correction if the instrument is to be interpreted correctly in relation to the surface. An altimeter set for an airport with relatively high pressure will indicate too high an elevation in an area with low pressure. (See Figure 13-3.) As a result, a pilot would tend to crash-land short of the runway or encounter obstacles he should otherwise clear easily. Conversely, an altimeter setting made in an area of low pressure indicates too low an altitude where the sea level

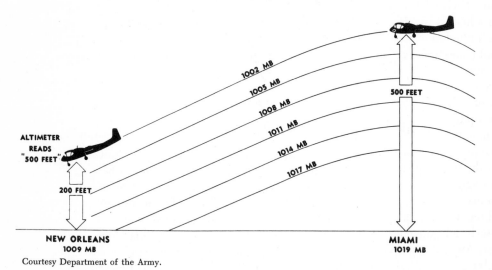

Courtesy Department of the Army.

Fig. 13-3   Effect of horizontal pressure differences on reading of aneroid type altimeter.

pressure is higher, and the possible result is a landing beyond the runway. Vertical air currents also affect aneroid altimeters, for they produce appreciable fluctuations in barometric pressure. A downdraft along a mountain slope is accompanied by higher pressure and therefore by an altimeter reading that is too high. This is another reason for extreme care when flying in the vicinity of mountains. An updraft not only tends to boost the airplane over the mountain but also produces an altimeter reading lower than the actual altitude, thus increasing the margin of safety. Where there is a choice it is better to fly on the windward than on the leeward of mountains. Other errors in altimeters result from temperature differences. In cold air the pressure decreases more rapidly with height, making the altimeter read too high; in warm air the pressure decrease is not so rapid and the altimeter of a plane in flight reads too low. Again there is danger in mountainous areas, where cold air may indirectly result in an altimeter reading higher than the true altitude. Altimeters which employ the principle of radar to indicate the elevation above the earth's surface are not subject to major errors due to pressure differences.

TURBULENCE

Atmospheric turbulence causes an uncomfortable ride and increases the strain on both aircraft and pilot, not to mention passengers. In its most violent forms it can be catastrophic. Four principal factors lead to turbulence: thermal, frictional, frontal, and that associated with extensive wind shear. Thermal turbulence is produced by vertical convection currents over a heated surface or by advection of cold air over a warm surface, and is accentuated in an air mass that already has an unstable lapse rate. Frictional (sometimes called mechanical) turbulence results from wind blowing over rough terrain. Its effects are often combined with convection currents when an irregular surface is heated or cooled unevenly. A strong flow of stable air across a mountain range frequently develops wave action with updrafts and downdrafts that extend to several times the height of the mountains and for a distance of 100 miles or more downwind. Turbulence in such a *mountain wave* is usually greatest at low levels and again near the tropopause to the lee of the mountains. (See Figure 13-4.)

Along a cold front the wind shift and the lifting of warm air above the cold may cause wind shear, that is, pronounced differences in wind speed or direction or both. The resulting turbulence frequently occurs near the westerly jet streams, where there are both horizontal and vertical wind shear. Aircraft sometimes encounter layers of turbulent wind shear when climbing or descending through a temperature inversion at any altitude up to the tropopause. Warm air moving over a ground inversion layer, as in a valley at night, creates a thin zone of wind shear that can be especially dangerous. Although turbulent conditions may have accompanying clouds as warning signs, they also occur in clear air. Clear air turbulence (*CAT*) is common in the vicinity of a jet stream but can be the result of any of the causes described above.

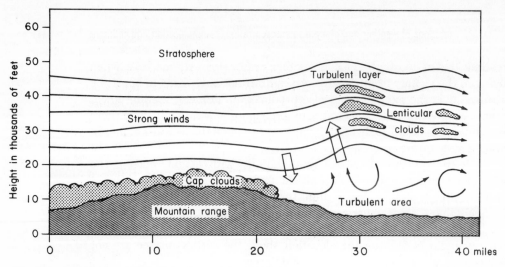

Fig. 13-4 Mountain wave turbulence in the lee of a mountain range.

Ice formation on aircraft is one of the great hazards to flight in the troposphere. Icing occurs when liquid water droplets are present in the air and the temperature of the exposed aircraft surface is at or below freezing. Clouds containing supercooled droplets are breeding places for aircraft icing. In turbulent air the droplets are large, and, when they strike the cold surfaces of an airplane, they spread out and freeze to form *clear ice*. In smoother air the small droplets freeze immediately upon striking the leading edges and take on a granular or crystalline form. This is known as *rime ice*. Often the two types occur together. Clear ice is more tenacious than rime and is prevalent in turbulent clouds. It forms most commonly at temperatures between 15° and 32°F and can occur where rain falls through freezing air. It creates a blunt edge on wings and other leading edges and thus interferes with their aerodynamic properties. Moreover, clear ice may add dangerously to the weight of an airplane. Snow and sleet fall from clouds in which icing conditions can be expected, and such clouds are to be avoided if possible. Freezing rain, on the other hand, falls from warmer levels and can be avoided by climbing into the warmer air. Rime ice tends to accumulate in the form of sharp projections from the leading edges and does not disrupt air flow so seriously. It is, nevertheless, dangerous.

In turbojet engines ice may form on guide vanes or other structures at the air intake, leading to reduced engine thrust and eventual turbine failure. In piston engines carburetor icing can occur in clear air at temperatures above freezing if the relative humidity is high, but it also forms in clouds. The expansion of air and vaporization of gasoline at the fuel

312

intake cause a decrease in temperature and condensation of water vapor. If the temperature drops below 32°F, the moisture is deposited as frost in the carburetor, reducing power or possibly causing engine failure. Carburetor icing is most common at air temperatures of 20° to 70°F in moist air.

FLYING IN STORMS

Flight through storms entails all the hazards of wind, turbulence, precipitation, low temperatures, poor visibility, and icing. Entry into a tornado is out of the question. Hurricanes are certainly not for routine air travel, but they have been entered for carefully controlled experiments and observations. Next in order of violence are thunderstorms, which because of severe turbulence, icing, and possible damage by lightning or hail are best avoided by flying above, below, or around them, depending upon circumstances. In a mid-latitude cyclone a variety of weather conditions may affect flight. Low ceilings and poor visibility accompany the typical warm front, and there may be hidden thunderstorms. Icing is likely in the cool upper levels, and in winter, sleet or freezing rain are hazards. Air mass weather in the warm sector of a cyclone may include fair weather cumulus, daytime convective turbulence, or thunderstorms. The cold front is usually the most dangerous portion of the mid-latitude cyclone. Frontal thunderstorms and a sudden change in wind direction and temperature are common features which bear upon safety and navigation. Occluded fronts tend to combine the flight conditions of the warm and cold fronts. Both warm- and cold-front occlusions have warm-front weather in advance of the occlusion, and both have upper-front weather like that of the cold front. (See Chapter 5, Occluded Fronts.)

In planning a flight the pilot has the aid of weather maps, upper-air data, and forecasts. His route and altitude are determined in relation to (and with respect for) weather conditions along the way. In flight, he is aided by radio reports, but he must understand basic meteorological principles so that he can analyze unexpected conditions and alter plans accordingly to assure maximum safety. In regions where there are few weather reports, he must be both an observer and a forecaster and the success of his flight may well depend on his ability to interpret observed weather phenomena in the light of the climatology of storms.

FOG DISPERSAL

Although all forms of transportation are affected by fog, the effects on aviation are the most serious. Several methods of artificial dissipation of fog have been tried with varying success. Natural dissipation of fog usually occurs as a result of evaporation of the water droplets. This suggests that artificial methods might employ some means of speeding up the evaporation process. Direct heating of the air over a large area is not feasible, but at an airport, burners may generate sufficient heat to clear the fog from a landing strip. During World War II the British developed *FIDO* (Fog Investigation and Dispersal Operation), a system for dissipating fog by burning oil dispensed from perforated pipes along the sides of runways. Installations employing the thermal principle have also been made in the United States. Shallow radiation fogs are more easily dispersed by this means than are other fog types. Fog being carried over an airport by wind is extremely difficult to deal with because it is constantly being renewed. In any case, large quantities of heat are needed to effect fog clearance and the cost is consequently great. As much as 100,000 gallons of oil per hour is required to operate an installation. Another method of fog dispersal is "drying" the air with hygroscopic materials. Calcium chloride is one such material. Sprayed into the fog it speeds up condensation and coalescence of droplets. This system also involves considerable cost, and has the additional disadvantage that the hygroscopic substance may be injurious to vegetation or ground installations and equipment.

Methods of physical removal of fog have been directed at causing the droplets to coalesce and fall out. Electrically charged particles of sand have been dropped through fog with limited success. Spraying large drops of water into the fog tends to produce coalescence of fog droplets but is generally impracticable. Sound waves and ultrasonic vibrations have also been used experimentally in attempts to effect precipitation of fog. Dry ice dropped from small airplanes is frequently effective in dispersing radiation fog. None of the methods suggested can alleviate low visibility due to smoke or dust. Selection of airport sites with infrequent fogs, use of "blind landing" equipment, and restriction of traffic at fogbound airports remain the best hopes for combating fog.

WATER TRANSPORT

Mariners have a long history of weather problems. Sailing ships depended on favorable winds, and history records many instances where wind was the crucial factor in naval engagements between fleets powered by sails. Strong gales probably accounted for several early voyages of "discovery" as well as for many lost ships. The discovery of America by Columbus was influenced, in part, by the trade winds. The pattern of prevailing winds and pressure centers over the ocean determined, to a large extent, the major trade routes of sailing days. Even today, when steam and motor vessels dominate ocean shipping, wind direction and

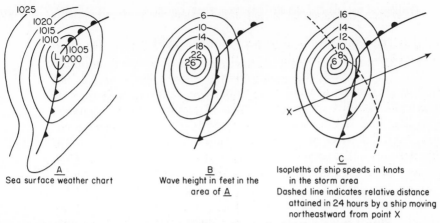

A	B	C
Sea surface weather chart	Wave height in feet in the area of A	Isopleths of ship speeds in knots in the storm area

Dashed line indicates relative distance attained in 24 hours by a ship moving northeastward from point X

After J. J. Schule, "Weather Routing of Ships," in *Meteorology as Applied to Navigation of Ships,* Technical Note No. 23 (Geneva: WMO, 1958).

Fig. 13-5 Relation of ship speed to wave height in the area of an extra-tropical cyclone.

force are important in the safe and economic operation of ships. Navigation is especially hazardous in coastal waters when strong winds are blowing. Small craft may be capsized by strong or gusty winds. On the open sea, a favorable wind can give increased speed to a ship, whereas a headwind slows the ship and increases fuel consumption. The pressure of wind against a ship varies as the square of the wind speed. A doubling of the speed increases wind pressure four times. Ships moving against headwinds must fight the relative wind speeds which represent the true speed plus the speed of the ship. Wind from the stern increases a ship's speed by about 1 per cent, but headwinds decrease the speed by from 3 to 13 per cent, depending on the size of the vessel and its load.* A longer route, planned in relation to winds and storms, can result in greater economy of operation, less time at sea, and a smoother trip.

In rough seas it is difficult to hold a course and sometimes is necessary to change the course in order to reduce the effect of waves and swell. Harbors in sheltered coastal locations, such as bays and river mouths, have always been desirable because of the relative absence of high winds and rough water, but even in the snuggest harbor damage can occur to vessels which are not properly moored. High or gusty winds make a landing dangerous. In cold climates, wind often piles up ice in harbors and increases the possibility of damage due to collision with ice chunks.

With the advent of the steamship, sailing has become largely a sport, for the most part confined to coastal and inland waters. But the importance of wind to sailing craft, both in attaining speed and in relation to safety, has not diminished. Erratic winds on mountain lakes or along rugged coasts make extreme care mandatory in operating small pleasure craft.

* Louis Allen, "Navigating with the Weather," *Bull. Am. Met. Soc.,* 32, 7 (1951), 245.

The fact that many pleasure-boat owners use their craft only a few days a year causes them to be unfamiliar with the principles of safe navigation as well as with local weather hazards. Sudden squalls have, all too frequently, brought disaster to small boats caught too far from shelter.

Next to wind, visibility is the most significant weather element in water transportation. Fog is the most common obstruction to visibility over water, although industrial smoke may intensify it in harbors. In the open sea, fog interferes with the accurate determination of the ship's position and increases the danger of hitting another ship, rocks, or icebergs. Along coasts where upwelling of cold water occurs, fog is common, and particular care must be exercised to avoid shallows or other danger points. Beacon lights afford some aid as warning devices, but foghorns have a greater range in dense fog. Modern foghorns are brought into operation when fog becomes dense enough to interrupt a beam of light between two fixed points. Radio, radar, and electronic devices for sounding ocean depths have considerably lessened the danger of collision or running aground in fog. Even so, dense fogs can bring harbor traffic to a standstill and many marine accidents due to fog occur every year.

Low temperatures affect loading and unloading activities and must be met with extra protection for cargo and passengers. If the temperature is low enough to form ice, otherwise navigable waters may become impas-

Fig. 13-6 The Coast Guard icebreaker **Westwind** leading supply ships through ice off Greenland. Official U.S. Coast Guard Photo.

sable. In arctic seas, ocean traffic is suspended for several months each year. At lower latitudes, icebreakers are employed to keep navigable channels open. On the Great Lakes, ice builds out from the shorelines and thus disrupts shipping, even though the lakes are rarely frozen over their entire area. The ice is generally thickest in protected bays; straits become congested with ice carried in by the wind and currents. Broken ice, or "slush," can damage steering gear and propellers and is not effectively moved by an icebreaker, for it tends to close around the ship. Heavy shipping moves on the Great Lakes for only eight or nine months a year, so that it is necessary to stockpile materials such as coal and iron ore in the navigation season to carry industry through the winter. In order to provide for the commencement of shipping as early as possible in the spring, the United States Weather Bureau operates an Ice Reporting Service from mid-February until the Great Lakes are completely opened. Dates of opening of navigation have been found to correlate with the mean temperatures for the preceding February. (See Figure 13-7.) In general, the

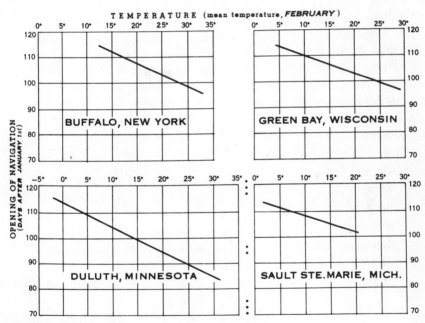

Courtesy U.S. Weather Bureau.

Fig. 13-7 Opening dates of navigation at selected Great Lakes ports in relation to mean temperatures of the preceding February in °F.

lower the February mean temperature, the later ice will be cleared from the ports. Forecasts from these relationships make it possible for shippers to ready their equipment with the minimum of delay and expense before operations begin.

Similar problems relating to ice on rivers, canals, lakes, and harbors occur throughout the higher middle latitudes. The net effect is to produce a seasonal rhythm in waterborne traffic with variations in the length of the shipping period from year to year and place to place.

Precipitation is ordinarily not a major factor affecting shipping. Loading and unloading are disrupted if perishable cargo is involved, and special protective measures are necessary for loaded cargo. Heavy rain or snow may affect visibility. Storms incorporate several of the adverse weather elements, and, depending on their severity, it is sometimes desirable to avoid them. Hurricanes, in particular, call for "evasive action." Wind speeds and sea swell are greatest at the front of a hurricane, making travel to the rear of the storm advisable. Cargoes must be carefully distributed and secured before rough seas are encountered. Where forecasts are available, it is often worthwhile to alter a ship's speed in order to arrive in port before or after a storm reaches the port. Since the danger of damage resulting from severe storms is greater near the coast or in poorly protected harbors, large ships usually head for the open sea when a storm with high winds is expected.

Radio weather reports and marine forecasts are broadcast from many coastal stations in North America and Europe as an aid to ocean navigation. Much of the interpretation of the local significance of these reports, however, is left to the mariner; indeed, valuable weather data upon which marine forecasts are based are contributed by ships at sea. Along the Atlantic Coast of the United States and Canada, reports from land stations to the west are fairly abundant, and they can be used to construct a weather map and make a forecast which is far more reliable than guesses based on weather signs. Off the Pacific Coast, weather reports from continental land stations are of limited value while a ship is at sea because the paths of the storms are generally from west to east. Between the Aleutians and the Hawaiian Islands there are no Pacific islands. It is therefore necessary to rely on sparse reports from weather ships, commercial vessels, and aircraft to analyze weather trends on the basis of observations.

RAILWAYS AND HIGHWAYS

Railroads would seem to be little affected by weather because of their permanent all-weather track systems. In fact, trains are likely to be on the move in storms which have brought automobile traffic to a halt and grounded all airplanes. But railroads are far from immune to weather hazards, and their operation must be constantly geared to weather changes. Severe storms may damage tracks, bridges, signals, and communication lines. Floods, heavy snowfall, and earth slides are related menaces. Heavy snow and avalanches are particularly troublesome in mountains, and it has been expedient in many cases to build expensive tunnels to avoid high-altitude weather as well as steep grades. Low visibility due to fog or precipitation calls for extra caution and decreased speeds. Passenger schedules are disrupted not only by the direct effects of bad weather on tracks and equipment but because many people forsake the airlines or highways for the train and extra time is consequently required for station stops. Passenger traffic to beaches, resorts, ski areas, and other holiday locations is closely related to weather conditions. Extra coaches or even extra trains may be needed when conditions are favorable, and, by the same token, a scheduled weekend excursion train may be nearly empty if the weather suddenly becomes unfavorable. Seasonal weather greatly affects tourist travel; the general movement in the United States is southward in winter and northward and westward in summer.

In the movement of freight on railroads, special attention must be given to perishable goods and livestock to prevent losses during unfavorable weather. There are seasonal variations in the types and quality of freight.

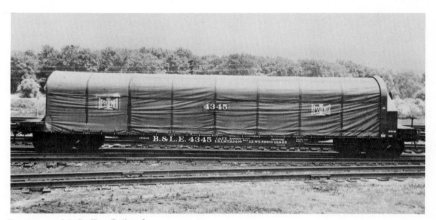

Courtesy Bessemer and Lake Erie Railroad.

Fig. 13-8 Railway flat car with a specially treated nylon cover to protect weather-vulnerable products.

Fresh fruits and vegetables must be moved immediately after harvest, the time of which is determined in part by weather. Freight lines serving ports which are icebound in winter necessarily experience much of the seasonal variation in traffic imposed on water transport. Perishable freight for export must be routed to other ports; nonperishable goods may be stockpiled.

The major consideration in the relation of weather to the use of highways is safety. Poor visibility, slippery surfaces, and gusty winds increase the hazards of driving. Snow, freezing rain, and fog create especially hazardous conditions calling for mechanical equipment in good working order and for caution on the part of drivers. Good weather, especially on weekends, brings large numbers of pleasure drivers onto the highways and traffic problems and accidents increase. Indeed, most accidents occur in relatively good weather. (See Figure 13-9.) Highway patrols experience fluctuations in activity which are closely correlated with fine holiday weather as well as bad weather. It does not follow that the alarming increase in traffic deaths is caused by the weather, however. Weather is a factor only insofar as it may create more hazardous conditions and a need for greater driving care.

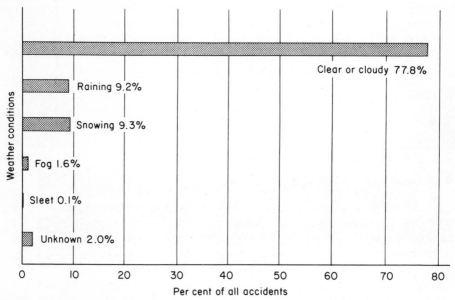

Data from *Wisconsin Accident Facts* (Wisconsin Motor Vehicle Dept., 1963).

Fig. 13-9 Percentage of motor vehicle accidents occurring in different weather conditions. Based on a survey of 71,848 accidents in 1962.

Many of the maintenance problems on highways and roads result from weather and climate. The expense of erecting signs to warn motorists of hazards associated with weather runs into huge figures. Unsurfaced roads suffer heavy damage from precipitation, and, when wet, are damaged by traffic. Even paved highways undergo erosion at the shoulders, which may lead to collapse of the roadbed. Floods can wash out bridges, under-passes, and even entire sections of road, or they may carry debris onto the highway. Gales blow trees, utility poles, and other obstructions onto the roadway. Alternate freezing and thawing causes frost-heave in the road surface and subsequent breakup of the roadbed under heavy traffic. It is

Fig. 13-10 Highway snowplow cutting through an avalanche on Red Mountain Pass in western Colorado.

often necessary to prohibit heavy vehicles from wet or thawing roads to reduce surface damage. When roads are icy, sand is applied to increase traction. Highway departments commonly keep containers of sand along steep grades that are likely to become icy. Snow is one of the most expensive highway maintenance problems in the middle and high latitudes and in mountains. Where drifting is common, snow fences or windbreaks along the windward sides of highways help induce drifts away from the road. Tunnels and snow sheds are built in mountain passes to avoid deep snow as well as avalanches. Because of the excessive cost of keeping them open with snowplows, some passes are closed for all or a part of the winter. Snow removal crews and equipment must be ready for immediate action in snow areas; great sums are expended in order to keep roads open for traffic.

The necessity for keeping city streets clear of ice and snow is even more urgent than on the highways. Sewers and gutters easily become clogged by heavy accumulations of snow. Besides being a traffic hazard, snowy streets are an inconvenience to pedestrians. Snow of great depth cannot be merely plowed to the side but must be hauled away. If the temperature is not too low, it may be removed by melting with water. Installation of hot-water or steam pipes under streets is a possible solution to the snow problem (hot-water pipes under certain sidewalks in Pittsburgh were able to melt a 31-inch snowfall in December, 1950, as fast as it fell), but it is a very expensive method of snow removal.

PUBLIC UTILITIES

Weather and climate produce erratic patterns in the demand for the services provided by public utilities and directly affect the maintenance of the services. Damage to wires or pipelines not only entails losses due to expenses of repair, but the affected utility loses revenue during the interruption. The use of gas, electricity, or the telephone commonly rises at the very times when maintenance problems are at a maximum. Consequently, utility companies must be organized to combat the worst conditions and to meet peak demands with speed and efficiency. Average consumption of electricity, for example, is only a statistic, for the vagaries of weather create wide variations in the amount used for heating, cooling, and lighting in homes.

The relation of weather and climate to hydroelectricity begins with precipitation on a watershed. It is important for a power company to know what volume of runoff to expect in planning power commitments. The influences of weather on runoff are discussed in Chapter 11. During dry summer weather it may be necessary to release more reservoir storage to meet the needs of irrigation, fisheries, or other water uses. Construction of power lines for the distribution of electricity, whether that electricity is developed by steam or water power, must take into account a great number of climatic effects on equipment. Wind causes the greatest damage to power poles and lines; strong, gusty winds blow over poles and snap lines, or blow trees and other debris into the lines. Hurricanes are by far the worst storms for overhead power lines, but even good winds for kite-flying are bad for power lines, if kites are not kept well in the open. Moisture conditions affect electrical transmission and the functioning of insulators. Wet snow, sleet, or freezing rain add weight to lines and poles and make them more vulnerable to wind. To remove ice from lines, power companies employ various methods of temporarily disconnecting a line from the main circuit and heating it with an artificially high power load. Power lines along highways suffer indirectly under conditions of ice or fog, for the possibility of automobiles and trucks running into poles is increased. Temperature fluctuations influence the operation of switches, transformers, and other equipment. In hot weather, lines expand and sag and are more easily damaged by high winds. Thunderstorms bring not only the dangers of wind and precipitation but also of lightning, which causes at least a temporary power failure if it strikes a line. Weather forecasting aids in anticipating heavy power demands and extra maintenance problems. As a storm or cold wave moves across the country, the load is often sustained by re-routing electricity around affected areas or by bringing emergency generators into use at a moment's notice. Line crews must be on the alert to keep the power system in operation as well as to protect life and property. In view of the many problems which weather imposes on overhead lines, it may well be asked if it wouldn't be wise to put the lines underground. From a meteorological point of view it would, but the cost would be exorbitant.

Photo by Jack Carver, *Bellingham Herald.*

Fig. 13-11 Telephone poles broken by wind following freezing rain. The weight of ice on lines made them especially vulnerable to a cold wind that blew at right angles to the lines.

The importance of weather information to gas companies is primarily in connection with consumer demand, although, as with other utilities, the maintenance of distribution facilities is rendered more difficult by severe weather. Delivery of natural gas over long distances cannot ordinarily be increased as rapidly as can electrical service, so that it is even more important to be able to anticipate future needs in the light of weather forecasts. Temperature, wind, cloudiness, and precipitation all affect the use of gas. Of these, the most important is temperature. (See Figure 13-12.) The demand for more gas resulting from a cold wave must

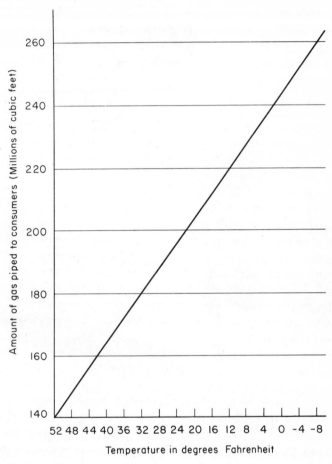

Fig. 13-12 Probability graph showing estimated 24-hour gas consumption as a function of expected average temperatures in a typical large city.

be met by dispatching gas from a remote source *before* the low temperatures occur. For the most efficient and economical service the gas dispatcher constantly refers to the meteorological conditions and forecasts for the area being served. Several gas companies have found it profitable to employ meteorologists who can interpret weather conditions specifically in terms of the problems of gas distribution.

Telephone and telegraph services have many of the same problems as power companies in maintaining their lines in all types of weather. Since telephone and telegraph lines are closely linked throughout the United States, it is often possible to channel communications around affected areas in times of emergency. In bad weather, especially during major disasters, the public makes heavy demands on communications systems, and these media must be geared to meet maximum traffic and poorest operating conditions at the same time. Microwave transmission eliminates some of the line problems but introduces new difficulties because transmission is affected by temperature and moisture conditions in the atmosphere.

Radio communication is freed, to a large extent, from the problems of line maintenance, although antennae are subject to the elements. Indirectly, radio transmission and reception are affected by power failures due to storms, and where communication is vital emergency power sources must be provided. Directly, the transmission of radio waves is influenced by atmospheric conditions. Lightning and other electrical disturbances cause static. Brilliant displays of aurorae are usually accompanied by poor radio reception. Changing temperature and humidity characteristics of the air alter the refraction of radio waves and thereby influence their propagation. Temperature inversions and steep humidity gradients near the earth's surface tend to produce an excessive downward refraction of radio waves, limiting the distance to which signals reach. On the other hand, long-distance radio reception would not be possible were it not for the downward refraction of radio waves by certain of the ionized layers in the outer atmosphere.

Municipal and industrial water supplies are closely related to precipitation and the hydrologic cycle. Year-to-year and seasonal fluctuations in the amount of water available result from variations in precipitation. Thus, a city water system must be planned in the light of dry years as well as of average years to provide basic minimum service. Where the ground freezes each winter, water pipes must be placed well below the expected frost depth. In some instances, in regions with permafrost, water mains, sewer lines, and hot-water pipes have been placed in the same insulated tunnel to overcome the threat of freezing.

Sewage systems depend directly upon the water supply and therefore are subject to all its problems, whether caused by weather or not. Temperature has minor effects on sewage disposal; the speed of chemical and biological activity is increased under high temperatures and decreases in cold weather. Storm sewers are ordinarily separate from sanitary sewers to minimize treatment and disposal problems. Their proper design and construction depend upon knowledge of rainfall extremes and potential runoff.

INDUSTRY

The influences of weather and climate on industry are so many and varied that they defy a complete listing, let alone a thorough analysis, between the covers of one volume. They may be divided into two general categories: those influencing location and those affecting operations once an industry has been established. Climatic factors influence the location of a factory because of their effects on transportation, raw materials, labor supply, housing costs, manufacturing processes, and waste disposal. The relative importance of climatic factors depends on the type of manufacturing in question, and climate is frequently overshadowed by more pertinent economic considerations. Food processing plants are likely to be located where the agricultural produce for manufacture is available. We can say that the availability of raw material is the primary factor, but certainly climate plays a fundamental role. Similarly, pulp and paper mills are located where there are abundant water supplies, which again presumes favorable climatic conditions. A factory demanding year-round access to water transportation would hardly be located on a harbor that freezes over for part of the year. The attractiveness of a climate to a large labor force may be a factor in inducing labor to move to a new area; at least it will be considered in the category of "fringe benefits." The cost of heating, or air conditioning, to provide satisfactory conditions for work and for certain manufacturing processes bears a direct relationship to climate. Factory buildings, warehouses, and other structures should be designed with climate in mind. Factories which dispose of wastes through stacks must be so located as to minimize air pollution over settled areas.

Weather conditions are reflected in almost every phase of operation of manufacturing plants. Storms cause workers to arrive late for work, hamper essential outdoor activities, cause damage to goods and equipment, or interrupt power. Some processes require rather well-defined temperatures, and special provision must be made to offset rapid changes in temperature. Atmospheric cooling towers and condensers afford further examples of the effect of air temperature on certain processes, notably in the chemical and related industries. Wind and low relative humidity increase the fire hazard at manufacturing plants, especially if combustible or explosive materials are being processed or stored.

The motion picture industry is an outstanding example of economic activity with highly specialized climatic requirements. In its early days, it depended on clear skies and abundant sunshine for photography; today, new types of film have somewhat reduced the importance of sunshine, but light and visibility remain vital factors in outdoor photography. Slight differences in the weather from day to day disrupt continuity in outdoor scenes. Wind blowing across microphones seriously impairs sound quality.

A sudden storm can cause great expense and loss of time to a movie company on location with valuable equipment and a large number of people. Yet a specific storm situation may be required for certain outdoor scenes. Both meteorological forecasts and climatic studies are used in determining the best time and place to photograph background scenes.

ATMOSPHERIC POLLUTION

Probably the most widespread problem confronting industrial meteorologists is that of atmospheric pollution around cities and factories, but it is not the problem of meteorologists alone. Weather and climate are not the causes of air pollution, but atmospheric conditions do greatly affect the rate of diffusion of contaminating agents, both horizontally and vertically. Since air pollution is far more common around cities than elsewhere and has increased with their growth, it is evident that it is a man-caused problem. Reduced visibility due to pollution is related to the greater urban activity on weekdays. One can often locate a distant city by its cap of smoke and haze. There are always some foreign materials in the air—in liquid, solid, and gaseous forms. The increase in pollution has come from a multitude of sources. Smoke, dust, gases, and vapors from industrial operations account for a large share; heating systems, incinerators, motor vehicle exhausts, and evaporation of volatile liquids such as gasoline are other sources. Many chemical effluents are unpleasant and create a distinct health hazard. Burning eyes and irritated nostrils are common symptoms of the effects of polluted air. Under extreme conditions of atmospheric pollution accompanying fog, the increased incidence of respiratory disorders and deaths from allied ailments has been directly attributable to chemical agents in the air. In December, 1930, sixty-three persons died as a result of severe pollution in the Meuse Valley in Belgium. Several hundred others suffered from respiratory illnesses and many head of livestock died. At Donora, Pennsylvania, in late October, 1948, twenty-one persons died under similar circumstances. During the period December 4–9, 1952, a layer of smoke varying from 150 to 400 feet in height blanketed the Thames Valley. In the Greater London area nearly 4000 deaths were charged primarily to sulphur dioxide effluents of industrial origin. In all these cases subsequent investigations revealed a high incidence of chronic respiratory diseases among residents of surrounding areas.

The meteorological effects of pollution are largely concerned with visibility and sunshine. Since many contaminants are hygroscopic they act as nuclei of condensation and create a haze or fog, further reducing visibility. Moreover, it appears that the water droplets thus formed are more stable than normal cloud droplets and do not evaporate so readily upon being heated. Oily substances, especially, tend to form a protective coating around a droplet, making it difficult to disperse. The combination of fog and pollutants has been termed *smog*. Solar radiation is appreciably reduced by polluted air in the daytime, and outgoing radiation is reduced at night. The net effect is a lowered diurnal range of temperature. Parts of the solar spectrum are transmitted selectively by different gaseous constituents in the air so that the quality as well as the quantity of insolation is impaired. Chemical reactions among various types of contaminants in the air produce new compounds that in some cases are more damaging than the original wastes. Certain of these reactions are photochemical, that is, they take place under the effects of sunlight.

Although it is comparatively easy to observe and describe the effects of atmospheric pollution, it is somewhat more difficult to explain the meteorological conditions which favor the stagnation of pollution-ridden air at certain times and places more than others. In general, stable air and light winds or calms are conducive to the concentration of pollutants at or near the source of contamination. Industrial areas where stable air resides for extended periods are likely locations for a pollution problem. For numerous reasons, industries are commonly concentrated in valleys and depressions for which stable air has an affinity and where temperature inversions are common. Temperature inversions are particularly suited to the formation of palls of smoke and industrial haze. As the warm fumes, gases, or airborne solids rise they are cooled adiabatically as well as by radiation and mixing. Since the air is warmer overhead in an inversion, they are soon at a temperature equal to that of the surrounding air. Therefore, they do not rise further. Cooling by radiation at night from the top of a smoke layer only intensifies the inversion and the concentration of pollutants increases at and below the top of the inversion. Stable air, especially with an inverted lapse rate, often is accompanied by radiation fog, which combines with the pollutants to form smog. As already indicated, hygroscopic particles may hasten the condensation process. If the inversion layer is well above the surface, a pall will form with less drastic effects, but it will nevertheless inhibit the passage of radiation and may eventually "build down" to the surface. The most intense smogs usually develop when the top of the inversion is within 1500 feet of the ground. Pollutants tend to be concentrated near the ground in a nocturnal surface inversion. By day, heating of the ground may create a layer of turbulent mixing which does not completely overcome the inversion. (See Figure 13-13.) Under such conditions the pollutants mix more uniformly through the layer below the inversion. Unstable air and strong winds are inimical to formation of dense smogs. Rising air currents carry wastes upward and winds disperse them through a large volume of air. Prevailing winds carry pollutants away from single sources and produce a strip of territory to the leeward that is subjected to a progressive decrease in intensity of

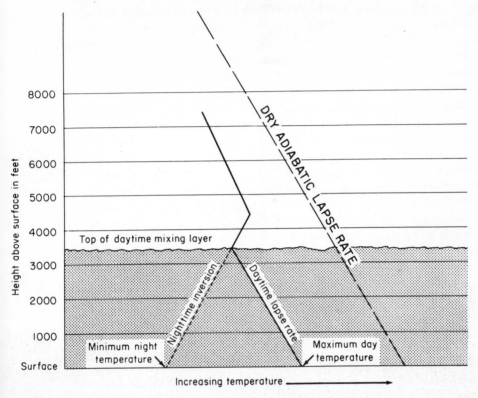

Fig. 13-13 Height of daytime surface-mixing layer in relation to temperature lapse rate.

pollution. Local winds, such as sea or valley breezes, may have a decidedly favorable effect in clearing away polluted air. But they may also have the opposite effect, even returning polluted air that has drifted away from its source.

The effect of precipitation on local atmospheric pollution is not as great as might be expected. Although some materials are unquestionably washed out by rain, wind and unstable air are more effective in cleansing the air during a storm. On a larger scale, however, much of the material dispersed into the air must eventually be returned to the earth by precipitation. Some scientists believe that carbon dioxide in the atmosphere is gradually increasing as a result of the large amounts of fossil fuels that have been burned over the past two or three centuries.

The obvious question at this point is: What can be done to alleviate pollution? The equally obvious answer is: Stop pouring every conceivable type of waste into the atmosphere, especially when stable air prevails. In the end this will have to be the solution, and industries are at work to perfect methods of retrieving wastes, many of which have economic

Fig. 13-14 Smoke released from a meteorological tower indicates wind currents moving in opposite directions. Data from towers such as this aid climatic studies of atmospheric pollution and other industrial problems.

value. More efficient combustion in heating plants and incinerators, better motor vehicle exhausts, and numerous other curbs can contribute to a reduction in pollution.

The atmosphere is an amazingly effective sewage disposal plant, but it can be overtaxed locally. Factory location can often take advantage of variations in the ability of the atmosphere to disperse pollutants. Areas with a high frequency of low-level inversions are particularly unsuitable for factories that eject large quantities of airborne wastes. High chimneys help to disperse effluents above the surface level, but their effective height is limited by both construction difficulties and atmospheric conditions. The contaminants of some industries could be more efficiently dispersed by piping them to a hilltop during periods when stable air prevails. Pollution can also be alleviated by restricting the release of wastes to periods of favorable meteorological conditions, that is, strong winds and unstable air.   **330**

CONSTRUCTION

There are two broad aspects to the relationships between outdoor construction projects and climate or weather: (1) influences on structural design, and (2) direct effects on construction activities. A given structure must be so designed as to withstand stresses caused by climatic factors such as temperature fluctuations, wind force, humidity changes, or loads of snow and ice. Selection of materials is also influenced by climatic conditions; certain materials are better suited to climatic extremes by virtue of their inherent strength or their resistance to damage by chemical or physical weathering processes.

Temperature is one of the most important climatic elements to be considered in construction design. Metals, in particular, expand and contract with changing temperature, and allowance must be made to prevent buckling of girders and supports during warm periods or contraction and possible breaks in cold weather. Railroad rails expand enough under high temperatures to disrupt their alignment and create a danger. Steel cables sag in warm weather and become taut in cold weather. Vertical metal towers expand more on the sunny side than on the shaded side, thus undergoing a diurnal bending that creates strains. Paints which reflect a large part of insolation help to lessen this problem. Reflecting paints and safety devices are provided for storage tanks to minimize the danger of overflow or bursting due to expansion of the contents. In general, extreme temperatures and sudden changes of temperature bring on the greatest troubles. Concrete, stone, and other types of masonry are subject to damage when temperatures drop rapidly to below freezing, especially if they are wet. The expansion of ice in cracks or in damp earth adjacent to masonry walls commonly causes structures to break up if they are not properly drained and reinforced.

Wind exerts a direct force on any structure in its path, and the maximum expected wind speeds are among the stress factors considered in designing bridges, towers, and buildings. Bridges are often located across gorges or in river valleys where they are exposed to unusually strong, gusty winds. Suspension bridges are particularly vulnerable to wind, for they tend to sway and to develop destructive undulations. A notable example was the first Tacoma Narrows bridge at Tacoma, Washington, which was destroyed by wind on November 7, 1940. On December 28, 1879, sections of the Tay Bridge at Dundee, Scotland, were blown down by westerly gales. A train that was crossing the bridge at the time fell into the water, killing all seventy-five persons aboard.

High towers, even if supported by cables, sometimes develop a "whipping action" and collapse under the force of strong winds. The total force of wind on an object in its path results from the impact of air on the exposed side and the lower pressure on the leeward. It depends on the size and shape of the object and is proportional to the square of the wind velocity. The full force of wind is never felt, even by flat surfaces, because the air tends to flow around them. Streamlining of surfaces can appreciably reduce the effect of wind pressure. Venting in broad structural members allows the air to pass through with less force also. Solid structures incorporate considerably more strength in order to withstand wind. Additional stress is placed on hollow structures as a result of the difference in pressure between the air inside and the wind outside. Vents help to equalize the pressure.

Relative humidity is significant in its effects on construction materials, preservatives, and paints. Metals are generally more susceptible to corrosion under conditions of high relative humidity. Chemical and physical deterioration of paints is speeded up by moist air, and masonry construction also disintegrates more rapidly under moist conditions. Rainfall not only enhances the destructive influences of moisture but also produces direct physical effects on exposed surfaces. Heavy rains erode earthen structures and cause floods which undermine foundations or carry away ground structures. Dams, canals, piers, and bridges must be constructed to withstand maximum flood stages. A competent engineer will make a thorough study of flood and rainfall records when designing these types of projects. Accumulations of snow create extra weight on horizontal surfaces; additional supports may be required to prevent collapse. Potential accretions of ice on towers, bridges, and cables also call for safety margins in design. When heavily loaded with ice, such structures are more vulnerable to the wind.

In the engineering design of construction projects, climatic records are of great value in determining the extremes to which the finished structure may be subjected. Actual construction work is related to both day-to-day weather and the climate. Much construction is seasonal, especially in climates where there are marked seasonal weather fluctuations. Economic efficiency dictates that work be planned carefully to take advantage of favorable weather and to avoid loss of time or damage to materials and equipment in bad weather. Climatic records of precipitation and temperature thus aid in scheduling various types of work. Concrete and mortar are damaged if frozen before they set thoroughly. If the amount of newly poured concrete is small, it can be protected by coverings or artificial heating. Frozen earth impedes some types of construction. On the other hand, in the tundra or muskeg, heavy loads can be moved over the frozen ground with less difficulty. Most machinery does not function well in temperatures below freezing, and special problems arise from the necessity for antifreeze, heaters, and closed cabs on mobile equipment. Metal parts break more readily in extremely low temperatures. Temperature also affects the efficiency of workers on a construction project. Very high temperatures appreciably slow the pace of manual work among the un-acclimatized and may lead to illness among men doing heavy physical work; low temperatures make more clothing necessary and thereby complicate manual tasks. Accidents are more numerous during periods of freezing temperatures or excessive heat than under normal temperatures. Housing and feeding of construction crews are also influenced by temperature.

Precipitation generally has an adverse effect on construction. Heavy rains pit newly laid concrete, erode earth embankments, and slow down or stop most earth-moving activities. Snow, sleet, and freezing rain create a variety of difficulties, depending on the nature of the construction. A heavy snow cover usually brings work to a halt. Heavy precipitation and fog reduce visibility and thereby increase the danger of accidents. Special facilities have to be provided for protection of materials and equipment subject to damage by moisture. Winds tend to increase the unfavorable effects of precipitation as well as the accident hazard on outdoor construction work, especially on tall structures such as towers, bridges, or high buildings. Partially completed structures are generally more easily damaged by strong or gusty winds. Certain kinds of construction activities are specifically affected by wind. Spray-painting is an obvious example. Drying winds prevent concrete and mortar from setting properly unless their surfaces are specially dampened.

CLIMATE AND BUSINESS

The primary goal of most businesses is to sell goods or services. Although many economic, social, and psychological factors influence success in selling, climate and weather are partially responsible for determining fluctuations in sales, and the type of goods or services in demand. Thousands of illustrations could be cited. A few will illustrate the nature of the relationship. In spring the sale of gardening supplies and outdoor sports equipment increases sharply during the first few warm days and continues to correlate broadly with the weather well into the summer. The housewife buys more salad vegetables and "lighter" items for family meals. Bathing suits, sports clothes, and other warm-weather apparel come into fashion. Drive-ins have an initial upswing in business which thereafter rises and falls with the vagaries of weather.

On a sunny day in summer, the sales of soft drinks, ice cream, cold meats, and other picnic items are likely to be great. Amusement parks will do a rush business, as will service stations, especially on a weekend. Motion picture theaters may play to empty houses as the populace treks to beaches or mountains; but, if the day is oppressively hot, their air conditioning will draw good crowds regardless of the quality of the film.

With the first cool spells of autumn, sales of fuels begin to rise and the demand for furnace repairs or installation grows. The first threat of freezing weather is accompanied by a rush of motorists to garages and service stations for antifreeze. Heavier clothing replaces summer fashions on the display racks of dry-goods stores. The effects of cold weather and storms on business extend into the winter. Fuel consumption rises, and, after a hard freeze, the plumber makes his rounds to thaw out pipes. A sudden storm induces many an unprepared customer to make a last-minute purchase of galoshes, an overcoat, tire chains, storm windows, or some other item which might better have been acquired months earlier. Goods related to indoor hobbies find a more ready market. The local grocery can expect a larger turnover when storms make travel to the larger shopping centers difficult or hazardous. The druggist who dispensed sunburn lotion to vacationers in the summer now sells it to skiers along with an infinite variety of cold medicines. Not only is there a marked relationship between the seasons and sales, but, from the above examples, it is clear that daily weather also affects the shopping habits of the public. A great deal of merchandising is geared to holidays and weekends. If the weather is unfavorable for a given product, sales will lag.

Besides seasonal variations in the retail market, numerous regional differences arise from climatic causes. Length of seasons and the average weather conditions determine to a large degree the nature of the market. Air-conditioning equipment for cooling homes finds a much better market in tropical and warm-summer climates than in cool regions, where heating systems and electric blankets are more in demand. An auto dealer can expect to sell a greater proportion of convertible cars in Florida or California than in Minnesota or Maine, whereas a sports shop will find few customers for sleds or skis in the southern states. The effects of weather and climate on retail businesses are generally transmitted to the wholesaler, who must have stocks on hand and make deliveries in advance of expected consumer demand. Moreover, the wholesaler must consider the possible effects of climatic conditions on goods in storage and in transit. If products are to be exported, the climate at the destination will have a bearing on the kind and quantity of goods which the exporter can expect to sell.

No general set of rules has thus far been devised to guide businesses in relating advertising and selling to weather conditions. The need for some types of goods has no relation to local weather changes but sales may nevertheless fluctuate as customers find the weather favorable for shopping trips. On the other hand, weather can create such a demand for some goods that customers will brave severe storms to obtain them. Success in retailing is further complicated by economic conditions, advertising, competition, fads, and fashions, but the wise businessman considers the climate and carefully notes the weather forecast in planning sales strategy.

ADDITIONAL READINGS

Ackermann, William C., "Application of Severe Rainstorm Data in Engineering Design," *Bull. Am. Met. Soc.*, 45, 4 (1964), 204–206.

Allen, Louis, "Navigating with the Weather," *Bull. Am. Met. Soc.*, 32, 7 (1951), 245–50.

Brooks, C. E. P., *Climate in Every Day Life*. New York: Philosophical Library, 1951.

Changnon, Stanley A., "Climatology of Damaging Lightning in Illinois," *Mon. Wea. Rev.*, 22, 3 (1964), 115–20.

Corey, C. P., "The Effects of Weather upon Electric Power Systems," *Bull. Am. Met. Soc.*, 30, 7 (1949), 239–41.

Dryar, Henry A., "Load Dispatching and Philadelphia Weather," *Bull. Am. Met. Soc.*, 30, 5 (1949), 159–67.

Haltiner, G. J., and H. D. Hamilton, "Minimal-Time Ship Routing," *Journ. of Appl. Met.*, 1, 1 (1962), 1–7.

McDermott, Walsh, "Air Pollution and Public Health," *Scient. Am.*, 205, 4 (1961), 49–57.

Pack, Donald H., "Meteorology and Air Pollution," *Science*, 146, 3648 (1964), 1119–28.

Petty, Mary T., "Weather and Consumer Sales," *Bull. Am. Met. Soc.*, 44, 2 (1963), 68–71.

Weather a Factor in Plant Location. Washington: U.S. Department of Commerce, Weather Bureau, 1961.

Webb, Willis L., "Missile Range Meteorology," *Weatherwise*, 16, 3 (1963), 100–107.

Influences of weather and climate have been reflected in man's dwellings since prehistoric times for the excellent reason that the primary function of housing is to shelter the inhabitants and the material contents against the weather. Whether one has in mind a small cottage, a mansion, or a giant skyscraper, atmospheric conditions are relevant factors in efficient siting, choice of materials, design, and air conditioning of the structure. Temperature, sunshine, precipitation, and wind are the chief elements requiring attention. Humidity, cloudiness, and visibility may also demand consideration. Although economic and social factors normally have a great influence on housing, principles of applied climatology afford a basis for many refinements in location and construction of buildings. Indeed, that which is economically feasible and socially acceptable in housing is determined in part by climatic circumstances.

CLIMATIC ASPECTS OF SITE

Assuming it has been decided to construct a building in a given city or rural area, local microclimatic conditions weigh heavily in the selection of the best, exact site. A good building site may possess microclimatic advantages which offset some of the disadvantages of the prevailing regional climate, that is, the macroclimate. Variable microclimatic conditions are commonly induced by local relief, but they may also be brought about by landscaping, adjacent build-

336

ings, water bodies, and industrial wastes. Since some of these controls of microclimate are likely to be altered by expanding settlement, especially in a city, it is advisable to anticipate possible major changes in an environment which might drastically affect the microclimate. Ideally, a complete site study should include the microclimate along with such matters as bedrock, drainage, land cost, or proximity to services. Unfortunately, detailed instrumental observation of the microclimate requires time and is not economically feasible except for the most expensive structures. The alternative is to apply known principles of microclimatology and to make reasoned inferences with respect to the climatic conditions at a particular site.

Wind is the most important climatic element in site selection, for it produces direct effects on a building and modifies temperature and moisture effects. How much shelter from the wind is desirable depends on the regional climate and on the type of building on the site. In warm and humid climates, free circulation of air helps to lessen excessive humidity and high temperatures; in cold climates, wind may have value in moisture control, but it also increases convective cooling. In either case, high-velocity winds are to be avoided if practicable, otherwise they must be allowed for in building design. Local relief is the most significant as well as the most permanent of the common controls of wind conditions at a specific site. Windward slopes, summits, and plains are likely to receive the full force of surface winds. Sites where topographic barriers produce a constriction in air flow often have strong and gusty winds. Valleys and slopes are subjected to the effects of air drainage and, possibly, mountain and valley breezes. These local movements of air can be of immense value in warm climates and in summer, but they may be annoying in winter. Selection of a site should take into account the directions of prevailing winds and their temperature and moisture characteristics, but a wind which occurs only a small percentage of the time may be more objectionable than all others combined. An outstanding example is a wind from the direction of sources of air pollution. The problem is not confined to cities. Few farmers would want their homes to the leeward of livestock pens or barns. Objectionable odors, pollens, dust, and even insects are carried by the wind.

Types of surface and ground cover to the windward modify wind force, temperature, and humidity. A forest, orchard, or park has a moderating effect on summer temperatures, but pavements and other bare surfaces magnify temperature extremes. Buildings in the vicinity modify both direction and speed of the wind and may create undesirable local currents. A cluster of large buildings absorbs heat during a warm day and radiates it at night. Summer nights may be abnormally hot in the area of its influence. Water bodies aid in reducing diurnal and seasonal temperature ranges and generate breezes. If they are too shallow, however, they warm readily and thus create oppressive relative humidities in their vicinities in summer. In winter in the middle and high latitudes, shallow lakes and ponds may freeze, rapidly losing their moderating effect.

Temperature conditions, other than those directly influenced by the exchange of air between the site and its surroundings, are controlled by sunshine and by elevation. Since the approximate location of the housing site is assumed to have been decided, latitude and its effects on duration of possible sunshine and noon angle of the sun are not variable factors. Average cloudiness may differ within a given area because of relief features, and industrial smoke may greatly decrease the effective insolation, another reason for selecting a site to the windward of industrial establishments. Maximum benefit from insolation is achieved by choosing a site on the slopes facing toward the equator, where the sun's rays are more nearly perpendicular to the ground surface. In contrast, poleward slopes receive the sun at low angles and may actually be in the shade for part of the day. In the Northern Hemisphere, slopes on the east and southeast are sunniest in the morning; west and southwest slopes are sunniest in the afternoon. Where maximum heating is desired, westerly exposures are better than those on the east because insolation is received at the time of highest air temperatures. An easterly exposure provides heating in the early morning; direct insolation is less in the afternoon, and cooling proceeds faster in the evening. Sites in deep valleys have a shortened period of possible sunshine, which may be a distinct disadvantage in winter. In a built-up area the difference in sunniness on opposite sides of a street is worthy of consideration. Nearby tall buildings may shut out most of the sunlight.

The effect of elevation on temperature–design relationships is closely related to relief. Except where differences of several hundreds or thousands of feet in elevation are involved, higher sites are cooled more by the freer circulation of air than by the effects of the normal lapse rate of temperature in the daytime. Air drainage and temperature inversions commonly disrupt the normal lapse rate at night. Under clear skies, a broad valley has greater extremes of temperature than adjacent slopes, where a temperature inversion provides warmer night air. Slope sites at or above the average level of inversions have the advantage of being above most of the associated evils such as smoke, haze, and radiation fog.

Precipitation differences will not be greatly significant in the normal range of site possibilities, unless there are wide variations in elevation and orographic conditions, in which case lee slopes will usually be drier. If there is considerable wind, some knolls and ridges produce the opposite effect as rain or snow are swept upward on the windward and deposited on the lee. An examination of the vegetation often aids in determining whether this is a common occurrence. Sites exposed to the wind will be most affected by driving rains. The pattern of snowdrifts depends on local eddies produced by obstructions. If deep snow is a winter problem, a site near a highway or street which is regularly cleared is better than an isolated one, unless one prefers to be snowbound. Where heavy showers occur or where there is a heavy runoff of snowmelt, flooding can necessitate excessive costs in design and maintenance of a building and its site. It is never wise to build on or near a river bank without thorough knowledge of the precipitation characteristics of the watershed and the resulting flood regime.

CLIMATE CONDITIONING

Even the best of building sites will be subject to weather changes, and other factors may make it necessary to use a site which is poor from the point of view of applied climatology. Nevertheless, proper orientation, design, and choice of materials for a house can overcome many of the climatic disadvantages of a site, the primary objective being to create a suitable climate in and around the house, that is, *climate conditioning*. Climate conditioning is concerned with landscaping and the placement of other buildings as well as with the design of the house itself. In its broadest sense, it includes certain aspects of the field of city planning, for groups of buildings and the associated streets and parks create their own microclimate. For many householders, convenience, architectural harmony, view, and cost of maintenance offset the minor advantages of a slightly better microclimate, but it is well at least to recognize the climatic factor in choosing a housing site.

HOUSE ORIENTATION

Orientation of a building with respect to wind and sun will, quite naturally, influence wind force, temperature, precipitation, and light effects. Narrow building lots in a residential section preclude much choice in orientation of a dwelling. Adverse climatic conditions will have to be compensated for in design and in the mutual protection afforded by closely spaced houses. Where there is greater freedom, it is expedient to orient buildings to achieve the maximum control over the microclimate. The broad face of a house will obviously receive greater wind pressure than will the narrow dimension. This may be desirable if high temperatures are prevalent but becomes a problem if winds are exceptionally vigorous or cold. Strong, cold winds on the side of the main entrance are particularly objectionable. Orientation with respect to both local and prevailing winds as well as to buildings or other windbreaks in the vicinity determines the relative effect of wind on different parts of a house. A wind rose showing average windspeeds and frequencies from different directions is especially useful if it is interpreted in connection with temperature and moisture data.

The rules which govern the relation of sunshine to site exposure apply equally to building orientation. In the Northern Hemisphere, the greatest amount of insolation is received by the east and southeast sides of a house in the morning and by the west and southwest sides in the afternoon. In summer, with increasing latitude, the path of the sun in the sky describes more complete circles so that the sun rises north of east and sets north of west; in winter the arc of the sun's visible path is shortened, and east and west exposures receive very little sunlight.

CLIMATE CONDITIONING THROUGH DESIGN

The climatic factors related to housing design are insolation, temperature, wind, and moisture. Insolation provides heat and light and has certain health-giving powers. Climate conditioning seeks to control its effects through such design features as shape, layout of rooms, placement of openings, insulating materials, overhangs, or roof orientation and slope. The functions of various rooms determine the most efficient layout with respect to the sun. For example, a kitchen and breakfast nook are best placed where they will receive morning sun, whereas the living room may benefit from afternoon sun, especially in winter. Bright sunlight can sometimes be a nuisance; the study and certain kinds of workrooms are better located on the north side of the house, where lighting is more even throughout the day.

By varying the ground plan from the traditional rectangle, it is possible to obtain considerably more sun control for various rooms. An L-shaped house can be oriented to provide a greater variety of sunny exposures than a square one covering the same ground area. Admission of sunlight to the interior need not be confined to windows in vertical walls on the sunny exposures. Skylights offer one method of increasing the light in a one-story house or on the top floor of a multistoried building. They are difficult to maintain, however. Clerestories are suited to rooms on the shady side of a building where sunlight is desired. The principle of the clerestory is illustrated in Figure 14-1. In combination with ceilings of the proper color and texture it can greatly improve lighting of northern rooms.

Unwanted bright sunlight is controlled from the interior by means of curtains or blinds over openings. Glass bricks and translucent windows also reduce glare while admitting light. Overhangs, awnings, and screens serve much the same purpose on the outside and have the added advantage of reducing heating of walls. In sunny climates of the middle latitudes overhangs can be designed to expose walls and windows in winter when

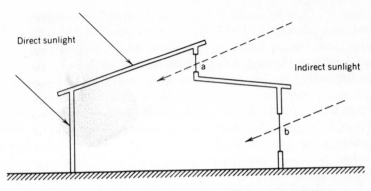

Fig. 14-1 Principle of the clerestory. Scattered and reflected light is admitted through the clerestory window at "a" and the wall window at "b." Direct rays of the sun are kept out by opaque roof and wall on the sunny exposure.

the sun is at a low angle but to provide noonday shade in summer. (See Figure 14-2.) The exact size of overhangs for the degree of shading desired is calculated from the noon elevation of the sun at different times of the year for the latitude of the site. In low latitudes, overhangs shade walkways and the ground around the house, thereby helping to reduce the temperature of the walls. Overhangs would have to be inordinately large in high latitudes to afford shade which is not usually necessary anyway.

Design features in a well-built house take into account possible extremes in outside temperature and aim to maintain indoor temperatures at a comfortable level with a minimum of artificial heating or cooling. Basically, this entails control of the processes of heat transfer: radiation, con-

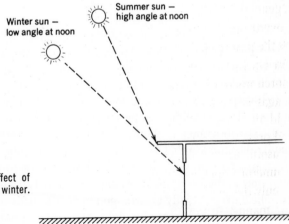

Fig. 14-2 Comparison of effect of an overhang in summer and in winter.

duction, and convection. These processes are affected by precipitation, humidity, and wind as well as by insolation and air temperature.

Solar heat is a blessing or a problem in relation to a specific house design depending on the climate and the season, and it is sometimes difficult to separate the benefits from the disadvantages. Well-insulated walls and roofs inhibit the passage of heat by conduction to or from the interior of a house. Light-colored and smooth surfaces reflect a greater percentage of sunlight than do dark and rough surfaces and consequently do not heat so rapidly under intense insolation. Through selection of materials for walls and roofs or the paint applied to them, it is possible to control solar heating to some extent. A light-colored surface will also reflect insolation in winter, but since there is less sunshine at that time this is generally not so important as summer cooling. Double roofs between which air can move freely are effective in reducing the flow of absorbed solar heat into a house in hot climates. Venting of attics has a similar though less marked effect. In semiarid and arid climates, flat roofs can be kept covered with water and thus aid cooling by evaporation. Short-wave solar radiation passes through clear air and windows with relative ease (even at low air temperatures) and upon being absorbed is converted into long-wave radiation which is partially trapped. Single-panel windows conduct and radiate a great deal more heat than insulated walls, however, and the gain in solar heat through large and numerous windows during short, sunny winter days may be more than balanced by losses at night or on cloudy days. Storm sash or double-pane glazing with the intervening space sealed airtight will reduce conductive loss. Cooling due to evaporation of water from the exterior window surfaces can also be reduced in this way. Drapes drawn over the interior of windows partially curb radiation losses. In general, the less sunshine at a particular site, the more glass is needed to overcome dark interiors, but it must be remembered that glass expedites the passage of heat in both directions.

Wind causes convective cooling, intensifies precipitation effects, and exerts direct force upon a house. Therefore house design should provide for insulation against too much cooling, tight construction to prevent the entrance of cold air or wind-driven precipitation, and over-all strength to withstand wind pressure. Under hot conditions, a movement of air through a building is useful in controlling temperature and humidity. Tropical houses have numerous openings to permit free flow of air. Native dwellings are commonly designed so that walls can be propped up or rolled up all around in a manner to provide shade but allow breezes to circulate. The tent of the desert nomad is a similar example of climatic conditioning through design. The flaps can easily be arranged to create shade and admit air by day and to restrict cool breezes by night. Movement of air through

Courtesy Standard Oil of New Jersey.

Fig. 14-3 Climate conditioning through design in a tropical rain forest. Farmer's dwelling in a clearing near Magdalena, Colombia.

Fig. 14-4 Climate conditioning through design in a tropical desert. Bedouin tent near Al Kharj, Saudi Arabia.

Courtesy Standard Oil of New Jersey

a house is modified by the openings and obstacles as well as by overhangs and the shape of the exterior. Various kinds of deflectors aid in directing air currents. For maximum airiness, floor-to-ceiling walls may need to be replaced by partial dividers or screens, for to have its maximum effect a breeze must pass through the house without being trapped in rooms on the windward. Some architects experiment with scale models of buildings in a wind tunnel before making final decisions on design details.

The design that allows free air movement may also admit precipitation carried along by the wind. Overhangs, louvers, and other types of deflectors help to overcome this. The attic venting that invites cooling air in summer provides an entry for rain or snow if not closed in the wet season or winter. Protection of the walls from precipitation is accomplished by overhangs except in the most violent storms. Walls need to be of tight construction and joints closely knit where there is danger of precipitation being blown into small openings. Even if it does not penetrate to the interior of the house, moisture will speed up deterioration of the outside walls. Canopies over entrances protect doors and shield the opening when it is in use. Vestibules extended beyond the main wall serve the same purpose and are more efficient in cold climates.

It was pointed out in the discussion of orientation of a house that the larger the surface exposed to the wind, the greater will be the total wind pressure upon it. Long eaves and overhangs tend to catch the wind and therefore increase the danger of wind damage. Loosely attached roof coverings of any type can be lifted and swept away by a fierce wind. Low, streamlined buildings of simple design are best for regions with violent winds. Departures from this principle call for compensating strength in structural members and walls. Possible destructive effects of flying debris to roofs, walls, and windows must also be taken into consideration. A part of the stress resulting from gale force winds is due to the difference in pressure between the outside and the interior. This can be reduced to some extent by louvered venting or by opening windows on the lee side. A well-built house can withstand hurricane winds, but the cost of "tornado-proofing" is normally beyond the range of the home-owner, who shares a calculated risk with his insurance company.

The most obvious aspect of moisture problems in housing is precipitation. Roofs and eave troughs should provide for rapid removal of heavy rains and for disposal of the runoff without damage to the surrounding grounds. If not properly diverted, runoff, carrying dirt, soot, or loose paint, may stain walls. Where there is danger of seepage along basement walls and foundations, tile drains will facilitate drainage away from the building. Water which enters crevices and subsequently freezes can be particularly destructive. Overhangs protect entrances, paths, and windows but must be designed with sun and wind in mind as well. Windows that are placed too low are subject to rain splatter and covering by drifted snow; doorsills need to be high enough to hold back a shallow flow of water which is likely to accumulate on a doorstep in a deluge.

In regions of heavy snowfall, roofs must be strong enough to hold the weight of several tons of snow. Some indication of the possible snow load can be obtained from climatic records. (See Figure 14-5.) The stress is especially great when rain falls onto a snow-covered roof. A steeply pitched roof will permit wet snow to slide off, easing the stress on the roof but creating a hazard beneath the eaves. On the other hand, gentler slopes will hold "dry" snow, which has valuable insulating properties in extreme cold. To obtain benefit from a cover of snow, the roof itself must be well insulated so that the snow is not melted by heat from the house. Otherwise, ice will form, reducing the insulating capacity. Moreover, melt water which flows down the roof is likely to form icicles along the eaves; adequate drainage of melt water is thus impeded and the danger of falling icicles is introduced.

Hail damage is usually greatest to roofs and windows. Roofing materials should be resistant to the pounding of hailstones. Shutters, or preferably

Fig. 14-5 Distribution of computed maximum snow load on a horizontal surface in Canada.

From an article by C. C. Boughner and J. G. Potter, "Snow Cover in Canada," *Weatherwise*, December, 1953, published by the American Meteorological Society.

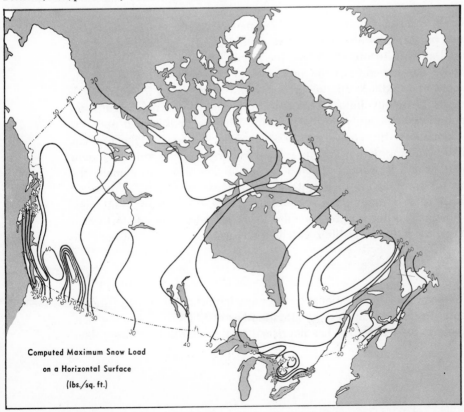

Computed Maximum Snow Load

on a Horizontal Surface

(lbs./sq. ft.)

heavy screens, afford direct protection to windows, although overhangs usually can prevent hail from striking windows beneath. Skylights are inadvisable in areas subject to hailstorms.

The influence of fog on design is closely associated with sunshine. In addition, frequent fogs enhance the danger of moisture damage to building materials and paint. Where air pollution is common, its chemical effects are greater when associated with fog, dew, or frost. Streaking of walls often results from precipitation of dirty fog particles. The choice of paint should be made with these factors in mind.

Lightning is hardly a moisture factor, but it does occur primarily with thunderstorms, and, where they are common, lightning protection should be an integral part of house design. A lightning strike damages house structure and electrical systems and may start a fire. The principle of protection involves provision of a direct and easy passage of the current to earth. Metal lightning rods attached to the highest parts of the roof and heavy cables to conduct the current to the ground serve this purpose. Utility wires, antennas, and other wiring attached to the house should be grounded, preferably on the outside. A *Code for Protection Against Lightning* has been developed by the National Bureau of Standards, giving requirements for adequate protection of houses of various designs.

AIR CONDITIONING

Rarely can site selection, orientation, materials, and design create the desired indoor climate at all times. Air conditioning is the last resort in the over-all attempt to provide a suitable indoor climate. In popular usage, the term has sometimes been restricted to the artificial cooling of the interiors of buildings. In the broader sense used here, it includes all attempts to modify indoor temperature, humidity, air movement, and composition of the air by artificial means. The demands placed upon air conditioning in the control of these elements depend on the outdoor climate, building design and its related factors, and the kind of indoor climate which is wanted. Though many of the principles remain the same, air conditioning of hospital operating rooms is quite a different problem from refrigerating a cold-storage locker. In residential buildings, the functions of different rooms influence requirements for comfort. Most importantly, individuals differ widely in their conception of comfort.

HEATING

Temperature is unquestionably the most important element of indoor climate. In the past much more attention has been given to heating than to cooling, for technology has flourished in the middle latitudes, where cold winters have been a greater problem than hot summers. Merely raising the air temperature in a room does not meet all the requirements for a comfortable environment; humidity and air movement are additional factors affecting the human response to air temperature. The concept of *effective temperature* is employed to combine the effects of air temperature, humidity, and air movement. It is defined as the temperature of calm, saturated air which would elicit the same degree of thermal comfort for a normally clad, sedentary person as that produced by the actual temperature, humidity, and air movement. An increase in air movement lowers the effective temperature; an increase in relative humidity raises it. Because the effective temperature varies with individuals, a composite is derived from the reactions of a number of persons. Figure 14-6 is a comfort chart

Fig. 14-6 ASHRAE Comfort Chart. The dashed lines indicate effective temperatures for different combinations of wet-bulb or dry-bulb temperatures and relative humidity values. For example, the effective temperature line for 80° passes through points representing 80° dry-bulb temperature and 100 per cent relative humidity; 86° and 60 per cent; and 90° and 40 per cent.

Reprinted by permission from *ASHRAE Guide and Data Book 1965.*

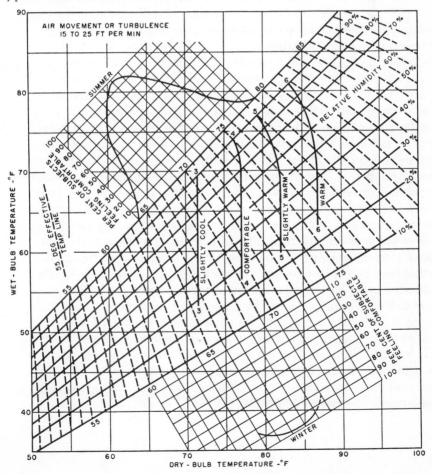

developed by the American Society of Heating, Refrigerating and Air-Conditioning Engineers. It shows combinations of wet-bulb and dry-bulb temperatures and relative humidity values which elicit various subjective responses from individuals who are adjusted to indoor conditions where the normal movement of air is associated with central heating and cooling systems. The chart indicates that nearly all persons feel comfortable indoors at an effective temperature of about 71°F in summer, whereas in winter the most acceptable effective temperature is 67° to 68°F. The effective temperature lines are based on comfort sensations of laboratory subjects in Pittsburgh, Pennsylvania, and do not necessarily apply in colder or warmer climates or among groups of people who are accustomed to other indoor conditions. For example, in Great Britain, where room temperatures are generally lower, the optimum effective temperature in winter is appreciably lower than in the United States. In the tropics comfortable effective temperatures are higher owing to a different pattern of climatic experience and customs in dress and diet.

Heating systems which depend upon forced circulation of air to distribute heat must be appraised in terms of effective temperature rather than simple air temperature. Cool air introduced into a room suffers a decrease in relative humidity upon being heated. Fortunately, the range of comfortable relative humidity is rather wide—between 30 and 70 per cent—so that there is no resulting discomfort, unless the difference between indoor and outdoor temperatures is large. When the indoor relative humidity is too low, water can be evaporated into the air, preferably under control in conjunction with the air conditioning system.

Another factor affecting the feeling of comfort in a room is the transfer of heat by radiation between the body and walls, floor, ceiling, and solid objects such as furniture. The loss of heat by radiation to cold walls may create a sensation of discomfort, even though air temperature is at the theoretical optimum. When wall temperatures are low due to cold weather, it is necessary to keep the indoor air temperature a few degrees higher than the standard in order to compensate for the radiative loss. Conversely, warm surfaces radiate heat to the body independently of the temperature of the intervening air and can maintain comfort, even though air temperature is two or three degrees below the standard. This principle is employed in panel heating, also known as radiant heating, which warms people and objects in the room by radiation from large surfaces (for example, walls and floors) having comparatively low temperatures of 85° to 130°F. Panel heating has the advantage that convective air movement is held to a minimum and heating is much more uniform throughout the room than when smaller, high-temperature heat sources are used.

The gradient between temperatures indoors and those of the outside air determines, to a large extent, what amount of heating is required, for even the best-designed house will lose heat to the exterior by conduction. Evaporation, the escape of heated air, and convective cooling by wind are also factors which need consideration in planning a heating system, however. Wind promotes both convective and evaporational cooling. Direction as well as speed is significant, since a house may be more vulnerable to these types of cooling on one side than on another. A house loses a part of its heat by radiation to cold ground surfaces, other buildings, and to the atmosphere. In the latter instance, clear skies will enhance radiative cooling, especially at night and in winter. Cooling of a house by evaporation occurs primarily during and after precipitation and is increased by low relative humidity as well as wind. Escape of heated air is controlled mainly by features of house design. Faulty ventilating systems often contribute to this loss. Fireplaces create a convection system which draws cool air into the room and carries warm air up the chimney.

Records of the pertinent climatic data are useful in determining the amount of heating required to overcome these cooling processes. Microclimatic observations in the immediate vicinity of a building are better than data from a weather station, which may be in a quite different situation. Nevertheless, regional temperature averages, ranges, frequencies of extremes, and heating degree-days are employed with some success in estimating the required output of a heating plant for a specific building. The term *heating degree-day*, widely used by heating engineers, is defined as a day on which the mean daily temperature is one degree below a certain standard. In the United States, the standard generally used is 65°F. Thus, a mean daily temperature of 60° for a given day would yield 5 heating degree-days. Total heating degree-days for a month, season, or year are found simply by adding the accumulated degree-days for the period. Figure 14-7 is a map of the average annual heating degree-days over Canada and the United States. This index of heating requirements does not take into account cooling by radiation, wind, or evaporation. For more accurate computations, research is needed to develop an index which will combine all cooling factors.

Questions involving the type of heating system, kind of fuel or power, operating costs, and efficiency are primarily problems for the heating engineer, but they have climatic relationships. The design and capacity of a heating system should be such as to meet requirements imposed by weather changes and extremes. Ideally, automatic control mechanisms should have sensitive elements exposed to outdoor as well as indoor conditions in order to avoid a lag in adjustment of the indoor climate. The amount of fuel necessary to operate a system is estimated in terms of the heating requirements, which, in turn, are closely correlated with weather conditions.

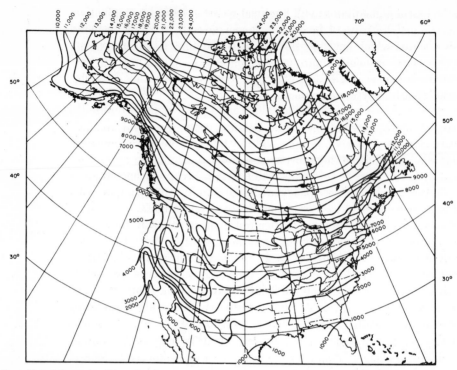

From United States Air Force, Geophysics Research Directorate, *Handbook of Geophysics*, Revised Edition, published by The Macmillan Company, 1960.

Fig. 14-7   Average annual heating degree days in Canada and the United States, base 65° F.

COOLING

Under summer or tropical conditions, the main objective of air conditioning is to reduce the effective temperature. The practical methods include lowering air temperature, lowering relative humidity, and increasing air movement. Design and orientation of a building should be exploited to the fullest to accomplish these aims at the lowest expense. If the desired conditions cannot be obtained, as for example in interior rooms or under extreme temperatures, some form of cooling mechanism may be necessary. Fans speed up air movement and promote cooling by increasing evaporation of skin moisture. At night, cooler outside air can be drawn into a room by exhaust fans placed near outlets at high levels. Adaptations of refrigeration units placed at air intakes actually cool the air and are most effective if combined with fans and used in a room that is closed except for intake and exhaust openings. Comparatively efficient units of this type have been developed which are no more expensive than heating systems. If heat is combined with high relative humidity, the effective temperature may be lowered by passing the air through apparatus which condenses a part of the moisture on cold coils or otherwise dehumidifies it. Air that is too dry can cause skin discomfort and irritate respiratory passages. In hot, dry climates air can be passed over water or through spray to increase its relative humidity and, at the same time, cool it by evaporation.

Cooling degree-days may be used as a basis for determining the amount of energy necessary to reduce the effective temperature of warm air. Although a cooling degree-day may be considered as a day on which the temperature is one degree above a desired base temperature, an expression incorporating a humidity value provides a more satisfactory index of the amount of cooling that will create comfortable conditions.

Under certain circumstances, an air-conditioning system may be called upon to cleanse the air of pollutants. Dust, soot, pollens, and other solid materials are removed by means of filters, by "washing" the air in a spray chamber, or by precipitating the particles on electrically charged screens. Objectionable gases are much more difficult to remove, although some are soluble in water and can be partially controlled in a spray chamber. Chemical modification of gases is practical only under extreme conditions and should not be necessary in a planned residential settlement.

ADDITIONAL READINGS

Aronin, Jeffrey E., *Climate and Architecture*. New York: Reinhold Publishing Corporation, 1953.

Conklin, Groff, *The Weather Conditioned House*. New York: Reinhold Publishing Corporation, 1958.

Housing and Home Finance Agency, Division of Housing Research, *Application of Climatic Data to House Design*. Washington: Government Printing Office, 1954.

Olgyay, Aladar, and Victor Olgyay, *Solar Control and Shading Devices*. Princeton: Princeton University Press, 1957.

Olgyay, Victor, *Design with Climate*. Princeton: Princeton University Press, 1963.

Page, J. K., "The Effect of Town-planning and Architectural Design and Construction on the Microclimatic Environment of Man," in S. W. Tromp, *Medical Biometeorology*. New York: Elsevier Publishing Company, 1963, pp. 655–70.

climate 15
and the human body

Human health, energy, and comfort are affected more by climate than by any other element of the physical environment. Physiological functions of the human body respond to changes in the weather, and the incidence of certain diseases shows a close correlation with the climate and the seasons. Our selection of both amount and type of clothing and food likewise tends to reflect weather and climate. Even our mental and emotional outlook is influenced by the state of the weather and the climate in which we find ourselves.

All human beings, however, do not react to identical climatic conditions in the same way; the relationship is complicated by individual physical differences, age, diet, past climatic experience, and cultural influences. Nor are all individuals equally adaptable to changes in climate. Nevertheless, by virtue of his cultural advancement man is the most adaptable to varying climatic conditions of all the life forms. Climate has probably been blamed for human failure more often than is justified by the facts, especially in the tropics, but it is unquestionably a factor in human efficiency.

Of the climatic elements which affect the human body, the more important ones are temperature, sunshine, and humidity. Wind exerts an influence largely through its effects on skin temperature and body moisture. Atmospheric pressure changes are registered in the circulatory, respiratory, and nervous systems. Such elements as cloudiness, storms, and visibility produce psychological reactions which may ultimately be expressed as physiological disturbances. In combination, the climatic elements constitute the climatic environment that directly influences human well-being.

Air temperature as measured by a thermometer is not, in itself, a wholly reliable index of the temperature the body feels. The body's response to air temperature is affected by the rates of conduction, convection, and radiation of heat away from the body and by cooling due to evaporation at the skin surface and in the respiratory tracts. The resulting temperature effect is known as the *sensible temperature*. It varies not only with the humidity factor and air movement but also from one person to another, and it is, therefore, not measurable by any instrument. However, the sensible temperature and the wet-bulb temperature are approximately the same when the skin is moist and exposed to calm air at normal dry-bulb temperatures, since evaporation will then be the principal cooling process. Thus, under warm conditions, low relative humidity tends to reduce the sensible temperature because the rate of evaporation is increased. High relative humidity, in combination with high air temperature, results in a lowered rate of evaporation and consequently a high sensible temperature. The familiar saying, "It's not the heat; it's the humidity," is not strictly true, for the feeling of oppression which we associate with hot, humid weather is dependent fully as much upon the high temperatures as on the high relative humidity. When air temperatures are low, evaporation from the skin becomes secondary to conduction as a cooling process. Both air movement and high relative humidity increase the rate of conduction away from the body. The sensible temperature is increased in summer and decreased in winter by high relative humidity. But it is decreased in all seasons by increased wind speed.

Attempts to derive an objective index of sensible temperature have been based primarily on air temperature and a moisture factor. Griffith Taylor used mean monthly temperature and rainfall data to plot *hythergraphs* (from *hyetos*, rain and *thermos*, heat) for specific stations. The twelve monthly values are plotted with the mean monthly rainfall as the abcissa and monthly temperature as the ordinate to produce a twelve-sided polygon. (See Figure 15-1.) Superimposed upon the graph is a "comfort frame" which encloses conditions which most Europeans find comfortable. Outside the comfort frame, conditions are characterized as too hot, too wet, too dry, and too cold.

Although readily available in world climatic statistics, rainfall data are not very satisfactory indexes of moisture for assessments of climate in relation to human comfort. Mean wet-bulb temperatures or mean humidity values show a closer correlation with subjective body responses under

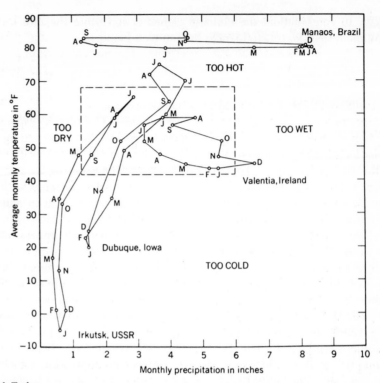

After method of Griffith Taylor.

Fig. 15-1 Hythergraphs for selected stations.

a given combination of temperature and wind conditions. They therefore afford a better basis for determination of the range of conditions that are comfortable to most humans. While the definition of the comfort zone varies with individuals, living habits, physical activity, seasons, and climates, nearly everyone finds conditions uncomfortable or oppressive when wet-bulb temperatures exceed 85°F. Dry-bulb temperatures below 60–65° are experienced as cool or cold by everyone regardless of the relative humidity. Thom has suggested a further refinement of the temperature–moisture relationship at the warm margin of the comfort zone.[*] In his formula, $DI = 0.4(t_d + t_w) + 15$, DI is the discomfort index, t_d the dry-bulb temperature in F°, and t_w the simultaneous wet-bulb temperature. Most people feel discomfort as the index rises above 70; everyone is uncomfortable when the index reaches 79. The comfort zone for a group of people is a generalization based on the comfort zones of the different

[*] E. C. Thom, "The Discomfort Index," *Weatherwise*, 12, 2 (1959), 57–60. The term "temperature-humidity index" has also been used to express this relationship. See "Temperature-Humidity Index," *Daily Weather Map* for August 10, 1960.

people in the group. Individual differences arise from variations in age, state of health, physical activity, type and amount of clothing, psychological factors, and past climatic experience. The normal, or group, reaction, reflects not only the composite of individual responses but also the local climate and the season; hence the comfort zone (that is, the range of comfortable sensible temperatures for the group) depends on climate as well as the characteristics of the group. Because it is based upon generalized statistics, it can tell little of the differing reactions of persons in different stages of acclimatization or of the effects of short-term weather changes.

COOLING POWER

Since the great variety of individual differences makes it impracticable, if not impossible, to obtain measurements of the sensible temperature the concept of *cooling power* has been developed to express the combined effects of air temperature and air movement in more objective terms. With respect to the human body, cooling power may be defined simply as the ability of the air to enhance the loss of body heat. Normal temperature of the human body is about 98°F. This is maintained by body metabolism and depends ultimately upon intake and digestion of food. On the other hand, heat is always being lost in order to keep the body from overheating. Ways in which heat is lost include evaporation of water from the skin, convective loss in moving air, radiation, conduction to objects in contact with the body, evaporation of water in the respiratory passages and lungs, loss due to cold air taken into the lungs, and minor loss to cold food or drink taken into the body. Through the normal range of air temperatures in which most people live, the most effective cooling is achieved by the evaporation of moisture from the skin, and this is the type of cooling over which the body has the greatest control. As activity is stepped up, so is metabolism and the production of heat. The body adjusts by increasing the circulation of blood near the skin and by perspiration, although people differ greatly in their ability to sweat. As long as evaporation can remove the secreted moisture it will have a cooling effect, but if the relative humidity is high and the sweating profuse, a feeling of discomfort develops. Sweat which drops from the body merely represents a loss of water and is not effective in cooling the skin. The most comfortable values of relative humidity lie in the range of 30–70 per cent. Increased speed of air movement along the skin surfaces aids evaporation. At temperatures below about 70°F, evaporation from the skin loses importance as a cooling factor, for the rate of perspiration is reduced. Radiation, conduction, and convection serve to reduce the temperature of exposed skin, but these processes are restricted by clothing. Heat loss from the lungs increases in relative importance as the air temperature decreases to extreme minima. At $-40°F$, the dissipation of body heat through the lungs may account for one-fifth of the total loss. As activity is increased, the volume of air breathed also increases, and, at very low temperatures, damage to the lungs and a serious lowering of body temperature may result.

Several formulas have been devised to express cooling power in terms of observed values of temperature, humidity, and wind speed. The most-used indices of cooling power are derived from special instruments, however. Measurements of skin and body temperatures of living subjects under controlled conditions yield more realistic results and promise, eventually, to furnish the basis for sound conclusions on the reaction of the human body to varying conditions.

As we have seen, the body loses heat through a complex combination of several processes. Temperature and wind speed, which are the primary bases of theoretical cooling power, are only two of the factors in actual sensible temperature, but they are the major factors when the air is cold. Considerable investigation has been carried on to determine the relationship between body heat loss and the combination of air temperature and air movement. Cooling effects due to low temperatures and wind have been called the dry convective cooling power of the atmosphere, or simply *wind chill*. When air temperatures are above that of the body, moving air heats rather than cools the body. The colder the air and the higher the wind speeds, the greater is the loss of body heat. Were it not for the gales frequently encountered, the deterrent effect of low temperatures on high-altitude mountain climbing would not be nearly so great. The chilling produced by a 45-mile-per-hour wind at $20°F$ is about the same as that of wind moving at 5 miles per hour with a temperature of $-20°F$.

CLOTHING AND CLIMATE

With respect to climate, the main purposes served by clothing are: protection against temperature changes and extremes, protection from excessive sunshine, and protection from precipitation. Clothing is also worn to protect the body against physical damage such as abrasion, cutting, or burning. With respect to culture, clothing is worn for adornment, prestige, fashion, custom, and other social reasons which vary from group to group as well as among individuals. Very often, the design and selection of clothing is dictated more by cultural than by climatic factors.

Clothing protects against the cold by trapping still air within its open spaces and in the layer next to the skin. Layers of "dead air" are good insulators because they do not readily conduct heat away from the body. Therefore, the fundamental aim in design of effective clothing for cold

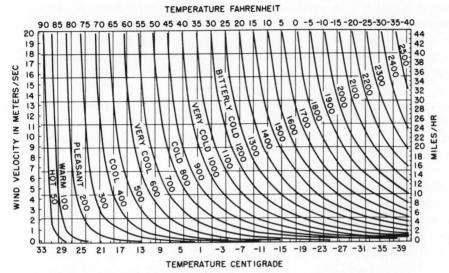

From United States Air Force, Geophysics Research Directorate, *Handbook of Geophysics,* Revised Edition, published by The Macmillan Company, 1960.

Fig. 15-2 Wind chill chart. Curves show rates of cooling in kilogram calories per square meter per hour for different combinations of temperature and wind speed. The cooling rate is based upon a body with neutral skin temperature of 33° C (91.4° F). When the dry convective cooling rate is less than the rate of body heat production, excess heat is removed by evaporation of perspiration. Under conditions of bright sunshine cooling is reduced. The terms denoting relative comfort are based upon individuals at rest.

weather is to provide insulation. Knit or loosely woven woolens are better than cotton cloth with a hard weave, and several thin layers of clothing are better than one heavy layer.

In order to be effective against wind chill, clothing must be reasonably impervious to the passage of air. Wind decreases the insulating capacity of clothing by forcing air into the openings and disturbing the still air. It also destroys the air layers between successive garments and between body and clothing by pressing the clothes against the body. Completely airtight materials are unsatisfactory because they do not provide for ventilation to remove moist air from near the skin. When clothing becomes wet from perspiration it loses much of its insulating power. In cold weather, wet socks are one of the first danger signs of possible freezing. This is one of the reasons for avoiding strenuous exercise in polar climates. Another is the fact that exercise sets up a bellows action in clothing, thus increasing convective heat loss. The ideal material for an outer garment in cold winds is one that will largely restrict the passage of wind but which will "breathe," that is, allow the escape of water vapor. Undergarments should be resilient enough to maintain their insulating properties against the pressure of the wind.

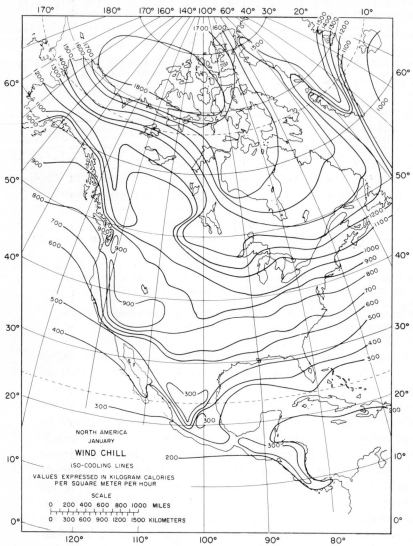

NORTH AMERICA
JANUARY
WIND CHILL
ISO-COOLING LINES

VALUES EXPRESSED IN KILOGRAM CALORIES
PER SQUARE METER PER HOUR

SCALE
0   200 400 600 800 1000 MILES
0   300 600 900 1200 1500 KILOMETERS

From United States Air Force, Geophysics Research Directorate, *Handbook of Geophysics,* Revised Edition, published by The Macmillan Company, 1960.

Fig. 15-3 Wind chill values for North America in January.

A rather obvious method of combating the effects of low temperatures and wind is the use of an electrically heated suit regulated by a thermostat. Heated suits have been used with some success by high-altitude fliers and certain sedentary workers, but they are generally impractical for persons active in the outdoors.

Special provision must be made to protect the eyes against snow blindness in cold climates. Eskimos use goggles with narrow slits that restrict the passage of light. Some form of cover is also advisable to protect the eyelids from the impact of blowing snow.

For protection against heat, clothing should be loose and allow free transfer of heat away from the body. One of the primary functions is to shade the skin from direct rays of the sun. Lightweight and light-colored materials that reflect insolation are best, and they need to be porous to allow maximum air movement adjacent to the skin. The wearing of coats and ties in hot summer weather is justified only by fashion; in terms of applied climatology it is indefensible. For temperatures above that of the body, insulating materials are of some value in preventing overheating. The desert Bedouin finds the same clothing that shields him from extreme insolation in the daytime useful against the cold night air. But in highly humid air, such clothing would be unsuitable. In any case, water vapor in the air absorbs a large proportion of ultraviolet rays so that the danger from that component of the solar spectrum is not so great in humid climates. Head covers in hot weather are especially important to prevent illness due to excessive heat and sunlight. They must permit free ventilation of the head, shade the eyes, and reflect sunlight. Footwear to insulate against hot ground is also necessary in hot climates, especially if the ground is dry. Warm-weather shoes should be porous to allow as much air movement as possible.

Clothing to ward off precipitation is usually of special design and not necessarily effective against accompanying temperatures, which must be combated by other clothing underneath. Completely waterproof garments made of rubber or oiled fabrics have the disadvantage of not allowing the escape of body moisture, and therefore become uncomfortable at any temperature. The so-called showerproof coats allow perspiration to escape but will not ward off heavy, continuous rain. A rain cape allows greater movement of air under its shelter but is more cumbersome when the wearer is working or encounters strong winds. Ideally, the material and the design of rainwear should prevent all rain or melted snow from passing through to the undergarments or body regardless of wind force and at the same time they should allow free escape of evaporated perspiration. For practical purposes, it is necessary to strike a compromise between the ideal and a utilitarian garment that will permit the maximum efficiency of physical activity. Rain clothes suitable for a policeman or sentry may be quite unsatisfactory for more active persons such as loggers. Although experiments in clothing design must take into account the variations and extremes of the weather elements, the type of activity performed by the wearer is also of major importance. There is no such thing as "all-weather" clothing. A great deal of discomfort is endured by persons who fail to modify the amount and type of their apparel to conform to changes in the weather or tendencies in their own heat balance.

WEATHER AND HEALTH

Weather changes and extremes produce a number of influences on human health, some of which result in illnesses arising from direct effects of atmospheric conditions on the body. Temperature extremes are the most common causes of illness brought on by weather. *Heat stroke* occurs when the body is not able to lose heat properly because of high relative humidity and air temperatures above that of the body; it can result in death. Symptoms are fever, nausea, dizziness, and headache. Treatment entails reducing body temperature with cold baths. *Heat exhaustion* is a milder form of heat stroke identified by dizziness, lassitude, and perhaps fainting. It is more common in crowded rooms than in the outdoors. When the body suffers an excessive loss of salts and water in perspiration, *heat cramps* may result. Adequate liquid and salt intake help to prevent heat cramps and also relieve the condition if it develops. Because of changes in metabolism and blood circulation, the appetite and digestion are impaired in hot weather; digestive disorders are more common in summer and in the tropics.

The most common direct effect of low temperatures is *frostbite.* The extremities and the exposed portions of the body are most likely to suffer and the danger is greater with increased movement. Perspiration, especially from the feet, accelerates heat loss as does the accumulation of condensed moisture about the face. Prolonged exposure to low air temperatures can alter the body's heat balance so drastically that death results. The precautions against wind chill, namely, adequate clothing and moderation of physical activity, serve to prevent frostbite. Low temperatures are an aggravating factor in a number of ailments such as arthritis, swollen sinuses, chilblains, and "stiff joints." Sudden lowering of temperature puts a severe strain on persons with cardiac disorders, although there is no evidence that climate directly causes such ailments. Indeed, virtually all physiological functions react in some manner to temperature changes.

Atmospheric pressure and relative humidity changes appear to bear a relation to certain kinds of pains, notably those associated with respiratory infection and muscular aches. The irritation of respiratory passages, which is commonly brought about by dry air, is further enhanced by wind and dust. Temperature and humidity are significant factors in the release of pollens and consequently affect the incidence of allergies. Very dry air is a major contributory cause of chapped skin and it inhibits the healing of sores and wounds.

To the extent that health is a function of nutrition, the influences of weather and climate upon diet indirectly affect human physiology. One facet of the influence results from the availability of different types of food in different climates. More important is the effect on appetite and selection of food. Temperature is the most significant consideration in this respect. Under cold conditions, the body requires a greater food intake to maintain heat; increased amounts of fats and carbohydrates are needed. Vitamins and minerals are, nonetheless, essential. Primitive peoples in the arctic achieve a balanced diet by eating virtually all parts of animals and fish. Men of more sophisticated cultures secure the proper balance through a variety of foods. Nutritional diseases may result from insufficient intake of calories, vitamins, or minerals. Adequate water must also be provided, and where it is obtained from melted snow, the deficiency in minerals has to be made up through foods.

Nutritional requirements in hot climates differ from those in the mid-latitudes in that more salt, water, and certain vitamins are needed. Whether these requirements are met is another question. Suppression of appetite may be a major factor in malnutrition in the tropics. There is some evidence that meat and eggs produced in the tropics are deficient in certain nutrients, notably vitamin B_1, presumably as a result of the effect of heat on the living animals. Still other deficiencies in food can be traced to leaching of tropical soils by heavy rains. Whether humans can improve their heat tolerance by controlling their diet is as yet an unsolved problem.

SUNSHINE AND HEALTH

Besides the obvious relation between sunshine and air temperature, the solar spectrum produces several effects on the human body. Infrared rays are absorbed by the body or clothing and converted to heat, thus offsetting much of the cooling power of the air. It is therefore perfectly natural to seek the shade in hot climates and the sunny exposures in cool climates. The visible part of the spectrum (light) affects mainly the eyes. The intense sunlight of the arid tropics or that reflected off snowfields can cause forms of blindness, headaches, and related discomforts.

Ultraviolet rays are valuable for their ability to form vitamin D in the skin and to devitalize bacteria and germs. These qualities explain in part why many health resorts are found in sunny locations. On the other hand, ultraviolet radiation can cause inflammation of the skin and sunburn to the point of illness. Combined with intense heat, ultraviolet rays are a factor in causing cataract of the eye. When the skin becomes pigmented (tanned) the pigment affords protection against further inflammation, but this adjustment differs greatly with individuals and races. Blonde persons are generally more susceptible to sunburn than those with darker skins.

The psychological reactions to sunshine are much more difficult to recognize—much less measure—than the physiological. Probably everyone longs to see the sun after several days of dark, cloudy weather. The cheering effect of a sunny day after a surfeit of gray skies is no mere illusion. Yet long periods of clear skies and glaring sunshine can induce ennui. Most people prefer change provided that the extremes do not become too great. Tourists and seekers after health regularly flock to sunny climates, especially in winter. A healthy suntan is commonly regarded as the mark of a successful vacation, although it is probably no more important than fresh air, change of scenery, and relaxation in promoting physical and mental well-being.

Tourist centers and resort areas are always proud to advertise whatever favorable sunshine data they can glean from climatic records. It is true that there are some large regional variations in duration of sunshine. Moreover, the intensity of sunlight is of primary significance in its effect on the body. At high latitudes and in the morning and evening hours, the low angle of the sun's rays makes sunlight much less potent. Smog and haze also detract from its power. At high altitudes, the air is much clearer so that solar radiation is more intense. Possible daily sunshine decreases with latitude in winter and increases in summer; the actual average duration varies with the climate, specifically with cloudiness. Figures 15-4 and 15-5 show the distribution of percentage of possible sunshine in the contiguous United States in winter and summer, respectively. It is evident that the drier climates are generally favored with more sunshine, but the claims of Florida are fairly well substantiated, especially in winter.

CLIMATE AND DISEASE

Many factors, such as cleanliness, nutrition, physical activity, and social contacts, act together in determining the incidence, severity, and spread of a disease. Climate is another factor, one which varies in importance according to the disease in question and the physiological and cultural characteristics of potential or actual victims. The climatic relations of all the common diseases cannot be discussed here; rather the aim will be to outline briefly the broad influences which weather and climate may exert

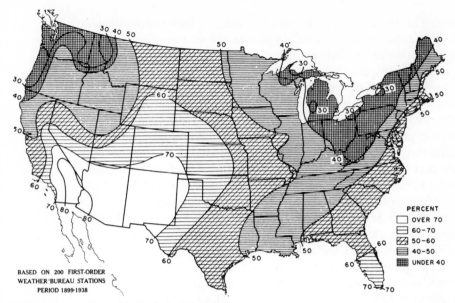

Fig. 15-4 Percentage of possible sunshine in winter (December–February) in the contiguous United States.

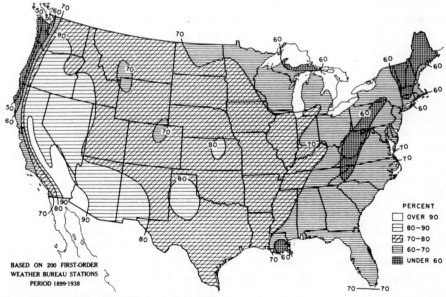

Fig. 15-5 Percentage of possible sunshine in summer (June–August) in the contiguous United States.

on disease. The relations are extremely complex. Much cooperation in research among specialists in branches of climatology and of medicine is necessary to determine the role of climate in causing, modifying, or facilitating recovery from a specific disease.

There are two basic aspects of climatic influence on disease: the relationship of climatic factors to disease organisms or their carriers and the effects of weather and climate on the body's resistance. Many diseases are associated primarily with certain climates or with a season because of the temperature, moisture, and other requirements of the microscopic organisms that cause them. A number of parasites which attack humans are confined to the tropics and subtropics, where they find suitable conditions of warmth and moisture. Scarlet fever is virtually unknown in the tropics, whereas leprosy flourishes there. Some diseases depend upon intermediate carriers and are restricted to environments favorable to those carriers. Yellow fever and malaria, for example, are spread by certain species of mosquitoes that thrive in tropical climates. Rocky Mountain spotted fever occurs in the summer when the tick carriers are active.

Many diseases follow a distinct seasonal pattern. (See Figure 15-6.) Pneumonia and influenza are common seasonal diseases of the mid-latitudes; their greater incidence in winter is probably due to the lowered resistance in the upper respiratory tract at that season. Measles and scarlet fever cases are most numerous in spring. Infectious diseases occurring chiefly in winter and spring are much more widespread among the population than those that have their maximum frequency in summer and autumn.

Few diseases are caused directly by climate. A given combination of climatic elements may modify the metabolic rate, respiration, circulation, and the mental outlook of the individual so as to either strengthen or weaken his resistance to disease. Chilling, for example, lowers body resistance to most illnesses. Even in the tropics, sudden decreases in air temperature may be followed by outbreaks of sickness. Persons who fail to adjust their rate of physical activity in high or low temperatures often suffer some degree of exhaustion and a predisposition to disease. Extremely low relative humidity and winds will fill the air with dust and irritate the respiratory passages, making them more susceptible to infection. Wind is also a factor in hay fever, since its speed and direction govern the transport of allergens. Occurrences of smog are frequently accompanied by an increase in respiratory disorders. The strain imposed by high-altitude pressures enhances development of a number of diseases.

Favorable atmospheric conditions can assist the body in warding off disease and in promoting recovery if the disease is contracted. Fresh air, sunshine, mild temperatures, and moderate relative humidity all have

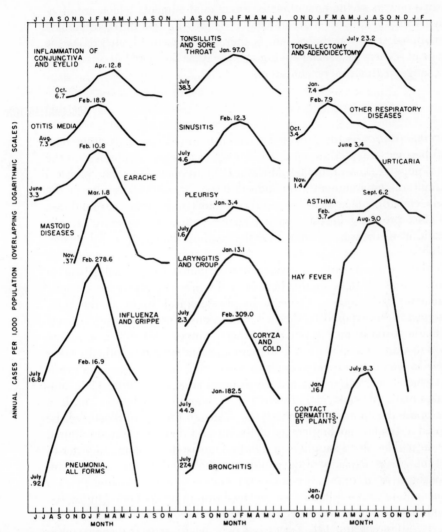

ANNUAL CASES PER 1,000 POPULATION (OVERLAPPING LOGARITHMIC SCALES)

INFLAMMATION OF CONJUNCTIVA AND EYELID Apr. 12.8
Oct. 6.7 Feb. 18.9

OTITIS MEDIA Aug. 7.3 Feb. 10.8

EARACHE June 3.3 Mar. 1.8

MASTOID DISEASES Nov. .37 Feb. 278.6

INFLUENZA AND GRIPPE

PNEUMONIA, ALL FORMS July 16.8 Feb. 16.9 July .92

TONSILLITIS AND SORE THROAT Jan. 97.0 July 38.3

SINUSITIS Feb. 12.3 July 4.6

PLEURISY Jan. 3.4 July 1.6

LARYNGITIS AND CROUP Jan. 13.1

CORYZA AND COLD July 2.3 Feb. 309.0

BRONCHITIS Jan. 182.5 July 44.9 July 27.4

TONSILLECTOMY AND ADENOIDECTOMY July 23.2 Jan. 7.4 Feb. 7.9

OTHER RESPIRATORY DISEASES Oct. 3.4 June 3.4

URTICARIA Nov. 1.4 Sept. 6.2

ASTHMA Feb. 3.7 Aug. 9.0

HAY FEVER

CONTACT DERMATITIS, BY PLANTS Jan. .16 July 8.3 Jan. .40

MONTH

From U.S. Department of Health, Education, and Welfare, *Long-Time Trends in Illness and Medical Care,* Public Health Monograph No. 48. (Washington: Government Printing Office, 1957).

Fig. 15-6   Relative seasonal variation in incidence of respiratory diseases and allergies.

therapeutic values. Fresh air and sunlight have long been recognized in the treatment of tuberculosis. Rickets and certain skin diseases respond to sunshine. The change of climate often prescribed for various kinds of illness is beneficial only if it is accompanied by rest, improved mental outlook, proper medical care, and good food. Moving to a location with a quite different climate may introduce problems that offset any actual curative powers of the new climate. Functional ailments which are obviously psychosomatic often are alleviated by moving to a different climate if emotional strain on the patient is thereby reduced. In such cases the change of scenery and social environment may be far more important than the change in atmospheric conditions.

ACCLIMATIZATION

Acclimatization is the process by which man (and animals other than man) becomes adapted to an unfamiliar set of climatic conditions. In the broad, popular sense it implies adjustment to all phases of a new physical and cultural environment, and indeed it is difficult to distinguish the purely climatic phenomena from other factors in strange surroundings. The chief problems in adjustment to a new climate frequently are not climatic at all but arise from homesickness, boredom, or social incompatibility.

In the narrower sense of physiological climatology, acclimatization entails actual changes in the human body brought about by climatic influences. It connotes a decrease in physiological strain as the body continues to be exposed to the new conditions. Temporary adjustments are made to daily and seasonal weather changes. But, when a person moves to a different climate, a more permanent adaptation gradually takes place. As would be expected from the foregoing sections, temperature is the element of greatest significance in acclimatization. Table 15-1 summarizes major physiological responses to high and low temperatures. In a hot climate the cutaneous blood vessels dilate so that more blood will be exposed to the low cooling power of the air and thereby maintain normal body heat. The blood supply is gradually increased in volume in order to meet the greater capacity of the capillary vessels, and it undergoes chemical changes. A larger number of sweat glands become active and there is a concomitant increase in thirst. Oxygen consumption declines. During the period of adjustment there may be physical discomfort, lack of energy, and an indifferent appetite. Persons in poor health may find their condition worsened by the strain. They are well advised to make the shift between two widely differing climates in gradual stages. In some cases a satisfactory stage of acclimatization may never be achieved.

Acclimatization is not so clearly defined in a cold climate as in a warm one. Residents of cold climates cannot withstand continuous exposure to extreme cold but they are less affected than nonacclimatized persons. Repeated contact with cold air leads to a decrease in the flow of blood through constricted capillaries near the skin. Blood viscosity and the number of circulating white cells increase; the liver enlarges; appetite and oxygen consumption both increase in a natural attempt to provide more

TABLE 15-1

Responses of the Human Body to Thermal Stress*

At low temperatures	*At high temperatures*
TEMPERATURE REGULATION	
Constriction of skin blood vessels	Dilation of skin blood vessels
Concentration of blood	Dilution of blood
Flection to reduce surface exposure	Extension to increase exposure
Increased muscle tone	Decreased muscle tone
Shivering	Sweating
Inclination to increase activity	Inclination to decrease activity
CONSEQUENT DISTURBANCES	
Increased urine volume	Decreased urine volume
	Mobilization of tissue fluid
	Thirst and dehydration
Danger of inadequate blood supply to exposed parts; frostbite	Reduced blood supply to brain; dizziness; nausea; fainting
	Reduced chloride balance; heat cramps
Discomfort leading to neuroses	Discomfort leading to neuroses
Increased appetite	Decreased appetite
FAILURE OF REGULATION	
Falling body temperature	Rising body temperature
Drowsiness	Impaired heat regulating center
Cessation of heartbeat and respiration	Failure of nervous regulation; cessation of breathing

° Adapted from Douglas H. K. Lee, "Proprioclimates of Man and Domestic Animals," *Arid Zone Research X, Climatology* (Paris, UNESCO, 1958), p. 108.

body heat. Sweating does not occur so readily and tends to be confined to certain skin areas, especially the palms, soles of the feet, and the axillae.

At high altitudes, adjustment must be made to both the lower temperatures and low pressure. Increased pulse and respiratory rates are the principal modifications which occur to offset the reduced oxygen supply. People who live at high elevations develop greater lung capacity and larger chest cavities than residents of lowlands.

Although the human body is capable of withstanding remarkable extremes of climate, it functions best under circumstances where there is a reasonable degree of comfort and freedom from strain on vital organs. In general, children and healthy persons are more adaptable to a change of climate than the aged or infirm. Fortunately, it is possible to lighten the strain of acclimatization by proper diet, clothing and housing, and by control of physical activity. Many questions concerning these and other factors which modify climatic influences still remain to be answered by research in physiological climatology and related fields.

ADDITIONAL READINGS

Buettner, Konrad J. K., "Human Aspects of Bioclimatological Classification," in *Biometeorology*. London: Pergamon Press, 1962, pp. 91–98.

Castellani, Aldo, *Climate and Acclimatization*, 2nd ed. London: J. Bale Sons and Curnow, 1938.

Lee, Douglas H. K., and Hoyt Lemons, "Clothing for Global Man," *Geog. Rev.*, 39, 2 (1949), 181–213.

Licht, Sidney, ed., *Medical Climatology*. New Haven: Elizabeth Licht, Publisher, 1964.

Monge, Carlos, *Acclimatization in the Andes*. Baltimore: Johns Hopkins University Press, 1948.

Provins, K. A., and C. R. Bell, "The Effects of Heat on Human Performance," in *Biometeorology*. London: Pergamon Press, 1962, pp. 359–65.

Renbourn, E. T., "Tropical Clothing, A Physiological Appreciation," in *Biometeorology*. London: Pergamon Press, 1962, pp. 91–98.

Stephenson, P. M., "An Index of Comfort for Singapore," *Met. Mag.*, 92, 1096 (1963), 338–45.

Thom, E. C., "The Discomfort Index," *Weatherwise*, 12, 2 (1959), 57–60.

Tromp, S. W., and others, *Medical Biometeorology*. New York: Elsevier Publishing Company, 1963.

Winslow, C. E. A., and L. P. Herrington, *Temperature and Human Life*. Princeton: Princeton University Press, 1949.

climatic change and cycles 16

In the preceding chapters we have examined some of the many relationships between climate and man's activities on Earth. For the most part, we have been concerned with the contemporary climatic pattern and its effects on life forms. Weather changes which collectively make up climate are taken for granted; in fact, the only constant thing about weather is change. No one denies the existence of diurnal and seasonal weather cycles, and cyclonic storms form and dissipate with a certain regularity. But there are several kinds of evidence that point to fluctuations in climate as well. The implications of a rapid secular change in climate are so numerous and so awful as to defy the imagination. Agriculture, industry, business, and all the rest of man's activities would need to undergo dramatic adjustment if the climate of the world changed very greatly during a generation. Gradual upward trends in mean temperature of only a few degrees could alter the vegetation pattern of the world, and major migrations of animal life might occur. Some plant and animal species might be extinguished. Continued warming in the polar regions would surely melt the existing icecaps and raise the level of the oceans. Some people become alarmed at the prospect of the latter development, for it is calculated that the water in icecaps and glaciers could raise sea level by 175 to 250 feet. Studies so far indicate that increased temperatures on the order of those experienced in the last century would have to prevail for 10,000 years to melt all the polar ice.

For the purpose of examining past climatic changes, periods of time and the associated evidence may be divided into three general categories:

1. Periods on the order of millions of years—*paleoclimates.*

2. Periods in the last several thousands of years, whose significance may be interpreted in terms of life forms of the recent geologic epochs. These are in the province of *geochronology.*

3. Historic time, the latter part of which incorporates the period of climatic records.

PALEOCLIMATOLOGY

There seem to be no grounds whatsoever for doubting that the climate of the earth has changed markedly since its creation about three billion years ago. The evidence becomes much more satisfactory as we work down through the eons, however. For lack of detailed data, we will dismiss the first two and one-half billion years at once. C. E. P. Brooks, a British climatologist, has set down a paleoclimatological calendar that shows a 150-million-year period of high temperatures through the Cambrian, Ordovician, and Silurian eras, that is, between 500 and 350 million years ago. (See Figure 16-1.) Since then, the general temperature trend has been downward, although there may have been significantly large variations. The lowest temperatures occurred during the last ice age, the Pleistocene era. The general cooling over the past 500 million years might be explained simply in terms of the gradual cooling of the earth from its earliest state as a ball of hot gases and fire-rock, if it were not for the evidence of definite fluctuations. Let us examine some of the evidence and the theories that attempt to explain it.

Paleoclimatology is based largely on evidence from rocks. It reaches back to Pre-Cambrian times about 500 million years ago and borrows its dating techniques from paleontology. Fossils and sedimentary deposits are studied to determine the approximate duration and geographical extent of temperature and moisture conditions. Since there are fossil evidences of life on Earth during the entire span of time covered by paleoclimatic studies, it follows that the climatic fluctuations must fall within the limits for sea life and probably for plant life on land as well. Thus, sustained temperatures of, for example, 200° or −100°F are most unlikely. To explain climatic changes since the Pre-Cambrian, several types of theories have been developed. One of the simplest and most persistent holds that receipt of solar energy by the earth has varied because of changes in energy release from the sun's surface, that is, the solar constant has changed. It was once accepted as fact that increases in net radiation would warm the earth's atmosphere and account for the melting of continental glaciers. G. C. Simpson, a British meteorologist, theorizes, however, that moderately increased insolation would permit higher moisture content in the air and cause stronger latitudinal transfer of air, thus producing heavier precipitation in polar areas. Increased summer cloudiness would inhibit melting of the accumulated snow and ice. Less insolation would lead to a weaker general circulation and a consequent reduction of precipitation. Thus, paradoxically, a lowering of the atmosphere's mean temperature might cause a retreat of glaciers, whereas a temperature increase would cause them to advance.*

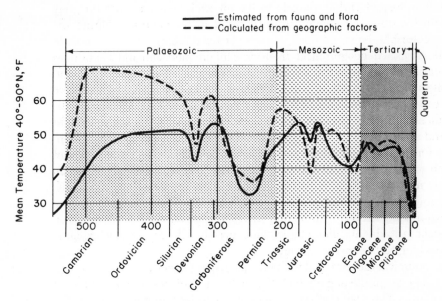

From an article by C. E. P. Brooks, "Geological and Historical Aspects of Climatic Change," *Compendium of Meteorology,* 1951, published by the American Meteorological Society through support extended by the Geophysics Research Division, Air Force Cambridge Research Center, Air Research and Development Command. Reproduced by permission.

Fig. 16-1 Variations in temperature in geologic time.

The oceanic circulation and the general circulation of the atmosphere are important factors in redistributing energy and maintaining the heat balance of the earth. Changes in the mean patterns of energy transport due to these systems could explain past climatic trends.

Another theory lends importance to volcanic activity, maintaining that volcanic ash clouded the sky at various times in the past and decreased the amount of insolation reaching the earth's surface. Closely allied theories postulate variations in amounts of atmospheric gases which ab-

* George C. Simpson, "Further Studies in World Climate," *Quart. Journ. Roy. Met. Soc.,* 83, 358 (Oct., 1957), 459–81.

sorb radiation. Carbon dioxide, water vapor, and ozone all tend to produce a greenhouse effect by allowing short-wave radiation to pass through to the earth but subsequently absorbing much of the long-wave radiation from the earth. An increase in carbon dioxide in particular is thought to produce slightly higher temperatures. Increases in the amount of carbon dioxide in the atmosphere in the past might have resulted from extensive plant decay and volcanic eruptions. Plass suggests that, more recently, the burning of large quantities of coal and oil has been adding more than six billion tons of carbon dioxide to the air each year and that this may explain the observed general upward trend in temperatures during the past century.*

The so-called geographical theories explain paleoclimatic change on the basis of changes in the world distribution of land and water area and changes in the elevation of land. We know, for example, that temperature decreases at the rate of about 3.3°F per thousand feet increase in altitude. If similar lapse rates prevailed in past geologic eras, changes in the height of land associated with major crustal upheavals might be directly responsible for regional glaciation and alteration in vegetative cover, both of which are important clues to past climates. Structural changes in ocean basins might significantly alter oceanic circulation and thus affect the heat and moisture balances. If one accepts the theories relating to shifting of major land masses (continental drift), the position of a continent in different latitudes at different geological periods offers a possible explanation of long-term climatic change.

Astronomical theories deal with four principal effects:

1. Changes in the angle which the earth's axis makes with the plane of the ecliptic. This would affect the seasons, especially in polar regions.

2. Changes in the eccentricity of the earth's orbit. Resulting variations in the mean distance from Earth to Sun could affect average temperatures on the earth.

3. Precession of the equinoxes. This refers to the regular change in the time when the earth is at a given distance from the sun. At present, the earth is closest to the sun in the Northern Hemisphere winter (about January 1st). About 10,500 years ago the Northern Hemisphere winter came at a time of the year when the earth was farthest from the sun. Other things being equal, winters should have been colder, and summers hotter, than they are now. In the Southern Hemisphere the reverse applies.

4. Shifting of the earth on its polar axis. The supposition is that the geographic poles migrated to their present locations from what are now lower latitudes, there being a corresponding shift of the attendant climatic conditions.

* Gilbert N. Plass, "Carbon Dioxide and Climate," *Am. Scientist*, 44, 3 (July, 1956), 311.

Thus far explanations of paleoclimatic change have not advanced beyond the stage of theory. It is unlikely that there is one ultimate cause of climatic change; rather several factors act together. One factor may be primarily responsible for short-term changes, but several factors may complement one another in producing secular trends or long-term fluctuations.

GEOCHRONOLOGY

The longest and most acceptable climatic record for the last few thousand years is found in *varves*, the annual layers of silt and clay deposited on the bottoms of lakes and ponds that are subject to freezing in winter and thawing in summer. The only material being deposited in a frozen lake is the fine clay which is held in suspension; the surface ice prevents other materials from entering. When thawing begins, fresh water and new sediments are introduced. Presumably because of climatic fluctuations, no two successive years have the same thickness of deposits. Thus, parallel dating of lake beds in the same region is possible through correlation of the thickness of the varves. Varves cannot be formed under glaciers because of the necessity for annual freezing and thawing, and, for this reason, a comparison of lake beds in once-glaciated areas enables geochronologists to determine accurately the dates of recession of glaciers. About 13,700 years are represented in the varve records of Scandinavia, where the oldest varves are in the south and the newest in the north, making it relatively easy to trace the retreat of the last ice sheet.

A second technique of geochronology is based on the annual increment of tree growth and is termed *dendrochronology*. Records in tree rings go back about 3000 years in living trees, but study of fossil trees and ruins may extend this back another 1000 years or more. A close relationship between growth rings and annual rainfall was demonstrated by A. E. Douglass in the southwestern United States, where fluctuations in precipitation have been fairly well charted. Studies by Douglass and others at the University of Arizona show four interesting features of climate over the past 850 years in the interior plains and plateaus of the United States and Canada. Almost the entire thirteenth century was dry, and the fourteenth was stormy. The last quarter of the sixteenth century was the driest period in the last 650 years. About 1670 there developed a remarkable change from long-term irregular fluctuations to shorter ones of only twenty or twenty-five years. The drought years just before 1900 and in the 1930's are examples of the latter cycles.

Dendrochronology has also been employed to date the comparatively recent advance and retreat of glaciers. Examination of cross sections of trees partly pushed over by glacier ice along the margins of its maximum

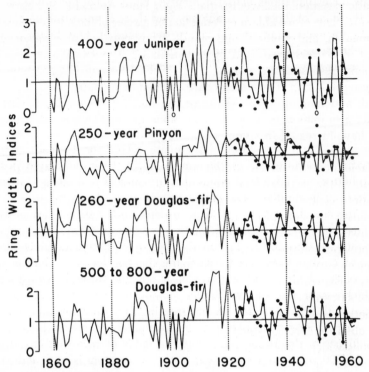

Fritts, Smith, and Stokes, "The Biological Model for Paleoclimatic Interpretation of Mesa Verde Tree-Ring Series," in "Contributions of The Wetherill Mesa Project," assembled by Douglas Osborne. *Memoir of the Society for American Archaeology*, Series No. 19 (Salt Lake City, Oct., 1965).

Fig. 16-2 Tree-ring chronologies from selected group of trees in Mesa Verde National Park, 1860–1963. The dots represent ring-width indices computed from local weather records. The agreement of the dot patterns with the measured ring-widths indicates the closeness of relationship between growth increments and climate.

advance but left alive in a tilted position reveals the exact year of the maximum advance of the glacier. While the tree was erect growth rings were concentric, but after tilting due to ice pressure the rings lost their symmetry. Narrow growth rings give evidence of periods when ice was close enough to a tree which remained erect to affect the temperature.*

One of the most fruitful fields of investigation into recent climatic changes is glaciology. Consistent trends in precipitation and temperature are reflected in the advance and retreat of glaciers. Most of the direct study of glacier fluctuations and climatic relationships has been carried out in the twentieth century. The foremost student of glaciation and

* Donald B. Lawrence, "Estimating Dates of Recent Glacier Advances and Recession Rates by Studying Tree Growth Layers," *Trans. Am. Geophys. Un.*, 31, 2 (April, 1950), 243–48.

climatic variation, the Swedish glaciologist Hans Ahlmann, first correlated measurements of ice ablation (reduction of glacier volume by evaporation, sublimation, and melting) and simultaneous weather observations. The extent of glaciers is affected by annual snowfall, duration and degree of temperatures above the melting point, and the amounts of incoming and outgoing radiation. These factors are affected, in turn, by cloudiness, wind speed, and humidity. The shape of the basin or valley containing the glacier also influences its movement; some glaciers cannot advance until they have increased in volume sufficiently to surmount topographic barriers.

Glacier observations by Ahlmann and his followers have shown that the climate of the arctic and subarctic became warmer in the first part of the twentieth century, the major change being in the higher latitudes. This trend may now be undergoing a reversal, however. At mid-century Pacific Northwest glaciers began to advance at rates greater than at any time in the previous hundred years. In the Cascade and Olympic Mountains advances varying from 10 to 350 feet annually were charted by aerial surveys. Expeditions to the Taku Glacier in southeastern Alaska in the early 1950's found that it was also advancing.

Another technique of geochronology utilizes *pedogenic* criteria, that is, data obtained through study of the development of soils. Examination of old soils which have been buried in river flood plains, along fluctuating lake shores, or under windblown deposits furnish some evidence of the nature of past climates, for climate is the most important factor in soil formation. A generalized method of climatic dating is possible through analysis of peat bogs. The most effective analysis has been accomplished by means of pollen studies. Under the microscope, pollen grains serve as identification of the plant associations that prevailed at various stages during the peat accumulation. The succession of plant types in peat shows that there have been several long climatic waves since the last glacial period, that is during the last 30,000 to 35,000 years. In the British Isles it has been possible to correlate peat studies with the cultural development of man.

Fossils of animals as well as plants aid in piecing together the history of climate over the past few thousand years. The bones of arctic mammals have been found far south of their present limits of distribution, and well-preserved remains of extinct animals occur in glacial ice in the Arctic. The mastodon is perhaps the best-known example. In western Europe remains of desert and steppe mammals have been unearthed.

A series of techniques not specifically illuminating the degree of climatic change but nevertheless invaluable in determining dates in the distant past are the methods of radioisotope dating. Because so many of the theories concerning past climates depend on a time correlation of two or more phenomena, radioisotope dating is especially useful in checking various types of evidence. The most important method for climatic study is the carbon-14 method discovered by W. F. Libby. It is applicable to plant and animal remains and even to carbon dioxide in air and water. Other methods depending on various radioisotopes have been developed to date rocks, and they extend dating backward virtually to the beginning of the earth's history.

CLIMATE DURING RECORDED HISTORY

The main purpose of considering the climates of thousands and millions of years ago is to determine whether there are any consistent trends or cycles which can be identified and projected into the future. The key to this secret has not been found. The best hope seems to lie in the examination of present climates and the climates of the past few centuries. During the entire period of written and inferred human history the data of geochronology overlap archaeology, documentation, and instrumental records to serve as a double check on supposed climatic changes. It might be naïvely assumed that recorded human history would lend itself readily to analysis of past climates. On the contrary, documental climatology deals largely with manuscripts written for purposes other than climatic description, and interpretation is difficult. Problems arise from changes in the calendar and lack of continuity of historical records for a given location. Writers have had a tendency to mention droughts, severe storms, or other extremes and generally have neglected periods of relatively stable climatic conditions. Nevertheless, records of crop yields or crop failures, of floods, and of migrations of people furnish useful evidence of the possible influence of a changing climate. Correlation with the geochronological evidence yields the following pattern since the birth of Christ.

As would be expected, there are more data for Europe than for other parts of the world. During the first century of the Christian era, the pattern of precipitation in Europe and the Mediterranean resembled that of today. This was followed by a wetter period ending about A.D. 350. The fifth century was dry in Europe and probably also in North America, where many of the western lakes dried up completely. In the seventh century Europe was both warm and dry. There was heavy traffic over passes in the Alps that are now filled with ice. Tree rings show a dry period in the United States at this time, and the Nile floods were low. The ninth century was wetter again, followed by warm, dry conditions in the tenth and eleventh centuries. Greenland was settled in 984 in a time of relatively favorable climatic conditions only to be abandoned about A.D. 1410. The first half of the thirteenth century was stormy in the North Sea and North Atlantic. A drought from A.D. 1276 to 1299 is believed to have driven the cliff dwellers out of Mesa Verde in Colorado. The fourteenth century was cold and snowy in northern Europe and northern North America. The Aztecs settled Mexico in 1325, when lakes were at higher levels than today. The early sixteenth, late eighteenth, and early nineteenth centuries were also wetter periods. Since the middle of the nineteenth century, Northern Hemisphere glaciers have retreated to their sixteenth-century positions, and sea level has risen by two or three inches.

RECENT CLIMATIC TRENDS

Finally, let us consider climatic changes in the very short period for which we have instrumental records. At the beginning of the nineteenth century there were five places in the eastern United States and twelve in Europe where satisfactory weather observations were being taken. Not until 1876 did the climatic record include any significant weather records taken at sea. Like all other forms of historical data relating to weather and climate, instrumental records fade away rapidly into the past, but instrumental climatology was fairly well established by 1850. One would expect that records of instrumental observations would bring an end to speculation on recent climatic changes. The statistician, treating the data objectively, should provide the facts on trends in temperature and precipitation, the two elements for which records are most abundant. But climatic records are not readily subjected to objective study. In the first place, weather observers are subject to human failings, and even small errors affect calculations that may involve equally small trends. The exposure and height above ground of instruments also materially affect results. Removal of a weather station to a new location practically destroys the value of its records for purposes of studying climatic change. But, even if a station remains in the same location for a century, the changes in vegetation, drainage, surrounding buildings, and atmospheric pollution are likely to produce a greater effect on the climatic record than any true climatic changes. Thus, very careful checking and comparison of climatic records is necessary to detect climatic fluctuations. In order to overcome some of the problems arising from changes in station location or in local environment the United States Weather Bureau has established a *climatological benchmark network*. (See Figure 16-3.) Chosen for their representative sites, continuity of past records, and promise of future permanency, these benchmark stations will provide basic data against which other climatic records can be checked.

Statistical analyses of temperature records in the United States show that, in the first half of the twentieth century, there was a general warming

Courtesy U.S. Weather Bureau.

Fig. 16-3 Climatological benchmark station network in the contiguous United States.

trend, but that the change was small. The average for many stations and for the year increased by less than 1F°, reaching a peak about 1940. Winter temperatures increased slightly more than those for summer months. However, the trend was not the same in all parts of the country. In the Pacific Northwest, northern Rockies, and the northern Great Plains, mean temperatures of the winter months decreased or showed little change.

World temperature trends were upward from about 1885 to 1940, the amount of rise being about 2F° in winter and less than 1F° for the year. Greatest increases occurred in winter over Arctic regions, where rises in excess of 6F° characterized the period 1917–1937. After 1940 the rate of increase slowed.* Low-latitude regions have experienced comparable trends. There, average temperatures have possibly increased slightly.

Additional information on climatic trends, partly inferred from evidence other than climatic records, indicates a greater warming in eastern Greenland and northern Scandinavia, where winters have been averaging 7 to 13F° higher than in 1900. This warming is expressed in the oceans also; codfish are found farther north in the Atlantic than ever before in history. Mounting evidence points to a correlation between climatic fluctuations and circulation systems in the oceans. But the relationship is reciprocal. Climatic changes may be reflected in water temperatures and ultimately

* John Conover, "Climatic Changes as Interpreted from Meteorological Data," in *Climatic Change,* ed. Harlow Shapley (Cambridge, Mass.: Harvard University Press, 1953), p. 288.

in oceanic circulation, which in turn affects the climate. It thus becomes difficult to distinguish between cause and effect.

Our heating systems, transportation, eating habits, clothing fashions, agricultural methods, and many other phases of our culture have so changed in the past generation that we cannot trust ourselves to evaluate climatic changes on the basis of personal reaction. It is entirely possible that the deep snow that reached Grandfather's knees in his youth impressed him more than the same depth would now because he had to walk to school and perhaps help with the farm chores morning and night regardless of the weather. Even where the average temperatures have risen as much as 2° or 3°, the change would go unnoticed by most individuals. Any lowering of heating bills is more likely due to improved insulation and heating systems than to climatic changes, and the increased use of cooling systems for homes and public buildings has resulted from

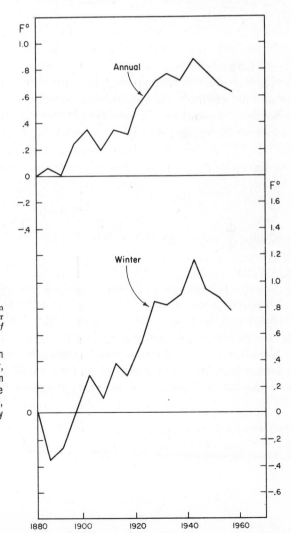

After J. Murray Mitchell, Jr., "On the World-Wide Pattern of Secular Temperature Change," in *Changes of Climate* (Paris: UNESCO, 1963).

Fig. 16-4 Trends of world mean temperatures, annual and winter, 1880–1960. Curves are based on successive five-year means relative to the 1880–1884 five-year period, using stations distributed as evenly as possible over the world.

their greater availability at moderate cost rather than because of a distinctly warmer climate.

CLIMATIC CYCLES

Although it seems clear that there have been climatic fluctuations in historic times, there is much less certainty about the regularity of climatic cycles. Even the well-recognized daily and seasonal cycles vary in length by large percentages. Daily maximums of temperature, for example, rarely succeed one another at intervals of exactly twenty-four hours. At high latitudes the daily cycle takes on a character much different in summer than in winter. The annual cycle often has seasons that are early or late; January and July are by no means always the extreme months in middle and high latitudes. The reversal of the monsoon in southern and eastern Asia is generally regarded as an annual phenomenon, but it occurs at widely varying dates. A great many supposed cycles with periods longer than one year have been uncovered by statistical manipulation, but none has a dependable regularity, and most are barely distinguishable from chance variations over long periods.

The leading theories that attempt to explain the climatic changes of recent decades attribute the variations to the effect of solar disturbances on atmospheric conditions. Examination of the variation in the number of sunspots (solar storms) over several decades indicates a sunspot cycle of about 11.3 years, but the cycle has been as short as seven years and as long as sixteen years. An increase in sunspot numbers has generally been accompanied by cooler, wetter weather and greater storminess; a decrease is associated with warmer, drier conditions. Thus, greater solar activity seems to produce lower earth temperatures. The explanation of this paradox may lie in the effects of variable insolation on the general atmospheric circulation.

No completely acceptable theory has been evolved to explain how solar variations are translated into climatic cycles, if indeed they are. One of the explanations relates solar disturbances to the general circulation of the atmosphere, and it has been elaborated by Willett.[*] Short bursts of ultraviolet energy and corpuscular energy emitted from the sun are believed to be absorbed in the upper atmosphere, and the resulting temperature variations at high levels are expressed as pressure differences and alterations in the "normal" pattern of general circulation in the troposphere. According to Willett, the vigorous bursts of ultraviolet radiation have their

[*] Hurd C. Willett, "Atmospheric and Oceanic Circulation as Factors in Glacial-Interglacial Changes of Climate," in *Climatic Change*, ed. Harlow Shapley (Cambridge, Mass.: Harvard University Press, 1953), pp. 51–71.

greatest effect in low latitudes, leaving the polar regions relatively cold and producing a zonal pattern of general circulation something like the hypothetical planetary winds and pressure zones. Corpuscular energy consists chiefly of charged protons and electrons, and its maximum emission comes with solar disturbances. Corpuscular bursts are diverted by the earth's magnetic field toward the magnetic poles and thus tend to heat the upper air of the polar regions more than the tropics, especially in winter. As a consequence, the zonal circulation is disrupted and there is a greater latitudinal transfer of air with accompanying storminess and temperature extremes. This theory does not require an appreciable change in average atmospheric temperatures but rather a modification of the general circulation wherein zonal circulation is interspersed with periods of nonzonal air movement and weather extremes.

FORECASTING CLIMATE

The logical extension of any proven secular or cyclical trend in climate is a forecast of future climatic conditions. Past cyclical changes offer one of the best possibilities for predicting future climate. So far no climatic cycles longer than one year have been well enough established to permit acceptable forecasts for several years in advance. If the apparent cyclical trends of the past two centuries repeat themselves, the last half of the twentieth century should be cooler and wetter than the first half in the United States. As always, one should expect years in which the weather departs from the average. Forecasts of climate, like weather forecasts, cannot be verified until the end of the forecast period, but data for checking theories of climatic change indirectly may be available sooner. For example, meteorological and solar observatories beyond the outer limits of the atmosphere could provide information on the fluctuations in ultraviolet and corpuscular energy.

If we accept Plass' theory concerning the effects of increasing carbon dioxide in the atmosphere, the over-all trend in climate during the next several decades should be toward warmer temperatures. The theory does not rule out the possibility of cyclical temperature variations superimposed upon the long-term trend, however. Coal and oil may be replaced by atomic energy within the near future. If that happens, the theoretical acceleration in atmospheric heating will be halted. Any forecast which depends on cultural factors must take into account changing technology, which is fully as difficult to forecast as natural phenomena. And who is to say that volcanic eruptions, geomorphic processes, astronomical or solar effects, or some other suspect or unknown cause of climatic change will not produce even more marked climatic fluctuations in the next few centuries than have occurred in the past?

ADDITIONAL READINGS

Abbot, C. G., *Solar Variation and the Weather*, Smithsonian Misc. Coll., 146, 3. Washington: Smithsonian Institution, 1963.

Brooks, C. E. P., *Climate Through the Ages*. New York: McGraw-Hill Book Company, 1949.

Callendar, G. S., "Temperature Fluctuations and Trends over the Earth," *Quart. Journ. Roy. Met. Soc.*, 87, 371 (1961), 1–12.

Changes of Climate, Arid Zone Research XX. Paris: UNESCO, 1963.

Curry, Leslie, "Climatic Change as a Random Series," *Ann. Assoc. Am. Geogrs.*, 52, 1 (1962), 21–31.

Dzerdzeyevskiy, B. L., "General Circulation of the Atmosphere as an Essential Link in the System: Sun-Climatic Change," *Soviet Geog.*, 5, 3 (1964), 37–52.

Ewing, M., and W. L. Donn, "A Theory of Ice Ages, I," *Science*, 123 (1956), 1061–66.

————, "A Theory of Ice Ages, II," *Science*, 127 (1958), 1157–62.

Fritts, Harold C., "Tree-Ring Evidence for Climatic Changes in Western North America," *Mon. Wea. Rev.*, 93, 7 (1965), 421–43.

Nairn, A. E. M., *Descriptive Palaeoclimatology*. New York: Interscience Publishers, 1961.

Namais, Jerome, "Short-Period Climatic Fluctuations," *Science*, 147, 3659 (1965), 696–706.

Öpik, Ernst J., "Climate and the Changing Sun," *Scient. Am.*, 198, 6 (1958), 85–92.

Plass, Gilbert N., "Carbon Dioxide and Climate," *Scient. Am.*, 201 (1959), 41–47.

Polozova, L. G., and Ye. S. Rubinshteyn, "Contemporary Climatic Change," *Soviet Geog.*, 5, 3 (1964), 3–37.

Schwarzbach, Martin, *Climates of the Past, An Introduction to Paleoclimatology*, translated and edited by Richard O. Muir. Princeton, N.J.: D. Van Nostrand Co., Inc., 1963.

Shapley, Harlow, ed., *Climatic Change*. Cambridge, Mass.: Harvard University Press, 1953.

APPENDICES

bibliography

Books on Meteorology and Climatology

Blair, Thomas A., and Robert C. Fite, *Weather Elements*, 5th ed. Englewood Cliffs, N.J.: Prentice-Hall, Inc., 1965.

Blumenstock, David I., *Ocean of Air*. New Brunswick, N.J.: Rutgers University Press, 1959.

Byers, Horace R., *General Meteorology*, 3rd ed. New York: McGraw-Hill Book Company, 1959.

Fleagle, Robert G., and Joost A. Businger, *An Introduction to Atmospheric Physics*. New York: Academic Press, 1963.

Geiger, Rudolf, *The Climate Near the Ground*, rev. ed. Cambridge, Mass.: Harvard University Press, 1957.

Gordon, A. H., *Elements of Dynamic Meteorology*. Princeton, N.J.: D. Van Nostrand Co., Inc., 1962.

Hare, F. Kenneth, *The Restless Atmosphere*. London: Hutchinson & Co. [Publishers], Ltd., 1953.

Haltiner, George J., and Frank L. Martin, *Dynamical and Physical Meteorology*. New York: McGraw-Hill Book Company, 1957.

Haurwitz, Bernhard, and James M. Austin, *Climatology*. New York, McGraw-Hill Book Company, 1944.

Haynes, B. C., *Techniques of Observing the Weather*. New York: John Wiley & Sons, Inc., 1947.

Huschke, Ralph E., *Glossary of Meteorology*. Boston: American Meteorological Society, 1959.

Kendrew, W. G., *The Climates of the Continents*, 5th ed. London: Oxford University Press, 1961.

Koeppe, Clarence E., and George C. DeLong, *Weather and Climate*. New York: McGraw-Hill Book Company, 1958.

Landsberg, Helmut, *Physical Climatology*, 2nd ed. Dubois, Pa.: Gray Printing Company, Inc., 1958.

385

Malone, T. F., ed., *Compendium of Meteorology*. Boston: American Meteorological Society, 1951.

McIntosh, D. H., *Meteorological Glossary*. London: H. M. Stationery Office, 1963.

Miller, A. Austin, *Climatology*. New York: E. P. Dutton and Co., 1953.

Neuberger, Hans H., and F. Briscoe Stephens, *Weather and Man*. Englewood Cliffs, N.J.: Prentice-Hall, Inc., 1948.

Petterssen, Sverre, *Introduction to Meteorology*, 2nd ed. New York: McGraw-Hill Book Company, 1958.

Riehl, Herbert, *Introduction to the Atmosphere*. New York: McGraw-Hill Book Company, 1965.

Tables of Temperature, Relative Humidity, and Precipitation for the World. London: H. M. Stationery Office, 1958.

Taylor, George F., *Elementary Meteorology*. Englewood Cliffs, N.J.: Prentice-Hall, Inc., 1956.

Trewartha, Glenn T., *An Introduction to Climate*, 3rd ed. New York: McGraw-Hill Book Company, 1954.

United States Air Force, Air Research and Development Command, *Handbook of Geophysics*, rev. ed. New York: The Macmillan Company, 1960.

United States Department of Commerce, Weather Bureau, *World Weather Records, 1941–50*. Washington: Government Printing Office, 1959.

Willett, Hurd C., and Frederick Sanders, *Descriptive Meteorology*, 2nd ed. New York: Academic Press, 1959.

Periodicals

Agricultural Meteorology. Amsterdam: Elsevier Publishing Company, quarterly.

Atmosphere, Bulletin of Canadian Meteorology. Montreal: Canadian Branch, Royal Meteorological Society, quarterly.

Canadian Weather Review. Ottawa: Canadian Meteorological Service, monthly.

Climatological Data (separates for 47 sections of the United States). Washington: U.S. Weather Bureau, monthly and annual summaries.

Daily Weather Map. Washington: U.S. Weather Bureau. Subscriptions through Superintendent of Documents, Government Printing Office.

Journal of Applied Meteorology. Boston: American Meteorological Society, bimonthly.

Journal of Atmospheric Sciences (formerly *Journal of Meteorology*). Boston: American Meteorological Society, bimonthly.

Local Climatological Data (daily and monthly data for many Weather Bureau stations). Washington: U.S. Weather Bureau, monthly and annually.

Meteorological Magazine. London: H. M. Stationery Office, monthly.

Monthly Climatic Data for the World. Washington: U.S. Weather Bureau, monthly.

Monthly Weather Review. Washington: U.S. Weather Bureau, monthly.

Quarterly Journal of the Royal Meteorological Society. London: Royal Meteorological Society, quarterly.

The Marine Observer. London: H. M. Stationery Office, quarterly.

The Mariner's Weather Log. Washington: U.S. Weather Bureau, bimonthly.

Weather. London: Royal Meteorological Society, monthly.

Weatherwise. Boston: American Meteorological Society, bimonthly.

World Meteorological Organization Bulletin. Geneva, Switzerland: World Meteorological Organization, quarterly.

abridged
meteorological
tables

Fahrenheit Equivalents of Centigrade Temperatures
(The column on the left contains 10 C° intervals; the single digits across the top are
1 C° intervals. Thus, 10°C = 50°F; 11°C = 51.8°F; 12°C = 53.6°F; and so on.)

Centigrade	Fahrenheit									
	0	1	2	3	4	5	6	7	8	9
—50	—58.0	—59.8	—61.6	—63.4	—65.2	—67.0	—68.8	—70.6	—72.4	—74.2
—40	—40.0	—41.8	—43.6	—45.4	—47.2	—49.0	—50.8	—52.6	—54.4	—56.2
—30	—22.0	—23.8	—25.6	—27.4	—29.2	—31.0	—32.8	—34.6	—36.4	—38.2
—20	— 4.0	— 5.8	— 7.6	— 9.4	—11.2	—13.0	—14.8	—16.6	—18.4	—20.2
—10	14.0	12.2	10.4	8.6	6.8	5.0	3.2	1.4	— 0.4	— 2.2
— 0	32.0	30.2	28.4	26.6	24.8	23.0	21.2	19.4	17.6	15.8
+ 0	32.0	33.8	35.6	37.4	39.2	41.0	42.8	44.6	46.4	48.2
10	50.0	51.8	53.6	55.4	57.2	59.0	60.8	62.6	64.4	66.2
20	68.0	69.8	71.6	73.4	75.2	77.0	78.8	80.6	82.4	84.2
30	86.0	87.8	89.6	91.4	93.2	95.0	96.8	98.6	100.4	102.2
40	104.0	105.8	107.6	109.4	111.2	113.0	114.8	116.6	118.4	120.2

TABLE A-2

Centigrade Equivalents of Fahrenheit Temperatures
(The column on the left contains 10 F° intervals; the single digits across the top
are 1 F° intervals. Thus, 10°F = −12.2°C; 11°F = −11.7°C;
12°F = −11.1°C; and so on.)

Fahrenheit					Centigrade					
	0	1	2	3	4	5	6	7	8	9
−100	−73.3	−73.9	−74.4	−75.0	−75.6	−76.1	−76.7	−77.2	−77.8	−78.3
− 90	−67.8	−68.3	−68.9	−69.4	−70.0	−70.6	−71.1	−71.7	−72.2	−72.8
− 80	−62.2	−62.8	−63.3	−63.9	−64.4	−65.0	−65.6	−66.1	−66.7	−67.2
− 70	−56.7	−57.2	−57.8	−58.3	−58.9	−59.4	−60.0	−60.6	−61.1	−61.7
− 60	−51.1	−51.7	−52.2	−52.8	−53.3	−53.9	−54.4	−55.0	−55.6	−56.1
− 50	−45.6	−46.1	−46.7	−47.2	−47.8	−48.3	−48.9	−49.4	−50.0	−50.6
− 40	−40.0	−40.6	−41.1	−41.7	−42.2	−42.8	−43.3	−43.9	−44.4	−45.0
− 30	−34.4	−35.0	−35.6	−36.1	−36.7	−37.2	−37.8	−38.3	−38.9	−39.4
− 20	−28.9	−29.4	−30.0	−30.6	−31.1	−31.7	−32.2	−32.8	−33.3	−33.9
− 10	−23.3	−23.9	−24.4	−25.0	−25.6	−26.1	−26.7	−27.2	−27.8	−28.3
− 0	−17.8	−18.3	−18.9	−19.4	−20.0	−20.6	−21.1	−21.7	−22.2	−22.8
+ 0	−17.8	−17.2	−16.7	−16.1	−15.6	−15.0	−14.4	−13.9	−13.3	−12.8
10	−12.2	−11.7	−11.1	−10.6	−10.0	− 9.4	− 8.9	− 8.3	− 7.8	− 7.2
20	− 6.7	− 6.1	− 5.6	− 5.0	− 4.4	− 3.9	− 3.3	− 2.8	− 2.2	− 1.7
30	− 1.1	− 0.6	0.0	0.6	1.1	1.7	2.2	2.8	3.3	3.9
40	4.4	5.0	5.6	6.1	6.7	7.2	7.8	8.3	8.9	9.4
50	10.0	10.6	11.1	11.7	12.2	12.8	13.3	13.9	14.4	15.0
60	15.6	16.1	16.7	17.2	17.8	18.3	18.9	19.4	20.0	20.6
70	21.1	21.7	22.2	22.8	23.3	23.9	24.4	25.0	25.6	26.1
80	26.7	27.2	27.8	28.3	28.9	29.4	30.0	30.6	31.1	31.7
90	32.2	32.8	33.3	33.9	34.4	35.0	35.6	36.1	36.7	37.2
100	37.8	38.3	38.9	39.4	40.0	40.6	41.1	41.7	42.2	42.8
110	43.3	43.9	44.4	45.0	45.6	46.1	46.7	47.2	47.8	48.3

TABLE A-3

Millibar Equivalents of Inches of Mercury

Inches					Millibars					
	.0	.1	.2	.3	.4	.5	.6	.7	.8	.9
15	508	511	515	518	521	524	528	532	535	538
16	542	545	549	552	555	559	562	565	569	572
17	576	579	582	586	589	593	596	599	603	606
18	610	613	616	620	623	626	630	633	637	640
19	643	647	650	654	657	660	664	667	670	674
20	677	681	684	687	691	694	698	701	704	708
21	711	714	718	721	725	728	731	735	738	742
22	745	748	752	755	759	762	765	769	772	775
23	779	782	786	789	792	796	799	803	806	809
24	813	816	819	823	826	830	833	836	840	843
25	847	850	853	857	860	863	867	870	874	877
26	880	884	887	891	894	897	901	904	908	911
27	914	918	921	924	928	931	935	938	941	945
28	948	952	955	958	962	965	968	972	975	979
29	982	985	989	992	996	999	1002	1006	1009	1012
30	1016	1019	1023	1026	1029	1033	1036	1040	1043	1046
31	1050	1053	1057	1060	1063	1067	1070	1073	1077	1080

Dry-bulb temp.	Saturation vapor press.	Wet-bulb depression										
		1	2	3	4	5	6	7	8	9	10	11
10	0.0631	5	—2	—10	—27							
12	0.0699	7	2	—6	—19							
14	0.0772	10	5	—2	—12	—33						
16	0.0850	12	7	1	—7	—20						
18	0.0933	14	10	5	—2	—13	—37					
20	0.1026	16	12	8	2	—7	—21					
22	0.113	19	15	11	5	—2	—12	—36				
24	0.124	21	17	13	9	2	—6	—20				
26	0.126	23	20	16	12	7	—1	—11	—32			
28	0.150	25	22	19	15	10	4	—4	—17			
30	0.164	27	25	21	18	14	8	2	—7	—25		
32	0.180	30	27	24	21	17	12	7	—1	—12	—42	
34	0.195	32	29	26	23	20	16	11	5	—3	—17	
36	0.211	34	31	29	26	23	19	15	10	3	—6	—25
38	0.228	36	33	31	28	25	22	18	14	8	1	—10
40	0.247	38	35	33	30	28	25	21	18	13	7	—1
42	0.266	40	38	35	33	30	27	24	21	17	12	6
44	0.287	42	40	37	35	32	30	27	24	20	16	11
46	0.310	44	42	40	37	35	32	29	27	23	20	15
48	0.334	46	44	42	40	37	35	32	29	26	23	19
50	0.360	48	46	44	42	40	37	34	32	29	26	22
52	0.387	50	48	46	44	42	40	37	34	32	29	26
54	0.417	52	50	48	46	44	42	40	37	34	32	29
56	0.448	54	53	51	49	47	44	42	40	37	34	32
58	0.482	56	55	53	51	49	47	45	42	40	37	35
60	0.517	58	57	55	53	51	49	47	45	43	40	38
62	0.555	60	59	57	55	53	52	50	47	45	43	40
64	0.595	62	61	59	57	56	54	52	50	48	46	43
66	0.638	64	63	61	60	58	56	54	52	50	48	46
68	0.684	67	65	63	62	60	58	57	55	53	51	49
70	0.732	69	67	65	64	62	61	59	57	55	53	51
72	0.783	71	69	68	66	64	63	61	59	58	56	54
74	0.838	73	71	70	68	67	65	63	62	60	58	56
76	0.896	75	73	72	70	69	67	66	64	62	60	59
78	0.957	77	75	74	72	71	69	68	66	64	63	61
80	1.022	79	77	76	74	73	72	70	68	67	65	63
82	1.091	81	79	78	77	75	74	72	71	69	67	66
84	1.163	83	81	80	79	77	76	74	73	71	70	68
86	1.241	85	83	82	81	79	78	76	75	73	72	70
88	1.322	87	85	84	83	81	80	79	77	76	74	73
90	1.408	89	87	86	85	83	82	81	79	78	76	75
92	1.499	91	89	88	87	86	84	83	81	80	79	77
94	1.595	93	92	90	89	88	86	85	84	82	81	79
96	1.696	95	94	92	91	90	88	87	86	84	83	82
98	1.803	97	96	94	93	92	90	89	88	87	85	84
100	1.916	99	98	96	95	94	93	91	90	89	87	86

TABLE A-4

Dew Point Temperature
(30.0 Inches of Mercury)

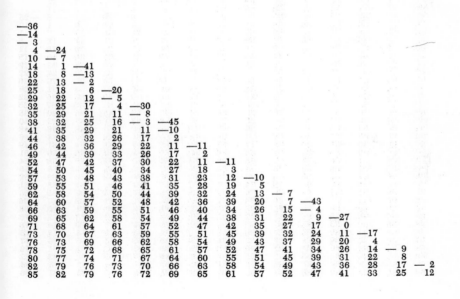

12	14	16	18	20	22	24	26	28	30	32	34	36	38	40
-36														
-14														
-3														
4	-24													
10	-7													
14	1	-41												
18	8	-13												
22	13	-2												
25	18	6	-20											
29	22	12	-5											
32	25	17	4	-30										
35	29	21	11	-8										
38	32	25	16	-3	-45									
41	35	29	21	11	-10									
44	38	32	26	17	2									
46	42	36	29	22	11	-11								
49	44	39	33	26	17	2								
52	47	42	37	30	22	11	-11							
54	50	45	40	34	27	18	3							
57	53	48	43	38	31	23	12	-10						
59	55	51	46	41	35	28	19	5						
62	58	54	50	44	39	32	24	13	-7					
64	60	57	52	48	42	36	29	20	7	-43				
66	63	59	55	51	46	40	34	26	15	-4				
69	65	62	58	54	49	44	38	31	22	9	-27			
71	68	64	61	57	52	47	42	35	27	17	0			
73	70	67	63	59	55	51	45	39	32	24	11	-17		
76	73	69	66	62	58	54	49	43	37	29	20	4		
78	75	72	68	65	61	57	52	47	41	34	26	14	-9	
80	77	74	71	67	64	60	55	51	45	39	31	22	8	
82	79	76	73	70	66	63	58	54	49	43	36	28	17	-2
85	82	79	76	72	69	65	61	57	52	47	41	33	25	12

Dry-bulb temp.	1	2	3	4	5	6	7	8	9	10	11	12	13	14
					Wet-bulb Depression									
10	78	56	34	13										
12	80	59	39	19										
14	81	62	44	26	8									
16	82	65	48	31	14									
18	84	68	52	36	20	5								
20	85	70	55	40	26	12								
22	86	71	58	44	31	17	4							
24	87	73	60	47	35	22	10							
26	87	75	63	51	39	27	16	4						
28	88	76	65	54	43	32	21	10						
30	89	78	67	56	46	36	26	16	6					
32	89	79	69	59	49	39	30	20	11	2				
34	90	81	71	62	52	43	34	25	16	8				
36	91	82	73	64	55	46	38	29	21	13	5			
38	91	83	75	66	58	50	42	33	25	17	10	2		
40	92	83	75	68	60	52	45	37	29	22	15	7		
42	92	85	77	69	62	55	47	40	33	26	19	12	5	
44	93	85	78	71	63	56	49	43	36	30	23	16	10	4
46	93	86	79	72	65	58	52	45	39	32	26	20	14	8
48	93	86	79	73	66	60	54	47	41	35	29	23	18	12
50	93	87	80	74	67	61	55	49	43	38	32	27	21	16
52	94	87	81	75	69	63	57	51	46	40	35	29	24	19
54	94	88	82	76	70	64	59	53	48	42	37	32	27	22
56	94	88	82	76	71	65	60	55	50	44	39	34	30	25
58	94	88	83	77	72	66	61	56	51	46	41	37	32	27
60	94	89	83	78	73	68	63	58	53	48	43	39	34	30
62	94	89	84	79	74	69	64	59	54	50	45	41	36	32
64	95	90	84	79	74	70	65	60	56	51	47	43	38	34
66	95	90	85	80	75	71	66	61	57	53	48	44	40	36
68	95	90	85	80	76	71	67	62	58	54	50	46	42	38
70	95	90	86	81	77	72	68	64	59	55	51	48	44	40
72	95	91	86	82	77	73	69	65	61	57	53	49	45	42
74	95	91	86	82	78	74	69	65	61	58	54	50	47	43
76	96	91	87	82	78	74	70	66	62	59	55	51	48	44
78	96	91	87	83	79	75	71	67	63	60	56	53	49	46
80	96	91	87	83	79	75	72	68	64	61	57	54	50	47
82	96	92	88	84	80	76	72	69	65	61	58	55	51	48
84	96	92	88	84	80	76	73	69	66	62	59	56	52	49
86	96	92	88	84	81	77	73	70	66	63	60	57	53	50
88	96	92	88	85	81	77	74	70	67	64	61	57	54	51
90	96	92	89	85	81	78	74	71	68	65	61	58	55	52
92	96	92	89	85	82	78	75	72	68	65	62	59	56	53
94	96	93	89	85	82	79	75	72	69	66	63	60	57	54
96	96	93	89	86	82	79	76	73	69	66	63	61	58	55
98	96	93	89	86	83	79	76	73	70	67	64	61	58	56
100	96	93	89	86	83	80	77	73	70	68	65	62	59	56

TABLE A-5

Relative Humidity in Per Cent
(*30.0 Inches of Mercury*)

15	16	18	20	22	24	26	28	30	32	34	36	38	40
2													
7	1												
10	5												
14	9												
17	12	3											
20	16	7											
23	18	10	1										
26	21	13	5										
28	24	16	8	1									
30	26	18	11	4									
32	29	21	14	7									
34	31	23	16	10	3								
36	33	25	19	12	6								
38	34	28	21	15	9	3							
39	36	29	23	17	11	5							
41	38	31	25	19	13	8	3						
43	39	33	27	21	16	10	5						
44	41	35	29	23	18	12	7	3					
45	42	36	30	25	20	14	10	5	3				
46	43	37	32	26	21	16	12	7	5	1			
47	44	39	33	28	23	18	14	9	7	3			
48	46	40	35	30	25	20	15	11	9	5	1		
49	47	41	36	31	26	22	17	13	9	5	3		
50	48	42	37	32	28	23	19	15	11	7	3		
51	49	43	38	33	29	24	20	16	12	9	5	1	
52	50	44	39	35	30	26	22	18	14	10	7	3	
53	50	45	40	36	32	27	23	19	15	12	8	5	2
54	51	46	41	37	33	28	24	21	17	13	10	7	4

TABLE A-6

Supplementary Climatic Data

T: Temperature in degrees Fahrenheit
P: Precipitation in inches

AFRICA

		J	F	M	A	M	J	J	A	S	O	N	D	Yr.
Accra, Ghana	T	80	81	82	82	81	79	77	76	77	79	81	81	80
	P	0.6	1.3	2.2	3.2	5.6	7.0	1.8	0.6	1.4	2.5	1.4	0.9	28.5
Addis Ababa, Ethiopia	T	59	61	63	63	63	61	59	59	61	60	58	57	60
	P	0.5	1.5	2.6	3.4	3.4	5.4	11.0	11.8	7.5	0.8	0.6	0.2	48.7
Algiers, Algeria	T	54	55	58	62	66	72	77	78	75	68	61	56	65
	P	4.4	3.3	2.9	1.6	1.8	0.6	0.1	0.2	1.6	3.1	5.1	5.4	30.0
Beira, Mozambique	T	82	82	80	78	73	70	68	70	73	79	79	80	76
	P	10.9	8.4	10.1	4.2	2.2	1.3	1.2	1.1	0.8	5.2	5.3	9.2	59.9
Bulawayo, Southern Rhodesia	T	71	70	69	62	61	57	57	61	67	72	72	71	67
	P	5.6	4.3	3.3	0.7	0.4	0.1	T	T	0.2	0.8	3.2	4.8	23.4
Capetown, South Africa	T	71	71	69	64	60	57	55	57	58	62	66	69	63
	P	0.7	0.6	0.9	1.9	3.7	4.3	3.7	3.3	2.3	1.6	1.1	0.8	24.7
Durban, South Africa	T	75	75	74	71	66	63	62	63	66	68	71	73	69
	P	4.3	4.8	5.1	3.0	2.0	1.3	1.1	1.5	2.8	4.3	4.8	4.7	39.7
Freetown, Sierra Leone	T	80	81	82	82	82	81	79	78	79	80	80	81	80
	P	0.5	0.1	0.5	2.2	6.3	11.9	35.2	35.5	24.0	12.2	5.2	1.6	135.2

		J	F	M	A	M	J	J	A	S	O	N	D	Yr.
Kano, Nigeria	T	71	75	83	88	87	83	79	78	79	81	77	72	80
	P	T	T	0.1	0.4	2.7	4.6	8.1	12.2	5.6	0.5	T	0.0	35.1
Mombasa, Kenya	T	81	82	83	82	79	77	76	76	77	79	80	81	78
	P	1.0	0.7	2.5	7.7	12.6	4.7	3.5	2.5	2.5	3.4	3.8	2.4	47.3
Stanleyville, The Congo	T	78	78	78	79	78	77	75	75	76	77	76	77	77
	P	2.1	3.3	7.0	6.2	5.4	4.5	5.2	6.5	7.2	8.6	7.8	3.3	67.1
Tamatave, Madagascar	T	80	80	79	77	74	71	70	70	71	74	77	79	75
	P	14.4	14.8	17.8	15.7	10.4	11.1	11.9	8.0	5.2	3.9	4.6	10.3	128.2
ASIA														
Ankara, Turkey	T	31	34	41	51	61	65	72	73	65	56	47	36	53
	P	1.3	1.2	1.3	1.3	1.9	1.0	0.5	0.4	0.7	0.9	1.2	1.9	13.6
Astrakhan, U.S.S.R.	T	19	23	33	48	64	73	77	74	63	49	36	27	48
	P	0.5	0.5	0.4	0.6	0.6	0.8	0.5	0.4	0.6	0.4	0.6	0.6	6.4
Baghdad, Iraq	T	49	53	59	71	82	89	93	93	87	76	64	53	73
	P	0.9	1.0	1.1	0.5	0.1	T	T	T	T	0.1	0.8	1.0	5.5
Bangkok, Thailand	T	78	81	84	86	85	83	83	83	82	81	79	77	82
	P	0.3	0.8	1.4	2.3	7.8	6.3	6.3	6.9	12.0	8.1	2.6	0.2	55.0
Bombay, India	T	75	75	79	82	85	84	81	80	80	82	81	78	80
	P	0.1	0.1	0.1	T	0.7	19.1	24.3	13.4	10.4	2.5	0.5	0.1	71.2
Hankow, China	T	40	42	50	62	71	80	86	86	76	67	55	44	63
	P	1.8	1.9	3.8	6.0	6.5	9.6	7.1	3.8	2.8	3.2	1.9	1.1	49.5
Inchon, Korea	T	26	29	38	50	59	68	75	77	68	58	43	30	52
	P	0.8	0.7	1.2	2.6	3.3	3.9	10.9	8.8	4.3	1.6	1.6	1.1	40.8
Jakarta, Indonesia	T	79	79	80	81	81	80	80	80	81	80	80	79	80
	P	11.7	13.5	8.4	5.6	4.3	3.6	0.4	1.5	2.8	4.5	5.7	7.6	71.3
Kashgar, China	T	22	31	45	59	69	76	80	78	70	57	41	27	55
	P	0.6	0.1	0.5	0.2	0.3	0.2	0.4	0.3	0.1	0.1	0.2	0.3	3.2

		J	F	M	A	M	J	J	A	S	O	N	D	Yr.
Irkutsk, U.S.S.R.	T	-6	-1	13	31	44	56	60	58	46	31	11	-4	28
	P	0.5	0.4	0.3	0.6	1.3	2.2	3.1	2.8	1.7	0.7	0.6	0.6	14.9
Lhasa, Tibet (12,090 ft.)	T	28	33	41	47	54	62	61	60	58	48	39	32	47
	P	T	0.5	0.3	0.2	1.0	2.5	4.8	3.5	2.6	0.5	0.1	0.0	15.9
Manila, Philippines	T	77	78	81	83	84	83	81	81	81	81	79	78	81
	P	0.9	0.5	0.7	1.3	5.1	10.0	17.0	16.6	14.0	7.6	5.7	2.6	82.0
Mukden, Manchuria	T	11	17	32	49	62	72	78	76	63	49	31	15	46
	P	0.3	0.3	0.7	1.1	2.7	3.3	7.2	6.7	2.5	1.4	1.1	0.6	27.9
New Delhi, India	T	57	62	72	82	92	92	88	86	84	79	68	59	77
	P	0.9	0.7	0.5	0.3	0.5	2.9	7.1	6.8	4.6	0.4	0.1	0.4	25.2
Peiping, China	T	25	29	42	56	69	75	80	77	70	56	39	29	54
	P	0.1	0.2	0.2	0.6	1.5	3.4	8.3	6.1	2.5	0.7	0.3	0.1	24.1
Shanghai, China	T	39	40	47	58	68	74	82	82	74	65	54	44	61
	P	1.9	2.3	3.3	3.7	3.7	7.1	5.8	5.6	5.1	2.8	2.0	1.4	44.7
Tbilisi, U.S.S.R.	T	32	38	43	52	61	69	74	74	65	56	44	37	54
	P	0.7	0.8	1.3	1.6	3.6	3.1	2.2	1.7	1.9	1.3	2.0	1.2	21.4
Verkhoyansk, U.S.S.R.	T	-58	-48	-26	4	32	54	56	49	35	4	-35	-54	1
	P	0.2	0.2	0.1	0.2	0.3	0.9	1.1	1.0	0.5	0.3	0.3	0.2	5.3

AUSTRALIA AND NEW ZEALAND

		J	F	M	A	M	J	J	A	S	O	N	D	Yr.
Alice Springs, Northern Territory	T	83	82	76	67	59	54	53	58	65	73	75	82	69
	P	1.7	1.3	1.1	0.4	0.6	0.5	0.3	0.3	0.3	0.7	1.2	1.5	9.9
Auckland, New Zealand	T	66	66	64	61	56	53	51	52	54	57	60	63	59
	P	3.1	3.7	3.2	3.8	5.0	5.4	5.7	4.6	4.0	4.0	3.5	3.1	49.1
Brisbane, Queensland	T	77	76	74	70	65	60	58	60	65	70	73	76	69
	P	6.4	6.3	5.7	3.7	2.8	2.6	2.2	1.9	1.9	2.5	3.7	5.0	44.7
Christchurch, New Zealand	T	61	61	58	53	48	43	42	44	48	53	56	60	52
	P	2.2	1.7	1.9	1.9	2.6	2.6	2.7	1.9	1.8	1.7	1.9	2.2	25.1

	J	F	M	A	M	J	J	A	S	O	N	D	Yr.
Dunedin, New Zealand	T												
	58	58	55	52	47	44	42	44	48	50	53	56	51
	P												
	3.4	2.8	3.0	2.8	3.2	3.2	3.1	3.0	2.7	3.0	3.2	3.5	36.9
Perth, Western Australia	T												
	74	74	71	66	61	57	55	56	58	61	66	71	64
	P												
	0.3	0.4	0.8	1.7	5.1	7.1	6.7	5.7	3.4	2.2	0.8	0.5	34.7
Sydney, New South Wales	T												
	71	71	69	64	59	54	53	55	59	63	67	70	63
	P												
	3.5	4.0	5.0	5.3	5.0	4.6	4.6	3.0	2.9	2.8	2.9	2.9	46.5
Wellington, New Zealand	T												
	62	62	60	57	52	49	47	48	51	54	56	60	55
	P												
	3.2	3.2	3.2	3.8	4.6	4.6	5.4	4.6	3.8	4.0	3.5	3.5	47.4
Wyndham, Western Australia	T												
	88	88	87	86	81	77	75	79	84	88	89	89	84
	P												
	7.3	6.0	4.6	0.8	0.2	0.2	0.2	T	0.1	0.4	2.0	4.1	25.9

EUROPE

	J	F	M	A	M	J	J	A	S	O	N	D	Yr.
Athens, Greece	T												
	48	49	53	59	68	76	81	81	74	67	58	51	64
	P												
	2.2	1.5	1.4	0.8	0.8	0.6	0.2	0.4	0.6	1.7	2.8	2.7	15.7
Berlin, Germany	T												
	30	32	39	46	55	60	64	63	57	48	38	33	47
	P												
	1.9	1.3	1.5	1.7	1.9	2.3	3.1	2.2	1.9	1.7	1.7	1.9	23.1
Edinburgh, Scotland	T												
	39	39	41	44	49	55	58	58	54	48	43	40	47
	P												
	2.4	1.7	1.6	1.6	2.2	1.9	3.0	3.1	2.5	2.8	2.4	2.1	27.5
Kiev, U.S.S.R.	T												
	21	24	32	44	58	66	65	66	57	46	33	25	45
	P												
	1.3	1.0	1.6	1.7	1.9	2.6	3.1	2.3	1.8	1.8	1.5	1.5	22.1
Leningrad, U.S.S.R.	T												
	17	18	25	38	50	58	64	59	51	41	30	22	39
	P												
	1.0	0.9	0.9	1.0	1.6	2.0	2.5	2.8	2.1	1.8	1.4	1.2	19.2
Lisbon, Portugal	T												
	51	52	55	58	62	67	71	72	69	63	57	52	61
	P												
	3.3	3.2	3.1	2.4	1.7	0.7	0.2	0.2	1.4	3.1	4.2	3.6	27.0
London, England	T												
	40	40	44	48	54	60	64	63	58	51	44	41	51
	P												
	2.1	1.5	1.5	1.8	1.8	1.7	2.4	2.2	2.0	2.2	2.5	2.1	23.9
Madrid, Spain	T												
	41	44	48	54	61	69	77	76	68	57	48	40	57
	P												
	1.3	1.3	1.6	1.7	1.7	1.3	0.4	0.6	1.5	1.8	1.9	1.4	16.5

		J	F	M	A	M	J	J	A	S	O	N	D	Yr.
Milan, Italy	T	36	39	47	55	65	71	75	75	67	56	45	39	56
	P	2.2	2.2	3.5	3.5	3.0	3.0	2.6	2.6	2.8	4.5	4.0	3.3	37.2
Odessa, U.S.S.R.	T	26	27	36	47	60	68	72	71	62	51	40	31	50
	P	0.9	0.8	1.1	1.0	1.3	2.1	1.7	1.2	1.1	1.1	1.3	1.3	15.1
Oslo, Norway	T	25	26	32	41	51	59	64	60	52	42	33	27	42
	P	1.6	1.3	1.5	1.5	1.8	2.0	3.0	3.6	2.4	2.6	2.0	2.0	25.3
Rome, Italy	T	44	46	51	56	64	71	76	76	70	62	53	46	59
	P	3.5	3.1	3.0	3.2	2.3	1.9	0.9	0.9	2.9	5.4	4.7	4.1	36.4
Vienna, Austria	T	27	31	38	48	56	63	66	65	58	48	37	30	47
	P	1.5	1.3	1.8	2.1	2.8	2.8	3.1	2.7	2.0	1.9	1.8	1.8	25.6
Warsaw, Poland	T	25	27	34	45	57	62	65	64	56	47	36	28	46
	P	1.2	1.1	1.3	1.5	1.9	2.6	3.0	3.0	1.9	1.7	1.4	1.4	22.0
NORTH AMERICA														
Angmagssalik, Greenland	T	21	18	22	27	36	42	46	44	39	32	27	22	32
	P	2.1	2.5	3.0	1.9	2.0	1.4	1.6	2.5	3.0	3.6	3.8	2.3	29.7
Boston, Massachusetts	T	30	30	38	48	59	68	74	72	65	55	45	33	51
	P	3.9	3.3	4.2	3.8	3.3	3.5	2.9	3.7	3.5	3.1	3.9	3.6	42.8
Chicago, Illinois	T	26	28	36	49	60	71	76	74	66	55	40	29	51
	P	1.9	1.6	2.7	3.0	3.7	4.1	3.4	3.2	2.7	2.8	2.2	1.9	33.2
Churchill, Manitoba	T	−16	−15	−4	12	30	42	55	53	43	29	7	−9	19
	P	0.4	0.3	0.7	0.7	0.6	1.4	2.5	2.4	1.9	1.5	0.8	0.6	13.9
Coppermine, N.W.T.	T	−19	−21	−14	1	22	39	49	47	36	19	−4	−15	12
	P	0.6	0.4	0.7	0.7	0.6	0.9	1.5	1.7	1.3	1.2	0.8	0.6	10.9
Dallas, Texas	T	46	50	56	65	73	81	85	85	78	68	55	48	66
	P	2.3	2.6	2.8	4.0	4.8	3.2	1.9	1.9	2.8	2.7	2.7	2.7	34.6
Edmonton, Alberta	T	8	11	23	40	52	58	63	60	51	41	24	12	37
	P	0.9	0.8	0.9	1.1	1.8	3.0	3.1	2.3	1.2	0.8	0.9	0.9	17.6

		J	F	M	A	M	J	J	A	S	O	N	D	Yr.
Halifax, Nova Scotia	T	24	23	31	40	50	58	65	65	59	50	40	29	45
	P	5.2	4.0	4.3	4.5	4.4	4.3	3.6	4.1	4.6	5.1	5.0	5.2	54.3
Havana, Cuba	T	72	72	74	76	79	81	82	82	81	79	75	73	77
	P	2.8	1.8	1.8	2.3	4.7	6.5	4.8	5.3	5.9	6.8	3.1	2.3	48.1
Mazatlan, Mexico	T	66	66	68	70	75	80	81	82	81	80	75	70	74
	P	0.2	0.3	0.1	0.0	0.1	1.2	6.6	10.6	11.9	1.2	0.7	0.7	33.4
Mexico City, Mexico (7575 ft.)	T	54	56	61	64	66	65	63	63	63	60	57	55	60
	P	0.5	0.2	0.4	0.8	2.1	4.7	6.7	6.0	5.1	2.0	0.7	0.3	29.4
Miami, Florida	T	67	68	70	74	78	81	82	82	81	78	72	68	75
	P	2.0	1.9	2.3	3.9	6.4	7.4	6.8	7.0	9.5	8.2	2.8	1.7	59.8
Mobile, Alabama	T	52	55	59	67	74	80	81	81	77	69	58	53	67
	P	4.6	4.6	7.2	6.4	4.9	6.2	9.7	6.4	6.2	3.0	3.4	5.5	68.1
Nome, Alaska	T	4	6	9	20	34	46	50	49	42	29	16	8	26
	P	1.1	1.1	0.9	0.8	0.6	1.1	2.7	3.8	2.8	1.6	1.1	1.1	18.6
Phoenix, Arizona	T	51	54	60	69	77	86	91	89	84	72	59	53	70
	P	0.7	0.8	0.7	0.3	0.1	0.1	0.8	1.1	0.7	0.5	0.5	0.8	7.2
Salt Lake City, Utah	T	28	33	40	50	58	67	76	74	65	53	38	32	51
	P	1.4	1.2	1.6	1.8	1.4	1.0	0.6	0.9	0.5	1.2	1.3	1.2	13.9
Sitka, Alaska	T	33	34	37	41	47	52	55	56	52	46	39	35	44
	P	7.8	6.7	6.1	5.5	4.2	3.3	4.3	7.2	10.4	12.8	10.2	9.1	87.4
Spokane, Washington	T	25	30	38	47	56	61	70	68	60	49	35	30	47
	P	2.4	1.9	1.5	0.9	1.2	1.5	0.4	0.4	0.8	1.6	2.2	2.4	17.2
SOUTH AMERICA														
Arica, Chile	T	71	72	70	67	64	62	60	60	61	63	66	68	65
	P						Negligible							
Bogota, Colombia (8678 ft.)	T	57	58	58	59	58	58	57	57	57	58	58	57	58
	P	2.2	2.3	3.7	5.2	4.2	2.1	1.8	1.9	2.3	5.5	5.1	3.1	39.4

		J	F	M	A	M	J	J	A	S	O	N	D	Yr.
Caracas, Venezuela	T	65	66	68	70	71	70	70	70	70	70	68	68	69
	P	0.9	0.4	0.6	1.5	3.0	4.0	4.2	4.4	4.1	4.2	3.6	1.8	32.7
Cuiaba, Brazil	T	81	80	81	80	75	72	73	75	79	82	81	81	78
	P	9.6	8.9	8.1	4.1	2.0	0.3	0.2	1.1	2.0	4.4	6.0	7.9	54.6
Manaos, Brazil	T	82	82	81	81	81	81	81	83	84	84	84	82	82
	P	9.8	9.1	10.3	8.7	6.7	3.3	2.3	1.5	1.8	4.2	5.6	8.0	71.3
Maracaibo, Venezuela	T	81	82	83	84	84	85	85	85	84	82	82	82	83
	P	0.1	0.0	0.3	0.6	2.3	1.9	2.2	2.3	3.2	4.8	3.2	0.6	21.6
Montevideo, Uruguay	T	72	71	68	61	56	51	50	51	54	58	64	69	61
	P	2.9	2.6	3.9	3.9	3.3	3.2	2.9	3.1	3.0	2.6	2.9	3.1	37.4
Rio de Janeiro, Brazil	T	77	78	77	75	72	70	69	69	70	71	73	75	73
	P	5.0	4.5	5.5	4.2	3.3	2.3	1.8	1.9	2.6	3.4	4.1	5.5	44.2
Sao Paulo, Brazil	T	69	69	68	64	60	59	58	59	61	63	65	68	64
	P	7.7	8.7	5.6	2.2	2.5	2.2	1.7	2.0	3.2	4.7	7.2	8.5	56.2
Ushuaia, Argentina	T	49	49	46	40	36	32	32	34	38	43	45	47	41
	P	2.0	2.6	1.9	2.1	1.5	1.2	1.2	1.1	1.3	1.6	1.5	1.9	19.9
Valdivia, Chile	T	62	62	59	54	50	47	46	47	49	53	56	59	53
	P	2.6	2.9	5.2	9.2	14.2	17.7	15.5	12.9	8.2	5.0	4.9	4.1	102.4
ISLANDS														
Apia, Western Samoa (14°S.; 172°W.)	T	80	80	80	80	80	80	78	79	79	79	80	80	80
	P	14.0	14.9	12.2	8.8	8.6	6.2	5.2	4.4	6.8	9.6	9.0	17.7	117.4
Ascension, South Atlantic (8°S.; 14°W.)	T	79	80	81	81	80	79	78	77	76	77	77	78	78
	P	0.2	0.2	0.7	0.5	0.3	0.4	0.5	0.4	0.4	0.3	0.2	0.2	4.2
Guam, Marianas (14°N.; 145°E.)	T	80	79	79	80	81	81	81	81	80	79	80	79	80
	P	4.4	1.2	2.6	3.9	5.7	5.4	8.6	11.0	12.6	13.8	7.6	4.3	81.1

		J	F	M	A	M	J	J	A	S	O	N	D	Yr.
Honolulu, Hawaii (21°N.; 158°W.)	T	72	72	73	74	76	78	79	79	79	78	76	74	76
	P	3.8	3.3	2.9	1.3	1.0	0.3	0.4	0.9	1.0	1.8	2.2	3.0	21.9
Laurie Island, South Orkneys (61°S.; 45°W.)	T	32	32	31	25	18	15	14	14	19	25	27	30	23
	P	1.3	1.1	1.7	1.5	1.0	0.8	1.1	0.8	1.1	1.2	1.0	1.0	13.5
Mauritius, Indian Ocean (20°S.; 58°E.)	T	79	79	78	76	72	70	68	68	68	72	74	77	74
	P	7.0	6.6	7.0	7.7	2.1	2.1	1.9	1.8	1.4	1.4	2.4	4.4	45.8
Noumea, New Caledonia (22°S.; 166°E.)	T	80	80	79	76	73	70	68	68	70	73	76	78	74
	P	5.4	3.3	8.5	6.5	3.0	3.4	3.0	2.5	2.4	2.3	1.5	2.8	44.4
Ocean Island, Pacific (1°S.; 170°E.)	T	83	83	82	83	83	83	82	83	84	84	83	83	83
	P	12.0	8.2	6.9	5.1	3.6	3.4	4.6	3.6	2.4	2.4	5.1	6.0	63.4
Tristan da Cunha, South Atlantic (37°S.; 12°W.)	T	63	64	62	61	57	54	54	54	52	54	58	61	58
	P	4.5	3.6	6.9	5.5	6.6	5.5	6.0	6.0	6.5	5.6	4.3	4.8	65.7

index

Y

Z

DATE DUE